The INSPIRATIONAL WRITINGS of CATHERINE MARSHALL

Something More

A Closer Walk

The INSPIRATIONAL WRITINGS of CATHERINE MARSHALL

Something More

A Closer Walk

Published in 1991 by

Inspirational Press
A division of LDAP, Inc.
386 Park Avenue South
New York, NY 10016

Galahad Books is a registered trademark of LDAP, Inc.
Published by arrangement with McGraw-Hill Book Co. and
Chosen Book Publishing Company Limited.

Library of Congress Catalog Card Number: 90-82770
ISBN: 0-88486-048-5

Printed in the United States of America

Contents

Part I
SOMETHING MORE

To

PETER CHRISTOPHER
and
AMY CATHERINE
children of the King, now with Him
and to
MARY ELIZABETH
and
PETER JONATHAN
whom He has loaned to us

Acknowledgments

I want to express my gratitude to my long-time editor and friend, Edward Kuhn, Jr., who believes in excellence, hard work, and humility for authors; to Elizabeth Sherrill for sensitive and penetrating critique; to Dr. William R. Felts of Washington, D.C., for much helpful information on medical details; to Marguerite Shuster, who contributed her insights as well as her knowledge of Biblical Hebrew; to my talented and versatile secretary, Jeanne Sevigny, who has patiently typed and retyped manuscript with unflagging enthusiasm; to Emma Mulrean and Frances Orgain, who also helped with last-minute typing; to my husband, Leonard LeSourd, for many constructive suggestions and for being always an honest and discerning sounding-board.

Finally, to all the friends who through the pages of this book have been willing to share so generously of their innermost joys, sorrows, and victories, I offer my deepest appreciation.

Contents

Foreword

*T*he other day I pulled a copy of my book *Beyond Our Selves* from the bookshelf and was startled to note again its date—1961. Thirteen years! It scarcely seemed possible! Writing it seems like only yesterday. Yet there have been so many changes that the thirteen years might have been fifty. For the world of the seventies is very different from the world of the late fifties and early sixties.

My personal world has seen changes too. In the Foreword of *Beyond Our Selves*, I wrote,

> Just at the point when I thought child-rearing was over, Len's three children have joined Peter John in calling me "Mother." . . . A man swimming a horse across a turbulent stream does not stop to take a picture of the experience. I'll get my colts across the stream, see them thoroughly dried off, well fed, and on their way—then perhaps the picture.

Well, it has happened. The colts are on the far bank. Jeffrey, a tot of five when I wrote *Beyond Our Selves*, is now a senior at the

McCallie School. Chester is a junior at Taylor University. Linda has graduated from college and has a job with Cornerstone, a Christian organization, in Washington. Peter John and his wife, Edith, minister to a lively, bursting-at-the-seams congregation on Cape Cod.

At times during the crossing, the stream was rough, the current swift, the wind shifty. Yet these thirteen years have been exhilarating, a learning process all the way. The pages that follow are not a photograph album of the crossing, but here and there snapshots are tucked in.

The setting of our lives has changed from Chappaqua, New York, to the east coast of Florida with frequent stops at Evergreen Farm in Loudoun County, Virginia, where my mother, after whom I modeled the heroine of my novel *Christy*, still lives, delighting in organic farming and conservation and enjoying her family and friends who come to her from all over the world.

The involvement of first, Peter John Marshall and then Linda LeSourd with facets of the rebellion of the young, together with the death of two grandchildren have forced me to reexamine my faith, groping for ever-surer foundations.

At further range, the rapidly changing worldscene, creating its own uncertainties, has challenged the tensile strength of our faith. Even in the early sixties most nations were full of hope. Surely, we thought, progressive education and our expanding social consciences would gradually eliminate the problems of society. As the dark side of human nature was educated out and away, together with the marvellous advances made possible by scientific knowledge, a golden age, Utopia, would eventually emerge.

Now we are in a position to see clearly that the progress we hoped for has not been achieved: we are not golden men living in a Utopia. Violence and crime have risen to new heights. The home and family units, the chief crucible from which our stability and creativity should have come, are a shattering vessel.

The present generation looks with skeptical eyes on both education and science and refuses any longer to regard either as a god. Standards of ordinary truthfulness, honesty, unselfishness, reverence for life, cherishing children, sexual morality previously accepted by past generations (even when individuals did not themselves measure up to those standards), are now under serious attack as not being necessarily desirable. Situation ethics have gotten us into increasing difficulty. Moral and sexual perversions are being flaunted in books and motion pictures, with crusades mounted to make the perversions "legal." Superstitious practices involving witchcraft and the occult have reappeared from the subterranean depths in which they had lain since the Middle Ages and are quite literally courting the Devil. Confusion reigns.

Principles, laws, institutions, positions of trust on which we have depended for structure, are crumbling all around us. Over most of the world a leadership vacuum has left men feeling rudderless with a sense of betrayal. Fear seeps like dank fog across the earth creating suspicion and mistrust, damaging relationships, and raising the specter of economic disaster.

Where do we turn for help in times like these? Is there nothing on which we can depend?

A long time ago when Roman civilization had also reached an impasse because of its corruption and state of decay, one small group of people who were certain they had the answer called themselves followers of "The Way." They were disciples of a Jew named Jesus who had been executed about the year A.D. 29 in an obscure province of the Empire under the Roman governor Pontius Pilate.

"Seek a new way." . . . The Way, they called it.

But is it really? If the way advocated by Jesus is the way for us today—then why hasn't it worked? Why hasn't Christianity eliminated poverty and war and brought us the good life? Because we have still never tried Jesus' way. Not enough of us. Not on a large enough scale.

Could it be that His way contains an answer that we have almost completely overlooked? Perhaps the reason we haven't found the answer all these centuries is that all the while it has lain in that portion of man we have mostly ignored—the spirit. Is it possible that the sole agent who can knit each human being back together, heal the wounds, and bridge the gaps between the heterogeneous elements of society is the one agent neither secular society nor the organized Church really takes seriously—the Spirit? By which I mean a specific: the divine Spirit tabernacling within each man's spirit—the Creative agent in life, writ small enough to live within each of us, to work through mind, body, emotions, will, and conscience, not only synthesizing them, but demonstrating a new and creative way—The Way—in every one of life's arenas.

The itinerant rabbi Jesus told us that we—you and I—would be living in the era of the Spirit of Truth.

We have never needed truth so desperately.

The pages that follow offer you experiences from my life and the lives of people well known to me as case histories of what happens in the twentieth century when we say "Yes" to the Spirit of Truth, allowing Him to invade us and lead us out into the light. These are men and women from all walks of life with backgrounds and temperaments as varied as humankind itself is varied. Their experiences come from every aspect of life—where evil strikes into the lives of "good" people, in matters of health, family relationships, rebellion, business and money, safety, remorse, resentments, and estrangements.

There are some surprises in this raw material from life. For the Christian the emphasis is usually on the original commitment to the religious life as symbolized by joining a church. Most sermons and religious books do not lead us to expect much to happen spiritually between our "entering in" and the end of life. The "rewards" are to come in afterlife.

Yet the true stories related here tell us that commitment is only our birth into the new life. Then begins learning and growth. The process of being molded into a mature person in Christ Jesus becomes more challenging with each year that passes. I am finding that the knowledge of God grows often by means of the very experiences that would sweep us downstream, the turbulence I would prefer to escape.

As we grow older the pace and dimension of physical life must wind down. But it is meant to be just the opposite with the spiritual life—growth at an ever-accelerating pace. The heights and depths of the spirit, and enthusiasm for God isn't for children. In the latter half of life the normal Christian almost breaks into a jog or a run. Excitement and aliveness build. An altogether new quality of joy is given to us. It has little to do with the circumstances of our lives—good or bad—but everything to do with knowing Him who is managing the circumstances. It is joy that has the feel of permanence, even of eternity about it. Deep within we know that nothing that befalls us today or tomorrow can ever defeat that joy.

There are other reasons for the joy too. How great it is to realize, for instance, that the Holy Spirit did not limit His revelations to the truths contained within the canons of the Old and New Testaments. "I have much more to tell you," this Jesus told His companions around the table during His Last Supper talk with them, "but you cannot bear to hear it now. When He the Spirit of Truth is come, He will reveal all."

All—more and more. Always something more.

No matter how late the hour, no matter how desperate the moment, we cannot despair; the joy and the riches He has promised us stretch like a shining road into the future!

Catherine Marshall
Boynton Beach, Florida
March 4, 1974

1.

Yes, God Is in Everything

*A*t last we were safely airborne. December winds buffeted the little Cessna 205 four-seater as if it were a helpless leaf tossing in the vastness of the sky. There was room only for the pilot and my son Peter, his wife Edith, and me. Directly behind Edith and me was the baby's casket—so tiny with a spray of pink rosebuds atop it. It was the casket of my first grandchild, Peter Christopher Marshall, who lived for only two weeks. The special flight was the only way we could make it that day from the funeral service in West Hartford, Connecticut, to the graveside service at Fort Lincoln Cemetery outside Washington.

Inside the plane the noise shut out conversation. Pictures kept intruding on my thoughts. So much had happened in only fifteen days. . . . Peter's first telephone call on December 3rd, "It's a boy, Mom." But his voice was not as excited as a man's should be over his first child. Then it came. "Something's wrong, Mom. 'Poor muscle tone,' the doctors say."

Lung congestion had followed, the threat of pneumonia. That Sunday Peter had crawled in under the oxygen tent to christen the baby Peter Christopher—"Christ-bearer" or "light-bearer."

I remembered that morning in Florida thirteen days later when the inner release to go to Connecticut had finally been given me. The message had been so clear, "Go—and crown My prince with thanksgiving."

Then that seemingly interminable three-and-a-half-hour delay at New York's Kennedy airport. Something was happening to the baby. I could feel it. Later I found out: Peter Christopher had stopped breathing; he had turned blue, then stony white. Loving hands had been laid on the baby in prayer and miraculously, he had begun to breathe again.

But not for long enough.

Sitting there in the bumpy little plane with the roar of the engines and the shriek of the wind in my ears, I could shut my eyes and remember my first glimpse of my grandson—pink and normal looking, that perfect round head with its suggestion of blond hair.

I had wanted to cuddle him—but first, I must do what He had told me to do. So there in the hospital room we offered up our sacrifice of thanksgiving, crowning His little prince with His own blessing.

Thirty-five minutes later, the young doctor had spoken. Simply, "He is gone."

Lord, I don't understand. When Peter Marshall died Your sure word to me was that "goodness and mercy would follow me all the days of my life." Lord, is this goodness and mercy?

Scarcely a person but knows similar earthly partings or heartache or loss. The mail I read day by day dramatizes our shared human plight: the young wife who had received one of those dreaded telegrams from Vietnam: "Killed in action"; a grandmother struggling to save her grandson from drug abuse; a husband with an alcoholic wife; a doctor's verdict of terminal cancer; a brush fire that destroyed one's home and possessions; a businessman cheated by a dishonest partner; a marriage breaking up in disillusionment and bitterness.

"How can God permit such things to happen?" is the cry that rises from our hearts. If He exists at all and is a loving God, He would not want such evils to befall us. Yet how could He be God and not have the power to prevent these disasters? These are the most difficult of all questions for those embarked on the Christian walk. Certainly for me this problem of evil has been a real stumbling block.

In my groping to understand, back in the forties during a long illness I "discovered" a body of Christian literature unknown to me. It was experiential, the true personal experiences of other people. Compared to most church literature which I knew so well—largely theory—this was exciting reading. I gobbled up everything that A. E. Simpson, Glenn Clark, Starr Daily, Rufus Mosley, Frank Laubach, Rebecca Beard, Dorothy Kerin, Roland Brown, and later on, C. S. Lewis and Agnes Sanford wrote. In addition, I began to search out the journals and letters of some who had lived in other eras—Brother Lawrence's *Conversations*, John Foxe, John Wesley, Hannah Whitall Smith, George Müller, Evelyn Underhill. These journals and letters proved a rich mine of personal experience.

I recognized that the experiential approach had firm New Testament precedent. For example, when John the Baptist sent messengers to Jesus to ask if He was really the long-awaited Messiah, Jesus' response was not a theological discourse. Instead, He pointed John to His miracles—the healing of all manner of disease, of the blind, the deaf. These facts were the evidence.

And I remembered the ringing words of Jesus' apostles to those who would silence them, "We cannot but speak the things we have seen and heard."[1]

But thrilling and helpful as those books were, there was one chapter in Hannah Smith's *The Christian's Secret of a Happy Life* over which I had stumbled. Able to accept and profit from all the rest of Hannah's book, my rebellion was violent against chapter twelve entitled "Is God in Everything?" I asked myself how God could be "in" the death of a three-year-old who wandered into the street in the path of a truck? Was God in war? In cancer? The answer that welled up inside me was a resounding "Certainly not!" Further, I even considered such submissiveness wrong when Christians confronted with such tragedies, intoned, "Then it must have been God's will" . . . and piously quoted old harassed Job, "The Lord gave, and the Lord taketh away; blessed be the name of the Lord."[2] To me this seemed an especially cruel and offensive form of piosity.

But despite myself there were two bits of Hannah's chapter twelve that stuck to my mind like glue. The first was an illustration. The author related how at an informal prayer and sharing meeting one night, a woman had risen and told this story. . . .

She had been much troubled by the seeming contradiction of a God supposed to have all power in heaven and on earth versus human instrumentality or "second causes." It seemed to the woman that stubborn, evil mankind was always messing up God's perfect plans. So she had pleaded with God to set her straight on this question.

The result had been an interior vision:

She thought she was in a perfectly dark place, and that there advanced toward her, from a distance, a body of light which gradually surrounded and enveloped her and everything around her. As it approached, a voice seemed to say, "This is the presence of God! This is the presence of God!" While surrounded with this presence, all the great and awful things in life seemed to pass before her—fighting armies, wicked men, raging beasts, storms and pestilences, sin and suffering of every kind.

She shrank back at first in terror; but soon she saw that the presence of God so surrounded and enveloped herself and each one of these things that not a lion could reach out its paw, nor a bullet fly through the air, except as the presence of God moved out of the way to permit it.

And she saw that if there were ever so thin a film, as it were, of this glorious Presence between herself and the most terrible violence, not a hair of her head could be ruffled, nor anything touch her, except as the Presence decided to let the evil through. Then all the small and annoying things of life passed before her; and equally she saw that there also she was so enveloped in this presence of God that not a cross look, nor a harsh word, nor petty trial of any kind could affect her, unless God's encircling presence moved out of the way to let it.[3]

So for this woman (and subsequently for Hannah Smith too), one of life's most thorny questions was forever settled: God is in everything. The events of our lives do come to us, moment by moment as from His hands, no matter how evil the instrumentality or second cause may appear to us to be.

The acceptance of this principle, Hannah Smith asserted, was the only possible basis for the Scriptural admonition (repeated over and over—Old Testament and New): "In everything give thanks: for this is the will of God in Christ Jesus concerning you."[4] And "everything," she insisted, did mean everything—bad things as well as good.

It was Hannah's warning that unless we do accept God in an all-inclusive "everything" we can know no contentment. In that case a life of faith and victory becomes a romantic mirage. For how can we accept or give thanks for what is less than good, or even evil, if we do not believe that God's shielding Presence has deliberately stepped aside to allow those forces to get to us? Even more, that His purpose in stepping aside is for good—not evil?

Well, the matter may have been settled for Hannah Smith. But not for me. I could not understand her explanation fully. I convinced myself I was hanging the matter on a hook for further consideration. Practically speaking, this was simply rejection.

But surely few are as stubborn as I! I held out on Hannah Smith's thesis from 1945 until 1972. Twenty-seven years!

In those twenty-seven years a great deal happened, including the worst I could imagine: on the morning of January 25, 1949, with only a few hours' warning, my husband Peter Marshall slipped over into the next life.

For the first week, I was supernaturally carried over and above grief. Then inevitably, I fell to the bottom of the pit asking, "Why? Why?" Even—"Have I been mistaken to put my faith in God? Has everything I've ever believed been wrong?"

In essence, my husband's death at only forty-six had thrown me squarely back once more against Hannah Smith's assertion that God *is* in everything—either to accept or refuse it. . . .

What is needed is to see God in everything, and to receive everything directly from His hands, with no intervention of second causes. . . .

An earthly parent's care for his helpless child is a feeble illustration of this. If the child is in its father's arms, nothing can touch it without that father's consent, unless he is too weak to prevent it. And even if this should be the case, he suffers the harm first in his own person before he allows it to reach the child. If an earthly parent could thus care for his little helpless one, how much more will our Heavenly Father! . . .⁵

But I was still not quite ready for that "completely restful" life of the spirit. Perhaps my mind, always questioning, always seeking the answer to "Why?" got in the way of the deeper life, the longer view.

I did understand and could accept the difference between God's ideal will and His permissive will. For the Creator refused to make His creatures puppets whose strings He could manipulate to force us to obey. He took the risk of giving us free will. Therefore, men are sometimes going to go their own stubborn way, bringing unhappiness, grief, and horror into human life. Upon those occasions, God "permits" the disobedience. Thus the permissive will of God is a fact of our life on earth.

In Peter's case, I am certain that it was not God's ideal will that he die of coronary occlusion at forty-six. Why then, did God "permit" it? I had some clues, but not the final answer.

In the meantime, I forced myself to stop asking "Why?" and face stark reality: I was a widow with a young son to rear without his father. So what was I to do next? What was God's ideal will for me right then?

Lovingly and surely, I was taught one of the greatest lessons any of us can ever learn. In essence, it could be summarized like this. . . . Sin is in the world. And sin is "missing the mark," missing God's perfect plan. There is so much of this missing the mark that it is going to impinge on every person's life at some points.

If God left us with only this, real happiness or victory in this life would be an impossible mirage. But the Gospel truly is good news. The news is that there is no situation—no breakage, no loss, no grief, no sin, no mess—so dreadful that out of it God cannot bring good, total good, not just "spiritual" good, if we will allow Him to.

Our God is the Divine Alchemist. He can take junk from the rubbish heap of life, and melting this base refuse in the pure fire of His love, hand us back—gold.

Out of that understanding I was led to claim for my personal crisis and for my young son the promise that, for me, is gold:

And we know that all things work together for good to them that love God, to them who are the called according to his purpose.[6]

The results of this claiming were amazing. Gently and tenderly, God brought to my mind the teen-age dream of wanting to write. "Now is the time," I seemed to hear God saying. "Go forward and I'll open the doors before you."

The words soon became fact. The first venture was my editing some of Peter Marshall's sermons. This became *Mr. Jones, Meet the Master*. I was hard at work on it within six weeks of Peter's death. A year or so later, thousands of people were reading Peter Marshall's words. Clearly the Lord was telling me, "Catherine, your job is to spread his message."

From that time the path has gone on and on through my delight in the editing and writing of eleven books. Of course, the "good" that God, the Alchemist, worked for me has gone far beyond merely a satisfying career as an author. Blessings have been heaped upon me, including eventually, eleven years after Peter's death, marriage to Leonard LeSourd and the challenge of taking on a new family—Linda, Chester, Jeffrey. The new family responsibilities in addition to my writing have taken all my resources of physical and spiritual strength and have given back a full life.

There have been many joyous experiences. Like that when my granddaughter Mary Elizabeth Marshall was born. On the second day of the baby's life, the head nurse on Maternity had bounced into Edith's room. "Of all the babies I've seen born in this hospital," she announced jubilantly, "yours has the greatest muscle tone!"

"It was like a direct message," Edith told us later. "That nurse didn't know about Peter Christopher. It was like the Lord saying, 'See, I've handed you a special joy. I've heaped it up.'"

My cup overflowed. . . . The total rapture of a one-year-old as she received her first doll. . . . The fun of painting Christopher Robin and Pooh Bear figures on a little girl's bedroom furniture, of reading to her and watching understanding grow and unfold.

In the midst of such joy it seemed to me that I could forget Hannah's challenge—that God *is* in everything, good and bad. I left it on the hook where I had hung it years before. I still wasn't convinced.

Then in 1971 a family crisis brought it to the forefront again. On July 22nd of that year a third child was born to my son Peter John Marshall and his wife Edith. It was apparent from her birth that Amy Catherine had suffered severe damage to internal organs because of some unknown genetic difficulty. Medically speaking, there was no hope.

The family decided that we could but pray in total faith, asking for a miraculous healing. We were joined by Peter's congregation on Cape Cod, by a group of sixteen who flew in for days of intensive prayer in a retreat situation, and by many, many others. If ever a family went out on the end of a limb of faith, we did. As for me, not since Peter Marshall's first heart attack had I thrown everything I am and have, every resource of spirit and mind and will into the battle for a human life.

Meanwhile, the sixteen people gathered there were experiencing in the space of a few days extraordinary answers to prayer: one of the group prayed for a little girl on the same floor with Amy Catherine at Boston Children's Hospital and later found that the child's miraculous recovery had begun that day; our daughter Linda experienced a cataclysmic reordering of her life, lifting her out of darkness and confusion into a new beginning; our friend Virginia Lively was given the key to her daughter's health; a woman's life, blighted twenty years before, which no amount of prayer, counseling, and psychotherapy had alleviated, was lovingly restored; a man's resentment against his father, festering since childhood, was healed; a floundering marriage was made right again.

It was as if the tiny baby Amy became a divine catalyst, calling forth a concentration of God's power and love for others.

After the retreat, I stayed at the Inn near Children's Hospital in Boston while Peter and Edith took turns keeping the vigil over Amy and driving back and forth to Cape Cod to be with Mary Elizabeth. Day after day we sat beside the baby who was stretched out on a slanting "Heat Bed" under a big light. Amy was hungry and would open her mouth expectantly like a baby bird, yet she was too weak to suck; she had to be fed intravenously, the seemingly endless tubes sticking out in all directions.

"She needs to feel loving arms," my heart kept telling me. Finally, the nurses assented and one morning carefully placed her in my arms, tubes and all. She cuddled up, nuzzling me. After that it became a ritual, and I was holding our baby only minutes before her heart stopped beating. Amy Catherine's time on earth had been but six weeks.

Had I long before received the truth of "Is God in Everything?," then I could have endured Amy's death in the spirit in which I had accepted Peter Marshall's. But the years of nonacceptance had taken a larger toll than I had realized. I fell on my face. There followed months of rebellion against God, sharper questioning than ever: what can we believe about healing through prayer?"

I experienced the most intense misery I've ever known. Life went gray. Nor was it all psychological or spiritual. Events in the exterior world began going against me. Things like: a major Hollywood studio purchased my novel *Christy*, then decided not to produce it. The fiction manuscript on which I was working was presenting problems so great that I began to see that after pouring myself into it for three years, I was going to have to suspend work on it. An almost wild succession of small, vexing personal inconveniences came on in waves: the dishwasher went out; the bathroom plumbing went awry; a truck driver backed into our mailbox and demolished it; the lawn developed chinch bugs; the car kept stopping cold on us.

> When sorrows come, they come not single spies,
> But in battalions![7]

wrote Shakespeare. It is true. Trials do have a way of piling up. The question is—why?

Once again I was brought back to Hannah's thesis. If we don't accept the circumstances God's permissive will has allowed and ask, "Lord, what is Your will for me in the midst of these circumstances?," then He permits the difficulties to heap up. For most of us that's the only way He can get our attention.

In my misery He had my attention all right. Obviously, I was meant to turn off my grumbling and wait upon Him. I was to listen and to learn.

Finally the words of truth began to break through. . . . "His loving allowance for us" . . . "Must see all of life as coming directly from His hands." Hannah Smith again! After twenty-seven years of rejecting her!

To explain the evolution of my belief to that moment when I knew that I'd made connection with the transcendent power of God, I must backtrack briefly. When still in my twenties a lung condition had put me to bed. After a year and a half of the four walls of my bedroom, desperation had set in. Every other way medically and spiritually had failed me. I had been forced to the Prayer of Relinquishment, "I stop demanding anything. I want only what You want for me, whatever it is." There I had touched the hem of His garment and found health. And is not relinquishment very close to the "acceptance" Hannah wrote about?

Yet I had been puzzled, as had others, about a seeming contradiction between relinquishment and praying with faith. For how can we pray "Thy will be done, whatever it is, even unto death," and mean it, and at the same time have faith for healing?

Suddenly, it was as if a searchlight played upon my own experience of relinquishment[8] to illumine it for me further. Having ascertained through reading of the four Gospels that God's will is for health (as Satan's is on the side of disease, death, and destruction), I had felt myself to be in accord with God's will in asking for healing. I loathed the idea of disease and of being sick and had self-righteously set myself not to submit to illness. Thus in my mind there was the sharpest kind of dichotomy between, on the one hand, disease and sickness—the Destroyer's territory, and on the other, wholeness of spirit, mind, body—God's kingdom.

Yet back in 1943 a year and a half of asking on the basis of that dichotomy and of "believing" to the limit of my ability (what I thought was faith) had resulted in—nothing. The reason was, I perceived now, that God would not allow me to get well *until I saw Him even in my illness.* Disease is of Satan's kingdom, but God had allowed it for me. Blame it on Satan, I might, but see God *in* it, I must. He would hold me at that point until I did.

He held me firmly right there, until out of desperation, I bowed to Him. That was all He required. I had dropped my human "reasoning"—the basis of my authority in asking—and had laid everything at the feet of the Creator: He had taught me through hard experience that as His creature, I had no authority of my own. When I finally acknowledged that, He raised me up speedily.

I realized then what I'd really been saying to Him. "I'll keep a certain amount of rebellion and pin it to a good cause (against disease)." Then I had added with due piety, "Of course, God, I only insist on this because I know it's Your will."

But God's reply had never varied. "You can't insist on anything. I will not let you harbor rebellion for any cause. Lay your arms down."

I had also been guilty of a Pharisaical stance in relation to my understanding of prayer, healing, and the like—a fearsome trap laid for those who have done their homework by reading a lot of books, attending many meetings, complemented by a minimum of experience. I cringed as I saw myself alongside that Pharisee in the temple,⁹ standing and praying with myself, "God, I thank thee that I am not as other men are. I've done so much reading and thinking and praying. I have more understanding than most of them."

My situation was perfectly set forth in this incisive statement in Romans 1:21:

> Because that, when they [rebellious men] knew God, they glorified him not as God, neither were thankful, but became vain in their imaginations, and their foolish heart was darkened.

No wonder God had been unable "to justify" me! No wonder I couldn't hear His voice at all until I had deposited my "understanding" along with my "proper rebellion" at His feet. Then I heard (I don't know about other people, but He doesn't always speak to me in King James English), "You did read the Gospels correctly about healing. But the important thing is not whether your ideas are right. Learn this: you can't trust in your own understanding any more than you can trust in your own righteousness. I am offended by even one odious whiff of intellectual or spiritual self-exaltation."

Thus it was that the searchlight playing on my healing through relinquishment lighted up some ugly facts about myself.

I saw that previous to being willing to bow before God and worship Him, lifting only empty hands, I had been steadily refusing to recognize the totality of God's authority in my situation. God *is* in everything—even illness.

I recognized better what Hannah had meant by God being "in" everything. Further, new light was shed on one of Jesus' teachings in the Sermon on the Mount:

> Are not two sparrows sold for a farthing? and one of them shall not fall on the ground without your father.
> But the very hairs of your head are all numbered.
> Fear ye not therefore, ye are of more value than many sparrows.[10]

The Greek word for "without" (verse 29) is a strong word implying more than sympathy or even empathy. I was told by those knowledgeable in New Testament Greek that this word "without" can be used not only as "without the knowledge or consent of" but also as "without the Father's *participating presence*."

Then I was given an insight on a facet of Jesus' teaching that had escaped me—His identification with every human being in need. The Gospel accounts show Him with a passion for helping those in trouble. He has not changed! The minute we need saving from anything, He stands ready in His role as Saviour.

He illustrated this identification in a variety of ways to show us that it is a real fact of our world. When we minister to someone hungry or poverty-stricken or ill or in prison, we are ministering to Him.[11] When we persecute others, we persecute Jesus.[12] When we receive and welcome one little child, we receive and welcome Him.[13] Frank Laubach has put this in a memorable way: "At the center of every need He stands pleading with us to help Him as He moves to help others."[14] He is not only "in" trouble and sorrow, but is there in a particular way—to have dialogue with us, to teach us, and then to rescue us.

Putting this together with the Sermon on the Mount passage, Jesus was telling us that since not even one insignificant sparrow can perish without the knowledge and consent of a loving Father and, more, His participating presence (since He stands waiting at the center of every need), then we should have no fear. Each of us is infinitely precious in the Father's sight, so much so that He knows every detail about us, even to the number of the hairs on our head.

Therefore, nothing can happen to us without His knowledge, His consent, and *His participating Presence* as Saviour. All of that Hannah had meant by God being "in everything."

Now, so many years later, God had given me this new insight to illuminate the heartbreak of Amy Catherine's death. Once again, I had been making the same errors: once again, I had been leading with my "understanding" that it was surely God's will to heal an innocent baby. As before, I saw Satan's work all over the physical problem, the tiny, genetically damaged body. And just as steadily, I was refusing to see God "in" the situation at all. So I had been attributing Amy's death to the combined factors of our failure in prayer plus the power of evil. Seeing it that way, I had not been able to receive the baby's death as from God's hands in a greater scheme of things not yet given to me to understand.

It was a shock to realize that as a result of this defective thinking I had actually ascribed more power to evil than to God. To the mind of Jesus, as consistently portrayed to us in the Gospels, this would be unthinkable. For any one of us to believe that His Father could be frustrated or vanquished by any rival power would surely call forth His sad, "O ye of little faith! How long must I bear with you?"

Nor is this the viewpoint of the Gospels alone. Like a great bell tolling and tolling over all the land, deep-throated, its echoes ringing in our ears, the consistent voice of the sovereign power of God reverberates throughout Old Testament and New. He is the God of the supernatural—omnipotent, omnipresent, omniscient in this life and the next. We cannot believe this and also think that our God is no match for the evil of the world.

Yet even believing in God's power doesn't help in our crisis situations if we cannot also believe that He wants to help *us*. Frequently, we hear people say, "I know God has power—'if it be His will' to use it . . ." Like that leper who pleaded with Jesus, "Lord, if You only choose, You can cleanse me."

Jesus' ringing response leaves no doubt: "I do choose. Be cleansed."[15] And Jesus is the portrait of God. Here is the One who leaves the ninety-nine sheep safely in the fold and goes out after the one lost lamb—because He cares.[16] By every word and deed, Jesus made it clear that His Father not only cares, but that no detail of any life is too insignificant for His loving providence.

The accounts of Jesus' miracles portray Him working out His Father's love for each man, each woman, each child. He went about demonstrating the Father's delight in restoring deranged minds to sanity, sight to blind eyes, hearing to deaf ears, the joy of unfettered motion to the lame and the paralyzed; in satisfying hunger, dispelling pain, curing diseases of all sorts—no matter how far gone or how hideous.

So often the styluses of the Gospel narrators etched the word "compassion." No wonder! In Jesus they had encountered a caring of such depth and magnitude, yet often stooping to attend to such minute detail, that language failed them in describing it. He who was the embodied revelation of God had the profoundest sense of the sacredness of human personality of any man in history. The Galilean's tender love for any human being in misery or pain or need is the Gospels' eternally true message about God. In the eyes of Jesus today, our Contemporary Lord, no set of facts in any century should ever shake this central core of truth about the character of His Father.

Yet as the twentieth century has progressed men have found the truth that God cares about each one of us increasingly difficult to believe. We need to be searchingly honest here. As children of a scientific age we have grown up indoctrinated with the concept of a mechanistic universe. Machines have all but taken over our everyday lives. The individual has come to feel lonely. Is anyone at home in the cosmos? Perhaps God *is* dead. And machines are not much company.

To loneliness is added helplessness. The individual feels like an all-but-worthless cog in the machinery of huge industrial bureaucratic nations. No wonder we find it a long leap from our century's framework of thinking to Jesus' sure teaching about the Fatherhood of God.

Yet whenever we are emboldened to accept and act on Jesus' revelation of the Fatherhood of God, always and always we find solid ground beneath our feet.

With a love and patience beyond imagining, God brought me slowly back step by step to take a fresh look at Hannah Smith's thesis, at what's wrong with grumbling about our lot in life—

even baby Amy's death—and at the relinquishment that brings such miraculous results. He seemed to be saying, "Now that you're fully persuaded of the value of relinquishment, you're ready for the next lesson. *But relinquishment is only a stopping place on the way to praise. It's as nothing compared with the power of praise.* Now begin to praise."

My thoughts went back to the Apostle Paul's "In everything give thanks: for this is the will of God in Christ concerning you."

"You mean, Lord," I asked, "that in the midst of tragic circumstances, by an act of will I'm to praise You? How can I make it real? Wouldn't it be just words, almost hypocritical?"

"Obedience means turning your back on the problem or the grief and directing your eyes and attention toward Me. Then I will supply the emotion to make the praise real."

One early morning not long after Amy Catherine's death I went out on the patio to begin. Hadn't nature always brought me closer to God? Birds sang in the branches of the fiscus tree in the back yard. The sky was still gray-white with the faintest suggestion of blue. I began to praise that first time hesitatingly, woodenly:

"Lord, I think I'll begin with the small irritations first—that truck driver demolishing the mailbox. Surely, I'm not supposed to thank You for *that*! I can see, Lord, as I talk to You that the mailbox is of no consequence. Looking at You puts petty problems into perspective in a hurry. I can feel Your humor that I took it so seriously. So thank You, Lord, for perspective. Thank You for humor. Thank You for You."

As I persisted on down the list, another instruction was given. "Now write down every situation in your life that seems less than good, that you would like to see changed."

That wasn't hard. I went inside to get my red notebook and a pen and proceeded to fill five pages. But what came next *was* hard: "I want you to go down the list and praise Me for every item."

"Lord, I can see praising You for bringing good out of all these things, but I still don't understand how I can praise You for the bad things. Doesn't that make You the Author of evil?"

"I am Lord over all—good and evil. You start praising. I'll supply the understanding."

Step by hesitant step, I was being led on an exciting spiritual adventure.

2.

The Golden Bridge of Praise

My first discovery was that I knew almost nothing about praise, neither what it was nor how to praise. Beyond some joyous hymns and a few "Praise Gods" and "We adore and worship Thee" with the lips, what then? We Protestants sitting so properly in straight rows of pews staring straight ahead, how can we know how to praise? The subject is mentioned occasionally as a nice worship exercise, a sort of icing on the cake as a gesture to God, but praise as the key to answered prayer, no. That was a new concept altogether.

A short time after I began my amateurish praise efforts with the five-page list, a new book came in the mail one day: *Prison to Praise*[1] by a former Army chaplain, Merlin Carothers. The author's thesis is that God steps in to change unhappy or even disastrous situations in our lives when we thank Him *for the situation itself*. This makes sense only when we see that life as it comes to each of us day by day is our schoolroom. That, in turn, can be true only when we at last understand that God is "in" every circumstance—good or bad—that He allows to come to us.

Growth comes at the point of our hang-ups and problems when we take an active step toward God who stands waiting for us at the center of the problem. The quickest way to go to meet Him is through praise. No wonder we meet Him there, for Scripture goes on to teach us that God actually "inhabits" (lives in) the praises of His people.[2]

Carothers concedes that when most people are first presented with the concept of praising God for unhappy situations, they are resistant and even incensed, as I was when I was told to offer praise after baby Amy's death. But Chaplain Carothers records incident after incident of miraculous answers to prayer following praise.

There is such a thing as the "fullness of time" for an idea. Following Carothers' writings on praise, books by other writers on the same subject began appearing on booksellers' lists, such as *Let Us Praise* by Judson Cornwall and *Praise the Lord Anyway* by Frances Gardner Hunter.

The Scriptural basis for this is not only solid but overwhelming, such as:

Rejoice evermore.
Pray without ceasing.
In every thing give thanks: for this is the will of God. . . .[3]

Continue in prayer, and watch in the same with thanksgiving.[4]

But out of many such passages,[5] it was the concept of praise as a sacrifice which began to show me the way:

By him [Jesus] therefore let us offer the sacrifice of praise to God continually, that is, the fruit of our lips giving thanks to his name.[6]

The fact that the word "sacrifice" is used tells us that the writers of Scripture understood well that when we praise God for trouble, we're giving up something. For sacrifice means "the surrender or destruction of something prized or desirable for the sake of something considered as having a higher or more pressing claim."[7] What we're sacrificing is the right to the blessings we think are due us!

We are also sacrificing our human desire to understand everything. Obviously, praising God for trouble makes no sense from the earthly side. Human reason asks, "Why should I thank God for dark and negative circumstances when He is the Author of light and goodness alone? So when we bypass our "right" to understand and offer up suffering to God in praise, the Bible is right in calling this a "sacrifice of praise."

When we offer thanksgiving in the face of circumstances such as Habakkuk set forth, that's a sacrifice.

Although the fig tree shall not blossom, neither shall fruit be in the vines; the labour of the olive shall fail, and the fields shall yield no meat; the flock shall be cut off from the fold, and there shall be no herd in the stalls:
   Yet will I rejoice in the Lord, I will joy in the God of my salvation.[8]

The Bible gives us many illustrations of praise being the hinge upon which great events turned. Just one example among many is the story of how King Jehoshaphat of Judah pleaded with God for help when the Moabites joined with the Ammonites to come against his little country. The answer came: Jehoshaphat and his people were to turn their back on their enemies and spend their time worshipping God . . .

And when he [Jehoshaphat] had consulted with the people, he appointed singers unto the Lord, and that [they] should praise the beauty of holiness, as they went out before the army, and to say, Praise the Lord; for his mercy endureth forever.
   And when they began to sing and to praise, the Lord set ambushments against the children of Ammon and Moab . . . which were come against Judah: and they were smitten.[9]

When we turn to the New Testament there are many examples. There was the time Paul and Silas were cruelly beaten at Philippi and put in jail under maximum security with their feet chained in stocks.[10]

In this crisis the prisoners gave themselves to prayer, which is understandable. But to praise? So exuberant did their rejoicing become that it flowed over from words of thanksgiving into songs of praise.

Praise for what? we might ask cynically. That their backs were raw and bleeding from the "stripes" so cruelly laid upon them! That they were in prison with all the city authorities against them? That with their feet in stocks, they couldn't even move around their cell? Thanking God for that? From any human point of view, it makes no sense. It's foolishness, maybe even hypocrisy. Foolishness, that is, so long as we are looking at the human circumstances and not at God.

Paul admits to us that anything about Christ's cross or about the crosses you and I bear in life is "foolishness" to the world. But he had learned that God allows us to have disappointments, frustrations, or even worse because He wants us to see that our joy is not in such worldly pleasures as success or money or popularity or health or sex or even in a miracle-working faith; our joy is in the fact that we have a relationship with God.[11] Few of us ever understand that message until circumstances have divested us of any possibility of help except by God Himself.

It is a stripping process that we experience as we go on in the Christian life. The process has gone by many names in Christian literature: "the dark night of the soul" . . . "inward desolation" . . . "the winter of the Soul" . . . "the way of the cross" . . . "the Valley of the Shadow" . . . "the Dispensation of Darkness."

Once we have only God to depend on—as Paul and Silas had at Philippi—then we can *with joy* "draw water out of the wells of salvation."[12] We draw out the precious water by rejoicing in Christ, our Deliverer, not in our circumstances or in anything about ourselves. Not even pride at our wonderful experiences or our faithfulness, or what we've learned, or even our joy.

About midnight, as Paul and Silas, still bruised and bleeding, turned their minds from self and sang their thanksgiving to the Lord, rejoicing in Him, an earthquake rocked the city of Philippi, shook the foundation of the prison, burst the gates and wrenched the chains from the walls. Two other miracles followed quickly. The jailer and his entire household became followers of the Way. And when morning dawned the city authorities in a complete about-face withdrew all charges and bade Paul and Silas "depart, and go in peace."

As the former prisoners strode on their way, Paul could exult, "I have learned, in whatsoever state I am, to be content."[13]

Out of such a framework, we would do well to listen to this giant among apostles when he admonishes us to

Rejoice in the Lord *alway*: and again I say, Rejoice . . . in every thing by prayer and supplication with thanksgiving let your requests be made known to God.[14]

Just to be certain that we fully understand, Paul carefully details for us some of the difficulties he had undergone in the midst of which he had practiced "rejoicing": official scourgings of thirty-nine stripes—five separate times; three times beaten with rods; stoned once; three shipwrecks; innumerable journeyings in peril of robbers and other enemies; weariness; pain; hunger and thirst.[15] Few of us can match Paul's list.

Even as God asked praise of Jehoshaphat and of Paul and Silas, so He asks it of each one of us. And the longer one ponders this matter of praise and experiments with it, the more evidence comes to light that here is the most powerful prayer of all, a golden bridge to the heart of God. No human situation is too burdensome, no circumstances too calamitous for praise to bring as marvelous results today as it did then.

Gladys, a missionary in Ecuador, has written me several times. One of her letters related her brother Clem's story. His marriage had broken up after the couple's only child, a three-and-a-half-year-old boy, had died in a drowning accident. Clem was an efficiency expert for an industrial consultant firm, traveling a great deal, usually staying in one place about three months until he could get a particular company's problems straightened out. Yet he was handling the problems of his own life with anything but efficiency; Clem was miserably estranged from God.

Clem's and Gladys's father had died suddenly when Clem was fifteen. Ever since, the boy had been angry at God. Whatever church services she and her brother would attend, he viewed every preacher and every congregation with a critical eye. Gladys had been praying for her brother's change of heart for twenty years. So far as she or anyone else could see, nothing had happened as the result of these prayers. Indeed, a deterioration process was apparent in her brother's life.

Then the Prayer of Praise came to Gladys's attention. She decided to praise God for Clem's life just as it was, believing that God was working in spite of outer circumstances.

Almost immediately a chain of unexpected events began. Clem's employer, based in Chicago, sent him to Seattle on a six weeks' consulting job. There he met some distant relatives who were retired missionaries. He had long talks with the missionaries, finding them easy to confide in. They took Clem to their church where for the first time he found the atmosphere to his liking—warm and friendly and loving.

Then Clem's work in Seattle was over and unwillingly he went back to Chicago. The rest of the story was in Gladys's letter:

Clem decided that he would get right with God someday, but he could do this best in Seattle where the atmosphere was more to his liking.

In the ensuing months Clem consistently put the cart before the horse by trying to solve his problems and *then* he would give his heart to God. Dejection set in.

At last there came an opportunity for him to be in Seattle over a weekend, staying at the home of the same relatives.

On that Sunday morning Clem awoke overwhelmed with the knowledge that Jesus loved him. At a Sunday evening service Clem was also aware that many of the people there were praying for him. That night the pastor asked anyone who wanted to hand his life over to God and to become a follower of Jesus to stand.

Secretly (so Clem told me later) he had told the Lord that he would go forward if the pastor asked. But he would not rise.

After the service, outside in the chuch parking lot, Clem felt that God was talking to him, "You have to have your own way even in this? You are saying, 'I will accept God on my terms.' The terms will have to be Mine, none of yours; or there will be no acceptance."

Clem drove as rapidly as he dared back to the relatives' home. "I can't hold out any longer," he annouced as he rushed into their living room.

It ended up with their shoving the piano bench to the middle of the room to double as an altar. There my brother knelt and handed his life over to the Hound of Heaven who had pursued him for so long.

Gladys's letter ended with these words:

Five months of praising God for Clem *just as he was* was more effective than twenty years of begging God in prayer to rescue my brother.

Or here is another incident. . . . Redeemer Temple in Denver, Colorado, is an unusual church. Its worship services are attended by a cross-section of Christians from the main-line Protestant denominations—Lutherans, Presbyterians, Methodists, Disciples of Christ—as well as by Roman Catholics. Many of these worshipers are still members of their own denominations and of a Sunday morning attend an early service in their own church before going on to Redeemer Temple. "It's because in this church the Book of the Acts is being lived out before our eyes," one of them told me, "that we can't stay away."

As in the Acts a large group in the church has been led to communal living. A group of hippies who had stumbled into Redeemer Temple one Sunday and subsequently had their lives turned right side up, were led to buy a run-down house in the heart of the ghetto and renovate it as the headquarters of a Christian commune. There at the "House of Grace" they minister to other hippies. The Redeemer Temple congregation enthusiastically agreed to sponsor and help finance it.

On Sunday, May 17, 1970, the sanctuary at Redeemer Temple was crowded to the doors. Suddenly a young man sitting in the center block of pews got to his feet and stumbled down the aisle toward the platform. His appearance suggested that he had come from the hippie commune. Since the services at Redeemer are more informal than most and often filled with surprises, no one reached out to stop the man.

But it was apparent to everyone that he was drunk. "My name's Clarence," he announced, his voice thick. "I'm a man of color and proud not to be a white, proud to be a Black Panther." He was waving a black beret aloft.

At first Pastor Lou Montecalvo had courteously stepped back allowing the young man the floor. As it became obvious that this was a canned speech filled with clichés and memorized hate talk, the pastor walked over to the intruder and put one arm around his shoulders. "Clarence, you're delivering your speech to the wrong people. We care about you here."

Gently, the pastor began leading Clarence back toward his seat, talking to him as they walked. "See all those people out there? They love you, Clarence, not for the usual human reasons, but because they know how much Jesus loves you."

The congregation was hushed. At the foot of the chancel steps, two ushers took over from the pastor and quietly escorted Clarence back to his seat.

Pastor Lou returned to the pulpit and began the morning prayer. But as he began to pray, the voice of the drunk man in the pew was heard again, muttering and complaining. It was rapidly becoming a duet between the complaining from the pew and the praying from the pulpit.

Then a strange thing happened. All over the church people began quietly praising God aloud. "Thank You, Lord" . . . "We praise You for what is happening . . ." First a quiet steady hum of voices, then an harmonious chorus of thanksgiving and praise. After a few moments of this, the chorus diminished again. Finally the voices ceased.

Then everyone saw—Clarence was no longer there. Somehow in the midst of the praise he had slipped out of the church. As the people were realizing this, a member of the congregation rose. "I believe that I have a word of prophecy for all of us. It's this: 'My children, this day I have been showing you, teaching you this lesson. Satan, the enemy, is routed by praise, and only through praise.'"

Then he sat back down and Pastor Lou quietly picked up again, incorporating into his prayer gratitude for the tremendous object lesson that pastor and people alike had just been taught. Not long afterwards, in the same church, Clarence rose and made a public apology for his behavior on May 17th. Then he asked for prayer for the Black Panther organization.

"We know," one of those who heard him told me, "that it is only a matter of time until Clarence will have his own personal confrontation with Christ and become one of us."

It was a sign of the spiritual maturity of the Temple people that they responded to this situation by:

Giving thanks *always for all things* unto God and the Father in the name of our Lord Jesus Christ.[16]

"Always . . . for all things" is inclusive. It offers us no loopholes, however awkward or irritating the situation, wherein we are not to praise. Even in the relatively minor emergency of an interruption to a worship service, praise wrought its own miracle.

Grim circumstances of quite a different nature faced our Dutch friend Corrie ten Boom and her sister Betsie during World War II in Ravensbruck, the Nazi concentration camp. The sisters had been hauled off to prison for aiding Jews in the Dutch underground in their native village of Haarlem.

Corrie is now a vigorous eighty-two, traveling and speaking all over the world. She remains one of the most enjoyable guests who has ever graced our home and has often regaled us with anecdotes of her prison life. One of my favorites is her flea story. . . .[17]

At one period of their imprisonment Corrie and Betsie were transferred from crowded cells (where they had been separated for months) to Barracks 28. Within the hour they discovered that their reeking straw bed pads were crawling with fleas.

"How can we live in such a place!" Corrie wailed softly.

Without answering, Betsie immediately began praying, "Show us, Lord. Show us how." Then a moment later excitedly, "Corrie, He's given us the answer! I read it in the Bible this morning. Here—read that part again."

It was in I Thessalonians. "Rejoice always, pray constantly, give thanks in all circumstances, for this is the will of God in Christ Jesus—"

"That's it, Corrie! We're to thank Him for every single thing about the new barracks."

"Such as?" Corrie was trying to look with fresh eyes at the half-dark, foul-smelling room.

"Such as being together here."

"Oh, *yes*."

"And having managed so far to hang onto that Bible."

"Yes—oh, yes. Thank You, Lord, for *that*."

"And for the fleas—"

"Betsie, I see no way I can thank God for fleas."

"But fleas are part of this place where God has put us. 'Give thanks in all circumstances,' it says. Not just pleasant circumstances."

So the two women thanked God for the fleas.

As the days wore on the prisoners in Barracks 28 discovered that there was an astonishing lack of supervision or interference. Corrie and Betsie used the unprecedented freedom to talk to the other prisoners, read the Bible to them, minister in myriad ways.

Then one day a supervisor tipped her hand as to why they were given so much latitude. Some of the women had called through the grilled door to ask the supervisor to come and settle a dispute. She refused, as did the guards. "That place is crawling with fleas," the supervisor said. "I wouldn't step through the door."

Corrie's mind rushed back to their first hour in the barracks and to their rueful prayer thanking God for fleas. When she looked up, Betsie was chuckling, her eyes sparkling, "So now we know why we were supposed to praise Him even for fleas. Even the fleas had to be His instrument for our good."

As time has gone on, I have begun to see why praise is such a miraculous key. As we begin our praising in each circumstance, ever-fresh insights follow. This much I already see. . . . Just as a genius in mathematics can skip over many interim plodding steps to get the answer to the algebra or calculus problem, even so praise is the genius-shortcut route to our answer—God. This is because praise is faith in action, faith in its most vigorous form. When we praise . . .

> We are letting self go by turning our backs (through an act of will) on the problem or grief where self has been most involved.
>
> We stop fighting the evil or less-than-good circumstances.
>   With that, resentment goes;
>   Self pity goes.
>   Perspective comes.
> We have turned our back on the problem and are looking steadily at God.

We are acting out our belief in the character of God—His goodness, His love.

We are acting out our belief in the present power of God—in His participating Presence.[18]

We have to experience the delights of it to know what glory His participating Presence adds even to life's unpretentious moments. Soon I made a discovery that thankfulness, as nothing else does, enables us to live in the present moment. Not often do any of us grasp one shining moment, live fully in its "presentness," and consciously enjoy it. I shall not soon forget one such moment. . . .

After dinner one evening my mother and I were comfortably settled in our living room. Through the room and around us flowed the music of a fine recording, the London Philharmonic Orchestra playing Mendelssohn's *Violin Concerto in E Minor*. As we listened, our hands were busy working on some table mats that were to be a gift. The singing, soaring melody was a delight not just to the eardrums but to the emotions.

All at once it happened. My heart overflowed with praise. Silently, I lifted all of it to Him, aware now of His presence. . . . *This quiet room, the comforts and the peace of it. No bombs are falling outside. No Gestapo is going to pound on the door. . . . By Your mercy and grace, Mother is still with us, the inimitable Christy, so gentle, yet so full of her own kind of ginger. You love her too. Isn't it great that she and I have such rapport that often conversation isn't even necessary! . . . This music, so glorious. It must be pleasing You too. Work for my hands to do, work that I enjoy. You know all about work with the hands. This moment—what delight—what an oasis—in the midst of busy life.*

The thankfulness bubbled up and up, and still I had not spoken.

Three evenings later at the dinner table I shared the experience with Leonard and Mother and in the telling, found tears in my eyes.

Then I marveled that such a quiet, unassuming moment had meant so much. Why, I wondered?

The word "consciousness" is probably the key to the answer. The thankful heart raised in praise and adoration, verbal or silent, becomes the vessel to hold the sense impressions and the distilled essence of the presentness of life.

In my sorrow after Amy's death, I had been promised that when I obeyed God by beginning to praise, He would show me how and why. Some of the understanding He has supplied has been given directly, some through others. At my request a friend who knows Hebrew and Greek made a study of Old and New Testament verbs and nouns denoting praise. Here are some of the insights which resulted:

> An arresting Biblical concept is that true praise and thanksgiving actually blesses and magnifies God; that what we do and our attitudes are important to Him for His sake, not just for ours.[19]

> The Hebrew root for "thank" also means "to acknowledge," "to confess." It is also related to the word for "hand," probably meaning the gestures used in worship.[20]

> Confession of wrongdoing goes hand in hand with praise because it is the other side of God's sovereignty.[21]

> Anything but praise attributes more power to someone or something than to God.

Now I began to see how God's Presence can be the catalyst to turn evil events and situations into good ones. We could compare it to the process that a photographer goes through to develop a negative into a beautiful print. (The word "negative" is intriguing here.) When we hold a photo negative up to a light, all objects are reversed: black is white, white is black. Further, the character lineaments of any face in the picture are not clear.

Once plunged into the developing solution, what photographers call "the latent image" is revealed in the print—darkness turns to light and lo, we have a beautiful picture.

Even so, we must begin by obeying Jesus' injunction "Resist not evil." So we stop fighting whatever form evil is at the moment taking in our life, even as the worshipers in Redeemer Temple did not resist the interruption of a drunken man.

"Resist not evil" however, does not mean mere passivity or submission. That would make us "slaves of sin," which is hardly what Jesus meant. When we praise by an act of the will, by our own free choice, first we accept present circumstances, then we take up a positive position. By beginning to praise God for the evil, we take our less-than-good situation and plunge it into the photographer's fluid—the Presence of God.

Even as the photographer has to wait while the chemicals in the solution do the developing work, we too have to wait—meanwhile continuing to praise—while the Spirit does the work. And as we wait and praise, often unable to see any change in exterior circumstances, we understand what Paul meant when he wrote, "I am become a fool in glorying."

Paul was right. There are times when paise makes any one of us feel foolish. I remember the pain, the agony, of my loss as I resolutely but awkwardly began the Prayer of Praise for my granddaughter Amy Catherine. "Lord, thank You for being with all of us during those weeks of Amy Catherine's battle to live. You certainly were a participating Presence, else that other little girl wouldn't have been healed, all those other great answers to prayer would never have happened.

"Lord, I see it: There's still a lot of selfishness and introversion in me, or I would be as overflowing with praise for those others getting blessed as I would have been if Amy had been gloriously healed. Thank You for showing me this." Now the pain was subsiding, the praise flowing more naturally.

"Lord, I see now what You mean about everything that happens being part of the lesson material in Your schoolroom. I really can praise You that You refuse to let us stay children, that you keep insisting on our growing up. Thank You for caring that much about us.

"And thank You most of all that Your love for each one of us goes right on despite our stubborn refusal to understand until You have shown us the light again and again."

The matter of praise is obviously still one of my growing edges. I am convinced that living at the point of praise and seeking it will lead us to the richest discoveries we have ever made.

3.

Forgiveness: The Aughts and the Anys

*J*oan is forty-six years old, a successful merchandiser of women's clothing, yet extremely unhappy. She resents her father to the point of hatred because she blames him that she never married. Her father so missed having a son that he pressed Joan into a too-masculine role from childhood on.

Roger, another acquaintance, is sixty, ill with a series of physical problems. He has drifted in and out of undemanding jobs beneath his ability. Roger's heart knows seething bitterness for a business partner who cheated him. Roger was the one who had to pay with a six-months' jail sentence. Constantly he harks back to this so that people do not like to be with him. His face looks so angry that children are always thinking he is mad at them.

In both Joan's and Roger's situation the inability to forgive has built to a point where all the people involved are frustrated and miserable.

Most of us are aware that Christ requires us to forgive. Yet forgiving is not easy when the other person is clearly in the wrong. This is especially true in actions that violate God's and man's laws and the good that God wants for His world. . . . The rape-murder of a little girl. Ruthless exploitation of a small country by a large and powerful one. The Dachau extermination camps. Did Jesus mean that we must also forgive evil of that kind? And if He did, how can we?

For years I attached a condition to my forgiveness: if the other person saw the error of his ways, was properly sorry, and admitted his guilt, then—yes, as a Christian, I was obligated to forgive him. Finally I had to face the fact that this was *my* pat set of conditions, not Christ's. For He said, "Forgive, if ye have aught against any. . . ."[1] "Any" can have only one meaning: anybody—everybody—all-inclusive. As for the particular wrongs we are to forgive, Jesus is just as demanding on us there too. His instructions are to forgive "aught." The dictionary definition of "aught" is "anything whatsoever." Again, all-inclusive.

The scope and inflexibility of Jesus' teaching on forgiveness staggered me. Obviously I was missing something. Basically two questions clamored for answers. First, how can a righteous God ask us to forgive a rapist, an exploiter, or a murderer with blood on his hands? Would not forgiving the unrepentant murderer be the same as saying that all value-judgments are wrong?

Secondly, approaching it from the psychological side, Jesus, we are told in Scripture, "knows what is in man." He understands human nature all through; furthermore, the Carpenter of Galilee is intensely practical. Therefore, He would not command human beings to forgive in a way that is impractical, cuts across all morality, and is frankly impossible for us.

Now I knew I was missing something.

When a pastor listens to an individual pour out his problems, often he sees clearly that at this point or that one, the person on the other side of his desk has been in the wrong. If the pastor has been trained in nondirective counseling, he will carefully withhold these opinions.

Even so, he is caught in a dilemma. The minister knows that a spirit of condemnation in him, even though unexpressed, will set up an immediate barrier to further confidences. Yet liberation for the needy one can only come from seeing himself as he really is and wanting to change. Without that there is no hope, as experience in a group like Alcoholics Anonymous has long demonstrated.

I remember Peter Marshall coming home from many such confrontations in his church office, marveling, "Nothing—but nothing—is as difficult as for one human being ever to bring another person to the conviction of sin. Why, oh why do we ever try it?"

And that's exactly what the Bible tells us. "When He (the Comforter, the Holy Spirit) is come, He will reprove the world of sin." . . .[2] Here we have Jesus telling us that convicting one another is not, and never was, our work: it's the Holy Spirit's business. The pastor can point to the ideal, even be specific about what the Bible teaches. Beyond that, each of us must receive illumination about his guilt from the inside.

But can we? Is there any way we can facilitate the work of the Spirit? I was given help on that by David du Plessis, a minister formerly of South Africa.

Back in 1961 when I was writing about David du Plessis' insight that there is no such thing as inherited Christianity because "God has no grandsons,"[3] I wrote of him as "a new friend." Now that the du Plessises live in the United States, we see them more often. In 1971, at a time when certain family prayers were still unanswered, David gave us an insight as powerful as the "no grandsons" one.

Over coffee in our living room he pointed out to us a verse of Scripture that had long puzzled me:

> Verily I say unto you, whatsoever ye shall bind on earth shall be bound in heaven: and whatsoever ye shall loose on earth shall be loosed in heaven.[4]

"For a long time I was puzzled," David told us, "about what 'loosing' and 'binding' meant. Then I found out: it means that by hanging onto my judgment of another, I can bind him to the very conditions I'd like to see changed.

"By our unforgiveness, we stand between the other person and the Holy Spirit's work in convicting him and then helping him. By stepping out of the way through releasing somebody from our judgment, we're not necessarily saying, 'He's right and I'm wrong.' Forgiveness means, 'He can be as wrong as wrong can be, but I'll not be the judge.' Forgiveness means that I'm no longer binding a certain person on earth. It means withholding judgment.

"How I wish," David continued, "that I'd been taught that from the beginning. My whole Christian life would have been different. Judge, judge—there are no more judgmental people in the world than Christians. It was certainly so in my life! When the Lord made me face up to that, He told me, 'You're not forgiving. You're a public prosecutor, judging everybody in sight. And I want you to be a public defender—not public prosecutor.'"

David put down his cup of coffee. "Weren't you and Len telling me that you're troubled by some unanswered prayers? Well, in my life I've found this forgiveness business a key to getting prayers answered. A couple of years ago I was going through one of those prayers-not-getting-beyond-the-ceiling periods and I prayed, 'Lord, I don't have enough faith. Give me the gift of faith.'

"'It isn't your faith,' the reply came. 'I can see faith even if it's as small as a mustard seed. No, it's something else. . . . When you stand praying—forgive if ye have aught against any. That's your trouble. That's why your prayers aren't answered. *You go about with a lot of aughts against a lot of anys.*'"

As David concluded his story, I thought to myself, "Our aughts against all the anys. . . . What a shaft of light!" So now we saw why certain of our prayers had not been answered and we set ourselves to the work of forgiveness.

My husband Len and I started on a systematic releasing of our "aughts against all the anys" in our respective lives. We agreed to spend about thirty minutes each morning, each with a cup of coffee in a separate room, getting our Aughts on paper. After that we would meet together for verbal prayer release of each person on our lists. Then we would tear the lists into small bits, put them in a large manila envelope. Eventually we would burn them.

Long ago we had learned the principle that it is necessary to get the past confessed and straightened out (as far as is possible) before we can live abundantly in the present. So we began as far back as we could remember, working on a different period of our life each morning, searching out people and situations buried deep in our unconscious.

For instance, since I've always been fascinated with history, many long-dead characters are as large as life to me, like the English Tudor king, Henry VIII. For reasons not altogether clear, I have always had a personal loathing for that man. On each trip to the British Isles, I could never seem to escape him. In the Tower of London, his coarse, obese presence hovered in the shadows as I would peer through the slit of a window to the green below where such a procession of his subjects had their heads chopped off at his instigation—Sir Thomas More, Bishop John Fisher, the aged Margaret Pole, and two of Henry's wives—Anne Boleyn and Catherine Howard.

Even in Scotland at the ruins of Dryburgh and Melrose abbeys, who should appear but Henry VIII! As I stood in the grassy aisle, the guide intoned, "In May, 1544 Henry VIII commenced what he called his 'rough wooing' of Scotland. The Earl of Hertford marched on the Border, looting, murdering, burning. Behind them in England, 3,219 abbeys already lay in ruins, which had added treasure to His Majesty, the King, of 161,000 pounds. Scottish abbeys, including Melrose and Dryburgh, were also soon put to the torch."

So that's why Dryburgh was a ruin! Even as my eyes reveled in the beauty of the stone fretwork looking like delicate lace against the sky, I seethed at the thought of all those cathedrals and abbeys destroyed by order of Henry.

Now back home in Florida, during one of those quiet thirty-minute periods of a morning, my "aughts" against Henry VIII kept hammering at me. How, I wondered impatiently, could someone I'd never known in the flesh be such a personal affront to me? And this historical Aught seemed too trivial to bother with. After all, this particular character had already been dead 425 years and more pressing forgiveness work awaited me nearer home.

But the answer came, "No, this is valid for you. Get on with the cleaning out. That's real emotional energy you've been spending on history. The point is not whether the target for your emotions is past or present, the dead or the living, valid or invalid. The point is to get into the proper relationship with Me: assume your creaturely role, and give back to Me the sole right to judge."

So . . . marveling at my own foolishness, I released His Majesty King Henry from my unforgiveness. After that, I could rejoice in no longer having to arraign Henry for his black deeds and let God handle that one.

On another morning, I tackled all my Aughts in connection with my hatred of war, like the armament makers of World War I, the Senate leaders who had defied Woodrow Wilson and blocked America's entrance into the League of Nations; more latterly, certain gentlemen of the Pentagon.

Some Aughts surfaced from my childhood. Childish resentments to be sure, but needing to be unloaded. My baby brother Robert had crawled in amongst my doll furniture, wrecking everything. Not only that, fascinated with dolls' eyes that open and shut, with an exploratory forefinger he had punched the dolls' eyes back into their heads. When I discovered sightless sockets looking up at me as Mrs. Eagen's and Mrs. Ogen's "eyes" rattled around in their heads, I was so angry that Mother had to restrain me from pummeling brother Bobby with my fists.

Mornings later an especially difficult Aught surfaced from Peter Marshall's first heart attack. Sometime before that attack he had stopped smoking. Nine days into his convalescence, the doctor had put a cigarette in Peter's mouth because he was so fearful of "nervousness." The passing of the years with all we know now about smoking and heart disease only made this Aught harder to release.

Then I came to that Aught from my first years in the writing-publishing world. On editing Peter's sermons from his manuscripts (meant only for oral delivery, hence not creafully annotated), a particular clergyman had not been given proper credit because I had not caught this in preparing the book manuscript. The publisher had received an angry letter. As one Christian to another, I had written the man a letter of detailed explanation (my fault—not Peter's) and apology, promising the proper credit line in the next printing and all subsequent ones. The only reply had been a terse, "From henceforward you will address me only through my lawyer." In the end, the retribution exacted had been a small sum of money. Curdled by the episode, this Aught had clung. Now it had to go.

As Leonard and I dealt with our respective Aughts out of the past and proceeded to present areas needing forgiveness, we had continually to guard against merely flashing around our negative opinions and analyses rather than relying on God to remedy the situation. But gradually we found that by dropping personal judgments we could clear out tons of emotional debris that had obscured the real issues involved.

It did not take many mornings to see that the contemporary parallel of my Henry experience involved that category of persons who had never injured me, but whom I would rather avoid. There are many ways of expressing the feeling. "He rubs me the wrong way" . . . "Oh, I don't know, some chemical reaction between us—not good" . . . "Just allergic to her, I suppose." That would not do in Jesus' eyes, I discovered. So those people, too, had to be released to be themselves whether or not I happened to like their looks, their habits, or their life styles.

Jesus' direction about love is clear: "You shall love the Lord your God with all your heart, soul, and mind . . . and love your neighbor as much as you love yourself."[5] In all honesty, we know how little genuine love we bring to God even in moments of what is supposed to be worship, how feebly and selectively we love our neighbor. The love God demands can only be the gift of God. Yet He cannot give us that gift so long as bitterness and resentment have slammed shut the door of the heart and unforgiveness stands sentinel at the door lest love open and enter. Forgiveness is the precondition of love.

The "how" of forgiveness is through knowing how to use our will—the rudder of our life. We are responsible for the set of this rudder; once we have willed a course of action, God will be responsible for our feelings if we will hand them over to Him. Otherwise, nothing we can do would change these feelings.

When I put that conclusion alongside David du Plessis' statement, "Forgiveness means, 'The other person may be as wrong as wrong can be, but I'll not be the judge,'" I saw that forgiveness is simply the decision of our wills to release a particular person, followed by verbalizing that to God. It can be a simple prayer like, "Lord, I release _____ from my judgment. Forgive me that I may have bound him and hampered Your work by judging. Now I step out of the way so that Heaven can go into action for _____." Obviously, there is nothing impossible about praying like that.

As for faith that such a nonemotional release would result in changes in the other person's life, I confess that we began with deficient faith. The process of releasing the Aughts seemed too simple, too pat.

We were about to be shown that when we follow Jesus' directions, the simplest ways are the most powerful.

Every human being has problems of relationship with other people. The other (positive) side is that in interaction between people we learn most of life's needed lessons. Yet grown-ups as well as children are inclined to avoid correction. Any of us can plan a life style which skirts around our foibles, hang-ups, and selfishness.

By 1959 after ten years of widowhood, with Peter John in college, I realized that I was developing exactly such a life style. Though I had decided to build a house and settle down in Washington, there were inner warnings. I saw that too much protected solitude was a danger to me. It jeopardized aliveness and those fresh discoveries that are part of spiritual growth. By then I also understood that even the most earnest prayer and disciplined Bible reading leaves out another whole area through which God reaches us—people. What to do about it?

Today many people who seek an answer to all this are entering into communal living so that interaction with others can deal with character flaws. In the fifties and sixties however, there were only faint rumblings of movements toward community living.

For my solution I had turned my eyes toward the Church of the Saviour. This was a small interdenominational church shepherded by Gordon Cosby. One of its requirements of church membership was a high degree of commitment not only to the Lordship of Christ but to the group itself. I had all but decided to take this important step when Leonard LeSourd and his three children walked into my life.

Soon it became apparent that for me God had planned a different sort of involvement and commitment. The house I was building was almost finished. Inside its insulated, climate-controlled walls I could have slipped into the rut of a padded middle age much too early. There I would have been secure from the jostles and jabs of normal family living. In that perfect step-down office adjoining my bedroom, I might even have completed my novel *Christy* in three or four years rather than the nine years it took.

But what growing pains of the human spirit (my own included) I would have missed! How little I would have understood of what life is all about compared to what I've learned during the hurly-burly years since. Though I have still had little experience with living in community (only an occasional retreat and a three-generation household) I now see the family as another one of life's important training grounds for learning how to deal with the Aughts.

So I sold the house and undertook the rearing of a second family. The years since have dramatized what I already knew, that I am no expert in child rearing, only a constant learner. I know that I share with other parents those situations in a family where varying interests and personalities whittle away at selfishness and impatience, force us to run the risk of sharing our innermost selves, so that we are bent and then rebent into flexibility. The bumps and bruises and turbulence are part of the price you pay for life's richness.

During the early years of my marriage to Leonard, some of the turbulence came from infighting between Chester and his young brother Jeffrey, two bear cubs, frolicking about the house, rolling over rugs, colliding with furniture.

There was the morning I heard loud noises from the direction of the boys' room. Then came the sound of a slap and a door banging. Chester and Jeffrey were at it again!

Chester's angry voice met me as I crossed the living room. "Jeff, open that door. Open it!"

From the bedroom side of the door came an impudent reply that further infuriated fourteen-year-old Chester. He hauled back his right foot and kicked the door. There was a crunch. With dismay I saw that the toe of Chester's shoe had punched through the wood paneling.

I rapped sharply on the door. "Jeff, unlock this door this instant—or I promise you such a scorched bottom you won't sit down for the next week!"

He slid back the bolt and stood there looking sheepishly at us.

"He hid my English paper and I have to turn it in today." Chester's voice was still shaking with rage. "He refused to give it to me."

"Did you do that, Jeffrey?"

53

"Yes-s."

"I'm disgusted with you. That's baby stuff." Then I turned on Chester. "When are you going to control that temper of yours? The door," I moaned. "Just look at that door! It's ruined."

Such a bear-cub scene was not made easier for me by Len's genial disinclination to punish for infighting. His attitude tended to be a relaxed, "Well, that's the way boys are."

Soon after Len and I were married and were living in Westchester County, New York, my new daughter Linda was entering the sixth grade. It became apparent that my stepmother role was not going to be easy. There was the usual playing of one parent against the other and the tussles over clothes and curfews most mothers have with their daughters.

In the sixth grade, Linda was bright and freckle-faced with the instincts of a tragic actress. This was the period when the fad was to wear dirty sneakers to school—preferably with no socks. One day Linda and I had just returned from purchasing a new pair of sneakers. Several minutes later, I looked out the front window and saw our daughter in the rock garden on her hands and knees, the shoe box open on the ground beside her, carefully dragging one white sneaker, then the other through the black soil.

Loudly I voiced my objections, "Do you really want to look as if you've come out of a pigsty?"

The gaze she turned on me was withering. "Mom, everyone wears dirty sneakers. I'll look ridiculous if mine are all new and white.

The emotional temperature was soaring, so I dropped the subject. That afternoon when I happened to be near the junior high school, I dropped in to see for myself. Classes were just changing. Sure enough, all the way down the corridor moved hundreds of pairs of dirty sneakers. Standing there, I remembered how humiliated I had been when Mother made me wear galoshes to school on a rainy day when my classmates didn't.

But sneakers and the like were minor points compared to something that neither Len nor I understood. When fun times were planned especially for Linda, such as a party or a shopping trip, immediately afterward she would turn into her worst self. This odd sequence happened so often that we knew a warped force was at work. It was as if she was saying, "Please, I can't stand any special demonstration of love."

On the other side, when punishment was necessary (usually the withdrawing of some freedom or privilege) no sooner was the discipline given than Linda would become a veritable angel with a winsome disposition.

Such behavior was especially discomfiting to a stepmother. The relationship to which I had looked forward was not what I had hoped. I felt like a rejected parent. Then I caught myself resenting this child and her attitudes. Since this was not my image of the "good mother," I tried to ignore or bury such emotions.

I still remember some moments of realization one Sunday morning in the First Congregational Church in Chappaqua. The winter sunlight was streaming in the tall arched windows laying long patterns of light across the white Colonial sanctuary. I was sitting there thinking about Linda. Suddenly in my mind and heart His voice was speaking to me with particular clarity and intensity. *Unless you love her, you don't love Me.*

"Lord, I know that's true." The thought stabbed me. "But *how* do we love a person when we hate some of the things they do? Please tell me how. And Lord, I have another problem. I can't manufacture love. Nobody can. I need help."

With the issues thus clearly drawn I struggled on. Over and over I would take a fresh grip on my willingness to love Linda, no matter what she did—all the way from minor infractions to slipping out of her bedroom window after midnight for a date with a senior football star five years older than she. As I willed to love, I asked God to take care of my emotions and make my love real. For a time it would work and our home would know contentment and harmony. Then another crisis would develop and I would fall on my face.

The difficulties that had surfaced in early adolescence grew until Linda was finding life all but unmanageable. For years, schoolwork had been difficult. Here was a bright girl whose grades seesawed wildly between A and Flunking. Almost every term report carried teachers' comments about "Poor attitude and motivation" and "Work not up to level of ability." Tutors and extra sessions and a prep school brought no demonstrable results.

During these years her father and I had tried everything we knew—guidance counselors, a child psychologist, counseling with Christian friends, group prayer, prayer at Linda's bedside while she was asleep—every type of prayer we could think of. There had been some minor breakthroughs, but Len and I knew that the root problem remained. It seemed to be centered in her will. She appeared to be unable to want to be any different.

In college the trouble grew. To academic difficulties was added the Youth Revolution of the late sixties. Linda plunged whole-heartedly into it: life pattern; clothing styles—levis, long hair, wire-rimmed spectacles; protest meetings, campus sit-ins, hitch-hiking to peace marches and rallies.

Most of us parents with children caught up in all this know the feeling . . . wondering whether our sons and daughters might be ensnared in experiences dark enough so that we would prefer not to know specifics. Especially when they were away from home, we told ourselves that "what we don't know won't hurt us," mean-while knowing full well that the ostrich never solved anything with his head in the sand.

Graduation day came for our daughter. Linda's father, grand-parents, and I got to the graduation scene to find a very tense girl on our hands. There was a thin veneer of happiness but flashes of irritation and anger kept breaking through to us. The strain in the relationship between Linda and me was obvious, her dissatisfac-tions deep. Watching the academic procession walk by on sneak-ers, dirty white shoes, T-thong sandals, with mortarboard caps tilted on the heads at every possible angle, I wondered what the other graduates were feeling. Were most of them unhappy too, with life somehow out of kilter, values all a jumble?

The scene left me with such heaviness of spirit that after our return home to Florida I spent one morning working on the release of all Aughts against Linda stretching back over the years to age ten. To my astonishment, I filled three pages. Neither Len nor I told Linda anything about our prayer of release.

We did not have long to wait to see results.

Several weeks later on Cape Cod during that tumultuous summer of 1971 came the climax to our long years of struggle with this particular situation. When my grandchild Amy Cath-erine Marshall was born on July 22nd with severe liver, kidney, and brain damage, a group of us gathered on the Cape for concentrated prayer. On an impulse I telephoned Linda, who was working in her grandmother's gift shop in Maine. Would she care to join us?

There was a moment's silence. Then, "Yes," she said, "I'd like to be there."

Afterward Linda told me that she wanted to come because I was the one who had telephoned and invited her. What happened when she got there literally reversed the direction of Linda's life. The details of the story are hers alone to tell. As is usually the case, people other than Len and me—her parents—were used by God as the catalyst for our daughter. The turning point that followed is best told in her words . . .

On the afternoon after my arrival at the retreat I was about to take a shower. A particular moment is crystallized forever for me. I had one foot on the bathroom rug, the other in the shower stall. At that instant like a bolt the realization hit me that one foot in, one foot out was an accurate representation of my life. Several times I'd gone through the motions of committing my life to God. Yet I did not have an obedient heart. I was living in outright rebellion against Him.

I sensed that this was the moment to decide—for Him, or against Him. There could no longer be any middle ground.

Standing there, I carefully weighed what choosing the Lord's side would cost me. Obviously, some things in my life would have to go. But I was tired of living in two worlds and not enjoying either. Desperately, I longed for His peace in my heart.

I took a deep breath and said aloud, "I choose You, Lord." Then I got in the shower. That shower was my true baptism.

The following day came many hours of agonizingly honest dialogue with us. We heard things we didn't want to hear. Tears flowed. After that I understood why the direction given me in the Chappaqua church—*Unless you love her, you don't love Me*—had been so difficult for me.

"I thought I wanted a loving relationship with you when you married Dad," Linda told me. "But resentment crowded in. The reason was that at a gut level I thought you were taking Dad away from me. I would no longer be Number One in his life."

During this long evening of honesty and confession among the three of us, many barriers came crashing down. For Linda it was the release of years of hostility and guilt. For us, it was a facing up to mistakes and fears and lack of understanding. To cap all of this emotional upheaval, Linda had a "believer's baptism" in the ocean followed by a communion service on the beach.

That was not the finish of this particular Aught-Any episode. I was to get my come-uppance the morning after the communion service.

During the intervening hours, my mind must have flicked at some secret thoughts along the line, "*All that* . . . all those years of agony she put her father and me through, then she's forgiven by God *instantly*. Isn't that too easy a forgiveness?" Ugly secret thoughts—except God knew.

The next morning I was awakened to the clear incisive internal message, "Remember My story of the prodigal son? You're in grave danger of taking the place of that elder brother.[6] That morning in Florida, you didn't quite mean business about finally releasing all those Aughts against Linda, did you? I heard and answered anyway. *Now let them go.* For now, take the lowest seat at My banquet table, below Len, below Linda. And I want you to confess all this to Linda this morning."

Thus I was properly zapped, as our boys would say. Humbly and a trifle haltingly, at breakfast I made my confession to Linda. She wept again, this time from joy, and then ecstatically hugged me.

Now that Len and I had released Linda of our Aughts against her, she was free to become the very person we had longed for. A new life began for her. For several months she stayed with Edith and Peter Marshall under their direction and guidance. Gradually she began to get answers to those crucial questions, "Who am I? Why am I on the earth? Where am I going?" Linda now lives in Washington where she is part of a unique Christian fellowship at Trinity House, living cooperatively and ministering to students and young career people.

All of this give and take with my new family enabled me to identify with many friends who were having trouble with rebellious teen-agers. One close friend, Sybil Jones, who lives in Virginia a few miles from our Evergreen Farm, was having a problem with her niece Fay. Because of the personal nature of the events, I have changed names and some unimportant details.

One night in Florida I received a call from Sybil. "Catherine, I just have to talk to you. It's about Fay."

As Sybil talked on, I was remembering Fay's family. I have known her parents, Loretta and Tim Randle, for many years and have watched with apprehension the way they have catered to their only daughter. Each Christmas would come a family picture of the three of them with the golden-haired Fay always the center of their adoring smiles. As the years passed the Christmas cards showed the child was growing up into a beautiful girl—a pert face, slender body, lovely. Except that when she was fifteen a look was developing on Fay's face that bothered me—a touch of arrogance in the eyes? Selfishness around the mouth? Or was I imagining?

We would see the three Randles in the summertime when they came to Virginia to visit my friend Sybil, who was Loretta's sister. Aunt Sybil had always been a sort of spiritual godmother to Fay. She read Bible stories to her as a little girl, taught her special prayers. Fay stayed with her Aunt Sybil while her parents took long cruises or trips abroad. During those periods she would try to provide the disciplined home life that Fay was obviously not getting. While the Randles were churchgoers, although only in a hit-or-miss way, they saw no connection between Christian faith and the way they structured their home. And whatever Fay wanted she usually got.

When Fay reached her seventeenth birthday that May she wanted a Corvette hardtop automobile. Her parents gave it to her. Then Fay began to want things not even they would give her—like drugs and weekend trips with boys.

Soon an ominous personality change developed in their daughter. Fay became withdrawn, moody, secretive. She had been a good student; suddenly she didn't seem to care. That was when they discovered the marijuana.

"I've no idea how long Fay has been smoking marijuana," Sybil told me. "As if that isn't bad enough, her father found a big supply of 'downers' in her room. When he discovered the marijuana and the downers—she had been using six or seven of them a day—he hit the roof. He took her car keys for a month. One night about a week ago Fay packed a bag and drove off in her Corvette. Apparently she had a spare set of keys.

"Her father almost went out of his mind," Sybil continued. "Days passed with no word from Fay. He alerted the police, then hired a private detective to find her." There was a long silence as

I prepared for—I did not know what. "Last Friday they found her and some boy named Bart living together in a dirty apartment in the French Quarter of New Orleans."

I commiserated with Sybil the best I could, promised to pray for Fay, and hung up the phone thinking, "How many, many parents are going through this same kind of experience!" I knew of ten or more friends who had watched in anguish as rebellious children left home. Some had returned; one had died of a drug overdose; two had been killed in car accidents, others injured with one paralyzed for life; some were still missing.

When Fay's father confronted her and her boyfriend in the New Orleans apartment, there was a stormy scene. "I'm tired of your respectable middle-class life," Fay shrieked at him. "It's phony. You and your friends kill yourselves with cigarettes and booze. Let me alone to do what I want to. Bart is the only real thing I've ever found in life. Except maybe Aunt Sybil."

Her father stared at her, at the long-haired boy beside her, then turned around and left. "I don't have a daughter any more," Tim told his wife when he got home. During the next few months his wife and friends watched him age ten years.

That Christmas no card came from the Randles.

But while Tim Randle had given up on his daughter, his wife and Sybil had not. They persisted in keeping in communication with the young couple.

The next summer while at Evergreen Farm, I had an unexpected visit from Sybil, visibly upset.

"I'm afraid I've done the wrong thing," she began. "Yesterday morning Fay and the boyfriend, Bart, arrived suddenly at my house. I had sent them some money to visit me, but they didn't tell me they were coming. They had hitchhiked all the way from New Orleans. I guess they've had to sell Fay's car.

"I greeted them lovingly, fed them a big meal. Then suddenly they asked where they were to sleep. 'Are you married?' I asked. They shook their heads. 'Then I'll give you separate rooms,' I said.

"'Separate rooms!' The look on their faces was something. 'You're a phony like everyone else,' Fay shouted at me. Before I could stop them they'd picked up their things and walked out the front door."

Sybil looked at me, her eyes full of tears. "Did I do the wrong thing?"

We talked and prayed together. The answer to our prayers was clear guidance: Sybil had done the right thing. She had showed them love, but since Fay and Bart sleeping together as an unmarried couple violated the moral code of Sybil's faith and her home, she had to ask them to take separate bedrooms.

During our time together I told Sybil about the Aughts against the Anys principle. For a long moment she considered the question: was there judgment and condemnation in her heart for Fay and Bart?

"Yes, I do think there is judgment on my part," she admitted. "But how can I honestly pray to get rid of it?"

We did it together. Then Sybil raised a new point. "My releasing judgment against Fay and Bart may help my relationship with them. But the real problem is between Fay's parents and these kids. And the Randles are coming to visit me next week."

Sybil had before her the formidable task of trying to bring the Randles to the point where they not only forgave and released their daughter from judgment, but did the same for Bart.

"You know, Bart isn't hard to like," Sybil confided to me as she was leaving. "Behind all that hair there's a gentleness and yes, even a sweet spirit. Fay calls him 'a hip beautiful person.'" Bart, too, had left a middle-class family situation in Arkansas in rebellion against his parents.

When the Randles came to visit there was complete stubbornness on Tim's part toward any reconciliation. Finally, Sybil bluntly told them that their hardness of heart would keep God from doing His forgiving work in all the lives involved. It had not been a pleasant time.

Months later she was on the telephone again, her voice jubilant. "Fay and Bart have moved into a small apartment just two miles from here. They hitchhiked from New Orleans weeks ago, both now have jobs. I had them for dinner last night. Do you know what they asked me? Did I know a minister they could talk to? I sure did."

The next letter had good and bad news. Bart's and Fay's talks with the minister had resulted in their deciding to get married. Living together unmarried had seemed racy and amusing. But they had few close friends and could find no real place in the community. There also came an inner dissatisfaction they couldn't define. They then had decided that marriage made more sense than they had thought.

So Bart and Fay were married one afternoon in a quiet church ceremony. The bad news was that Fay's parents had refused to come to the ceremony.

I had trouble sleeping that night, grieving over the Randles' unforgiving stubbornness. What was the Lord trying to tell parents through experiences like this? That what we have called love for our children is largely sentimentality, not strong enough to be redemptive? That the permissive giving of so many material possessions to children is really a form of self-gratification without the quality of love Paul talks about in the thirteenth chapter of Corinthians?

Fay's mother, it turned out, had desperately wanted to go to the wedding, but felt she should not come without her husband. Heartbroken by the situation, she thought of Sybil's words about their hardness of heart and the necessity of releasing their Aughts against Bart and their daugther Fay.

The morning of the wedding, Loretta Randle alone in her quiet bedroom took two important steps. She gave her life to the living Lord she had never known. Then she spent two hours getting on paper her Aughts against Fay stretching back to about age ten. She had not realized how many resentments against Fay she had acquired.

Loretta felt lighthearted, happier than she had been in years. So she persuaded Tim to work on his Aughts too. He found it especially hard to release Bart, who in his eyes had "seduced his little girl." All of this was done with no communication with Fay and her new husband Bart. Slowly, painfully, hundreds of miles away they were being released from judgment.

There came the memorable day in Sybil's living room when Fay and Bart were reconciled with her parents. Fay asked her father's forgiveness for the harsh statements she had made that day in New Orleans. She hugged her mother—and wept. Then to Sybil's astonishment her niece knelt at her feet. "Aunt Sybil," she said revealingly, "you were right that day—when you wanted to put me and Bart in different rooms. One reason I got so mad was because I knew you were right. That's the reason Bart and I came here to live because we felt you were the one person we could trust. You stood for something and deep down we wanted what you had."

Later Sybil wound up her report to me with a little vignette. "The Randles," she wrote, "arrived two days ago for a week's visit. From my window I can see Bart with Tim Randle out by the front fence. Bart is handy with tools, so Tim has enlisted his help in making a new gate for me. Already there's an easy camaraderie between the two men. Isn't it great the way this has turned out! How can I ever thank you for the Aughts and the Anys?"

After we had seen such miracles of restored relationships, I began to understand why Jesus gave us the Aught-Any command immediately following His clarion call to "have faith in God" and His challenge to get on with a mountain-removing faith.[7] The sequence can mean only one thing—that our Aughts, big or just pesky, are always the chief block to prayer power.

Once we see this truth, many examples spring to mind, such as that of Stephen, that personable, eloquent young man who became the first Christian martyr. As the murderous stones flung by a frenzied mob bruised flesh and broke bones and the bloody stones piled up at Stephen's feet, Saul of Tarsus stood watching, holding the witnesses' outer garments so that they could better hurl stones at the condemned man. Saul heard Stephen's last words before death, "Lord, lay not this sin to their charge." So it was Stephen's release of his Aughts against his executioners that made it possible for heaven to go into action for Saul of Tarsus.

Shortly thereafter, as Saul traveled toward Damascus, heaven opened to bring Saul to his knees in one of the most dramatic turnabouts in recorded history. He would become Paul, missionary-traveler over all the known world, great apostle to the Gentiles, and spiritual father to all of us in the Western world.

As each of us bemoans the severing of so many relationships, we may recognize that we can't really expect anything else when we leave God out of our lives. As always, Jesus challenges His followers to be out in front showing the way: "Forgive, if ye have aught aginst any. . . ."

There's no way to get our world back together again except as each of us begins with himself and with his own family.

4.

The Law of the Generations

*F*or years I felt the same despair as everyone else under the continual barrage of articles and true-life situations telling of estrangement between parents and children and issuing dire predictions of the imminent demise of the family.

The cover of a national news magazine dramatized it, a picture of a father, mother, son, and daughter—square, robotlike people, with the caption, "The U.S. Family: 'Help!'"

Statistics followed: one in every four marriages now ends in divorce; a high 70 percent rate of divorce exists in some California communities; 40 percent of all married women with children hold out-of-home jobs; half a million teenagers run away from home each year; the rate of school drop-outs is steadily rising; the "new morality" with utter rejection of premarital chastity has been accepted by a large percentage of young people.

During the 1960s the world's youth had center stage. The young had become our obsession: either they were glorified, with even their hair and clothing styles copied by their elders, or they were feared, resented, and blamed for everything. After a while it became apparent that neither extreme could be right since we had found so few solutions.

It was about then that I was startled to find in the Old Testament a brief but applicable description of society's plight in our time:

> Thou shalt beget sons and daughters, but thou shalt not enjoy them; for they shall go into captivity.[1]

All of us know the ways in which we do not enjoy our children. We are afraid of what is happening to them. Or we feel cut out of their lives. Then there's the basic fear that our children will "go into captivity." In the seventies we are discovering that the captivity of drugs, of the occult, of sexual promiscuity, is every bit as real a captivity as it was for the Israelites who were physically carried into Babylon centuries ago.

How different is this from those other descriptions in Scripture of parents who do enjoy their children, described joyfully as "a fruitful vine by the sides of their house" . . . "a quiver full of arrows" . . . "the crown" of old age . . . "olive plants round thy table."

Startled by how pointedly and powerfully the Deuteronomy verse speaks to our hearts today, I sought out the original setting of the words. The author and compiler of Deuteronomy[2] has Moses speaking them as part of a prophetic warning as given him by God. The forty years of Israel's wilderness wanderings were over. The second generation then stood poised, ready to enter the Promised Land. Moses would soon die; he would not enter Canaan with them. Before formally commissioning Joshua as his successor, the venerable leader gave a farewell charge to Israel. This charge is the book of Deuteronomy.

Reading this book is like looking through a window into the amplitude of Moses' spirit. In his speech there is no note of an old man's sentimental nostalgia, rather the entire thrust is into the future. Warm with feeling and persuasively eloquent, Moses focused on this one significant point:

> See, I have set before you life and death, the blessing and the curse . . .
>
> Therefore choose life . . .[3]

The rest of the Old Testament narrative tells us what happened: all too often the descendants of those to whom Moses had given his charge did not "choose life." History records that these descendants did go into captivity literally as well as spiritually.

Each generation then, as now, has a choice: life or death . . . the blessing or the curse.

"Why shouldn't I do as I please—as long as it doesn't hurt anyone else?" we are hearing frequently today.

The truth is that whether we are young or old, we cannot do as we please and not hurt other people in the process. As Dr. Francis Schaeffer, philosopher and theologian, states it, "Man is drowning in cosmic alienation." Scripture continually insists on the principle of our connectedness as a fact of human life: "We are . . . every one members one of another."[4] In this Law of the Generations, as I call it, we are linked to previous generations behind us. Our ancestors are in our genes, in our bones, in our marrow, in our physiological and emotional makeup. We, in turn, will be written into the children who come after us.

I was at home alone one night recently when I heard a noise in the kitchen. Dropping my mending in my lap, I tensed, listening for any other sounds however faint. Those cat burglars I'd been hearing about . . . was someone there?

Hearing nothing more, I went to investigate. The kitchen was so dark! Suddenly, I felt that familiar prickling at the base of my neck.

Then came a surge of annoyance at myself. "You're not going to let that fear of the dark return," I told myself sternly. Resolutely, I walked into the kitchen and flipped on the light. A tray had toppled from its place beside the refrigerator.

Most of my life I've struggled with an assortment of fears, many of them foolish ones. As I sought through prayer for a reason for so many fears, I was pointed back to my father's mother, Grandmother Sarah.

My girlhood recollections of this grandmother are rather negative ones. I remember that she spent most of her days sitting in a comfortable chair in the bay window of the living room, often with a huge Bible open on her lap. She used it as a sort of scrapbook; it bulged with clippings, cards, letters, and snapshots tucked between its pages. The expression on her face was usually dour. I cannot recall any of her grandchildren sitting in her lap to be cuddled.

Yet Grandmother Sarah had an immense capacity for friendship and hospitality. I can remember no meal in that home without guests and boarders, not even breakfast. She and the two daughters who ran the house were superb cooks in the best of Southern tradition.

But I began to see that the overall effect of my grandmother's fear-ridden personality on me was not good. My mother remembers a significant event that occurred when I was six weeks old. Grandmother and Grandfather had agreed to baby-sit for me one night while my father and mother went to a lecture.

"About midway in the evening, an usher handed a note to the lecturer," Mother recalled. "He asked if a Mrs. Wood was in the audience? If so, there was a message for her at the door of the auditorium. There stood your grandfather. 'It's the baby,' he panted. 'She's cried herself blue in the face.'

"He and I started for home almost on a run. Halfway home I could hear you screaming. Yet the instant I dashed into the room and picked you up, the crying stopped as though a faucet had been turned off. You were frightened and my presence reassured you. Grandmother had searched so fearfully for an open safety pin, a Florida mosquito chewing on you, or a rash, she had made you more afraid. She was so tense."

Can it be that a baby's sensitive antenna can pick up the tone of people surrounding him? If his family is happy and their relationship harmonious, the baby's reaction is contentment; if there is strong negativism like fear, the baby senses this and protests. Child psychologists and those who work with babies in institutions affirm that this is exactly so.

As I grew up, I discovered the nature of Grandmother's fears. Since she thought the night air dangerous, she would not allow Grandfather to raise any windows in their bedroom winter or summer. Many a morning we would see Grandfather stagger pasty-faced and dripping with perspiration from the sweatbath of their stifling sleeping quarters.

To this was added an abnormal fear of thunderstorms. As the skies would begin their fireworks, Grandmother Sarah would dash for her feather bed, cover herself with a comforter and stay there until the last bit of lightning had faded and the last drop of rain had fallen.

Later, when I was about eleven, Grandmother Sarah kept me and my younger brother and sister while my father, dangerously ill, spent three months at Johns Hopkins Hospital with Mother there beside him. It was a time of real fear and tension for all of us. At this impressionable time of my life, I somehow focused on Grandmother's fears of night air, drafts, thunderstorms, the dark, washing hair too often, staying out in the sun—things which seemed to me ludicrous and absurd. Such phobias were the last things I wanted to imitate.

Yet so strong is the Law of the Generations that even what we scorn can still come down to us. In my case it was not Grandmother Sarah's particular fears—rather simply an overinclination to fear. In my life it centered on a dread of germs and illness; a horror of mice or small dead animals, and during my childhood, fear of the dark, ghosts, and the like.

The time came when I realized that in Jesus' eyes, fear is a sin since it is acting out a lack of trust in God. Then my attention was drawn to that part of the second commandment which follows the injunction not to "make for yourself a graven image": "For I the Lord thy God am a jealous God, visiting the iniquity of the fathers upon the children unto the third and fourth generation. . . ."[5]

I had always wondered about this: was that fair? Or like a loving God?

But now in the light of the revelation about my fear and Grandmother Sarah, I saw that the Exodus verse was simply stating a fact of life. And I *was* the third generation from my grandmother to be beset by those petty fears.

As is often the case when we are being taught something, this matter of sins being passed down from generation to generation seemed to be everywhere I looked in the Bible.

We are accustomed to the idea that we pass on to our children a physical inheritance—color of eyes, color of hair, even certain diseases: tendencies toward gout, diabetes, certain skin diseases. Handing down a material inheritance is such standard practice that the laws of every country make careful provisions governing wills, probate, death and inheritance taxes. I began to ask myself, is it possible that our spiritual inheritance is as real as the others?

It soon became apparent that just as we can inherit either a fortune or debts, so in the spiritual realm we can inherit either spiritual blessings or those liabilities (unabashedly called "sins" in Scripture) that hinder our development into mature persons. These blessings or liabilities do not come to us solely by heredity. Obviously they are also passed on by example and by teaching—conscious or unconscious. For instance, I think of a mother with a habit of keeping an untidy bedroom; her daughter now fights a continual losing battle with cluttered closets and drawers.

I've a friend who can scarcely go to sleep at night without reading herself to sleep; her father before her had the same habit, as do both her grown sons.

My husband Leonard dislikes tomatoes, sweet potatoes, liver, broccoli; so do sons Chester and Jeffrey. My grandmother used heaping teaspoons of sugar in her coffee or tea; my father did too, and also my brother.

These are trivial matters. Above this lowest level, more serious bequests are handed generation to generation. . . .

A man whom I'll call Sam found himself hindered by a terror of any emotional involvement with other people. At an office farewell party for a secretary who was moving to another city, the girl began to weep as she opened her gifts and read the enclosure cards. Even though she was weeping from gratitude and fond memories, Sam was still uncomfortable and found himself sidling out the door. "But this is silly," he told himself. "Why am I doing this?"

It was a pattern he had repeated over and over—this ducking out of emotional scenes. As he pondered this fact, a picture came into his mind. . . . It was a dinner table scene in his boyhood home. Angry over criticism directed at her, his mother had jumped up from the table and flounced out of the house. For a minute or two the father just sat in his chair, weary and lifeless. Finally, he left the table to seek out his wife to placate her. The scene ended with husband and wife returning home arm in arm, surface harmony restored. But there would be other occasions when Sam heard his mother crying and saw his father retreat out the back door to sit in the car and smoke a cigar.

Sam realized that these scenes had been repeated over and over through his growing-up years. How he had dreaded them! Whenever possible he had left the house. He sensed that his father had wanted to retreat from those scenes as much as he had. Now he could understand better one of his father's traits that had long puzzled and annoyed him, a sort of peace-at-any-price stance in any situation involving disagreements.

About three months after this revelation, Sam was caught up in a mild argument with his wife. He did not know that she was unusually tired from a difficult day. When she burst into tears, they were both startled to see their shy six-year-old son hastily leave the living room and run up the stairs. Sam followed the child. He found him in bed rocking his body rhythmically back and forth in the way he had comforted himself as a very small child.

"Oh no!" the father thought as the significance of the chain reaction now into the third generation was borne in upon him. His son knew nothing of the similar episodes in his father's life when he had fled from emotion. Nor of his grandfather's tendencies along this line. Yet here was the child acting out the emotional hang-ups of his father and grandfather. It was uncanny! As he sat on the edge of the bed comforting his son, then and there Sam vowed to find the way to break this particular inheritance; surely this bondage to the fear of negative emotion had harassed his family long enough!

Intellectually, Sam knew that many of life's greatest experiences take place in emotional confrontations involving people. Yes, the man knew that, but the little boy still in the man remained terrified of all emotion.

Up to that time in Sam's life, he had had little use for religion. Yet one day at the noon hour, impulsively he slipped into the back of a church. There were several other worshipers sitting throughout the sanctuary. He could feel growing within him a desire that seemed ridiculously emotional—to stand up, walk down that long aisle, kneel at the altar railing and say, "God, I need You."

But he could also feel rising resistance. What if he got to that altar and actually shed tears? These people sitting there . . . if they saw him kneel weeping at the altar, would they not think him some kind of exhibitionist?

A deep instinct told Sam that this was a true crisis point in his life. Here he was, again backing off from emotion.

Knowing that the answer had to be "yes" if that vicious chain was ever to be broken, resolutely he got to his feet, walked down the aisle and knelt. Immediately, he forgot all about the other people. He even shed a few tears, but they were glorious tears, a moment Sam could never forget. The chain *was* broken and though not everything was healed instantaneously, that day in the church was the beginning of a new level of maturity for Sam and his family.

All of this gave me ample proof that the Law of the Generations is a fact—the sins or the blessings of the fathers *do* come down to the children.

It is the nature of sin to divide, to build walls, resulting in strained relationships or estrangement. I wondered if the Law of the Generations might give not only clues to the difficulties between the generations in our time, but even constructive answers. How might we pray so that the negatives could be transformed to positives?

In the process of searching for an answer, I was surprised to find that the last words of the Old Testament have to do with these problems between the generations. They are words of great promise. At the last days, God promised to send another prophet who

> . . . shall turn the heart of the fathers to the children, and the heart of the children to their fathers.[6]

The date of the Book of Malachi has been placed at about 450 B.C. The writer mentioned Elijah as the forerunner of that "Sun of righteousness" who would "arise with healing in his wings." All these centuries later we know who the Sun of righteousness is, the greatest of all the prophets—the Lord Jesus Christ.

At the beginning of His public ministry Jesus made it clear that He had not come to destroy the Law, but to complete and fulfill it. Jesus would recognize the Law of the Generations, like all other law, as part of His Father's world. But until then there had been that missing dimension, exactly the question I had asked. After we struggle and find that we can't keep the law by our own effort, then what? Is there any hope for us?

It is at this point that Jesus gives us the good news of His Gospel: He who is Truth and therefore is above the Law, will do for us what we cannot do for ourselves. So there is not only hope, but a real answer. We cannot turn the hearts of our children to their parents, but Christ can.

It was my son Peter who helped me to apply these new insights about my fears and Grandmother Sarah at a time several years ago when both of our families were coming to grips with the negatives in the Law of the Generations. No doubt Peter's position in the intertwining generations put him in the perfect position to help me with my fears. We found that our prayer work fell into three parts.

First, having brought into the light all remembered dark heritage from previous generations, I had to forgive all these ancestors and release them from my judgment.

Second, Peter prayed that I be cut loose from these negatives. As I remember it, his prayer went something like this:

> Lord Jesus, You have told us that Your Word is the Sword of the Spirit,[7] that it is sharper than any two-edged sword known on earth. Whatever You say to us cuts deep and lays bare even the thoughts and intents of the heart.[8]
>
> You've also assured us that You came to earth to loose all bonds, to set every captive free.[9] Lord, Mother has been captive to these fears that we've been laying out before You. Yet You've declared that where the Spirit of the Lord is, there is liberty.[10]
>
> So now, Lord, I take that Word and claiming it and wielding it as the Sword of the Spirit that it is, in Your Name and by Your power I hereby cut Mother free from every chain and shackle from the past. I release her now to her rightful heritage—the glorious liberty of the children of God.[11] Thank You, Lord Jesus, thank You. Amen."

This powerful prayer led naturally into the third step, praising God for every part of this experience. For we found that the release would not be final unless I received it in faith, and as I had been discovering, praise is the swiftest, surest route to faith.

So now I began to understand how Christ makes the Law of the Generations work for us. It was our friend, the late Starr Daily, who gave me some further insights about what our part is in this process.

For many years Starr, originally an expert safebreaker, had been in and out of penal institutions, finally pronounced hopeless by the judge who sentenced him to prison for the third time. Later, in the penitentiary hellhole, he experienced one of the most dramatic conversions of the twentieth century. After the prison doors opened for him in 1930, he wrote ten books, gave innumerable lectures, conducted hundreds of interviews with youthful criminals.

Out of the totality of Starr Daily's great contribution to prison reform, I'm concerned here with but a single facet of what he learned—how a change in the attitudes of parents can effect changes in a son who is in prison. A number of his examples[12] demonstrated to me that the Law of the Generations works positively in as precise a way as it does negatively.

The father of a twenty-four-year-old prison inmate sought an interview with Mr. Daily one day to ask for help. "I've tried everything with my son," the man mourned. "There's nothing left but God."

"Well, He's quite a leftover," was the dry reply.

Wordlessly, the man handed Starr Daily a summary of his son's record. It looked bad indeed:

> . . . excessively quick and bright in intelligence, but infantile in emotional reactions and responses. Reformatory, jail, and prison record of nine years. Type of crime: sex offenses, burglary, robbery, forgery, confidence games, picking pockets, purse snatching, drug and narcotic peddling.

"Looks hopeless, doesn't it?" the father commented.

"Don't you believe it," Starr told him. "While there's life, there's hope. It's up to you."

"Up to me!" the father almost shouted back. "What do you mean by that? What can I do at this late date?"

The father and mother made no pretense of being "religious"; they went to church twice a year, on Christmas and Easter. The home had always swung between two extremes—great leniency when the parents were in good humor and not busy, and unusual severity when they were out of sorts or rushed.

Starr next prescribed a spiritual rehabilitation program for the couple. "I'm going to be hard on you," he told them, "because I sense that you mean business."

The program was to be carried out in a way that would funnel into it tremendous spiritual power: husband and wife were to be "in agreement" about what they were trying;[13] they were not to discuss it with anyone, keep all of it a secret between them.[14]

Then Mr. Daily wrote out a prescription for the couple. In relating this particular story Starr did not detail the prescription. However, it was not too difficult to cull out of Starr Daily's writings[15] the sort of spiritual rehabilitation program he recommended:

1. Rise early enough to start the day by giving one hour to the program. During this hour, use only the Bible and a notebook and pen or pencil. Start with reading the Gospel of John. Jot down in the notebook:

    Any verse or promise about faith.

    Make notes about the character traits and attitudes of Jesus, remembering that when you want to know what God is like, look at Jesus.

    Together try conversational prayer aloud—no "thees" and "thous," honest straightforward talk about anything that comes to mind.

2. Begin to focus on the fact of Jesus' identification with anyone in need. Keep reminding yourself that He stands at the center of each person's need ready to help, to be the Saviour.

    Pick out three situations each day in which you in secret and silently pray for another person, visualizing the Saviour spreading His light within them and their affairs.

    Then practice trying to trust other people—not because they necessarily deserve trust, but because you are trusting the Spirit of the Lord in them.

3. For now, do not ask anything for your son. He is God's child as well as yours; God loves him even more than you do. Turn him over completely to that light of Christ within him.

    Whenever you think of your son, picture the light spreading as God does His own work within this boy.

Mr. Daily explained to this father that he and his wife were the key to the situation in the sense that the Law of the Generations enabled God to use them as His divine catalyst to change their son.

"As you work on this program," Starr explained, "you'll be reclaiming your spiritual parenthood. You see, God's order for the home is that husband and father must shoulder spiritual along with financial responsibility. In a real sense the man is to be God's representative—priest or prime minister, as you will—for his own household. When the man takes this rightful place, then God promises His protection and blessing for that home."

"My wife's been the spiritual one in our family," the man objected.

"Maybe that's part of your problem. With both parents alive, in God's eyes there's no such thing as the woman being the spiritual head of the house. When that happens, strength and vitality go out of Christianity every time."

"Why? I don't get it."

"When a father thinks so little of God that he leaves any slight gesture toward Him up to his wife, how important are children—especially boys—going to think religion is anyway? Maybe," Starr added gently, "that's part of the problem with your boy."

The father ruminated on that for a moment. At last he said slowly, "Looks like I've got a lot of work to do."

The father left with new hope. But it took him and his wife two months really to get under way with the program Starr Daily had assigned them. Disregarding the initial awkwardness and unreality they felt, they took up prayer separately and together.

Though these parents did not understand why, during these months they no longer worried about their son. Later on, they understood that Starr's prescription had helped them put first things first: they were actually living out the Scriptural promise, "Seek ye first His kingdom of God, and His righteousness; and all these things shall be added unto you."[16]

Three and a half months passed. The father had long since finished the Gospel of John and had gone on to the Acts. One morning he had gotten to Chapter 10, where he was reading the story of the Apostle Peter and the Italian centurion Cornelius. Suddenly, a particular verse leapt out of the page at him:

God hath shewed me that I should not call any man common or unclean.[17]

His eyes were riveted to the words. An insistent thought kept hammering on his mind for admittance. Was God trying to give him a message through that verse?

The story was plain enough. Peter was given a vision of a huge sheet let down from heaven filled with all manner of creatures including some that the Jews regarded as unclean. The meaning: Peter was to disregard the Jewish taboo on certain foods. This led into the larger truth that Gentiles who wanted to ally themselves with the infant Christian church did not have to become Jews first. That, in turn, burst into a truth so big—here the father held his breath—that it embraced the whole world: God was asking Peter and all of us to love everything He had made, all His other creatures and one another. Nothing—no one—is to be refused the grace and love of God. So that had to include his son, the boy in prison.

Since God had accepted and welcomed him, the father, God expected him, in turn, to have the same openness of heart toward his son.

A warmth the man had never before felt flooded his heart. Here was a message to him straight from God. He would hold fast to that and no longer believe the prison official's negative prognosis about his son. Now he could receive every thought of his son into his mind with thanksgiving.

Here is Starr Daily's brief summary of what happened:

As this father turned from fear of and doubt in his son and looked steadfastly at the good with more and more praise, the boy began to respond to the new parental conviction and attitude. And it was done *"across space" without personal contact.* When the father visited his son six months later, the young man was cured of his criminal mind and well on his way to total rehabilitation.

When the parents (and especially the father) allowed God to become the Head of their home, the immutable Law of the Generations worked just as Starr had predicted—from sharply negative, the situation was turned upward to a glorious positive.

I have been fascinated to read about what happened in one entire family where the blessings of the Law of the Generations were joyously fulfilled through many generations.

In her delightful book about "the uncommon union of Jonathan and Sarah Edwards"[18] Elisabeth D. Dodds gives us a composite portrait of the Jonathan Edwards family. Edwards, the Puritan, has been wrongly pictured as an overly serious ecclesiastical sourpuss, remembered chiefly for a single sermon, "Sinners in the Hands of an Angry God." The full picture of him is very different.

Sarah Pierrepont and Jonathan Edwards were married in 1727 after a courtship of four years. Edwards was over six feet tall, towering over most of his contemporaries. His bride was a vibrant brunette with erect posture, gracious manners, and a gift for conversation that put people at ease.

The Puritan view of marriage was not the restrictive and spiritless one usually assumed. Most Puritans had a healthy viewpoint toward marriage, sex, and family life. Sarah's wedding dress was "no white wraith mistily drifting toward some vague spiritual experience . . . but she wore a peagreen satin brocade with a bold pattern as she stepped joyfully toward her lover."

Sarah and Jonathan were to have eleven children. Edwards believed in rising very early, so everyone in the house was routed out even in the dark winter predawn for prayers by candlelight. The family heard the father read a chapter from the Bible and then ask God's blessing on the day ahead.

Each child had chores. As the child's taste developed, his or her tasks were chosen as largely as possible on the basis of special talents and wishes. For example, Esther gardened, while Mary claimed that she was the champion maker of chocolate. The house functioned efficiently because all these highly individual children were taught to work together.

Courtesy was the rule. The parents approached the discipline of their children united; this may be one reason why the children, in turn, married happily.

One Samuel Hopkins, who spent many months with this family, wrote in his quaint style:

Sarah carefully observed the first appearance of resentment and ill will in her young children toward any person whatsoever, and she never connived at it. . . . Her system of discipline was begun at a very early age. . . . She wisely reflected that until a child will obey his parents, he can never be brought to obey God.

Edwards always gave one hour a day of complete attention to his children. Toward evening, he would take his place in his chair, one with a high back, unmistakably the father's. No one else presumed to sit in this particular chair. During this hour the children could ask questions, get help with lessons, or anything else they wanted.

Today it staggers us even to think about the work involved in such a household. How did Sarah Edwards stand up under this? Her security and fulfillment came from her certain assurance of her husband's love and the place of great honor always given her in their home. Jonathan treated Sarah with total courtesy and serenely expected that each child would follow his example. His wife always sat next to her husband at the table. Their children were able to observe daily the small affectionate demonstrations of their parents' love for one another.

About four o'clock on fair afternoons, Edwards would emerge from his study and suggest that Sarah join him in a horseback ride. The couple would ride together in the hills above the river. Edwards would test the day's harvest of ideas against Sarah's practical intelligence.

Sarah depended on her husband for her own spiritual replenishment. Whenever she felt an acute need of it, she would dive into his study during the day, confident that no matter how intent he was on his writing, he would put down his pen and turn to her with a lighted face. She fed on his leadership in family prayers and on the quiet times she and Edwards spent together on devotions after the children were in bed, a time together that put a benediction on the bustle of the daylight hours.

In those Colonial days, most women lost their looks early. Not so, Sarah. Her husband appreciated her beauty and her style. Everything she did was with flair. She took the trouble to tie her hair with a ribbon for breakfast and found that extra time to arrange bouquets of the daylilies, pansies, and pinks she grew.

Though the Edwardses had little money, Jonathan once spent eleven pounds for a gold chain and locket for his wife. So unusual was this for the time that his parishioners were critical of what they regarded as an overly lavish gift.

On another occasion, Sarah went through a bad emotional time for a number of weeks. Long before anyone had thought of psychotherapy, Jonathan had Sarah sit down and tell him everything she could remember about the weeks past. Using a shorthand system he had invented, he took down her words in full. By promptly reliving the difficult weeks, Sarah was able to put into perspective the pressures which had built up over fourteen years of neverending household demands. From then on, she sailed through strains that might have sent another woman into bitter seclusion or whining invalidism.

In this family where "the hearts of the fathers and the children" were so visibly turned one to another it is possible to see how God blessed them down through the generations "unto thousands of them that love me, and keep my commandments."[19] In 1900 A. E. Winship tracked down 1400 of the Edwards' descendants and published a study detailing what astonishing riches this family had contributed to the American scene. By 1900 this single marriage had produced:

    13 College presidents
    65 Professors
   100 Lawyers and a dean of an outstanding law school
    30 Judges
    56 Physicians and a dean of a medical school
    80 Holders of public office:
       3 United States senators
       Mayors of three large cities
       Governors of three states
       A vice-president of the United States
       A comptroller of the United States Treasury

Members of the family had written 135 books ranging from *Five Years in an English University* to a tome on *Butterflies of North America*. They had edited 18 journals and periodicals. They had entered the ministry in platoons, with nearly 100 of them becoming missionaries overseas.

The Edwards family is a beautiful showcase of how God fulfills His promises when we do our part. For the greatest blessings that God has to give us are never offered just to the individual. Always, "the promise is unto you, and to your children . . ."[20] And the early Church held up as the ideal not individual salvation but household salvation, thus demonstrating the outworking of the Law of the Generations in the love and interrelatedness of the Christian community.

God is sending us a ringing call to understand that we cannot escape the blessing or the curse of the generations. If we will allow Him to, our Lord

> . . . shall turn the heart of the fathers to the children, and the heart of the children to their fathers. . . .

Here is God's singing, soaring promise of what this could ultimately mean to nations of splintered families.

"The generations" can start to assume their creative function *at any point.* Even if most of one's life is in the past and certain children and grandchildren are acute problem cases, yes, even then God can turn this curse that goes down through the generations into a blessing. Moreover, this redemptive work can even work backwards, as in Peter's prayer for me, when my son was the instrument used to stop the fear inheritance up through an older generation as well as down to the generations to come.

For each of us—no matter what our situation or how we feel we have failed—there is hope.

> See, I have set before you this day life and death, the blessing and the curse . . .
> Therefore, choose life.

5.

The Joy of Obedience

*H*ave you ever gotten an inner nudge to do something but resisted it? Then later you found out why you should have obeyed the nudge? Most of us have experienced this.

Of course, we are right to be careful about obeying hunches, because they can come from selfish desires or from negative forces outside us. On the other hand, when a person has asked God to take over his life and guide his actions, disregarding the inner Voice can be costly. I have heard story after story dramatizing how the Lord tries to reach us with His wisdom and help.

The latest comes from Nancy De Moss. She and her husband Art,[1] on that unforgettable Sunday night, September 3, 1972, were living in a spacious English Tudor house not far from Valley Forge, Pennsylvania. The De Mosses have seven children.

The week before Labor Day weekend, Nancy received a telephone call from her sister Lynne. She and her husband were going on a short trip for the holiday. Would Nancy be willing to keep their baby? With seven De Moss children in the sprawling house there was always room for one more. Nancy readily agreed. She thought the eleven-month-old Brandon was one of the most beautiful babies she had ever seen, tow-headed with big blue eyes and a smile that melted everyone who saw it.

But this time taking care of Brandon turned out to be difficult. The baby was restless from teething. For two nights the entire household got little sleep. On Sunday Nancy decided to move the baby's crib from the guest room (where it was proving difficult to hear him) to the playroom down the hall.

While the family was at dinner that evening, Ginny, a good friend of Nancy's sister, dropped in. "I've come to take Brandon home with me," she told the family.

When Nancy protested, Ginny explained, "Lynne had asked me to keep Brandon. I was the one who should have taken him. I just know it. But we had something on for the weekend and I let this loom too large in my mind and turned her down. Ever since I've known that was wrong."

"But my sister will be home soon," Nancy said, "and I don't mind keeping the baby a bit."

"I know. But Lynne asked me to keep Brandon in the first place."

When Nancy saw that nothing she could say would change Ginny's mind, she agreed and Ginny drove off with the baby.

Later on that night Art and Nancy had been asleep several hours when they were awakened by violent pounding on the door.

"The house is on fire!" The housekeeper's voice was shrill with fear. "Get out! Quick! I've got the children out!"

Art and Nancy stumbled to their feet. The hallway was thick with swirling acrid smoke. Shouting the children's names, they groped their way to the front door. Figures were clustered on the lawn, orange-red in the light of the flames from an upstairs window. Counting over and over, Nancy at last was reassured— all seven outside, safe.

They crowded around her, all talking at once . . . "The smoke made me cry, Mummy" . . . "We got out by the back stairs" . . .

It was one of the children's statements that sent a sudden chill up Nancy's spine, "When I passed the playroom door, Mom, it was *full* of fire right up to the ceiling."

The playroom! . . . Nancy looked up to the flaming square of window.

"It seems to have started in there," the housekeeper said.

And Brandon—Brandon would have been in the playroom where no human effort could have reached him.

In telling me the story, Nancy's eyes opened wide at that point. "I still get shaky every time I think, what if Ginny hadn't come—"

I too blinked in realization. "It certainly puts a frightening priority on obeying those inner nudges," I commented.

"Yes, it does—except that Ginny said it was more like a distress signal, then after that like an inner shove. She's been pondering for sometime now how a person gets God's guidance. In this situation the signal was loud and clear. She was restless that particular Sunday afternoon. Her thoughts kept going to Brandon and her refusal to take him in the first place. But the child was obviously all right with us. Then suddenly Ginny had this strong feeling that she *must* go and bring Brandon back to her house.

"She was afraid she would sound silly to us. It could be embarrassing. She tried to shake off the feeling, but by dinnertime Ginny knew she had to obey. Instead of calling me, she left a message with the housekeeper to have Brandon's things ready. She knew that if she came in person, I couldn't turn her away without the baby. And you know, later investigation proved that the fire *had* started in the playroom exactly where Brandon would have been sleeping. So the baby's life actually hung on Ginny's determination in obeying what she so deeply felt."

As I pondered this story in subsequent days, I remembered how often Jesus had told us that we would be wise men and women to obey His instructions. He even went on to say that when we go through great difficulty—such as torrential rain and floods and storm winds beating against our house, it will not collapse and we won't be in real danger—if we obey Him.[2]

Yet how difficult it is for most of us to believe that the obedience God asks of us is for our benefit. A story like Nancy's makes it clear that it is *not* obeying that poses the appalling risk. No wonder Jesus had so much to say about obedience!

Unlike earthly kings, God does not want our obedience out of fear. Our obedience to Him is the fruit of lives growing in the rich soil of love and trust. Our obedience is to be at once both the result of our loving God and also the proof of our love.[3] As with our human love, we are going to be capable of loving only to the extent that we abandon ourselves to another with no reservations.

Nancy's story made me eager to search out Jesus' words on obedience. I found an amazing assortment of riches promised those who learn the joys of obedience.

Salvation is given to those who obey.[4]

When we purpose in our will to obey Jesus and tell Him so, then we shall know whether Jesus' teachings are from God or merely His own.[5]

We become members of Jesus' family when we obey Him.[6]

The Father will come to a man who obeys and make His abode within him.[7]

Jesus will manifest Himself to those that obey.[8]

The Holy Spirit is given to those that obey.[9]

Our deeds will be blessed when we obey.[10]

As we obey Jesus, the Father will shower us and our affairs with His love.[11]

Certainly, these are impressive dividends from obedience. But what exactly are we to obey? Since Jesus often mentioned His commandments, I found it helpful to read the Gospels through, setting down in a notebook the commandments which Christ Himself gave us. There are a remarkable number of them and many are surprisingly precise.

In addition, Scripture clearly points out other kinds of obedience God requires of us:

1. To law and governmental authority.

As citizens of transient earthly kingdoms (along with the eternal kingdom of God) we are voluntarily to subject ourselves to law and the national government over us.[12]

2. To the individual's Christian fellowship—what the Bible calls "the Body," meaning the true Church, the Body of Christ on earth, we are to "be subject one to another."[13] Thus the individual's inner guidance is to be checked against the wisdom of the group mind.[14]

3. To our human family.

Depending upon our individual position in the family unit, God asks of us obedience and responsibility in a chain of Divine Order which He has established. . . . Christ is the Head of each human family.[15]

The husband is under Christ's authority as he assumes leadership of his home and final authority over the children of the household.[16]

The wife is the helpmate to the husband, protected by him from stresses outside the home and even from any abuse from children. God would elevate woman, not plunge her into servitude. Rather, her husband is to honor her with an unselfish love even as "Christ loved the Church and gave Himself up for her."[17]

Children are to obey both their parents "in everything, for this pleases the Lord."[18]

This Divine Order gives us necessary safeguards so that the individual does not mistake the Shepherd's voice. With such solid support, we can relax into the freedom of a living Lord's dealings with us individually. It is when we try to hear Christ's Voice for the daily decisions that we begin to know Jesus personally. Most people are astonished at His interest in the details of this relationship: how well He knows us, all the little things we thought we had successfully hidden; how realistic and relevant are the directions that He gives us.

Substituting a type of superspirituality for Jesus' homespun practicality can be one subtle way many of us try to keep a safe distance between Him and us. C. S. Lewis humorously illustrates this by telling us one way we can "render our prayers innocuous": make sure that they're always very "spiritual," that we are concerned with the state of another's soul, for instance, rather than his rheumatism.[19]

It may turn upside down one's preconceived notions about Jesus to realize that He *is* concerned about rheumatism and not especially interested in the lofty generalities in which we tend to take refuge. The Bible also tells us that He is concerned about the fall of sparrows and the baby's teething and our little habits that have us bound more than we realize.

Insomnia may seem an odd affliction through which to learn the Lord's definition of obedience.

Not long ago I was still one of those unfortunates struggling with sleeplessness. In 1955 my physician had suggested a mild sleeping pill as the best solution. After years of using these, I was aware of the still small Voice on the inside calling the pills into question. But I kept ducking. There was the fear, not even admitted to myself, that if I listened to the inner Voice, He would say something I didn't want to hear.

On those sleepless nights when my churning mind would not be turned off, wearily I would finally get up to find the cylindrical plastic bottle with the tiny capsules, pink on one half, blue on the other. Sometimes half-aware of a "Stop" on the inside, I would pause even as my hand reached for the bottle. "But I'm so exhausted," would run the counter thought. "Surely this isn't the time to fight spiritual battles. I need sleep to get on with that important work tomorrow." Once again I would take the sleeping pill.

Then one morning in 1972 en route to the airport to catch a plane, I realized that I had left the sleeping pills at home. I thought, "Great! God has a wonderful sense of humor. The joke's on me! So this is the way He's going to give me the breakthrough I've been wanting." Then I asked Him to see to it that I slept naturally.

As usual, His ways were not my ways. That night I did not sleep at all. Dawn found me weary from tossing and from praying in what seemed to be a vacuum and fighting a losing battle with self-pity. But leaving the pills behind had uncovered in a stark way how overdependent I was on barbiturates.

Upon returning home, my prayers took the form of direct questions: "Lord, am I hearing You correctly on this? Is this false guilt I have about something really unimportant, like these foolish little pills?"

When His answer finally came, there was no difficulty about recognizing His voice, "Yes, pills are foolish. But the more important point is, you desire sleep more than Me. Therefore, lay your cherished sleep on My altar. Make this your alabaster box of ointment poured out for Me."

His words rang true, like the notes of a clear bell perfectly in tune. Obviously He was applying to my life His "If you love Me, keep My commandments." I realized then that obedience was going to be the key to some fresh new understanding. I was also to find that this is the way to get understanding rather than by the intellectualizing, library-digging route—obey first, then the illumination comes.

That September afternoon I searched through the medicine cabinet for all the sleeping pills. There was a large supply on hand. Taking a deep breath, I flushed them away and watched as the swirling mass of pink and blue disappeared from sight. Then I told God that I was going to depend on Him alone for sleep.

There followed eight rough days and nights. My dependence on God was real enough but so was my sleeplessness. How was it, I would marvel over and over, that both body and mind could be so fatigued, yet I would be unable to sleep? Isn't it man's natural state to sleep?

Quickly I found that continued loss of sleep was resulting in oversensitized nerves day and night. The slightest noise was amplified many times. . . . Someone would turn the pages of a magazine and for me it would be a loud rustling flip-flop. A bug would hit the windowpane and I would jump. I would turn over in bed and the freshly laundered sheets crackled in my ears. I couldn't even nap of an afternoon. Something was inhibiting the sleep mechanism.

That God would let the struggle be so brutal came as a shock. Having taken what I fondly considered a positively heroic step in dumping the pills, I had expected my reward: an instant miracle.

I was given one, though not what I had expected. Even in the midst of my deepest fatigue there was no real temptation to go back to the sleeping pills even for one good night's sleep. The set of my will was firmly held by Someone else, astonishing to me because it was not of my doing.

I was learning about the part the will plays in our relationship with God. First, there is that period of initial struggle of the will when we know full well that a decision has to be made. God won't force it on us; it must be entirely our choice.

Once the struggle is resolved to the point of saying "Yes" to Him—especially when it's accompanied by some irretrievable step such as the pill-dumping—then the struggle in the will subsides. Grace is given an individual at that juncture, at the point of the decision previously made. God regards it as a binding contract. It's as if by saying "Yes" to Him we pick up the ball (the will) and throw it to Him. He takes it then; he carries the will for us.

Even so, during these days I was given no relief on the sleep front. In an effort to understand, I began doing some reading about sleep. Some scientists believe that the brain has both a sleep center and a wakefulness center,[20] much as one's heart action is regulated by one set of nerves to stimulate activity, another set to reduce activity. It is theorized that natural sleep comes through reducing the wakefulness center's activity partly by withdrawing nervous impulses to the brain. Artificial sleep from pills comes through a chemical that enters the blood stream and may depress or inhibit the waking center's activity, thus changing the brain's chemistry. So for me, long use of even mild sleeping pills obviously had knocked my sleep mechanism all askew.

The nights seemed endless. I would hear a dog barking somewhere, then the electric refrigerator clicking off. There would be the sound of a train in the distance, the five-after-two-in-the-morning freight. The engineer was blowing his whistle for that long straight stretch just before town.

The long periods of wakefulness required sharp disciplining of thoughts and emotions. I had had a lifetime tendency to let my thoughts sink to the bottom every time I let my mind go fallow. Now a new level of obedience was being asked of me where negative or critical thoughts, doubting and worrying must be turned off immediately. After a few nights I noticed that I could take more authority over the negativism. This then, was another bonus of obedience.

I was also having to battle another byproduct of barbiturates. These drugs tend to inhibit dreaming. In sleep experiments[21] those deprived of dreaming begin to show nervous and behavioral disturbances. Since much of my dreaming had been inhibited, conflicts and tensions had been building up in my unconscious.

It was a great night when I got three to four hours' sleep. When I did sleep, my dreams seemed continuous and wild and persistently pointed to two deep anxieties—rejection and danger. In an effort to understand, I wrote down the dream of September 23rd:

I am the preacher's wife in a church in which an elaborate wedding is being solemnized—more gala than solemn. There are tickets to present at the church door and a fashion show is also to be part of the affair.

I am acutely aware that I am not part of the "in" group. I seem to have arrived late and am incorrectly dressed. There is some discussion as to whether I am to be allowed into the church without a ticket. Fashionably dressed women are milling all around me looking at me curiously.

The dream ends without my knowing whether or not I will be admitted inside to see the ceremony.

There were also many dreams in which there was actual danger:

A group of us have been told that something important (unidentified) is missing. We are asked to go and get it. We have to walk a long way—uphill and down, through several houses, in one door, out another. I feel threatened. Some of the women argue with me, some are belligerent.

There are even physical threats—one especially vivid one: as we pass through one house near the front screen door, the man of the house warns, "Look out! Pull your hat over your forehead. And watch the angle that you open that door."

On the porch a rifle is mounted on a stand to the left of the door. It is connected to the door like a booby trap, so that when the door is opened to a certain angle the gun fires.

I wake up shivering with fear.

Sometimes resentment would rise in me. "All right, Lord," I would protest, "I obeyed You and look where it's gotten me. I've been miserable ever since."

Eventually the answering insight came, "When you obey, I do more than handle one little thing. You've been demanding an instant miracle for sleep; I want a healing of the whole woman. You've been asking for *one* blessing; obedience is the door through which I plan to flood you with blessings."

Following that, on the eighth day came the first breakthrough. After the worst night of all, I slept a little toward dawn and awoke with a single clause in my mind, presented to me in an authoritative and luminous way: *Blessed assurance, Jesus is mine.*

I recognized it as an old gospel hymn, one I had not thought about for years. When I looked it up and got all the words, God's message to me was plain and oh, so welcome:

> Blessed assurance, Jesus is mine!
> Oh, what a foretaste of glory divine!
> Heir of salvation, purchase of God,
> Born of His Spirit, washed in His blood,
> This is my story, this is my song,
> Praising my Saviour all the day long. . . .[22]

This came as if in direct answer to the rejection aspect of my dreams. Obedience had helped me identify and face the rejection. Here was God's reassurance of His love and care for me, as if He was saying in terms of sleep, "You may fall tranquilly asleep any time you need to, for I love you."

So obedience in the little area of pills had led to the beginning of this deep healing of a basic need. The last line of the hymn pointed me to the next step in the healing—praise. That now-familiar way of praise—the open door to God!

After that, the threat-fear aspect of my dreams diminished, then disappeared altogether. In their stead delightful dreams of promise surfaced. Such as the one on September 30:

> I am wandering from room to room in a large house. In the spacious dining room is a large and beautiful rug, and on it an intricately designed carved mahogany table, with portraits on the walls. An air of mustiness pervades everything as if these rooms have long been in disuse. Though I have never seen such a room, in the dream I have the impression that it is mine.
>
> Going on to the adjoining room, I stand looking at tall cupboards with glass doors all around. They are filled with china and glassware that I recognize as belonging to me, but these possessions have not been used in a long time. I stand staring at all of it wonderingly, thinking how beautiful it is and what happiness to know that it will now be used again.

Whatever else this meant, certainly there was implied the picking up again of joyous activities that had somehow been set aside.

The quantities of china and glassware suggested entertaining as a reactivation of human relationships in a creative outgoing way and an end to the unconscious mind's conviction of rejection.

The ninth day saw real victory, the wonderful feeling of sinking blissfully to sleep without fear and resistance.

Now, all these months later, I can say, "Yes, it's natural to sleep." And how great not only to be free from the chains of dependence but to know that lifelong problems are being healed.

Yet the road to freedom had to be through that low door of obedience. Best of all is the closer fellowship with the Lord that always follows obeying a specific He asks of us.

After such an experience the Shepherd usually allows us a plateau for rest and refreshment. Then we learn that this obedience is a steady daily discipline and that the discipline is for life. But being fickle creatures, we use our freedom of will sometimes to take back what we've already handed over to the Lord.

It took my friend Pat Baker several years to conquer the cigarette habit. But finally breaking the habit was the least of her rewards. She was given insights about her own personal motivations, about the difference between real and counterfeit sacrifice, about how important it is to let God design the blueprint for obedience rather than trying to fabricate it ourselves.

After many tries, Pat had at last achieved a four months' conquest of the smoking habit. The victory had come through a simple step of obedience. For weeks Pat had been feeling God's inner "Stop" each time she reached for a pack of cigarettes. There came a day when she said "Yes" but added, "If I'm going to have to quit, You'll have to do this for me." Lying on the dresser before her was a pack of cigarettes. Deliberately, she left them there. Every time she was tempted to pick one up, she would think, "If this were my idea to stop, I'd already have a cigarette in my mouth by now. But it's just not me at all."

She found it exhilarating—the most joyful experience of her life. Then one evening she and her husband Dick had an argument. In a spirit of rebellion, Pat fled the house and drove around town trying to dispel her anger. All at once, she found herself reaching for a pack of cigarettes her husband had left on the front seat. Even as she did so, she was saying on the inside, "Lord, I know You've told me to stop. And I really will stop—but not quite yet."

For a year after the argument with her husband, Pat found herself waging a losing battle in her struggle with tobacco. She asked prayers from all and sundry friends. Some of them suggested that one way of tackling the problem was to probe why she had started smoking in the first place. Yet Pat could find no answer to the question.

At last she got to that point of desperation I knew so well. "O Lord, I want to be free. I really do. And I won't take the cigarettes back this time." There was no immediate answer.

Then one Sunday afternoon she felt as if she was coming down with a cold. She decided on a nap. When she awakened she instantly recognized that there was something not of herself in the clear thought in her mind, "Get up. Get dressed. Go down to the Bethany Church."

Pat was inclined to argue, "Lord, that's a wild church. I'm an Episcopalian. I've never been in that kind of place—" Then more humbly, "Lord, if this is really You and this is what I'm supposed to do, would you please let Dick agree to it?"

Ordinarily her husband Dick would say in a situation of this kind, "Don't be ridiculous. You've been out three nights this week. Be sensible and go back to bed."

This time however, when she told him of this strange nudging, he answered, "Go ahead, I think you should."

When Pat got to the church she found that some sort of evangelistic services were going on. She slipped into the back hoping that she wouldn't be noticed. After all, this was a small town. What would her fellow Episcopalians think of her attending this kind of church?

Then the preacher's words caught her attention. He was speaking about Cain and Abel and about Abel's "more excellent sacrifice."

"Perhaps," the young preacher said, "Cain never had liked the idea of killing innocent little lambs as a sacrifice to Jehovah. Why would Jehovah ask them to do that? Wouldn't it be better to wait until he understood why, and then obey?

"Meanwhile, if God wanted a sacrifice, how about that beautiful mound of fruits and vegetables he had grown! Those perfect bunches of grapes! Those luscious pomegranates and figs! Surely Jehovah would like those!

"You see, the problem with Cain," the young preacher summarized, "was that he was offering a sacrifice all right, one that he had thought up, but *not the sacrifice God had asked for.*"

Sitting there listening, Pat thought of all her multitudinous church and civic activities, of her generous giving of time and money, of her sacrifices during Lent. But the clear counter-thought came to her, *None of this is any good unless you do the particular thing I'm asking you to do.*

"O Lord," Pat answered in her thoughts, "I hear You loud and clear, but I can't do what You're telling me to do. I've tried. I just can't."

Now the evangelist was giving an altar call, but it wasn't the usual one. "All those," he said, "who came here expecting God to do something for them, come forward to receive it."

That sounded the right note to Pat. She knew that being there hadn't been her idea in the first place. "But," she struggled with herself, "I'm just not going down there. I know that young man will shout like those other evangelists do. . . . Lord, do they *have* to be so loud about it?"

Moments later she was astonished to find herself kneeling at the altar rail. The evangelist made his way to her first of all. Without saying a word, he knelt quietly on the other side. Pat looked across the rail at him, surprised at his quietness. Finally he said, almost whispering, "The Holy Spirit never gives one of us a message for another person in order to hurt or embarrass them. The message is always given to help another. Do you understand that?"

"Yes, I do," Pat replied, marveling at the way the young minister was speaking directly to her thoughts.

"Would you like to hear what God has for you this afternoon?"

She nodded.

"Well, He's ready to deal with you about your problem with nicotine."

Pat stared at him in astonishment. How could he possibly know that? She listened wide-eyed as he began telling her when and why she had started to smoke. "It started when you were a teen-ager and it grew out of the soil of rebellion. Even then, God was calling you, but you weren't willing to listen. Now He has a special gift of the Spirit for you, one that He wants you to use in a particular ministry for Him. If you're willing to get rid of the nicotine, He'll reveal more to you of what this is all about."

Then the evangelist told Pat how to get free. "If you will resist the nicotine for three days, the Lord will do the rest. At the end of that time, He promises to reveal something of the particular kind of work He's calling you to."

As she drove home that night Pat thought, "Well, I suppose I can do anything for three days." But she was to find even three days so much more difficult than it had been the first time. Now it was a moment-by-moment battle.

On the third day, a friend whose marriage was in trouble came to thank Pat for helping her find her way out of darkness several weeks before. Immediately, Pat realized that she had allowed her bondage to cigarettes to interfere even with helping other people. She had been so preoccupied with herself and her hang-ups like smoking that there had been no time or mind-space for anyone else. The impact of her friend's gratitude brought Pat tears of remorse followed by a surge of joy and a strong resolve that bolstered her resistance.

From that point, Pat found herself free of the desire to smoke—when she was awake! But strangely, she began to dream of smoking.

The dreams were so vivid! She could taste the cigarettes and smell the smoke, and would wake up with the knowledge that she had been fighting the desire to smoke on unconscious levels. Out of this experience Pat learned that we have to be of one piece—not divided between the conscious and the unconscious—before a prayer can be finally answered. In her case, Pat had been delivered from smoking on the surface; now a deeper work was going on in her unconscious.

Dreams by night and insights by day revealed to her what the evangelist had suggested: the smoking had started through insecurity during her courtship days. Now she was able to remember what had goaded her to start smoking—nothing more than several paragraphs in one of Dick's letters. He was then at the University of Florida and, to tease her, he had written glowingly about another girl.

Pat had overreacted with anger and jealousy. Wanting to rebel against Dick and her whole life, she chose cigarettes as the best symbol of rebellion. Hadn't her mother always made *not* smoking a symbol of virtue? Before she and Dick could resolve the quarrel, Pat had started smoking.

The battle of the cigarettes is four years behind Pat now. Depending on the Lord (instead of cigarettes) in moments of friction and stress has brought Pat not only joy, but a steady stream of deepening insights to help other people with their problems.

When Jesus says, "Follow Me," not a one of us is going to drop his fishing nets to leave all and go after Him—unless he feels he can trust Him. One memorable sentence quoted by the Quakeress Hannah Smith sums it up, "Perfect obedience would be perfect happiness if only we had perfect confidence in the power we are obeying."[23]

So we're back full circle to the only basis there is for obedience—love and trust. It may seem hard to be asked to have this kind of confidence before we have had personal experiences of God. But He also helps us out of that dilemma. The moment we "purpose in our heart" to obey Him, at that instant He comes to help us. His incomparable gift is the ability to obey, to move out into what usually looks like uncharted and dangerous country.

That's the way it was for Abraham long ago. The Lord had told him to uproot himself and his family: "Get thee out of thy country, and from thy kindred . . . unto a land that I will shew thee . . . and I will bless thee . . . and thou shalt be a blessing."[24]

There was the word of command. There was the promise of blessing. There was no option to ask "Why?" or "Please explain everything to me." Always and always the understanding comes after the obedience.

So Abraham obeyed. "He went out, not knowing whither he went." He did not need to know because God knew. And the result of this "blind" obedience has blessed uncounted millions down all the generations.

6.

"To Sleep!
Perchance to Dream . . ."

I dreamed last night . . .

In a living room I saw a pedestal-stand about two feet tall! On it had been placed the head of a woman. From a distance it looked like one of those marble busts that one sees in palaces or museums.

But this bust was different. It had been severed from the body of a living woman and placed atop the pedestal.

In my dream as I looked on, a female figure appeared in the room. She looked at the bust as she passed within a few feet of it. Then she uttered just two words, "It stinks."

I keep wondering, what is the dream trying to tell me?
Seemingly gruesome in imagery, I was to learn later that it held a potent spiritual message.

Few of us attached importance to dreams until the rising influence of psychiatry began to pique interest in the subject.

Even those who have never been near a psychiatrist's office now know that patients are asked to take their dreams seriously enough to capture them on paper and consider them.

Even so, the average person wonders from time to time if dreams have anything rational and constructive to say to us. Or are they the result simply of eating too much pizza or of something one saw on the Late Late Show?

On the other side, I have heard of instances where scientists or inventors, unable to finish an experiment or a project because of something eluding them, decided to "sleep on it." And somehow as they slept, the unconscious served up the solution needed—sometimes directly upon awakening, sometimes in a dream.

Yet most have regarded these experiences as flukes. What about the bulk of dream material? Isn't it mostly just garbage-pail residue of daytime experiences?

Clearly, psychoanalysts do not think so. It was in 1900 that Sigmund Freud published his book *The Interpretation of Dreams*, for the first time connecting dreams with the unconscious in an empirical study. Among physicians and the public in general, Freud's book met with contempt: it took eight years to sell the 600 copies of the first edition.

As time went on, dream interpretation came to be an accepted part of psychotherapy. Even so, I could uncover little on the subject in Christian literature. The Church for the most part was ignoring the subject. This was strange when we consider the thread of dream material all through the Bible. I had no sooner become interested in the subject than I realized that the Bible is a veritable storehouse of dreams. How had I previously overlooked this! Jacob dreamed of a ladder from earth to heaven; another time of spotted he-goats mating with the flock. Joseph dreamed of his brother's sheaves bowing down and worshiping his sheaf; later, he interpreted the Pharaoh's dreams. The child Samuel's dream; Amos's dream of a plumb line; Isaiah's of his lips touched with the live coal from the altar; Ezekiel's dream of the valley of dry bones. The book of Daniel—full of dreams. Such an amazing amount of material!

The gist of the Bible's message is that God frequently uses dreams as a medium of revelation.

If there is a prophet among you, I the Lord make myself known to him in a vision, I speak with him in a dream . . . in dark speech.[1]

Nor is there any diminution of this emphasis on dreams in the New Testament. We see the Wise Men being warned in a dream not to go back to Herod but to return to their country another way; Joseph told in a dream to take the young child and his mother and flee to Egypt. We see Pilate's wife frantically sending her husband the message, "I have suffered many things this day in a dream because of him [Jesus]."[2] A major tenet of the early Church was turned on its head by the Apostle Peter's dream picture of the sheet let down from heaven with all manner of birds, reptiles, animals—clean and unclean—in it. And the last book of the Bible, Revelation, is almost entirely dream and vision material of John, then an old man.

Why does the Church in our time pay so little attention to dreams? For a number of years, Freud's viewpoint that the unconscious was concerned mainly with sexuality dominated the field. Perhaps the trouble was that, blinded by Freud's emphasis, the Church could not find a connection between the scriptural emphasis placed on dreams as the vehicle for all manner of messages—dreams thus being one way of God speaking to man—and the Freudian doctrine of sexuality.

As the years have gone on and Freud's dream theories have been amended and enriched by the works of Alfred Adler and Carl Jung and others, as well as a decade of work in sleep laboratories,[3] I discovered that a few men here and there in the Church have been constrained to take another look at the biblical emphasis on dreams. Two of them, Morton T. Kelsey,[4] and John A. Sanford,[5] both Episcopal priests, have experimented, often successfully, in helping troubled people make use of dream material. (At the time I discovered this, little did I realize how much this was shortly going to mean to me personally.)

It's a big subject and generalizations are dangerous. Those who worked in the field warn that we must not try to work out pat formulae to help us interpret our dreams. The point is that the psyche, the total mental and psychological structure of a person, is not just the repository for dead memories but is living and fluid; it will not be pigeonholed any more than the Spirit of God acting upon the psyche can be pigeonholed.

Having warned us, they nevertheless come to our aid with some helpful suggestions. . . . The unconscious, usually "thinks" or translates thoughts into pictures. These pictures usually take the form of either parables or cartoon-like story material. The parables are in many respects reminiscent of the stories and symbols Jesus used in his parable-stories; in other dreams they are akin to the kinds of stories in the folklore of all peoples. Often our dream cartoons or parables are woven into a story or playacted out on an inner stage while we sleep.

The unconscious mind does not think analytically, but symbolically or pictorially. Dream symbols are provocative in their wide variety and above all, in their originality.

We've only to take note of a few of our dreams to know that with our conscious mind we never could have put together such highly original imagery. In some images, there is great simplicity, but the originality is in the way the dream uses them. Here are some symbols from my own dreams and those of others close to me:

> The dreamer is in a rose garden eating rose petals, but carefully; eating the petals will make him intoxicated.

> A child's wicker toy basket is turned upside down over a flame to quench it.

> A flight of newly constructed stairs has no place to set one's feet because all the treads are missing.

> My house is burning, but is not consumed.

> A snowstorm of small squares of fresh white paper falls from the sky.

> A toilet is made of several huge shells.

> A large pair of scissors is used as a murder weapon.

> I see a baby in a tiny boat on a rushing stream.

We wonder where such highly original imagery comes from. In part, the experts say, from conscious sights, impressions, and thoughts passed on into the 90 percent of the psyche below the level of consciousness, then screened, condensed, and translated into dream images.

But beyond this personal area, Freud, Jung, and others believed that the unconscious draws its material from the race mind—what Jung called "the collective unconscious." It is at this point that many dream figures and images connect us with the symbolism used by Jesus, the folk stories of all peoples, and the world's fairy tales.

It reminds us of that memorable little statement inserted in the Gospel of John. "He [Jesus] knew what was in man."[6] Therefore, it shouldn't surprise us that He deliberately chose to use symbolism which would speak to both the conscious and unconscious levels of men of all nations in every century. Notice how Jesus used objects in the external world to teach us truth about the internal world even as our dreams do:

A candle covered by a bushel basket.

A plank sticking out of a man's eye.

Pearls being thrown before hogs.

Digging up a treasure in a field

A minuscule seed growing into an immense tree.

A woman hiding starter-dough in a barrel of flour.

Fishermen with a dragnet pulling in unimaginable varieties of fish.

A serpent lifted high on a stick.

Though some dream symbols come out of this collective unconscious like visions replete with signs and sounds wafting out of some far country where we were once at home, our dreams are often intensely personal and self-reflective. Something deep within seeks to give us a message. Different characters in our dreams are usually parts of our own being.

Aspects of our personality we have ignored or even cast out of our consciousness now seek to be heard. This is so even when the dream figure is of the opposite sex from the dreamer. Psychology teaches us that every man carries within his dominant masculine psyche some largely unconscious feminine traits, what Jung chooses to call "the anima," just as every woman possesses some masculine traits, "the animus." Thus a feminine figure in a man's dream may be trying to point him to "anima" qualities of sensitivity, of the emotional life, of the willingness to love and be loved.

The kind of help our dreams can give us is as varied as people's temperaments and needs. Pat Baker[7] fighting her cigarette problem for example, found that dreams helped her become a believer in a personal God who could comfort and guide her. Married at eighteen, Pat had become pregnant almost immediately. Throughout her pregnancy, she had been deeply troubled, feeling in no way ready for the responsibilities of motherhood. She had a hunger for faith, yet doubts about a personal God. During all those months, the cry of her deep spirit had been, "How can I rear a child when I myself have no answers to what life is all about?"

During childbirth, while Pat was under anesthesia, she had a strange dream. She was sitting in the audience in a theater with a large stage before her. The figures who appeared on the stage looked like cartoon characters come to life. Mrs. Baker described every vivid detail of this dream:

On stage right appeared a woman slowly pushing a baby carriage across the stage. The baby, a girl, was sitting up in the carriage with knitting needles and a ball of yarn trying to figure out a knitting pattern. The baby's face was tense and worried trying to understand the pattern.

As the mother pushed the carriage on, the baby was making progress: another part of the pattern would be finished. The scene before me was so huge that I could clearly see the knitting in the baby's hands. By the time the carriage was almost across the stage, all the pattern was figured out except one stitch. Then the whole tableau —mother, carriage, baby and all—fell off the end of the stage.

Watching, I could feel the drop—kerplunk! in the pit of my stomach. I heard myself saying, "Oh no! God, You can't let that happen. You can't let that poor baby die without figuring that pattern out."

Then I heard a male voice offstage chuckling reassuringly, as if to say, "Don't worry about it. I've got it all figured out."

I then also understood that the baby would know that she wasn't going to be left with that one stitch of the pattern missing. I felt inside myself a relieved, "Oh! Thank God!" as a great peace swept over me.

Then as though to dramatize before my eyes the truth of the reassurance, almost immediately the stage came back into view. There was another mother, another carriage, another baby like the first scene, only this time the baby was peaceful. No strain on her face.

I saw the same knitting in the baby's hands, but now with the missing part of the pattern figured out and an additional one added. This time the mother and baby did not fall off the stage.

Before this, it had never occurred to Pat Baker to take dreams seriously. As if to make certain that she would not discount her dream because of the anesthesia, she was given a detail-by-detail repeat of this dream two more times—once while still in the maternity ward, and then again after she returned home from the hospital. This was the confirmation she needed.

The dream's first gift to Pat was peace of mind. It also helped her to believe in the existence of God in a way she never had before. At a deeper level and after meditating on the dreams prayerfully, Pat realized that the baby in the carriage was a part of her being: *she* was the one who in the first dream couldn't figure out the complicated "knitting" of life; she was the one afraid she would fall off the stage of life.

The second time across the stage, she had figured out life's pattern and she did not fall off. Thus the new mother was given total assurance that the One whom she could not see but had heard as the Voice offstage, knew what was going on in her life and had everything under control. With His help, she and her husband would be able to rear their daughter.

In those rare instances when dreams do warn of a coming event, the purpose is never to frighten or discourage us. The Creator's work through the unconscious, as elsewhere, is affirmative, directed toward a constructive end. Therefore the dream warnings present possibilities we are meant to avoid, seldom actualities.

Dr. Glenn Clark told of how Stella Holbrook, a Minneapolis woman,[8] dreamed that she saw her best friend, a Mrs. Simpson, walking back and forth in a room holding her head between her hands. She had gone insane. Horrified by the dream, Stella was unable to sleep for the remainder of the night. Early the next morning, she telephoned the friend saying that she had to see her. When they met, Stella told her, "You are in deadly peril. You must see a doctor immediately."

"But I've never felt better in my life," the friend, Mrs. Simpson, remonstrated.

"No matter. I plead with you to see a doctor. I've never had a dream so real."

As much for her distraught friend's peace of mind as anything, Mrs. Simpson made an appointment with her doctor. He found a brain tumor located where it would probably cause insanity without prompt surgery. Mrs. Simpson was stunned. Her friend had dreamed the truth after all. But it was the rest of the dream that made her recoil in horror. In Stella's dream, Mrs. Simpson was stark raving mad. So wouldn't it turn out that way—surgery or no surgery?

With this double burden of fear heavy upon her, Mrs. Simpson stopped off to see Dr. Clark on her way to the Mayo Clinic. His advice to her was first, to clear out superstition. "There's no power," he told her, "in the psychic realm of foretelling the future that can stand against God's power. You must vigorously reject any form of superstitious attachment to this dream."

Then he added that *the dream warning had been given so that the event foreseen would not have to come to pass.* "To foresee a thing in time," he suggested, "is just like foreseeing a thing in space. You would not run head-on into it, would you? You'd make a detour around it."

Having agreed between them how to make a detour by means of prayer, Mrs. Simpson went on to Mayo's. The earlier diagnosis was confirmed. They were preparing for the operation when it was decided to ask both Dr. Judd and Dr. Will Mayo to examine the patient. Dr. Will was one of those doctors who studied the person along with his symptoms. In conversation with Mrs. Simpson, he discovered the quality of her faith.

The great surgeon seemed to withdraw into his own thoughts. After a moment of silence, he spoke slowly, thoughtfully. "Any brain surgery is drastic, carries its own risk. There's one other way to proceed. You're the sort of person who may be capable of this other way. The human body is a marvelous creation. When helped by faith and prayer, sometimes it can take care of its own problems. I wonder?" He paused and looked at her long and hard. Mrs. Simpson almost had the impression that he was listening.

"Yes, I believe this is the way. My advice is, let's not operate right away. Mrs. Simpson, I want you to go away for three months. Live quietly, in as healthful a manner as you know. Apply all the faith you have during this time. Then let us here at Mayo see you at the end of three months."

So Mrs. Simpson went to a mountain cabin and devoted herself to a three-months' prayer journey toward health. Day by day she sought, on the one hand, to close every separation between her and God; on the other, to open every facet of her being to healing.

In September she returned to the Mayo Clinic. New X-rays plus carotid angiograms left the specialists puzzled; the tumor was no longer there. Yet in June it had been as big as a hen's egg.

Other doctors were called in, including first, Dr. Judd, and then Dr. Will Mayo. After Dr. Judd had studied the X-rays and exhaustively examined the patient, he seized Mrs. Simpson's hands in excitement. "This," he exclaimed, "is a great miracle." Dr. Will was equally joyous. "I think this calls for a celebration," he said.

About the time I was realizing how pinpointed dreams can be, I met the Reverend Morton Kelsey, Episcopal priest and Notre Dame professor. I then read some of his books and asked if he would be so gracious as to give me help in learning to interpret my dreams.

He replied that he would be happy not only to give me his thoughts on specific dreams, but also some general principles of interpretation. I was to send him eight or ten dreams written out. We would then agree on a date for a long telephone conversation.

The telephone conference was eventually set up for three o'clock on the afternoon of July 18, 1973. With Professor Kelsey's permission, I recorded our forty-five-minute conversation. Morton Kelsey was speaking from South Bend, Indiana.

"First," he commented, "let's put any work with dreams in this framework. . . . The only way anyone should go into the unconscious is, first, to ask Jesus Christ for His power and direction and protection. Personally, I find that without Him I'm in danger even going to the grocery store without His direction, let alone trying to teach a college class.

"Then some general guide lines:"

Ninety-five percent of dream material refers to the dreamer rather than to the one being dreamed about.

Realize that the process of dreaming is, in itself, therapeutic.

One of the greatest dangers in dream interpretation is thinking that you're getting guidance for other people. Almost always it's about *you*.

When one dreams of a husband or wife, it may not necessarily refer to the mate, rather what one is "married to" emotionally and spiritually.

An often helpful procedure is:

Write down your dream immediately upon awakening; if necessary, interrupt your sleep to write it down. Keep a pencil, pad, and flashlight by your bed for this purpose.

Later, write down the main events happening in your life just then and any major fears or worries. You will need this framework for interpretation of your dream.

As your will consents to taking dreams seriously, you'll be able to remember more and more of them. The more dreams we write down immediately upon awakening, the more the unconscious will serve up.

After writing your dream down, talk it out with some trusted person. Let his reflection add wisdom to interpreting your dream.

Third, turn your attention to a study of symbolism, analogies, and images. A good place to begin is to review (perhaps with notebook in hand) the Bible's rich symbolism.

Most of us soon find that our thinking and training has not been in such directions: when we were young, we probably read too many Dick-and-Jane-type stories about going to the supermarket, the dentist, or helping the nice teacher change her flat tire, so now our imaginations need reawakening and nourishment. A deliberate return to the reading of the mythology and fairy tales of all nations and of books like *Hiawatha, Gulliver's Travels, Alice in Wonderland,* C. S. Lewis's[9] novels will help to reconnect us with an important part of ourselves and also assist us in interpreting our dreams.

Take the significant insights or questions into your prayer life. This will provide material for meditation.

During meditation it is helpful to confront the other person or persons in your dream (almost always part of you) and enter into imaginative dialogue with "them." Then invite Christ into this three-way dialogue for His thoughts and directives.

Following these general guide lines, I was eager for Morton Kelsey's observations about my dreams of rejection and danger during the sleeping-pill crisis. "Your dream of September 23rd and the following[10] are both classics," the voice on the phone had a quality of joy, even laughter. "The first one involved an elaborate wedding. How often Jesus spoke of weddings! A wedding is the union of opposites. Nothing about a real mating of opposites was possible for you until after the pill-dumping.

"Your dream wedding included a fashion show. It is reminiscent of the prodigal son on whom the father placed the 'best robe.' The wedding, you wrote, was 'more gala than solemn.' God is not dour or grim-visaged about His religion; His grace takes from us the burden of 'oughtness' and duty, releases us to worship Him joyfully as a feast, a banquet, a celebration. When He has a wedding feast, He does it in top style!

"You were 'incorrectly dressed' . . . you didn't have on the right wedding garment. Remember that on September 23rd you were still working through the aftermath of the pill-dumping. You were not quite ready for the celebration. So the dream ended without your knowing whether you were admitted to the wedding scene."

Then Professor Kelsey went on to discuss the dream involving physical danger.

"'We had to walk a long way,' you wrote. In late September with acute insomnia still with you, the road was seeming very long indeed.

"The rifle on the porch is a reference to the sleeping pills, I feel sure. The dream's gun booby trap was meant to be a warning. Your victory was not yet complete. By returning to the pills you could fall back again. 'Look out: Watch it! This is a life-and-death matter,' the dream was saying . . ."

"By September 30th, you had won your victory, so this is a dream of promise. The house is a typical dream symbol representing one's total being.

"The dining room is for feeding people. What have you done in your writing except to feed people! You wrote, 'a carved table' on a 'beautiful rug' . . . 'portraits on the wall.' You are going to feed people beautifully.

"'The tall cupboards . . . filled with china and glassware' unused for a long time. The years of the sleeping pills had cut you off from part of your own being. Now you can use a lot of content and rich creativity in your psyche you had even forgotten you have.

"I'll make a prediction, Catherine. . . . What you write in the future may have more significance than what you've written in the past."

"Morton," I answered, "I hope you're right!"

A little later I switched the conversation to the Head-on-the-Pedestal dream.[11] "I have some ideas about it," I said, "but I'm very curious about yours."

"All right," came the voice over the telephone. "First, a random comment. The female figure's 'It stinks' reminds me of Martha's almost identical statement at the tomb of her brother Lazarus. . . . Also, do you know C. S. Lewis's *That Hideous Strength*?"

"I have a copy," I replied, "but haven't read it yet."

"You'd better!" Again the chuckle came over the phone. "In the first chapter an Englishwoman dreams of a French prisoner visited in his cell by a rather coldly cynical man. The visitor unscrews the man's head and carries it away."

"I'll start the book tonight."

"All right. Now first, most dreams want us to look inward. Therefore, the head on the pedestal is your head. And the female figure is probably also another part of you.

"Now one or two questions to you, Catherine. Have you had trouble with always wanting to *understand* before you step out in simple obedience?"

"Always. Most definitely. In relation to healing and lots of things about the Holy Spirit, thinking I need to understand has been a real stumbling block."

"Second question, which do you value most, the intellectual process or the emotions?"

"The mind—far and away. I think the emotions can really lead us astray."

"True in part," Morton Kelsey retorted. "Well, I think the dream was issuing you a stern warning. It was saying, 'The head needs a body to be whole—not just the emotions, but the *entire* person.' You see, Christianity is the world's earthiest religion. Centuries ago even very spiritual monks knew that working with their hands—gardening or erecting buildings, working vineyards or even winemaking, copying manuscripts, whatever—was as much a part of true worship as prayer. The use of the whole person, you see."

"Then the dream was saying that I am wrong to place the head, the intellect, on such a pedestal?"

"Correct," came the voice over the phone.

"And that when we sever the mind from the rest of us, the end result is that we die—even intellectually—and so begin to decay? And"—I paused—"stink."

"Right. Your prayer-meditation on this dream could include at least two questions: first, at what points are you resisting the real thrust of the Holy Spirit in your life because of an overemphasis on the mind?"

"Ouch! Now you've put your finger on one of my hang-ups with some aspects of the Holy Spirit Movement."

"A lot of us have the same difficulty. . . . Now, ask yourself the second question: 'Lord, what must I do to get my head back on my body, to begin functioning as a whole person? What is my first step in that direction?'"

I was beginning to see what he meant. "My dreams are providing lots of material for meditation."

"Not just for you personally either," Professor Kelsey replied. "For instance, hasn't the twentieth century created a society where the head rules—education, science, and technology supreme? We thought we could cleave the head from the body— divorce, 'put away' the spirit, the conscience, the imagination, and emotional life and get a Utopia. Maybe instead we have a civilization that could be summarized with a quite inelegant 'It stinks.'"

Dream therapy of a poignant nature was given to Tom Dowling, whom I met in 1967 at the first *Guideposts* magazine Writers Workshop. As the background for Tom's dream, it is necessary to fill in certain details of his life. . . .

The Dowlings lived in California. In September 1958 Tom had taken his wife Babs to Hawaii on a vacation trip to help her recover from a spinal fusion operation. The young couple had left their four children in the care of Tom's father. On the fourth day tragedy suddenly struck: Babs suffered a severe cerebral hemorrhage and after the necessary brain surgery was unconscious for thirty-five days. After consciousness slowly returned, it became apparent that the young woman was paralyzed. Sight and hearing were left to her and she could on occasion speak a word or two. That was all. In the agony and shock of what had happened to her, Babs was in such desperate need of love and reassurance that Tom stayed by her bedside for the first fifty days, even sleeping there in a chair at night. Often, so often, he would reach for her hand or pat her cheek, and the gratitude in her eyes spoke volumes.

In November the paralyzed woman was flown back to a hospital in San Mateo County. Babs lived for just over two years, never recovering from the paralysis. Part of the agony was that her mind was so sharp. She knew what was going on around her. Yet since she couldn't move even a finger, existence became a living death, like being buried inside one's mind. Babs' dark brown hair turned to white.

During the two years there were three major operations and twelve minor ones. Shouldering all home responsibilities and the care and rearing of their four children along with his job, Tom managed to spend forty hours a week at his wife's side. Sometimes he would lift Babs into a wheelchair and take her to the hospital roof so that she could feel the sunshine on her face. Occasionally on a Sunday afternoon he would take her home for a few hours to be with the children and to see that home was being kept ready for her.

When death came to Babs, Tom was holding her hand, whispering a prayer of benediction into her ear. It seemed a merciful release for her and for him.

But Tom soon discovered that he had no release. He was tormented by a dream that kept repeating itself. Though Tom remarried in 1961 and was happy with his new wife, Ginny, the dream recurred sometimes twice a week. Soon he developed serious insomnia. Here is Tom's version of the dream that refused to be turned off:

> I am hurrying to the hospital. When I get there I cannot find Babs' room. Frantically, I go from floor to floor, room to room, calling her name. My panic and frustration grow by the minute because I know how much she needs me.
>
> Finally I stumble into the right room. There she is as always, unable to move, sobbing my name.
>
> Then I awaken in a cold sweat, tears on my face. The nightmare has drained so much emotional energy I can hardly get out of bed and go to work.

Then came the 1967 *Guideposts* Workshop. Tom Dowling was one of twenty-four writers out of 1200 applicants chosen for the week at a country estate on Long Island Sound, a scene of many religious gatherings. In this relaxed setting, companionship and a deep level of communication grew among the five *Guideposts* staff members and the writers from all over the country.

Although most of the time was spent on developing writing skills, there was an early morning prayer time for those interested. Each participant was asked to pick two people from the group to pray for. They could keep the names secret if they wished. Later on, Tom found that a writer from Texas, Dot Main, had chosen him because she sensed that he had pressing needs, though she had no idea what they were. Tom never told anyone at Rye about his nightmare problem.

Looking back, I see the hand of God in almost everything that happened that week. One of the Workshoppers' big discoveries was that writing grows out of life: get the life set right and enriched and creative production rises to new heights. Beyond that, how better to summarize what happened then to say that the Holy Spirit was there that week in fullness and power? Prayers were answered, problems resolved, lives changed.

At the end of the Workshop, Tom left for California feeling that this had been the greatest week of his life. When his wife Ginny, met him at the San Francisco airport, she took one look at him, saw a new calmness on his face, and exclaimed, "Tom, something wonderful must have happened to you!"

A few nights later Tom dreamed again. . . .

As so often before, I am hurrying to the hospital. (Strange! I always know I am dreaming, but can do nothing about it.) *Oh God! Not again—please. Don't let it begin all over again.*

But this time when I reach the hospital there is none of the usual frantic searching. I go directly to Babs' room. She smiles up from the bed and oh, joy! extends her arms to me! She is no longer paralyzed!

She takes my face in her hands and calls my name and great waves of joy, unimaginable joy, rise up in me.

She asks me to put her in the wheelchair as I'd done so often before. I start pushing her toward the elevator to the roof thinking she'd like to soak up some sunshine, but she says, "No, not the roof. Take me in *there*."

I turn in the direction she is pointing and find a room full of people. It's the library at the retreat house on the Sound where my little Workshop group met each day.

As I wheel Babs into the room, the people come to greet her. Great rays of light, love-light, radiate from her as she holds out her hands to each of them!

My happiness is beyond belief. There are tears of happiness in my eyes. Yet there's much more joy to come. . . . When Babs has greeted each Workshopper, she says, "I want to stand."And suddenly she's on her feet!

Then the scene shifts to Oakland, where Babs was born. We're walking beside Lake Merritt as we used to long ago. She's laughing and twirling like a girl full of life and happiness. Then she puts her head caressingly on my shoulder— and the dream ends.

Tom Dowling added, "When I awoke, I bolted straight upright in bed. My usually heavy heart felt feather-light, gay. There was the unmistakable feeling of having been in God's presence. The messages of the dream were so plain:

Babs was no longer paralyzed and was extremely happy.

God had let me know that He loves me.

There is an assurance—a knowing—that I'll never have the nightmare again.

And Tom never has, from that time to the present. The deep wounds to his emotional life and his psyche reaching into the unconscious that Tom had sustained from Babs' terrible illness had been healed—permanently.

Let's suppose the Church and its leaders want to return to the Scriptural view of the importance of dreams. How could we of the laity play a part?

One experience from a Fellowship-Prayer Group in Chappaqua, New York, provides some hints. . . . One of the members, Jean Nardozzi, shared with the others her desperate feelings of exhaustion and her difficulty with sleeping. Because she is a kindergarten teacher with two separate groups of 30 five-year-olds each morning and 30 each afternoon, Jean called herself "a walking disaster area."

For two Wednesday nights the group prayed for Jean. On the third Wednesday, Jean told her friends, "I had a strange dream last night. I'd like to know what you make of it . . .

Some people were holding a baby and indicating that it was mine. In the dream I acted astonished because I didn't know I *had* a baby. The child had been totally neglected, was pitifully thin and undernourished.

Then the dream gave me a message over and over, "The poor thing needs milk."

Two people present gasped simultaneously and both started to speak. Then it came out that in prayer during the interim week (with no communication between the two), each had been given identical guidance for Jean: "She needs milk."

In addition, one of the two, Elizabeth Sherrill, recalled that the morning she had been given this message, she had also been pointed back to Numbers 12:1–10, the story of Aaron and Miriam's criticalness of Moses, particularly to verse 6:

> Hear now my words: If there be a prophet among you, I the Lord will make myself known unto him in a vision, and will speak unto him in a dream.

As events turned out, Jean was led to travel to Boston for an appointment with a specialist, a nutritionist. Among other findings the nutritionist discovered serious calcium deficiency in Jean's system. In passing, the doctor remarked that calcium is one of nature's best soporifics, adding, "The old folk remedy of warm milk at bedtime has that basis in fact." The patient left with diet lists along with necessary supplements.

Within a short time Jean felt like a new person with her sleep improving night by night.

An incident like this reveals that we don't need to be sleep-laboratory researchers or trained analysts to get on with letting God show us how to use our dreams. It is encouraging to recall that our lives are set in the era prophesied by the Old Testament prophet Joel:

> And it shall come to pass in the last days, saith God, I will pour out my spirit upon all flesh. . . . and your young men shall see visions and your old men shall dream dreams.[12]

"All flesh. . . ." It had not always been so. In Old Testament times only the privileged few ever had the gift of the Spirit—only certain prophets, priests, and kings. From this elite group the only true dream interpretations had come. So the Bible's message for our times seems to be: not only will the Spirit of Truth use dreams and help us to understand them, but He is the Interpreter *par excellence*. And His help is available to every one of us.

At first we may be able to interpret only a fraction of the dream material that comes to us. But if we persist in taking our dreams into our prayer life and acting upon what we understand, we will experience an unfolding progression. In the years ahead I believe there will be exciting experimentation on this subject among Christians. God will lead us through our dreams to all sorts of provocative discoveries about our hidden selves in His plan to refashion us into whole people.

7.

The Fallen Angel

*I*s Satan alive and well on planet earth? You be the judge.

It happened a few years ago. . . . In the space of a few weeks incidents of striking similarity were related to me separately by two close friends. One came unexpectedly from Lamar, a man in his early thirties; the other I heard from Jennie, a young housewife, in the middle of a tape-recorded interview with her on another subject altogether. At the time I could never have guessed that this was a door opening, urging me on to investigate a subject about which I had been largely ignorant.

The first incident was in a letter from Lamar.

. . . On this particular Saturday, an acquaintance afflicted with a creeping paralysis so that he was mobile only in his wheelchair had been visiting in our home.

Dick attended services in our church and had been prayed for often at his own request at healing services—with no apparent results.

Dinnertime approached and my wife asked him to stay to dinner. Ten o'clock came, ten-thirty. Still our guest made no move to leave. By then I had shared everything I knew to share with him.

"Dick," I told him, "tomorrow's another day." Reluctantly, our guest left and my wife and I went to bed.

During the night I dreamed that I was still talking to Dick. This was one of those crystal-clear things; even the words I spoke to Dick. "Have you ever heard a word, Dick, that comes down to us in many churches—'exorcism'? Do you know what it means?"

I woke up with a start and my voice not only had awakened my wife, but she actually jumped about a foot off the bed.

As I opened my eyes, my attention was drawn to a figure standing in the opening of the closet, the door having been left widely ajar. He was tall and lean with the statuesque, stately figure of a young man. His silhouette was sharp because he seemed to be dressed all in black.

But it was his face to which my attention was drawn. He had cropped black hair, high cheekbones, a pointed chin— clean shaven—piercing eyes that were glowering at me with rage. It was a face full of evil. Instantly, I knew this was Satan.

I was chilled and frightened. All I wanted was to get him out of that room. From somewhere deep in me came the words, "In the name of Jesus Christ, begone! Satan, go!"

Even as I stared, within a few seconds he disappeared.

Later on, I went to see Dick and found out that he had been deeply involved in the world of the occult. He even had two spirits whom he called by name and who were now so familiar that they would wait upon him in various ways. When Dick flatly refused to submit to exorcism, I began to see why no amount of prayer effort or caring had worked for him: while he wanted to be healed physically, he did not want to let go his love affair with the occult.

The last I heard of Dick, he had stopped coming to church.

You know me so well you'll realize that I'm not the type given to visions. But this experience has done one thing: since then I've never had any slight doubt about the existence of Satan.

My instant reaction was "How wild!" The experience may have settled the matter of Satan as an incarnate spirit for Lamar, but for me it raised a lot of questions. Was Lamar telling me that he had actually seen a creature—Satan? If I hadn't known Lamar for some years and eaten many a meal in his home, I might have written his "vision" off as the hallucination of a disturbed person. But this particular friend's level-headedness and love for life were in total contrast to the strange, dark, and unappealing world of his nocturnal experience. I wanted nothing so much as to slam the door on that world.

But the very next week while in the midst of a long recorded interview with Jennie (whom I have known well for five years or so) came another story. Here it is as I took it from the tape:

On a particular night I went to bed, then later was awakened by a light coming in my room. At the foot of my bed stood this man about six feet two. He had a black butch haircut and dark features and eyes. He just stood there looking at me.

Now since I came to know Jesus eight years ago, I've had many problems, yet I've never known such an out-and-out fear as I knew it at that moment. Through my mind went the thought, "Oh my God, who is that?"

The thought had no sooner crossed my mind than I knew that Jesus Himself was standing beside me protectively on the right-hand side of my bed. And strange thing, He had His staff in His hand. As if in direct answer to the question in my mind, He explained the dark man standing at the foot of the bed. "He is the personification of Man."

Well, I'd never heard that word before, but I knew what it meant. My immediate reaction was, "I've got to get up out of bed and call someone to pray for me."

That too, brought a response. It was like the Lord saying, "No, you've got to face him sooner or later." Only please understand that this was not in external words—it was all interior.

So I stayed in bed and screwed up my courage to look at the dark man again. He stood there unmoving, radiating— what shall I call it?—the personification of evil. I couldn't have been more grateful for the feeling of Jesus' presence and the security of that staff in His hand. Then Jesus said, "He has to appear to you personally so that you can learn that everything that the devil and man can do to you are not going to harm you as long as you stay close to Me. *Don't ever again let any of his life live in you or have any power over you."*

As I began letting my mind roam over all the wonderful changes that had come to me in the last eight years and the fullness of my life in Christ, that personification of evil standing at the foot of the bed was instantly gone. Then I went to sleep, peacefully and lovingly.

Two details of my friend Jennie's description struck me especially: the phrase "the personification of Man" and her insistence that in her vision Jesus was holding a staff. I wondered if a staff in His hand had significance in connection with moments when we face evil?

Beyond that, my emotional reaction to Jennie's confrontation with Satan was the same resistance I had felt to Lamar's experience. Still—here were two friends whom I knew to be wise and solid persons. I trusted them completely, yet they had presented me with what I regarded as "far-out" stories.

I had also been noticing that every time I read a book review page or saw the ads, more and more titles of the type of *Rosemary's Baby* were being published. Publishing houses had whole lists of titles on Satan and the occult. Entire stores were being given not only to occult books but to hundreds of items, trappings of the occult such as masks, candles, incense, charms, games, zodiacal highball glasses, napkins, tarot cards, and witches' hats.

"Just a fad," I thought. All of it went so directly against my experience of God as being all-love and goodness that I had decided to keep my eyes solely on Him as my personal answer to the rise of the Satan cults. But when first one close friend thrust the distasteful Satan subject on me, then another, I saw that I couldn't continue to duck it. Having a new respect for the importance of obedience, I realized that I was being asked personally to take a look at the kingdom of evil and become knowledgeable about it.

"All right, God," was my response. "If you're telling me that Satan is real and on the march and attacking today, and that You want me to look at him and hear what You have to say about all this, I'll do it. But please be with me every minute because I'm not looking forward to this."

Up to this time, I had read little about Satan except in the writings of the late C. S. Lewis, eminent Cambridge scholar and convert to Christianity from atheism. In *Mere Christianity*, Mr. Lewis had hit the Satan subject head-on:

> I know someone will ask me, "Do you really mean, at this time of day, to re-introduce our old friend the devil—hoofs and horns and all?" Well, what the time of day has to do with it, I don't know. And I'm not particular about the hoofs and the horns. But in other respects my answer is, "Yes, I do." . . . If anybody really wants to know him better, I'd say to that person, "Don't worry. If you really want to, you will. Whether you'll like it when you do is another question."[1]

Neither of my friends, Jennie nor Lamar, had in any way sought an experience of Satan. And C. S. Lewis was right, they didn't enjoy Satan. Still, questions had been raised and would not be put down. Given a devil at all, I realized that he must be spirit. Therefore, I resisted the idea of external manifestations, like horns and a tail and being dressed in a ludicrous red suit. Satan's appearance would be of less importance than his character. How was I to research Satan's character?

The obvious place to begin was to see what God had Himself chosen to reveal to us in Scripture about Satan and the problem of evil. I set myself to spend thirty minutes on this study early each morning before breakfast. Propped up in bed with a cup of coffee, a clean notebook, a chain reference Bible and full concordance, I began.

Right away I was surprised. The first reference I turned to described Satan as a beautiful creature, once a magnificent archangel called Lucifer, "the shining one," or "the son of the morning." Some Bible scholars surmise that Lucifer was the greatest of the heavenly creatures who led all the rest in glorifying God. But the time came when Lucifer began to covet this worship for himself:

> How art thou fallen from heaven, O Lucifer, son of the morning! . . . For thou hast said in thine heart, I will ascend into heaven, I will exalt my throne above the stars of God. . . . I will ascend above the heights of the clouds; I will be like the most High.[2]

When this shining angel broke his relationship with the Father, he led a revolt in heaven. The Book of Revelation hints[3] that Lucifer may have enticed one third of the heavenly hosts to revolt with him. After all, their angelic leader still had his superior intelligence, his attractive persuasiveness, and his power.

At that time Lucifer's name was changed to Satan—"adversary" or "resistor." I wrote down some of the other names I found for Satan. The names tell us a great deal about the ex-Lucifer's character:

Enemy
Tempter
Destroyer
Liar
Unclean spirit
Foul spirit
Accuser of the brethren
God of this World

As I thought about it, I realized that God must have known that this awful perversion of His beautiful creation had been possible. Ironically, it was because God had lavished so much on Lucifer that the tragic reversal came about.

But the Lucifer disaster did not dissuade the Creator from His eternal intention to create truly free man. For man He made a special place, the garden-planet Earth set like a blue and green jewel in the gray cosmos.

Man would be perfect physically, equipped with a body exquisitely formed, from the chromosome pattern of each cell to the human eye with its retina composed of seven delicate layers of molecular and nuclear tissue, ganglion cells, and nerve fibers; from the chemical complexity of the blood with its own transport system for bathing and nourishing every cell, to the brain marvelously constructed with some 100 billion neurons and at least two times that many glia. Neuroscientists like Dr. Francis Otto Schmitt have shown the human brain to be so complex that it makes a sophisticated electronic computer look like a child's toy.[4]

But more important than man's incredible body was God's plan that his judgments would partake of the Creator's own goodness and love, so that human beings would know unimaginable happiness and fulfillment.

So God looked on His creation—man—and pronounced that creation "very good." Yet by giving us the attributes of personality, especially a will with which to choose, He deliberately ran the risk that men or angels might reject His plan.

That is exactly what happened. By the time planet earth had been formed, the archangel Lucifer had already become heaven's rebel. Our little planet became the stage for the fight to the death between Satan and his cohorts and God the Father.

The conflict began in Earth's springtime. God had warned Adam and Eve that if they ate of the fruit of the Tree of Knowledge, they would surely die. Even as Satan had wanted to be like God, so now he sought to transfer the same rebellion to the mind and will of Eve first and then Adam. . . . God didn't tell you the truth, the serpent suggested, "for God doth know that in the day ye eat thereof, then your eyes shall be opened, and ye shall be as gods. . . ."[5]

Man decided to take his chances on Satan. The result was tragedy for that first man and woman and for every descendant down the long ages since. For man's decision to eat the fruit of the Tree of Knowledge was to set his will against God's to enthrone himself "as a god" independent of his Creator.

It was as if my right arm "decided" that it no longer needed the rest of the body, so it would separate itself and take up life on its own. The severed arm would die.

But physical death was only part of it. It was man's spirit that made him the crowning accomplishment of creation. *That* was why man was told that he had dominion over the animals, "over every living thing that moveth upon the earth."[6] It was because Jehovah had "created man in his own image" that the writer of the Book of Hebrews, echoing the Psalmist, could say lyrically:

Thou madest him [man] a little lower than the angels; thou crownedst him with glory and honour. . . .

Thou hast put all things in subjection under his feet. . . .[7]

That same spirit that enabled man to worship, to make decisions and moral choices, to plan, to remember, to assimilate ideas and store up knowledge, to reason—not only meant that there was a great gulf fixed between man and the rest of the animal kingdom, it also meant that man's spirit would be dependent for its real life on the Spirit of which it was a part. To the Tempter, Jesus said, "Man shall not live by bread alone."[8]

As a result of man's disobedience, death entered life, precisely as God had said it would. Not just the cessation of the heartbeat and the decay of the flesh that marks the end of every man, but all the interim ills that lead up to death—sickness, disease, pain, weakness, accidents, famine, pestilence, plague, fear, loneliness, hatred, jealousy, hurt, cruelty, torture, murder, suicide. Now began the long history of man's inhumanity to man—man now bound tightly, stultified by the fallen divided nature which he himself had chosen. And because God had given man true freedom of choice, He could not and would not forcibly overrule that.

Man might have been left there. The story could have ended as the poet Edna St. Vincent Millay has it in her heartbreakingly beautiful sonnet sequence *Epitaph for the Race of Man.*

> Here lies, and none to mourn him but the sea,
> That falls incessant on the empty shore,
> Most various Man, cut down to spring no more;
> Before his prime, even in his infancy
> Cut down, and all the clamour that was he
> Silenced; and all the riveted pride he wore
> A rusted iron column whose tall core
> The rains have tunneled like an aspen tree. . . .
> Whence, whence the broadside, whose the heavy blade? . . .
> Strive not to speak, poor scattered mouth; I know.[9]

But it did not end that way. God's love yearned over His deluded creatures. "God's impossible Love," as C. S. Lewis called it in one of the most brilliant, witty, and penetrating books on Satan ever written, *The Screwtape Letters.* He puts these words into the mouth of the influential demon Screwtape as he instructs the underling tempter Wormwood:

> ". . . He really loves the human vermin and really desires their freedom and continued existence. . . ." [Then, catching himself and realizing that this is heresy in the under-

world's theology] . . . "The reason one comes to talk as if he really had this impossible Love is our utter failure to find out that real motive. What does he stand to make out of them? That is the insoluble question. . . ."[10]

Out of God's "impossible Love" a rescue plan was evolved, surely one that only the three Persons of the Godhead together—Father, Son, and Holy Spirit—could have conceived: Jesus would leave for a time that perfection of communion and communication that He had always enjoyed with the Father and the Holy Spirit, and come to earth clothed in flesh, born of a woman like all the sons of Adam. Jesus would be God revealed, the God-man walking the earth demonstrating what the Father is like—His love and compassion, His reverence for all life, His power to unbind, to set free, to remake.

The plan became fact at a specific moment in time, thus dividing all history into two parts—B.C. "Before Christ" and Anno Domini, "In the Year of Our Lord." The God-man's teaching was incredibly impressive, had the sure touch of One who spoke "with authority." His miracles, even His enemies grumbled, had the world following after him.[11] It is at that point that people reading the Bible for the first time are in for a surprise. The writers of Scripture insist that the real point of Jesus breaking into human history was neither His teaching nor His miracles; rather, that Jesus came to earth for the purpose of dying and being resurrected to life on the third day.

Thus His death and resurrection was the Master Plan to win back for man all that he had lost in Eden. As the last Adam, Jesus would mount His cross taking all of us, Adam's heirs, with Him into the death of the old, now-spoiled creation. Thus He would accomplish a perfect exchange. As Derek Prince, British-born Greek scholar and author, has summarized it in a single memorable sentence, "Jesus took the evil that was due to us and the entire Adamic race that we, in return, might receive the good that was due to Him by eternal right."[12]

Jesus went to His cross as the willing agent of the divine plan. Nevertheless, His agony in Gethsemane shows us that humanly He shrank from the torturing hours ahead. All His growing-up years in Nazareth He had seen crucifixions. When Jesus was about twelve, He could scarcely have helped seeing the crucifixion by Varrus, Prefect of Syria, of 2000 rioters after the death of Herod the Great. The field full of 2000 crosses would have made an indelible impression on any sensitive boy. How well He knew that the nails used in crucifixion (square, one-third inch on each side) were real enough, as real as the pain and the agonizing thirst, the cramps, and the ultimate asphyxiation. Even so He considered that "to this end was I born, and for this cause came I into the world."[13] Therefore, He was "obedient unto death."

The victory was God's for on the third day Life poured back into the dead and mutilated body of Jesus. The crucifixion and resurrection are history's watershed. Those who speak of some sort of "spiritual resurrection" are missing the point. For the first Adam or the last Adam or for any of us sons and daughters of Adam still in the flesh, nothing short of the resurrection of the flesh would have been any victory at all. Satan would not have been deceived; Jesus' surprised, incredulous disciples would not, and neither would we.

Satan knew defeat now. Henceforward any man or woman could look at the Tempter unflinchingly and say, "You're a liar, a defeated foe, a bluffer, and a washout. I stand here in the name of Jesus—the Christus, the Victor—and on His finished work. Begone—." There is nothing for the Tempter but to slink away.

Thus the Bible nowhere teaches us to believe in Dualism, the philosophic premise that two equal and independent powers— one of them good, the other bad—eternally vie for supremacy in the world. It is easy even for the Christian to attribute more power to Satan than he has and thus fall into heresy. Rather we are told that our earth is enemy-occupied territory. The Rightful King has landed and has already won the decisive victory. But we are still living through the mopping-up stage of the battle. The time will come when Christus, the Lord Emmanuel, will finally ring down the curtain on all remaining pockets of rebellion and guerrilla warfare to establish His kingdom openly for all to see.

Satan still has one ace card to play. If he can keep any man from believing the truth about Jesus Christ—who He is, the Life He holds out for mankind, the fact of his (Satan's) defeat—Satan can then keep that man in bondage to his dark kingdom. For though I have a million dollars in a bank account in my name, if through some chicanery I am persuaded that I do not have it and make no overt move to use it, the money in the bank does me no good at all.

Thus the Accuser of men employs unbelievable craftiness and resourcefulness, artifice and deceit to keep mankind from knowing the truth and acting upon it. With him the technique of lying has been honed to a fine art. His ways of camouflage and duplicity are almost limitless. After all, this was Lucifer, the magnificent archangel, with his great intelligence, only now turned totally to negative designs.

Nor does Satan give up on us even after we become followers of Jesus. He never gives up so long as we inhabit these vulnerable bodies in this uncertain life. After we become Christians, his aim is to oppose and stymie us so that our spirits will be stunted short of maturity. He also wants to keep us ineffective so far as spreading to others the good news of freedom in Christ Jesus.

Satan cannot create anything new, cannot create anything at all. He must steal what God has created. Thus he twists love and God's wonderful gift of sex into lust and sadism and myriad perversions. He disfigures the heart's deep desire to worship God and persuades us to bow before lesser gods of lust or money or power.

"But," the protest rises within us, "if Christ won the victory, then why isn't the war with Satan over? Why doesn't God simply wipe Satan out?"

It's a valid question. God's luminous answer was given me one morning: "Because the Father is determined that all the sons of Adam will, for as long as possible, have a second chance to reverse that decision made in Eden." Jesus bought this second chance for us. The Father is determined that His Son's tremendous sacrifice will not go for nothing.

C. S. Lewis in his book *Mere Christianty* expresses the same thought in different words:

> . . . Christians think He [God] is going to land in force; we don't know when. But we can guess why He's delaying. He wants to give us the chance of joining His side freely. . . . I wonder whether people who ask God to interfere openly and directly in our world quite realize what it will be like when He does. When that happens, it's the end of the world. When the author walks onto the stage the play's over. . . ."[14]

So it is as if nothing had changed since that moment eons ago when man was presented with his stark choice: would he believe God or Satan? . . . Which one had his happiness at heart? . . . Would he let go his connection to Life in God and set up on his own? Time is still holding its breath for our answer now. Which way will each man, each woman, decide now?

"But," some may protest, "I never consciously made any such decision." We do not need to. That is the state we are all in just by being born of the flesh into the race of man and inheriting our father Adam's nature just as surely as we inherited the color of some ancestor's eyes. And it would be just as useless to protest that inheriting a sin-disposed nature seems scarcely fair, as to protest the color of our eyes or the race that dictated the skin's color.

The truth is that whether we are millionaires directing a financial kingdom or youthful idealists in revolt against a materialistic world, or quite ordinary citizens content to live self-centered lives of quiet mediocrity, until such time as we grasp our second chance, reverse the fiasco-decision made in Eden and get reconnected to Life, we remain vulnerable to Satan's cunning approach and to his designs. When I understood that, then I could see why the phrase which had been given to my friend Jennie, "the personification of Man" was so appropriate. Satan remains the personification of adamic Man even as Jesus is the Personification of the new Man. Each of us can escape the bondage of Satan's kingdom for the freedom of Christ's kingdom only when he resolutely sets the rudder of his will so to do.

That's why the moment of decision for Christ is so vital. That's why the angels themselves rejoice when even one lost lamb is brought back on the shoulder of the Good Shepherd.

As my morning study progressed, I began to see why God had insisted on this distasteful chore. A good hard look at evil as it is presented in the Bible and an obedient following through of the whole story left me with one overwhelming impression—a great feeling of confidence and victory. The Bible story of the conflict between good and evil is not downbeat at all, but upbeat; it is the story of the total defeat of evil because of the absolute power of Christ.

But God had wanted me to study this subject for myself until I was not only aware, but fully persuaded of the reality of the kingdom of evil. Sooner or later a lot of tough experiences, doubts and temptations were going to be thrown at me (and at other people close to me) and it would be essential that we know how to fight them.

An additional reason why we dare not pretend that Satan does not exist is that God has deliberately placed Himself in the position of depending upon us human beings to tell His good news and to spread His kingdom on earth. We cannot get on with this task without being hindered by Satan at every step of the way. Satan's tactics fall into many categories, among them higher spiritual temptations, sexual temptations, and what we might call his harassment techniques.

An endlessly used Satanic weapon in his spiritual arsenal is that of discouragement, often interlocked with a degree of self-pity and depression. During our early years in Washington when Peter Marshall often battled discouragement, I remember our quoting at one another one of Hannah Smith's favorite maxims: "All discouragement is of the devil." Of course the remedy is to realize the source of the depression and to remind oneself that spiritual reality can never be gauged by feelings.

Other strategies of the devil include presenting sin as a virtue; the old ruse of exhibiting the bait and concealing the hook; suggesting "you aren't accepted by God, else you wouldn't continue to be tempted"; keeping Christians musing on their hang-ups and sins; using the seduction technique—good to bad in tiny steps.

Satan sometimes lays the groundwork for sexual sins by encouraging self-pride in a leader and his achievements. This then is followed by the leader being flattered by "opportunities for service" and overextending himself. Family relationships suffer in the wake of too much travel for meetings and speaking engagements. As the home life deteriorates, then the Tempter at times arranges "a plant" such as an immensely attractive married woman in deep distress who comes seeking the leader's help. When a liaison follows and becomes public news, the disastrous side effects of this situation always cause great rejoicing in hell. Among them, groups of disillusioned people who leave the church—"If that's Christianity, I want no part of it"—as they judge the church by the fallen leader rather than by Christ and His perfection.

The third category of Satan's strategem dips into the realm of the bizarre. For instance, on a day when a well-known evangelist was preparing to preach one of his rare sermons on Satan, he was dictating notes into a recording device when, suddenly, the machine caught fire. We might be inclined to think, "Wouldn't the machine have caught fire if the minister had been dictating on say, 'God's love'?" Perhaps—except it gives us pause as we go on to experience this sort of harassment over and over whenever we are about to unmask Satan by writing or teaching or preaching.

The following list is taken from the experiences of Christian leaders, all of whom I know:

> The living-room chimney of a house catches fire the last day before a book manuscript on Satan is to be delivered to the publisher.

> En route to a Christian meeting there is trouble with impossibly bad traffic and with the car. In addition to time delays, the leader loses his peace of mind, becomes irritated, and loses effectiveness.

> Mechanical difficulties are notorious. Tape recorders and amplifying systems often go wild or cease to function.

> As the time for an important talk or service approaches, the minister's family grows irritated and edgy. A spirit of contention enters the home. There are minor accidents.

Usually, these vexations are not serious trouble, more like a sort of nasty bullying. Even a few experiences with such obstructionist tactics, however, and we begin to see that the warfare spoken of in the Bible is absolutely real:

> For we are not fighting against people made of flesh and blood, but against persons without bodies—the evil rulers of the unseen world, those mighty satanic beings and great evil princes of darkness who rule this world; and against huge numbers of wicked spirits in the spirit world.

> So use every piece of God's armor to resist the enemy whenever he attacks. . . .[15]

In the thick of battle a soldier needs to be able to identify the enemy. In the old days warriors were identified by their uniforms or by a standard held aloft. So how can we Christian soldiers learn to identify the enemy Satan? From my study, I was able to draw the following antithetical lists to help us know what God wants for us against Satan's aims. Lining it up like this enables us to see it more readily. . . .

Satan	Jesus
Seeks to do his own will.	Always obeys the Father's will.
Aims to bind and blind men.	Yearns to free men and open our eyes to see.
Lies interminably.	Is the Truth.
Takes himself very seriously, cannot bear taunting or levity.	Often uses the light touch.
Wants us to live in darkness and hide portions of our life from others.	Wants us to live in the light.
Wants us to doubt and disbelieve God's word.	Longs for us to have faith that He always keeps His word.
Works to make us ignore, disbelieve, or choose for ourselves what to believe in the Scripture.	Steadily assures us that the Scripture is the Word of God.
Pushes us to disobey God.	Says, "If you love Me, you will obey my commandments."
Urges us to use God for selfish purposes.	Longs for us to be used by God to help others.
Tells us, "My body belongs to me."	Tells us, "The body is the temple of the Holy Spirit."
Wants sickness and disease.	Wants wholeness of body, mind, and spirit.

Spares no effort to bring us sorrow and grief.	Wants our joy.
Desires our death.	Eagerly bestows life stretching on into eternity.
Condemns and accuses us.	Assures us, "I came not to judge the world, but to save the world."
Pushes us toward self-contempt.	Assures us that each man is of infinite worth to Him.
Fosters discontent and grumbling.	Urges contentment and praise in all situations.
Urges us to think that we can get virtue in one big slug for life.	Desires that we depend on Him minute by minute for what we need and claim our "daily bread."
Urges us to concentrate on the sins of others.	Tells us to look at the beam in our own eye and remove that first.
Wants us to hang onto resentment and bitterness.	Tells us to forgive others in the same way God forgives us.
Urges us to have our fun now, try to forget about paying for it.	Influences us to pay now in time or effort, then fun later is assured.
Attempts to get us to hide our sins and make excuses for them, thus encouraging their festering within.	Wishes us to run to Him, bring our sins into the light and have them forgiven, cleansed, and forgotten.
Labors to have us believe that temptation *is* sin.	Assures us that temptations rightly handled strengthen us.
Wants us, when we fail, to wallow in discouragement or despair.	Encourages us in failure to ask forgiveness, accept it, rise, and go on.

Aims for us always to wear a mask and act a part; be all things to all people.	Plants in us the desire to be true to ourselves; to let others know where we stand.
Wants our faith always to be for the future.	Wants us to cultivate a present moment faith.
Seeks steady procrastination.	Teaches us that *"Now* is the moment of salvation."
Strives to have us preoccupied with "what ifs?" (what might happen); to be hagridden by the future.	Is concerned with what we do in the present; wants us to offer up the *present* moment to God.
Urges us toward a false, lofty superspirituality.	Wants us to live out daily "Without Me ye can do nothing."
Delights in a "moderate" religion with no extremes.	Wants the total man—"Thou shalt love the Lord thy God with *all* thy heart and with *all* thy soul and with *all* thy mind."
Works for churches to be divided into "clubs" or factions with "party spirit."	Leads us toward unity amid diversity of gifts of the Spirit amongst the people in the Church.
Wants us to see all morality as relative, no final truth or falsehood.	Insists that He *is* the Way, the Truth and the Life; God's laws are absolute.
Labors to destroy all law, God's and man's.	Fulfills the law and the prophets and adds righteousness to it.
Labors for war.	Desires peace, the fruit of righteousness.

I was soon to find out that this period of instruction was not going to be limited to quiet bookwork. Lessons from life were just around the corner.

8.

The Unholy Spirit

*I*t was from a pair of hippies, Carrie and Jeff Buddington, that I first heard the term "the unholy spirit." I met Jeff and Carrie in September, 1969 in the small Cape Cod church where my son Peter is pastor. It was a surprise to hear Peter welcoming to the platform to receive into the church such a young couple, "swinging" in appearance, rather than the typical older retired couple of that Cape Cod community.

After the formal part of the ceremony was completed, Peter turned to the congregation. "Because Jeff and Carrie have traveled such an extraordinary route to arrive at this point of commitment, I've asked them to share a little of their story with all of us."

Jeff, tall and broad-shouldered, spoke of how long he had run back and forth across the United States seeking the answer to what life was all about. Carrie, hair flowing to her shoulders, spoke softly of how she had come out of the jungle of drugs to find the reality of God. As they talked, people were leaning forward with interest. I was so intrigued that after the service I asked for an interview. Our two-hour talk together later that week proved to be memorable and revealing.[1]

As I replay today the tape I made of that two-hour conversation, I can still see the scene in Edith's and Peter's living room: the warm afternoon sun streaming through the windows reflecting back from the silver-gray shingles outside; Carrie, hair swinging, sitting on the davenport with legs tucked under her like a little girl: both Jeff and Carrie surprisingly articulate.

The first part of Carrie and Jeff's story parallels the experiences of thousands of today's youth. . . . They had met in 1968 at a California commune. Jeff was from Massachusetts. After one semester of college, he had restlessly ricocheted from job to job—selling insurance, building pipe organs, designing stage sets, even a circus big top stint. Carrie was a Californian who had gotten hooked on drugs—marijuana, acid,[2] speed,[3] in that order—during her senior year in high school.

At the time the two met, each was on speed. "I found out in a hurry," Carrie explained to me, "that speed makes you paranoid. All of life becomes one big fear trip. It also gives you this delusion of grandeur.

"But where I got hooked was, coming off it, crashing, is so awful you keep staying up because you can't bear to come down. If you ever do, you ache inside. Your guts get really up-tight. Your nerves are on end. You get cramps. You can feel the heat coming off your head—'bzzy-bzzy'—like being plugged into a high-tension wire."

"Drugs do one good thing for kids, though," Jeff added. "They show that there's a world other than the material one. Maybe that's part of the reason so many kids these days have finally let go of two hang-ups of the older generation. First, the kids see no point in trying to accumulate things. Second, they know now that science doesn't have the answers to life they once thought it did. So science can never again be their god.

"Carrie and I had more in common than just thrill-seeking. We were on this big search for some meaning in life. We still thought that happiness meant the way you lived externally, that if things around you were the way you liked them, then you would be happy."

They found very few answers to their big questions in the commune. The forty members (eleven children among them) had erected a large hexagonal lodge of logs on the 240 acres of Oregon woodland[4] where the commune hoped to escape civilization and the Establishment. Meant for a central meeting place as well as sleeping and eating quarters, the lodge had homemade furniture, a cast-iron stove for cooking, even a library of some 500 books. There was no electricity or running water—only the streams in which to bathe and wash clothes. The men dug a well. All possessions were shared.

Carrie added, "It wasn't long until we discovered that we weren't going to eat if we didn't work. And the work wasn't going to get done without a routine." The rule was made that everyone had to work at least four hours a day. They planted a vegetable garden, fished in the river, kept chickens and goats. Since the winters were severe, trees had to be cut and the wood sawed and split for firewood.

Carrie and Jeff started living together in a tepee they had built. "But something was still missing," Jeff explained. "Carrie and I spent hours in that tepee huddled beside a little fire, watching shadows on the slanting walls, trying to figure out what it was that still eluded us. We were like people stumbling around in the Los Angeles smog.

"The reality we continued to seek in the LSD visions was increasingly hideous. Eventually we got tired of seeing ourselves as we were—like people with naked bodies covered with warts and souls all deformed—and we knew it. But we couldn't find any way to change ourselves.

"Then we began having bad acid trips. I remember the first. It was a foggy day. Carrie and I were walking down this hillside and the big old oak trees were dripping—one of those spooky days. I began to feel something evil reaching out to possess me.

"Crazy thoughts appeared in my mind. I kept seeing a kind of crude black basalt male figure with a hawk's head and a male phallus, a coiled snake on his arm, strange hieroglyphics all over him—and I kept having this urge to get down on my knees in front of it. It was as though I was being asked to take part in some ceremony that I knew nothing about. It seemed to me like something very very ancient. I could feel the control over myself slipping away. Something was eroding my will. Carrie felt the same thing."

Carrie interrupted, "It's like this evil power had been there all along, only he hadn't shown himself at first. He waits until you're well hooked; only then does he reveal himself. And he wants you to think that it's O.K. to play childish games with the drug-taking, that it's spiritual and beautiful—the lovely psychedelic colors, all that.

"But it's counterfeit spirituality, and believe me, it isn't beautiful. It's more hideous than anyone can imagine."

Jeff grimaced in remembrance. "The second of the bad trips was at Thanksgiving. The entire commune was crowded into the lodge, taking acid together. That day we were acting out being 'married' into the brotherhood of man. Outside it was raining steadily. There was a fire going, and the rhythm of drums.

"Suddenly Carrie and I had a loathsome feeling about the whole thing. So did one other couple. The four of us left the lodge and went to the tepee. We sat there huddling together, cold, miserable, too drugged even to build a fire.

"That night we knew that the answer we'd seen in drugs was really a mirage, just wasn't there. We knew then why so many kids commit suicide."

The Oregon winter was severe that year and there was sickness. So few could work that firewood almost disappeared. Their one chain saw was broken too. The situation was desperate.

Then came the miracle. One morning out of nowhere several strange men appeared with saws and axes. "We've come to cut wood for you," they said. The visitors worked all day until they had a big pile of firewood.

"Who are you?" commune members kept asking. "Why are you doing this for us?"

"We're Christians," was the answer. "We have our own little community about fifteen miles up the road. We came because the Lord Jesus told us that your firewood was almost gone."

"But why?" they persisted. "How could God care about us and our commune?"

"Because He loves you."

The experience rocked the hippies as nothing else had. Jeff and Carrie and a few others went up the road to find out more about this brand of Christianity.

"It was in this Christian community that we began at last to find answers," Jeff told me. "The key was the Holy Spirit. We'd had some experience of spirits, you see, we'd encountered the *unholy* spirit—"

"Holy Spirit—unholy spirit," I interrupted, fascinated. "I've never heard it put quite that way." I said the phrases again, listening to the sound of them. "How would you explain the difference between the two spirits?" my voice on the tape recorder asked Jeff.

"Well, we found that the unholy spirit does have power in the world, only it's a power each individual has to allow him. Once a person decides to play around with him and opens the door, the unholy spirit can be overpowering. He can perform 'miracles' and has a lot of tricks: power over nature, power over the elements. But it's a power without any love. It wants just one thing, just one—to destroy."

Carrie spoke up. "The Holy Spirit has power too, greater power than the unholy spirit. He too, waits on our wanting Him. But He's different. He's all love—real love. And He's—*for* us."

"What's the basis," I asked, "of your being so sure that the Holy Spirit has more power than the unholy spirit?"

"Because," Carrie promptly answered, "He enabled us to kick drugs when we'd been on them for so many years. That's a *real* miracle!"

Jeff continued, "Next, He took away the old haunted, fear-ridden 'me.' Inside each of us was born this new being, what the Bible calls 'a new creature in Christ Jesus.'"

"It's not a case of trying to be like Christ, to imitate Him," Carrie went on. "Who has the strength to do that? Through the Holy Spirit, Jesus comes to live in us and to do His own work."

"The next step," Jeff went on, "was to find a church. We remembered one that had occasionally come to our rescue with a meal or a warm bed. So we went barreling there, pretty eager, I guess. To our astonishment we found no sense of life or power there. More than that, they seemed almost scared of the change in us. They wanted to help us when we were on drugs and out of work, sure. A change of clothes, a hot meal, good advice, concern. But real change? Real power? God really doing what He said? Wow! They backed off like crazy."

"Tell me about the change," I said. "How did it start?"

"Well," Jeff said, "one day, all by ourselves, we had our own Pentecost and accepted Jesus. Later we were both baptized in the creek and also legally married. People came from everywhere for the wedding—hippies still on acid and straight people. We spent the whole day telling them all, 'Jesus is the One you're searching for.'"

The Buddingtons spent four months in the Christian community, learning. "That new person born in us had to start from scratch and go to school," Jeff said. "But it was so great! When you go up on acid, there's always that terrible coming down again. With Jesus, you just keep going up, gradually and surely. You keep growing and learning step by step how to meet and overcome your difficulties. There are problems with self-discipline, of course, but joy all the way. It's that 'living water' for sure.

"Other hippies followed us to the Christian community. The big difference between the two groups is this: in the hippie community they're still doing their own thing; in the Christian community, they're doing His thing."

This was not the end of the story. Christ as the new Life within them led Carrie and Jeff to Cape Cod to teach for a time in a home for retarded children, then on to become part of another Christian community whose calling is teaching, retreats, help, counseling. They've been there ever since—learning, growing, giving.

On July 9, 1970, Catherine Heidi Buddington was born, by the grace of God, a healthy, normal baby. Then on June 5, 1972, Daniel Jeffrey was born; in November, 1973, Ruth Anne, also strong and normal. And still Jeff and Carrie go on from strength to strength as they dig deeper into Christian disciplines and learn to show others the way.

The childish games with which Jeff and Carrie started out to explore evil's terrain are being played by millions of people today. Witchcraft, the occult, Satan worship, sorcery, spiritualism, tarot cards, horoscopes, are currently big business over most of the world. Among the more popular courses currently offered in many high schools and universities are telepathy, precognition, clairvoyance, and other aspects of scientology; spiritism, I Ching, and witchcraft.

There are now an estimated 10,000 full-time and 175,000 part-time atrologers in the United States. Horoscope readings are computerized. Almost every newspaper and periodical in the nation now regularly prints them. In France 60,000 sorcerers are said to be taking in $200,000,000 a year. A national magazine estimated that in 1970 there were 500 witches in Manhattan alone.

This fascination with the occult climaxed in the early months of 1974 when Warner Brothers released the film *The Exorcist*, producing what *Time* magazine called *Exorcist* fever.[5] All over the United States serpentine lines waited for hours outside theaters to see the horrifying movie about a little girl possessed by the devil. Once inside, audience reaction repeatedly included screams, hysteria (some requiring hospitalization), blackouts, heart attacks, vomiting, at least one miscarriage, and speedy exits. In New York City a boy ran from the theater toward a nearby church, tearing off his clothes and shouting, "Exorcise me! Exorcise me!" Longer-range effects included people believing themselves possessed, acute insomnia, nightmares.

Exorcist fever uncovered an American public with a morbid fascination with despair, pain, and gore. William Blatty's book from which the film was taken sold almost 4 million copies (in addition to the 5 million previously sold) in five week immediately after the movie was released; the motion picture is, reputedly, going to be the top money-maker of all time, exceeding *The Sound of Music* and *The Godfather*.

Most of this upsurge has come since 1967. A brilliant young Englishman, Os Guiness, whom I met at L'Abri, Switzerland in the summer of 1972, had researched the new interest in witchcraft, the occult, Satan, and kindred subjects. He could find almost no major works on these subjects for the last two hundred years. History books treated black magic and the occult as curious extinct phenomena: the Enlightenment following the Renaissance, together with the rise of modern scientific knowledge, had effectively silenced witches and laid the ghosts.

Then in 1967, like the cap blown off a volcano after centuries of molten churning underground, there erupted into the open a torrent of publications on Satan, Satanism and all kindred subjects. The underworld's debris has been spewing up ever since.

"Why 1967?" I asked Os Guiness.

"I don't know," was his cautious reply. "Except perhaps that year was, in some strange ways, evil's 'fullness of time.' Between June 5th and 10th occurred an event clearly foretold in Scripture[6]—Israel's six-day war when Old Jerusalem and sacred sites such as the Wailing Wall were repossessed."

"But what connection——? I don't see——"

"Scripture prophesied that event as the beginning-of-the-end times—an accelerating warfare period between good and evil, God and Satan."

This conversation later gave me much food for thought. We are living in a period when evil is getting more evil while good is no longer satisfied with pallid goodness. In the last ten years a movement of the Holy Spirit has swept through the Catholic church and most branches and denominations of the Protestant church. It may well be that the rising popularity of Satanic activities is the unholy spirit's terrified counterattack against the moves of the Spirit.

Other thought-provoking facts about 1967 have been given me by knowledgeable educators. In the United States at least, autumn, 1967, was remarkable for two phenomena: a widespread, dramatic upswing in drug experimentation among the young and the real start of the campus revolution.

Be that as it may, I marvel that so many moderns, particularly the young, can be taking witchcraft and devil worship seriously. As Andrew Greeley, a Roman Catholic priest teaching sociology at the University of Chicago wrote: "What the hell is going on? God is dead but the Devil lives."[7] One answer must be that this generation has revolted against positivism. They no longer believe in religion, humanism, or even the imperialism of science that claims to be the only valid form of knowledge. In the words of one graduate student,

> Let's face it, science is dead. While the newspapers and magazines were giving all the attention to the death of God, science was really the one that was dying.

The second reason why so many moderns now "believe in" Satan may be that large numbers of people have been simply bored with life, seeking a costless thrill, and unsuspecting that there was any real world of evil or of good either. Having been taught the doctrine of relativism (that is, that there is no real or final good or real evil) they expected their exploration to end in fantasy. It came as a shock but also a strange relief, to discover that evil is real. A relief in the sense that people in this machine age were beginning to wonder if anything was real except our machines. One student expressed it in this question, "Is there anything so powerful that it can even make us real? I mean *really real*."

Professor Mircea Eliade of the University of Chicago defines the sacred almost in the precise words of the student: "That is exactly what the sacred is, the really real."

It should come as no surprise that the modern existentialist is not interested in second-hand philosophy or theology. To him, the "really real" is what he or another person experiences first-hand. Thus if some come to a belief in the reality of the world of the spirit via the negative underside (as the Buddingtons did in order to get to the God-ward side), at least we can be grateful that they *are* finding reality.

History proves that there are two sets of experiences which will flush out the power of evil and make Satan surface—one is to reconnoiter deeply in evil's territory; the other is to become a follower of Jesus.

So long as we remain secularists—whether just conventionally good members of society, or even church members who deny the supernatural aspect of religion—then probably we shall give no particular thought to Satan. If we consider the devil at all, we are likely to dismiss him as an outmoded, nonsensical symbol. Incidentally, Satan, like any other saboteur, would prefer to keep it that way. Disbelief in his existence is his best camouflage. If I have a mortal enemy who is intent on destroying me, my ignorance of such an enemy only makes my danger greater.

But I had learned Scripture's observation that Satan is not only real, but that each human life is in dire danger from the unholy spirit.

Be sober, be watchful: your adversary the devil, prowls around like a roaring lion, walketh about, seeking some one to devour. . . .[8]

And Jesus, speaking to the Pharisees:

> Ye are of your father the devil, and the lusts of your father
> ye will do: he was a murderer from the beginning. . . .[9]

Moreover, our danger from Satan is to our physical bodies,[10] our families,[11] our possessions,[12] along with the eternal part of us—our spirits.

Meanwhile, my eyes were progressively being opened to substantiation of these Scriptural lessons by events all around me in contemporary life. Occasionally we can catch the Destroyer in the very act of trying to destroy.

Derek Prince, whom I know well, recently related such an incident.[13] At a preaching mission in Chicago, Mr. Prince had emphasized the dangers in playing around with the Destroyer's toys—ouija boards, tarot cards, going to fortune-tellers or mediums—even when we tell ourselves that we are taking none of this seriously.

He had commented that something like going to a fortune-teller just for a "joke" is quite like entering a lion's cage to count the lion's teeth for fun. Where there has been such dabbling, the speaker urged repudiation with a prayer for cleansing and if necessary, the Church's ancient rite of exorcism.

After one of the services, a woman approached Derek Prince, confessing that she had been a medium, and asked him to pray with her. As he looked into her eyes, he sensed duplicity. Knowing that his prayer for her would do no good unless she was ready to make a clean break with Satan, Derek suggested that she was not yet ready.

A day later she came again asking for prayer, this time insisting that she had changed her mind about spiritualism and had repented. Though Derek found himself nagged with doubts about her sincerity, finally he agreed to pray with her. But he found it hard going, like a series of obstacle courses all the way. After a few moments, he told the woman that he wanted to take a little rest, so he withdrew a few steps away and was leaning against the altar rail, thinking and asking for God's direction.

Suddenly he was jerked out of his reverie. A loud, clear voice of a different timbre from the one the woman had been using made him whirl around. He saw her pointing a finger at him. "I see you in a car and it's wrecked against a tree."

Derek Prince's reaction was trigger-quick. Recognizing now what he was really up against, with great firmness of voice he said, "You spirit of divination, I refuse to accept that from you. That's Satan's lie. I will *not* be in any car that's wrecked against any tree."

Later, telling of this incident, he concluded by saying, "Had I not been on my guard, had I begun to believe this woman, I would have been in real trouble. The woman was seeing and describing Satan's destiny for me. By admitting this idea into my mind, I would have submitted myself to Satan's plan."

The Bible not only spells out the peril of Satan's life plan for us, but goes on to give us a plan of defense. For our reassurance, God has made us sure promises of help and deliverance. . . .

Submit yourselves therefore to God. Resist the devil, and he will flee from you.[14]

. . . God is faithful, who will not suffer you to be tempted above that ye are able; but will with the temptation also make a way of escape, that ye may be able to bear it.[15]

And Jesus . . . spake unto them, saying, All power is given unto me in heaven and in earth.[16]

Thus reassured that God has made us "a way of escape," what are those defense tactics?

First, it's a blessed relief to learn, as Carrie and Jeff Buddington discovered through hard experience, that while "the unholy spirit does have power, it is a power each individual has to allow him." That freedom of choice God gave man is so real that the unholy spirit cannot violate it. He must therefore persuade or deceive us.

Satan can call God a liar, he can flash before our dazzled eyes all the supposed sin-fun imaginable, but if we do not agree to his blandishments, give him the nod, he remains helpless. Although the divine part of man—the inner core of him, his spirit—is sacred, nevertheless God has made each man the keeper of his inner castle. We do not therefore have a built-in protection against evil. But we have been given truly free wills. That is why it is possible to hand over so much to Satan and why to do so places us in such jeopardy.

When we understand the factuality of this free will, then we'll be more likely to perceive why it's so dangerous to hand over to Satan any ground in our life on which he can stand. What I have come to call "the beachhead trick" is a favorite one of the enemy.

During World War II the term "beachhead" came into popular usage. A beachhead is that first landing on an island or a shore on which the whole battle may depend. Once that toehold on land is secured, it is usually only a matter of time until the rest of the island or country or even empire falls.

Just so—my life, my body, my affairs are as an island empire that the unholy spirit hopes to win en route to his ultimate objective of my eternal soul. To do that, he too must first gain a beachhead in my life. With that toehold, then he can take his time about gaining control of the rest of me and my affairs—yard by yard, decision by decision. But the analogy breaks down at one important point. In war, through physical overpowering, the victor can force his opponent to bend to his will, whereas God has kept from the unholy spirit the ability to force any human being against his will. Either Satan has to be granted permission by God (as in Job's case), or we have to give Satan the beachhead voluntarily, else he can't have it.

But who in warfare would be foolish enough voluntarily to give a beachhead? We do. We're foolish enough. How often we fall for the Destroyer's beachhead arguments, finding them amazingly appealing. . . .

A little sinning is a good thing, the father of liars suggests to us. Not enough to sink us, of course. Just enough to be easier to live with and more socially acceptable. Anyway, who wants to be Mr. Goody Two-Shoes?

Another day, another approach. Don't we realize that a civilized person doesn't want to be "narrow" in morals, ethics, or religious belief? True, we agree, it is a sunny day on the beach, sparkling sand, fluffy clouds floating in a blue sky. Spiritual warfare? What made us even think about such a thing?

Then comes the whispered argument, "All of life has to be a compromise." We can even take it from there for Satan. Of *course* a little ground here and there, not be rigid about everything.

How else would conflicting points of view ever reach agreement on anything?

Then there's always "moderation" and "normal"—such reassuring words when compared to "fanaticism" and "extremist." Above all, who wants to be tagged "religious fanatic"!

Thus we succumb to Satan's beachhead strategies. Once he has this bit of ground, then he uses it to stand on for further assaults. I have received tremendous help by keeping this picture of the tempter's beachhead strategy in my mind's eye. It reminds me how dangerous is the initial bit of sinning on any given front.

We are creatures of habit patterns for good or ill. In other words, we do not make a series of equal and independent decisions, rather one decision leads to another. Unfortunately, the natural inclination which we have inherited from our father Adam toward making the wrong choice means that this phenomenon works more easily downward than upward. Any parent or teacher concerned with children knows this well. For instance, it is easier to let a child be sloppy and to allow careless habits to develop than it is to fight uphill toward his becoming an ordered, neat person.

Moreover, each repetition of a downbeat choice makes the next one easier and bothers us less as sin's inevitable deadening process sets in. Even after collaborating with the enemy by handing over the beachhead, we think ourselves still in control, able to call a halt to the enemy's advance any time we choose. Instead, Jesus warns us that "whosoever committeth sin is the servant [or slave] of sin."[17]

Notice how clear-cut Jesus was about His own total refusal so to collaborate with Satan (Jesus is speaking here to His apostles at the Last Supper):

Hereafter I will not talk much with you: for the prince of this world cometh, *and hath nothing in me.*[18]

Jesus had given no ground because He knew how deadly playing with Satan is. Just as a physician would not dare ignore or underestimate the malignancy of a few cancer cells, even so in God's eyes there is no harmless little "white" evil.

The second defense God has provided for us is what Scripture calls "the armour of light."[19] So long as we stay in the light we're safe because Satan cannot endure light and will not come near it.

A true incident has become an unforgettable symbol of this for me. Some years ago *Guideposts* magazine editors received a short manuscript in the mail. The writer, whom I'll call Mary, was married to Bill W., a traveling salesman, and was the mother of three children, the youngest a baby girl. She and her husband were both active in their local church, where the couple had met and grown fond of an attractive young man, John Ames. On those Sundays when Mary's husband was out of town on one of his frequent business trips, John would give her and her children a ride to church.

Nothing was wrong with that, except that soon it was becoming a habit. Mary found herself looking forward to seeing John and thinking of him often.

An inner warning signal went up for her as she remembered Jesus' words about lust beginning inside us—in the thoughts and the will. "I'll duck this," she decided. She and the children went early to church to get there ahead of John's proffered ride.

The strategy worked the first Sunday. But on the next one when Bill was out of town, John started early for Sunday School too—and picked them up.

On both sides the attraction was intensifying. Even sitting across the room from one another in a group of people, Mary was acutely conscious of John and of his eyes often on her. An electric sexual attraction was developing between them, no question about it.

One night Mary forced herself to face the issue. "I made myself think through the end results if John and I kept on the road we were going. A romantic interlude, nothing more? To think so would be kidding myself. Rather, probably a broken home. My husband's life cruelly hurt and twisted. Worse still for our children. And tawdriness as my reward. On the other side was the frightening intensity of the electricity between John and me.

"In desperation, I dropped on my knees. 'Oh God! This is too much for me.' It was a cry wrung out of me. 'I can't fight any more. I turn this battle over to You.' That night I slept calmly."

The next day with her husband still out of town, Mary spent the entire day cleaning closets, drawers, cupboards, windows. In some way, it must have been symbolic.

That evening after the children were in bed, John Ames appeared at the front door. "Bill's not home," Mary told him. But he came in anyway.

Mary didn't ask her caller to sit down. She remained standing in the center of the room bathed in a cone of light from the electrical fixture overhead. There was an awkward interlude during which John Ames made persistent small talk, his eyes fastened on Mary. As she concentrated on Jesus as represented by that light, she felt herself becoming less aware of John and more and more aware of the enveloping light of God all around her.

Finally her caller noticed the baby asleep on the sofa. "Don't you want me to carry her to her crib?" he asked.

Mary nodded, but did not follow John into the darkness of the adjoining bedroom. Somehow she knew that she must not. There in the darkness John's arms would reach for her as inevitably as—No, *she must stay in the light*. As long as she stood in the light, the values she really cared about—her marriage, the home she and Bill had made together, their children—would be safe.

John remained in the bedroom for what seemed like an eternity, waiting for her, Mary thought. At last he emerged. For a long moment he stood looking at Mary, indecision written on his face. At last reluctantly, he left.

"Then I understood," the author wrote, "the truth of the Scriptural teaching that there's nothing wrong with being tempted. It's what we *do* with the temptation that matters.

"My tumultuous feeling for John Ames did not disappear overnight. But as I prayed more about it, the entire episode just faded from my emotions, leaving no trauma, no scars, no regrets—just praise to God for delivering me from a serious temptation."

Mary had found for herself the reality of "the armour of light." That protecting armour is, of course, Jesus Himself as prophesied in Isaiah's beautiful words:

The people that walked in darkness have seen a great light: they that dwell in the land of the shadow of death, upon them hath the light shined.[20]

So, as His disciples, we are urged:

For ye were sometimes darkness, but now are ye light in the Lord: walk as children of light.[21]

We walk as children of light when we insist upon transparent openness and honesty, no dark secrets, no duplicity, lies, or double-dealing. It was from my spiritual mentor, the Quaker Hannah Smith, that I learned the valuable lesson that hidden sin—no matter how carefully denied, glossed over and secreted away—will give Satan his beachhead and result in our inability to stand victoriously before the enemy or any of his cohorts.[22] The emphasis here is on any accursed thing being tucked back in our lives, hidden out of sight. We may have almost forgotten about it, but Satan never forgets. For us, the result will be failure every time. This is the reason that Jesus had so much to say about the necessity of light and our coming to the light. When men's deeds are evil, they love darkness rather than light.

But he that doeth truth cometh to the light, that his deeds may be made manifest, that they are wrought in God.[23]

So it helps to stay aware of this principle: whenever we prefer to keep something secret or hidden, tucked away in the darkness, we do well to question our real motives.

Truth is the name of a third defense against the Destroyer pointed out by Scripture. The cynic would always echo Pilate's sarcastic question to Jesus, "What is truth?"—the assumption there being that all truth is relative, so there is no final clear-cut truth. But this is Satan's position, not Christ's. Jesus' words echo down the centuries, "*I* am the way, the truth, and the life."

Naturally, Satan could never agree to clarity. The saints of all ages are in agreement that the unholy spirit delights in fuzziness. He would have us believe that we are being properly humble when we intone, "I hope my sins are forgiven" . . . "Well, Yes, I think I'm a Christian. I try to be." Jesus wants us to *know* that our sins are forgiven and that we are Christians.

Thus one of our greatest weapons is not just defensive, but offensive: the use of Scripture as truth hurled in Satan's teeth, wielded as the "sword of the Spirit." Jesus' repeated use of "It is written" in His wilderness temptations is a vivid example. Of course, in order to use Scripture in this way, we have to get the habit of reading it so that the truth cast in the cadences of the great English of the Bible sinks deeply into heart and mind. I have found that when I do my part, then the Holy Spirit can do His. So often it has happened! It is as if the Helper searches through the library stacks of my unconscious where all manner of information has been filed away (much of it long since forgotten by the conscious mind) and produces the particular "It is written" needed for the moment of battle. Always Satan flees before this. He flees because the unholy spirit has final respect for the authority of Scripture. Though the Destroyer loathes truth, he recognizes it, thus tipping his hand about those eons spent in the presence of God. Certainly this should give us pause at a time when the authority of the Bible has been so generally called into question.

Satan and his lackeys always recognize and must bow before Jesus, who is our Deliverer. Long before even Jesus' apostles recognized that He was more than an exciting Teacher and Healer, the unclean spirits (demons) who had taken up abode in human beings recognized Him as the Son of God. So over and over in the Gospels we hear an unclean spirit crying out, "What have I to do with thee, Jesus, thou Son of the most high God? I adjure thee . . . that thou torment me not."[24] Each time Christ was able to cast out the unclean spirit because He is the only One who has never given any ground to Satan.

Usually we think we deserve a "little fun" by a fling into sinning when life has handed us some injustice or when we have stuck faithfully through some protracted trial. A degree of self-pity joins the blown-up pride of our self-congratulation at having been so patient and reliable. Many of us have found out to our sorrow what a deadly brew this is. Our eyes are completely off Christ and on ourselves. Out of this little mess Satan has worked some great triumphs.

But what if we are already in the middle of such a mess? What if one's life is snarled up by habit-patterns, bad human relationships, fears that one can't get rid of, debts, and illness? What then? Is there any hope?

There certainly is! That's precisely the good news Christ brings us. . . .

So also the Lord can rescue you and me from the temptations that surround us. . . .[25]

Behold, I give unto you power . . . over all the power of the enemy; and nothing shall by any means hurt you.[26]

Because thou has kept the word of my patience, I also will keep thee from the hour of temptation. . . .[27]

When we bring our misdeed into the light of Jesus' love and forgiveness and renounce it, we have taken the first step. The renouncing part is especially important when we have been toying with ouija boards, spiritualism, witchcraft, fortune-telling, and the like, even though this be years behind us. In order to belong to Christ, we have to make a clean break with the accoutrements of Satan's kingdom by renouncing them. Once that break is made, then we are free to "turn around" and accept Jesus' forgiveness.[28] Thereupon Satan loses his beachhead and we are again free.

But Satan, the liar, will throw everything into the fight to blind us to this final power before which he is helpless—the finished work of Jesus on His cross, the sacrificial Lamb, His blood shed for us. God's wish is that no matter what we've done, we feel guilt only long enough to bring it to the Light of the World to be dealt with. Satan's aim is to bog us down through the emotion of guilt, somehow convince us that *our* sin is too rarefied to be forgiven (an odd form of inverted human ego!), thus making us feel estranged from God and inept in serving Him.

The opposite of Satan's lie is given us in a ringing declaration in Colossians:

. . . he [Christ] cancelled the regulations that stood against us . . . when he nailed them to the cross, when he cut away the angelic Rulers and Powers from us, exposing them to all the world and triumphing over them in the cross.[29]

I remember how Peter Marshall once made this truth real and personal. One evening a friend had questioned him about God's judgment. Did he really think that there was going to have to be an accounting for each of us?

"Yes, I do think so," Peter answered promptly. "The Bible makes it quite clear. I think I may have to go through the agony of having Old Scratch, the accuser, recite my sins in the presence of God.

"But I believe it will be like this: Jesus, our High Priest, will come over and lay His hand across my shoulders and say to God, 'Yes, all these things are true, but I'm here to cover up for Peter. He is sorry for all his sins, and by a transaction made between us, I am now solely responsible for them.'"

Suddenly Peter smiled. "And sister, if I'm wrong about that, *I'm sunk.*"[30]

But we're not sunk. Glory be to God!

9.

The Enigma of Healing

Most of us feel no need of facing the question "Does God heal directly today?" until we are personally confronted with some physician's blunt finality: "There's nothing more we can do."

Those were the precise words my friend Sandra was hearing so incredulously that night—February 8, 1966. I did not learn of this sequence of events until later when Sandra Ghost (now a close friend. Yes, her name really is Ghost) shared it with me. Arriving at the hospital room where her little son lay, Sandy had encountered Dr. Gallo.

"Mrs. Ghost, there's been no improvement in Kent's condition since this afternoon," the distinguished-looking, dark-haired doctor told her. "No question of the diagnosis—a cerebral hemorrhage. He's still in deep coma."

Over his shoulder Sandra could see the slight form of her two-year-old son, usually unable to stay still for an instant. Now there wasn't a flicker of movement anywhere—from his toes to his blond head.

Dr. Gallo asked gently, "You did call your husband in Louisville?"

"Yes, I did. Bill caught the first plane possible. He should be here at ten o'clock."

"I must warn you. . . . Kent may not hold on until your husband gets here. Mrs. Ghost, you may go in now." He paused. "There's nothing more we can do."

The words spoken so slowly for emphasis struck Sandra like a physical blow. Their impact detached some part of her mind and sent her thoughts spinning backward to that first day when she and Kent, his hand clinging so tightly to hers, had walked through the front door of the National Institutes of Health on the outskirts of Washington, D.C. What relief she had felt! To think that this great research arm of the United States Government had been willing to take on their son's case of acute lymphocytic leukemia. Why, this place was one of medicine's frontiers. In these vast government buildings they were finding answers. Surely, she told herself, only God could have made the connection between the Ghost family in Louisville, Kentucky, and NIH. Therefore, the fine and compassionate doctors on Two-East (the leukemia unit) would discover the key to the healing of Kent's leukemia.[1]

And in the two months since, the doctors had indeed proved themselves compassionate. In fact, the warmth of everyone around NIH—laboratory technicians, housekeeping detail, clean-up crews, and Mr. Botts, the gentle black elevator operator who "God-blessed" all his passengers—had steadily reassured her.

So how could Dr. Gallo be saying so seriously, "There's nothing more we can do"? For what he meant was, "Kent is going to die and I can't prevent his death. Medicine, science, the best we know, has no further resources to give you."

Her thoughts reeled and staggered. "But that can't be! This is the twentieth century. I—Sandra Ghost—am a twentieth-century woman. I have relied on science. Science can do *anything*."

But she only stared at the doctor, nodded her head, and murmured, "Thank you, Doctor." For an instant she watched the physician's back retreating down the long corridor almost at a trot, as though eager to be away. Then she hurried into Kent's room.

This was Intensive Care with Di-Gi on duty, a nurse whom Sandra had learned to know well during the two months. Every ten minutes Di-Gi was taking vital signs: would Kent respond to the beam of light flashed directly into his eyes? Any sign of consciousness by grip or response? Any change in temperature? Blood pressure?

But there was no visible response—none at all. Her child was so still and so white, his legs so limp. Almost the smell of death was in this room. Was Sandra imagining it? No, this was no illusion; she saw it in the nurse's eyes.

Sandy kept a grip on her emotions through two of the ten-minute periods. Then she broke down, sobbing quietly.

Di-Gi understood. "Some black coffee would help," she suggested, "help me too. Why don't you go down to the Snack Shop for two cups?"

The distraught mother realized the nurse was using psychology on her, but she also knew that some activity would help. "Sure," Sandra agreed, "good idea."

On Sandy's return from the Snack Shop, she was surprised to see Mr. Botts running the elevator; it was rare to see him on night duty, rarer still for her to be the only passenger. As the doors slid shut and the elevator mounted, Mr. Botts asked as he always did, "And how's my little man?"

This time the question brought quick tears to Sandra's eyes. She shifted the sack with its two steaming cartons of coffee to her left hand in order to grope for her handkerchief. "Mr. Botts, Kent's bad. He's—not expected to live." Then from deep inside her came a request that she was surprised to hear herself making, "Will you—would you pray for Kent?"

At that moment they arrived at the second floor and the elevator doors opened. Sandra was no more than three steps into the hallway when she heard Mr. Botts's voice behind her, "Get back on the elevator, would you? Let's pray *now*. Please get back on."

Wordlessly, Sandra obeyed. The elevator doors shut, only this time Mr. Botts left the elevator stationary at the second floor.

"Lord Jesus," he prayed, "I ask you to heal this child as you healed me when the doctors told me I would never walk again. The Church prayed and You heard their prayers, and there's nothing wrong with me now. I ask You to do for this child what You did for me since the Good Book says, 'God is no respecter of persons.'

"Lord, enter this little boy's body. Heal Kent, Lord, and let him walk again. And Lord Jesus, give Kent's mother here Your strength. She needs it so much. . . ."

Was there more of the prayer? Sandy could never remember, only that she was aware of God's love in that elevator as she had never before felt it. And wasn't it odd that during what had seemed to her a long stretch of time, no one had rung for the elevator? Fumbling for words, she tried to thank Mr. Botts. Then she ran left down the corridor and through the double swinging doors to Kent's room. As she went, she glanced at her wrist watch—six minutes before nine.

"Any change?" she asked the nurse.

Di-Gi shook her head. "No change."

As the two women sipped coffee, Di-Gi talked. Sandra discovered one reason for this nurse's special depth of compassion. She had been through trouble too: her mother and her younger sister had died in an automobile wreck just two months before. Sandra wondered why Di-Gi was not angry with God or bitter. She had the feeling that the nurse knew Him.

As they talked, two sets of vital signs were taken. At the third, Di-Gi seemed startled and made no attempt to hide it. "His blood pressure! Coming down fast, toward normal."

Almost immediately, Kent stirred in the bed. His eyes fluttered open. Recognizing his mother, he turned toward her, "Mommy, I'm thirsty."

Di-Gi restrained her excitement long enough to finish taking all the vital signs and recheck them, then she ran for the doctor on duty. He made it to Kent's room in record time.

By the time Bill Ghost arrived from the airport, Kent was fully conscious, sitting up in bed, sipping a soft drink through a straw, anticipating his Daddy's coming.

During the night hours Kent continued to improve. The next day, February 9, Dr. Robert Gallo appeared to be in sharp disagreement with a battery of neurologists. Though the parents at NIH are always considered a part of the "medical team" for their own child, the Ghosts were surprised to hear the physicians openly discussing their differences: Dr. Gallo could not possibly have been correct in his diagnosis, the neurologists insisted; no patient could recover from a cerebral hemorrhage as quickly as Kent Ghost had.

Dr. Gallo stood his ground. Yes, he reiterated, his diagnosis had been correct. He had performed the requisite spinal tap. Nor had a vein been punctured during the tap, thus accounting for blood in the test tube.

Finally the neurologists would not be appeased unless they performed another spinal tap, so Kent was wheeled away to a treatment room. There Dr. Gallo was vindicated: yes, the little boy had had a brain hemorrhage.

Two days later, Kent was riding the rocking horse in the playroom at NIH, unaware of the doctors and nurses who kept drifting by the playroom door, staring at him. . . . "Can you believe that's Kent Ghost?" Between his turns on the rocking horse, he would ride Mr. Botts's elevator up and down, down and up, and each time a jubilant Mr. Botts would pat "his little man's" head, make gleeful remarks or hum under his breath, all the time looking as though he possessed a secret too marvelous to contain.

My first reaction to Sandy's story was joy. My second was, then why doesn't God always come to our rescue as He did to Kent Ghost's? Here is a query asked not so much by non-Christians nor even by the Christian who has never admitted healing into his understanding of the whole Gospel, but by those of us who have long struggled with this matter of healing through God's intervention.

I first asked the question in 1943 when, because of a lung condition, I too heard the doctors say, "Sorry! Nothing more we can do right now. Just lie in bed and rest."

So I was bedridden during 1943, 1944—winter . . . spring . . . summer . . . into autumn. During the long, tedious days I was doing a lot of praying and thinking. Since the birth of modern scientific inquiry, men had come to rely on the orderliness of nature, what science calls "the uniformity of natural causes." I could see how Christians had picked up this concept and applied it to Christian thinking. An idea can often be as catching as a virus. Such was the case with an idea that surfaced in the late 1930s and was verbalized from thousands of pulpits through the decade of the 1940s. It could be summarized like this. . . .

"We are accustomed to the fact of physical laws—discoverable, definite, immutable. When we drop an object from the top of a tall building the object always drops because the law of gravity always operates. In the spiritual realm too there are laws just as discoverable, just as precise, always operative.

"Therefore, the way to get on with spiritual research to find out how prayers are answered and healing effected is to discover these spiritual laws and apply them. The results will then be just as certain as in the realm of the physical laws."

It was an exciting concept. Many of us had turned to it with relief. It had given us a way to go. It was like having in our hand the latest AAA strip map for our spiritual journey. If we followed the directions carefully from point A to point B and then C and D, our destination was assured.

Lying in bed feeling half-alive, my need was great. I set out eagerly to find those spiritual laws governing healing. After studying the New Testament, I would then delve into what I could uncover from human experience as recorded in books and in any sort of verbal contemporary sharing for which acceptable proof was offered.

So methodically, I started searching out each of Jesus' healing miracles and analyzing them. I was groping for some common denominator in these healings by which I could uncover the principles or secrets I could apply to my situation. Thirty-seven miracles are detailed in the gospels in addition to thirteen separately recorded times when Christ healed "many" or "multitudes" or "great multitudes."

In order to make a comparative study of Jesus' dealings with the sick and the afflicted, I ruled wide sheets of paper into seven divisions, like this:

The Case of	The Trouble	Means Used	Time	Patient's Part	Other's Part	Christ's Instructions
The deaf man (Mark 7:32-38)	Deafness and severe speech impediment	Jesus' touch on afflicted part with saliva and His word of authority	Immediate cure	None	Friends brought man to Christ, begging that He lay hand on sufferer	Forbade man or his friends to tell others about it

My conclusion from this study could be summed up like this.
. . . Jesus came to earth to reveal His Father's nature and His will
for mankind.[2] Jesus saw sickness and disease as intruders in His
Father's world, part of Satan's work,[3] therefore evil all the way.
Consistently, He fought disease just as any dedicated physician
fights it.[4]

I could find no Gospel record that the Master ever refused
anyone who came to Him and asked for healing, though He did,
upon occasion, select one to be healed out of a group—such as
the man at the Pool of Bethesda[5]—thus obviously, leaving other
sufferers around that Pool unhealed.

He did not once say in regard to health, "If it is God's will."[6]
There is no beatitude for the sick as there is for others like the
bereaved, those who suffer persecution, the peacemakers.[7] Nor
did there ever fall from Jesus' lips any statements that ill health
would further our spiritual growth or benefit the Kingdom of
God. Rather, He not only wants to heal our diseases, He also
wants us to stay healthy.[8]

So I asked myself the question, "Then did Jesus intend for these
healings to go on after His ascension—even into our own time?"
According to the New Testament, He certainly did! How else could
we interpret His words, "Verily, verily I say unto you, he that
believeth on me, the works that I do shall he do also; and greater
works than these shall he do because I go unto my father."[9]

All of this added up to what seemed an unassailable "yes" on
the side of healing through the direct action of God today.

Yet this study, including that wistfully well-ordered chart of
Jesus' healings, were disappointingly frustrating in uncovering
any rules or methodology for healing through prayer. At first
glance, faith on the part of the sick one or his relatives or friends
(such as Mr. Botts for Kent Ghost) seemed to be necessary. But
closer scrutiny told me that while sometimes Jesus placed great
emphasis on faith, at other times faith was never mentioned. For
instance, what about those crowds whom Jesus healed?[10] Did
every person in those crowds have faith? It isn't likely.

Perhaps going to Jesus and *asking* for healing could be put
forward as a rule? No, because many were healed who never
asked, like the man with the withered hand[11] or the sufferer at
the Pool of Bethesda.[12]

Well then surely, I thought, some degree of goodness must be necessary? Not a bit of it! Here Scripture's message is resoundingly clear: all humankind is born into this earth life with the same stain. "All have sinned, and come short of the glory of God."[13]

And this "coming short" is such a great gap that it can never be filled by human effort: "Not for thy righteousness, or for the uprightness of thine heart, dost thou go to possess their land. . . ."[14] "Not by works of righteousness which we have done, but according to his mercy he saved us. . . ."[15]

Jesus healed out of pure compassion because He was ever—and always will be—"The Father's Restorer." True, after Jesus healed the man at the Pool of Bethesda, He told him that now he would be wise to repent and change "or something even worse may happen to you."[16] But the healing came before the man's change and in no way seemed dependent on it.

Though I was learning, I could find no uniform dependable act or attitude on the part of the sick person that would provide certain healing. At that point I began wondering if things of the spirit could really be pigeonholed and categorized in the way that has been such universal procedure in the physical world? I was beginning to doubt it.

Even so, my search went on into the second phase, the area of human experience since New Testament times. Of several such areas I investigated, I'll mention only one—the healings at Lourdes in southwest France. This has been a healing shrine since a fourteen-year-old peasant girl, Bernadette Soubirous,[17] had a vision of Mary, the mother of Jesus, on February 11, 1858. The girl was told to dig in the earth at a certain place where she would find a spring. She was instructed to ask that a healing shrine be built over the spring.

Bernadette obeyed. Digging in the dry earth, she was astonished to find a trickle of water appear, no bigger than a finger. Over the days, the spring grew larger and larger until today it pours out thirty-thousand gallons of water every twenty-four hours. More than forty-five thousand sick people go to Lourdes each year, most of these as a last hope.

Investigation convinced me that there have been healings so remarkable as to fall clearly into the category of "miracle." The first one in 1858 was that of the eighteen-month-old boy Louis-

Justin Bouhohartz, a neighbor of Bernadette. Dying from a disease that Dr. Dozous, the local physician, had said "hesitates between meningitis and infantile paralysis," the little boy had intermittent convulsions with high fever, was unable to sit up, walk, or stand. Feeling that she had nothing to lose, the child's mother plunged him into the icy spring for fifteen minutes and took him home with his little body stiff and blue. The next day, Louis-Justin was walking and eating normally.

Dr. Dozous, who had attended the boy and given him over to death, watched the icy bath and its results, and this convinced him. Incidentally, Louis-Justin lived to be a very old man.

Over the years other miracles have followed, stories that fascinated me as I read of them.[18] The distinguished scientist Dr. Alexis Carrel has left us with an impressive eyewitness report, his observation of the healing of the eighteen-year-old Marie Ferrand from advanced tubercular peritonitis between two-forty and three o'clock on a July afternoon in 1903.

At the time, Carrel was on the faculty of the Medical School of the University of Lyons. Born into a Catholic family, he had become first a Stoic, then a disciple of Kant, then skeptical of any belief in a supreme being. All religious concepts had been ground down and finally destroyed by intellectualism, especially the rigorous German system of Higher Criticism. Any attempt to discuss primary causes seemed useless to Carrel; rationalism satisfied his mind all the way.

Out of this background, having heard so many rumors of cures at Lourdes, the young doctor decided to accompany a trainload of pilgrims to observe, analyze, examine, and discredit these vaunted cures. On the train he was summoned to the side of Marie Ferrand, who was apparently dying. He learned that there was a history of tuberculosis on both sides of Marie's family. After examining the girl, Dr. Carrel concurred in the diagnosis of her hometown doctor—tubercular peritonitis too far advanced to risk surgery.

Dr. Carrel examined Marie again after she got to Lourdes and before she was taken to the Grotto. He found her with an emaciated white face, a pulse racing at 150 beats a minute, an abdomen markedly distended with viscera and fluid, ears and nails of a pale greenish hue, her nose and hands cold. He scarcely expected the patient to live long enough to be carried from the Lourdes hospital to the Shrine.

Later on at the Grotto Shrine, Dr. Carrel stayed close by the girl thinking that she might need medical help. As he watched, astounding changes took place: the lines and shadows on her face began disappearing as color returned; the blanket over her distended abdomen was flattening out while her heartbeat was slowing down to a regular pace. One of the nurses offered her a cup of milk which she drank eagerly. Then she began moving her legs without any discomfort.

Still incredulous, Dr. Carrel reexamined Marie that same evening. She was sitting up in bed. Her pulse was now a steady 80 beats per minute. All traces of distension, hard masses, and fluid had disappeared from her abdomen; hers was the flat, slightly concave stomach of an undernourished girl.[19]

Witnessing this case changed Alexis Carrel's life in several respects. Upon his return to the University of Lyons, he decided that he could no longer call himself truly scientific if he failed to speak out about what he had observed at Lourdes. He was promptly summoned into the office of the Dean of the Medical School. "With such views, sir," he was told, "you can hardly expect to stay on as a member of our faculty."

"In that case," Carrel replied, "I must look elsewhere."

That was why Alexis Carrel left France to come to the United States, first to the University of Chicago, then to New York as a member of the Rockefeller Institute for Medical Research. There in 1912, he received the Nobel Prize in physiology and medicine for his contribution to the surgery of blood vessels.

The Catholic Church—at first as skeptical about Lourdes as was the medical profession—had finally seen the point of detailed medical substantiation. Thus, in 1885 a Medical Bureau had been established for professional examination and verification of alleged healings. Later an International Medical Association (nicknamed AMIL) with five thousand doctors from thirty countries was added to support the Medical Bureau and the scientific study of Lourdes cures.

Of the many apparent healings at Lourdes, only 1200 in eighty-nine years have passed the Medical Bureau's rigid standards, with probably an additional 4000 genuine cures not finally substantiated because of incomplete data in the Bureau's files.

Out of the total, only sixty-two have been submitted to the Catholic Church's Canonical Commission, finally to be pronounced "miraculous."

This rigorous medical substantiation gave me in Lourdes an ideal modern showcase to set alongside the New Testament in searching for that common denominator or set of spiritual laws in healings. Yet a careful scrutiny of the Lourdes healings left me with the same confusion as had the Gospel search. Try as I might, the why or the how of the Lourdes healings could not be pigeonholed or categorized any more than the New Testament ones. For among those gloriously healed at Lourdes have been some roustabout sinners all but dragged to the healing Grotto, while others who apparently fulfilled every prayer condition departed with their physical infirmities unchanged.

Some of the ill suffered severe pain at the time of healing; others were healed with no physical sensation.

While persistence on the part of the sufferer often appeared to be a factor, some have been cured at the Lourdes Grotto at their first bath in the springs.

The conclusion from all of this was clear: there was no neat set of spiritual laws, no cut-and-dried pattern I could follow to insure the return of the health I so desperately wanted. But back in 1944 I was not yet ready to admit to such a conclusion. I tried every way I knew: confession and spiritual housecleaning, asking for the gifts of faith followed by collecting faith passages of Scripture, memorizing affirmations, practicing positive thinking—and so on.

Finally, having prepared myself in every way I knew, with all the faith I had, I asked Christ to heal me. Then I waited impatiently for the next physical checkup and set of X-rays, certain that a loving Lord had observed my stupendous efforts and would respond.

The blood tests and X-rays were taken. Receiving the report two days later was always a traumatic experience for me . . . a racing heart, a pulse I could feel in my dry throat as I picked up the phone and dialed the number.

The doctor's voice revealed no such excitement. "No change in the X-rays; markings just the same. Sedimentation rate, ah—the same. Just carry on!" And he hung up.

No change—after all that! Incredulously, I sank back on the pillows. I had come to the end of self-effort and the sign before my face read DEAD END.

I hit bottom. And there I met God at the place where He had been waiting for me all along: where I knew that I wanted Christ's presence in my life more than I wanted health. Never mind healing, I wanted to be certain that God wasn't dead, that Jesus Christ lived, that He was real, and that I had been received by Him.

I poured all this out before Him, "God, I don't understand You at all. I've tried. You know I have. You told us that 'Your ways are not our ways.' That's certainly the understatement of the ages! Even so, I don't understand why You're so hard to find. But here I am. I want You to take me over and do what You like with me. I'm no good as I am, so I'm not giving You much of a gift. But if You want me to lie here on and on, like a vegetable—all right, that's up to You."

There was no fine theological language in this prayer and certainly, no graciousness in the gift of myself. But it was honest, probably the most straightforward prayer I had ever made. Finally, I meant business with God. In the years since, I've learned that our Lord waits patiently until we stop playing games with Him. The instant we leave off our childish fooling around, He knows it and responds. It had taken me eighteen months of trying everything else, but at last I wanted the Giver more than His gifts.

That did it! The connection was made. At 3:00 the next morning, I awakened suddenly to a feeling of crackling power in the darkness. There followed an experience of the Risen Christ. Since I've described this elsewhere,[20] I shall not repeat the details here except to say that I saw and heard Christ with the eyes and ears of the spirit. And my observations of His personality, of what He said, and of my replies and reactions, were even more specific than most of my contacts ever are with my fellow human beings in the flesh.

The results in my body were observable too. The next set of chest X-rays revealed healing. Every X-ray thereafter showed more healthy lung tissue until finally the healing was complete. Nor has there ever been any relapse.

Surely there is no joy like that first rush of discovery in experiencing for oneself that the Lord is alive in one's life, so much more alive and real than any of us. And I had stumbled into that revelation in the last way I would have thought logical—through the relinquishment of myself to Him.

At that point I caught a glimpse of God's sense of humor—His revelation of Himself had outmaneuvered logic.

10.

The Roof on the House

When one touches a live electric wire, there's no mistaking the instantaneous power that jolts the body. In the same way, when through relinquishment, I had touched the power of the Risen Christ in my quiet bedroom in the middle of the night, it had been as startlingly obvious.

We have Jesus' promise from His own lips that the Holy Spirit will lead us into all truth,[1] including all puzzling questions we need answered about healing. My problem was that often I was not content to have the Good Shepherd lead me into truth; like a rambunctious sheep, I kept running on ahead, nosing around the pastureland, always thinking that the truth I sought must surely lie immediately on the other side of the nearest hill.

That is how I acted back in 1944 after my return to health. In no time, I had all but forgotten about the necessity for relinquishment. In my joy over experiencing the presence of the risen Lord, I rushed to pray for all manner of neighbors and friends who were ill. This included Kenneth Grey, a neighbor on Cathedral Avenue in Washington who was dying of a brain tumor; an appealing small boy in the last stages of leukemia; a friend in our church with cancer.

I hope that my prayers brought comfort to the ill and to those around them. But they had no appreciable effect on the disease of the sufferers. In each case the illness took its course and the sick ones died.

That was deeply discouraging. Once again I had to go to God to ask Him my mistake. "Go back and look carefully at the way I've led you," I was told.

So I studied all the efforts in 1943–1944 that had failed to bring results:

My effort	*God's response*
Tried to find blanket laws.	No methodology; He deals with each one of us as His child, and each case individually.
Tried to make myself worthy.	"All [your] righteousness are as filthy rags to me."[2]
Tried to have faith in faith, and to work up faith by positive thinking, affirmations, and picturing.	He showed me that this is putting faith in a technique rather than in a Person— Jesus.
Demanded healing as my "right" as a child of God who thought she had met the conditions.	"You have no rights or righteousness in yourself, only in Christ Jesus."[3]

I saw that my demanding spirit, with self-will as its rudder, had blocked the answer to prayer.

"Now take a close look," I was told, "at how Jesus Himself handled the problem of will."

I was startled to find that Jesus (before His resurrection and glorification) insisted upon His helplessness:

The Son can do nothing of himself, but what he seeth the Father do. . . .[4]

. . . I do nothing of myself; but as my Father has taught me, I speak. . . ."[5]

Thus Jesus' helplessness meant a total dependence upon His Father for everything.

But His *will*, what of that? Since Jesus' perfect humanity was as real as His divinity, His would have been a strong human will, stronger than any of ours. Over and over He reiterated that He had handed over that will:

"For I have come down from heaven not to carry out my own will, but the will of Him who sent me. . . ."[6]

And to His disciples He said:

"My meat is to do the will of Him that sent me. . . ."[7]

And at the end, He was "obedient even unto death."

Given Jesus' dependence on the Father, together with His laying down of self-will, then I asked myself, "Why didn't Jesus have to go through the process of relinquishment (for most of us a lengthy and agonizing process) each time He wanted to stretch out His hand and heal some sufferer?" Reading between the lines of the Gospel records, I believe He did relinquish His will each time, then immediately looked to the Father for what to do. But for Him it was neither an agonizing nor a lengthy process because He was altogether clear of our sticking points: does God really love the individual as we understand love; does He really have final power to break or overrule so-called "natural law"? Most of us have never settled these basic dilemmas. Jesus had.

So persuaded was He of His Father's complete love, trustworthiness, and Omnipotent power over all evil that He could make these relinquishments quickly. And just as quickly there flowed back from the Father to Jesus the particular Word to give the sinner or the sufferer along with the necessary faith. Thus occurred the resultant miracle healings. With us it takes longer—hours, weeks, sometimes years of trying everything else.

Meanwhile, as though to keep me seeking in the direction of relinquishment[8] and to let me know that this had not been just one woman's isolated experience, instance after instance kept coming to my attention in literature and history, in journals and letters, and by word of mouth. One of the most convincing and dramatic was Maude Blanford's remarkable recovery from what was diagnosed as terminal cancer fourteen years ago. A friend in Louisville, Kentucky, first put me in touch with Mrs. Blanford.

Attached to a brief typed outline of her story was an impressive statement signed by Mrs. Blanford's physician, Dr. Oscar J. Hayes, making it all but impossible to dismiss the patient's recovery as one of those occasional "remissions" as medical men usually speak of them. I was excited enough to fly to Louisville to get the details from the woman herself, now gloriously restored to health.

In the dining room of our mutual friend, we three women sat around the table sipping coffee as I questioned Maude Blanford. There was no trace of gray in her reddish hair, though she is middle-aged now, a motherly type, comfortable to be with.

"How did your trouble begin?" I asked.

"In my left leg," was her prompt reply. "The leg had been hurting me for two years. I thought it was because I was on my feet eight or ten hours a day. Finally, when I couldn't stand it any longer, my husband and I decided that I should see a doctor."

As the Blanford's family doctor examined her, he became increasingly sober. Her leg was not her only problem. On the patient's lower abdomen there were lumps—large, firm tumor masses.

"I'm going to have to send you to a specialist immediately," he told Mrs. Blanford. The unspoken word hung in the air between them, "malignancy."

The specialist to whom Mrs. Blanford was sent discovered uterine hemorrhaging. Mrs. Blanford read in his eyes the poor prognosis. "I must warn you," he told her, "I suspect that this is extremely advanced."

"But Doctor," the patient pleaded, "there must be some way you can stop it. I'll go through *anything*—radium, surgery—"

"Mrs. Blanford, I promise you I'll do everything I can."

On July 7, 1959, the patient was admitted to the hospital for seventy-two hours of radium treatment in an effort to stop the hemorrhaging—without success. So in August she was given an additional seventy-two hours of this treatment. "The effect of the radium was total misery," she told me, "like having a hot oven inside me."

On September 29th she underwent surgery. Three days later, as she pleaded with the surgeon, Dr. Hayes, for the truth, he admitted, "The malignancy is extensive and we removed as much as we could. Lymph nodes are affected—that's why the pain in your left leg. One kidney is nonfunctioning because of blockage of the ureter. There is an area of metastasis in the liver. I am sorry. I am so sorry."

Maude Blanford was sent home, apparently to die. She was put on strong narcotics and tranquilizers to control the pain, and she was supposed to come back into the hospital for radium at regular intervals. Over a six-month period, she consumed $1,000 worth of pain-relieving drugs—Zactirin, sometimes Thorazine, and morphine.

Meanwhile, the sick woman began reviewing her spiritual resources, not to make her peace with God before death but for His help to continue battling for life. Mrs. Blanford had no church affiliation and no knowledge of the Bible. She did discover within herself a childlike (though untested) belief in the Person of Jesus Christ.

On the first Saturday of January 1960, she suffered a cerebral hemorrhage and remained unconscious for twelve days. Afterwards, she related a vivid image that had come to her. She saw a house with no top on it. The partitions between the rooms were there, the furniture in place, but there was no roof. She remembered thinking, "Oh, we must put a roof on the house. If it rains, all the furniture will be spoiled."

When she came out of the coma, Mrs. Blanford was bewildered. Instinctively, she turned to the Lord to ask Him in prayer what the vivid image had meant. "Christ showed me," she explained almost matter-of-factly, "that without Him as my covering, my body had no protection. Therefore, my life was in danger. But at that time I didn't know how to get the roof back on the house."

But Maude Blanford's fallacy, as mine had been, was that all her attention was focused on her danger, her roofless house. So despite all her prayers between then and July 1960, day by day her condition worsened. Breathing became so labored that she was reduced to speaking in whispers.

Still she kept struggling back and back for the radiation treatments. Then came Friday, July 1, 1960; she remembers it well. As the radiologist examined her, she asked anxiously, "Is it getting any better?"

"No, as a matter of fact—" his voice trailed off. Mrs. Blanford could read pessimism in his eyes. "I dare not give you any encouragement."

A few minutes later as Maude Blanford's son-in-law helped her into the car and she lifted her bad leg onto the seat, she broke down and wept. "For the first time, death looked good to me. Maybe I couldn't fight any more. I just hoped the Lord would take my quickly." It was a complete handing over of herself for God to do with as He pleased.

As He pleased . . . a bell of remembrance rang in my mind. My thoughts went spinning back to that September night in 1944 when I had ceased my frantic human striving and laid down my will almost in the same words she had. Only my situation had not been as stark as Maude Blanford's. For me, the alternative to healing was just having to lie in bed year after year; for her, it was death.

I leaned forward, eager to learn the result of this Prayer of Relinquishment. Had she made contact with the Source of power?

"That last visit to the radiologist and my turning myself over to God," she continued, "had been on Friday, July 1st. Well, I didn't have long to wait."

Monday, July 4th dawned beautiful but hot. That afternoon Joe Blanford made a bed for his wife outdoors with chairs and cushions. As the ill woman rested, hoping for the relief of a breeze, into her mind came some Scripture which she was not aware of ever having read. . . .

Is not this the fast that I have chosen? to loose the bands of wickedness, to undo the heavy burdens, and to let the oppressed go free, and that ye break every yoke? . . . Then shall thy light break forth as the morning and thine health shall spring forth speedily. . . . Here I am. . . .

As Maude Blanford quoted this, I found myself looking at her in astonishment over the rim of my coffee cup. "But I thought you didn't know the Bible that well?"

"I didn't. I'd never read the Bible and I didn't even know that verse was there. When I was given those verses in my mind, I was also told, 'Isaiah 58.' My husband had to hunt up a Bible that had gathered dust on a spare-room shelf for years. Then I had to search and search to find the part called 'Isaiah.' But when I found the great verses just as I had heard them, even that 'Here I am' on down in the ninth verse, I knew the Lord Himself had spoken to me."

In the next few days the ill woman felt an intense desire—like an authoritative inner summons—to get outdoors and absorb the beauty of the good earth. She found a way to express this to her husband: "Joe, I want to go fishing."

That made no sense to him. Suppose his wife died on the way to the lake? The back road was rough. His wife would have to be carried down the steep hill to the lake.

Finally Maude Blanford's insistence that God had told her to do this won her husband over. He allowed some neighbors to take her to the lake. That first day she stayed at the lakeside all day until six thirty. Just watching a breeze ripple the water, looking at the clouds and the wheeling birds and the distant hills brought a refreshment of spirit. That night she was relaxed for the first time in many months and slept soundly.

After that, the lake trip became routine. In three months' time, Maude Blanford was climbing up the hill to the road by herself. Then that inner Voice told her to begin walking upstairs slowly, praising God on every step. Still lifting her left leg with difficulty, at each step she would murmur fervently, "Thank You, Jesus."

Following that came the insistent instruction to undertake a few household chores. So she would sit in a chair and dust a mahogany tabletop saying, "Thank You, Jesus. Isn't that wood beautiful! Thank You for giving me the strength to lift my arm."

Then she tried putting a small amount of water in a pail. Sitting in a light chair, she would mop the floor in the area immediately around her, then inch the chair along and mop another spot. "Thank You, Jesus. I praise You for helping me do this. Is this the way we get the roof back on my house?"

Not that all pain or difficulties were over. She was still on heavy narcotics, still experiencing much nausea as the aftermath of the radium.

About this point she commented to me, "I learned a lot about the difference between self-effort which is the result of our human will to live and the self-effort that's obedience to what God tells us to do. We have to cooperate with *what we see God doing*, as Jesus put it."

She was so right. After our relinquishment, when the initiative passes to God, we need to follow willingly, obediently, trustingly. There must be no running out ahead of Him, but also no lying back limp or passive either. Instead we learn to listen and we follow.

About this time Mrs. Blanford was led to another type of nourishment. The doctor had ordered vitamin therapy and iron sulfate. Iron, she learned, is one of the best oxygen carriers to body tissues. After one of her conversations with Jesus, the insistent direction came: to slough off disease, your body's cells need all the oxygen they can get. He directed how much to increase the dose of iron sulfate.

The next morning as she was preparing breakfast for her husband, she said to him, "Honey, I've been healed." He lowered the morning paper and looked at her quizzically as she told him what had happened. His silence told her that he didn't believe her; so far as Joe Blanford could see, his wife looked exactly as before—except happier.

Mrs. Blanford knew that she was being ordered to share this faith with others, rather like those lepers whom Jesus had healed being told to go and show themselves to the priests. To obey, she had to relinquish false pride and risk a degree of embarrassment. Though not a churchgoer, Maude Blanford went to a small Baptist church near her home. The clergyman allowed her to stand in the service and tell her story. "I have no idea how long I talked," she reminisced. "I do remember seeing tears on different faces in the congregation."

Even so, it took time to rebuild her body-house—nine months for her bad leg to be near normal, three years for evidence of the cancer to leave her. As her body created new cells, the vicious malignant ones were sloughed off as waste. The "football" in her side disappeared. Vitality returned.

One problem remained, however. She still had so much pain. In April she went to her family doctor. "Is there anything more you can do for me to kill this pain?"

To her surprise, she saw tears in the doctor's eyes. "No," he had answered slowly, "there's nothing more I can do except give you the drug by hypodermic."

Suddenly she knew. . . . After all her other relinquishments, the one she faced now was the toughest of all: could she let go the drug crutch? Did she have the courage to say to God, "O.K., I'll even take the pain, if that's what You want for me"?

It was going to take a year of struggle to make that decision. On the 27th of April, 1961, Mrs. Blanford was returning on a long bus trip from a visit to her son in West Virginia. At a five-o'clock rest stop, as she popped the pain-killing pill into her mouth, she knew that at last she could say, "Yes, Lord" even to this: it would be her last narcotic pill.

So it turned out. Not that all pain left immediately. But what remained was bearable and gradually it faded away.

Two years passed during which period Maude Blanford had no contact with any doctor. Then when she called Dr. Hayes again over some small unrelated matter, the surgeon shouted in astonishment, "Mrs. Blanford! What's happened to you? I thought you were——"

"You thought I was long since gone." She laughed.

"Will you get in here to my office and let me examine you?"

"Look," she retorted, "why should I spend a lot of money for a complete examination when I'm a perfectly well woman?"

But Dr. Hayes insisted. "Mrs. Blanford, I promise you that if you will let me examine you, this one will be on me."

What the doctor found can best be stated in his own words:

I had lost contact with Mrs. Blanford and had assumed that this patient had expired. In May of 1962 she appeared in my office. That was two and a half years following her operation and her last X-ray had been in July 1960. She had had approximately one-half of the X-ray treatment usually given, which certainly was well below what would be required for any effect.

The swelling of her leg was gone. She had full use of her leg; she had no symptoms whatsoever. . . . Her examination was completely negative and no evidence of cancerous disease could be found. . . .

She has been seen periodically since that time for routine examinations. . . . She is absolutely asymptomatic. . . . This case is most unusual in that this woman had a proven, far-advanced, metastatic cancer of the cervix (epidermoid carcinoma) and there should have been no hope whatsoever for her survival.

(Signed) O. J. Hayes, M.D.

A follow-up examination nine years later by Dr. Hayes in January 1972 was followed by the same conclusion—"absolutely no evidence of any cancerous tissue."

Dr. Hayes, Mrs. Blanford, and the Record Librarian of St. Joseph's Hospital in Louisville were kind enough to allow me access to the medical data on her case. We lay people with meagre medical knowledge little realize the extent to which we are shielded from abhorrent details. I've no desire to expose them further. It is enough to say that the greater part of this patient's body was in a pre-death, putrescent state, riddled all through with metastatic cancer.

When I expressed appreciation to Dr. Hayes, the surgeon reiterated, "I'm only stating the facts. Truth must be served. Not that I understand it. I've no medical explanation to offer for Mrs. Blanford's return from certain death."

The puzzle in a case like Maude Blanford's is, why relinquishment? Why does God insist on our laying down our wills even when what we are clamoring for also happens to be His will for us?

I believe that the answer lies in this direction. . . . God is interested in more than our recovery from a specific illness; He is intent on our learning how to obey Him in the totality of life. Back in 1943–1944 my personal desire for health was the focal point of reality for me. Perhaps so much of me had been packed into that eager longing that there was no room for God to enter and do anything at all so long as my myopic thinking was equating "life" with the health I wanted.

Everything turns here on what constitutes life. In the end God's answer was infinitely more inclusive and richer than mine. So long as I was assuming that fullness of life corresponded to what I was striving for, I was actually deifying my own goal. And "Thou shalt have no other gods before Me" had to apply to my personal desire-world. There was nothing for it but to "put away" that most beloved of all idols inscribed "What I want." The scrapping of a treasure is always painful.

Our struggle with giving up self-will goes right back to the beginning of man's history on earth. It is significant that the fruit of the tree that Adam and Eve insisted on eating at all costs was the Tree of the *Knowledge* of Good and Evil.

The temptation to hang onto self-will is tagged "man's autonomy" and the bait is our covetousness for understanding. It is a temptation to which I, for one, have succumbed as often as most people by always wanting to know "Why?" I've even handed myself accolades for that. Doesn't that show that I'm a seeker, even a spiritual researcher? Didn't even Solomon ask for the gift of wisdom?

No, it doesn't prove much of anything except that I'm like my Mother Eve. She could have offered up the same rationalizations. . . . "And when the woman saw that it was a tree to be desired to make one *wise* . . . she. . . . did eat."

Wisdom . . . understanding—all tempting bait. Except for the thoughts God chooses to share with us, it's still forbidden fruit. So long as we wear the garment of flesh, we can never understand the mind of our Creator.

At the time of the Protestant Reformation, men like Luther, Zwingli, Calvin, Farrel, and others kept insisting that the Biblical view of Man's Fall was that every part of Man fell, including his mind. Indeed, once we admit the Fall at all, what other view makes any sense?

Yet the Western world's humanism rests upon the opposite view. Our virtual deification of human intellect goes straight back to Thomas Aquinas (1227-1274), the intellectual and spiritual father of the Western nations who taught that while man's will fell from grace, his intellect did not. This is the same teaching that reached its height in the eighteenth-century Age of Reason.

When we realize that it was the eighteenth-century which gave America her legal and constitutional documents, we can see why the Aquinas views are so deeply imbedded in our thought. His dogma was even accepted almost completely by the Church. Along with the United States, Britain and other Western nations have inherited from Aquinas a mind-set driven to such depth that we are all but unaware of it.

Whenever anyone sets up his reasoning against God's, he is going the Aquinas way of humanistic autonomy, even though he may piously call it faith. The only true wisdom is facing up to what we actually are—creatures—and then yielding ourselves to the love and wisdom of our Creator. This yielding is relinquishment. And as we relinquish our own defective, incomplete human judgment, it feels like death because it *is* death—the beginning of the end of the old Adam in us.

The psychologist Fritz Kunkel has called this "The Crisis"—the major crisis of egocentricity. For many years prior to the crisis the basis of life has been—openly or secretly—"My will be done." The result has been increasing rigidity, an inability to change ideas or life patterns, and a decreasing ability to handle life's burdens. The ego becomes a hard shell around the person, layer by layer, deed by deed. Now there remains but one way to crack the shell—exterior circumstances. To the person hiding within, these appear to be tragic, surely the end of everything.

A marriage is in difficulty. Health or financial resources are lost. There are misunderstandings between friends. Someone is taken by death. Then

> he comes to realize the deeper meaning of the great paradox, "He that would save his life must lose it." . . . It seems to him to be a real death . . . for the Self, the only form of life that he knows, must disappear, and therefore, he believes its collapse is death. Thus he believes he faces the end of his life. . . . It is true, indeed, that one must lose that which *seems* to be his life—the system of mistaken ideas and values which are embodied in his Ego—in order really to live, to release into life the creative, enriching, productive powers of the true Self. . . .[9]

Yet . . . doesn't this complete laying down of one's life seem to be a denial of the need for faith? After my book *Beyond Our Selves* was published, I began receiving letters like this:

> . . . you mentioned in your book that we must give in to God's will. I am confused. . . . Does relinquishment mean that we can never be sure about praying for any definite thing? If so—how can that be faith? . . .

Indeed, many stories of healing in the Bible seem to indicate that just the opposite of relinquishment—an insistence on life—was the key to Christ being able to heal. In the cases of the woman with an issue of blood[10] and the palsied man carried by four friends and let down through the roof,[11] healing apparently had nothing to do with relinquishment; rather there was an intensity of desire in both cases.

Though the importunate widow in Jesus' parable on prayer[12] was not seeking healing, she was trying to make contact with the Source of help. Clearly, Jesus was here praising the strength of the widow's determination.

And in the instance of Marie Ferrand on the train to Lourdes? The girl was too ill to be struggling with relinquishment or anything else except her next breath.

These people were not "relinquishing" in the usual sense. They were, instead, going to incredible lengths to insist on healing, letting nothing discourage them.

It was the extraordinary experience of our friend Virginia Lively that shed great light on this seeming contradiction.

I've known Virginia for nine years. She's a housewife (now a widow) in Belle Glade, Florida who does her own cooking and cleaning, saves grocery stamps, and has to watch her weight. She and I have had dozens of meals together, visited back and forth, gone on retreats and prayed together often. Virginia has a homespun quality including a sense of humor that bubbles up in an infectious laugh. She is about the last person I would expect to have any far-out spiritual experience.

It happened in 1950 after her father Roy Wolff had been in the Tampa Tuberculosis Sanatorium for seven months. The sixty-three-year-old man's illness had been discovered almost by accident. A casual visit to the T.B. truck going the rounds had revealed three cavities about the size of silver dollars in the top of his left lung.

That was bad enough. But Mr. Wolff's condition did not respond to treatment and he was losing ground. The crisis came in October. Mr. Wolff's latest X-rays gave a grim prognosis. INH (Isoniazid), almost a miracle drug for many tuberculosis patients, had effected no change in the patient's diseased left lung. The three cavities had enlarged into what looked like a figure eight.

The physicians at the sanatorium dared give the drug for only six more weeks. The patient was too old to undergo surgery; they could hold out little hope.

Virginia and her mother and sister were together when they got the news. At that time not a one of them knew how to pray. Roy himself had little use for religion. He had not attended a church service all his married life because as a boy he had been "churched to death."

True, Virginia and her husband were church members, active at fund raising, church committees, and bazaars. Civic-minded church activists, neither husband nor wife had even taken subjects like prayer or healing into serious consideration. It would never have occurred to Virginia or her mother or her sister Doris to ask God to step into Roy's case and change medical facts.

One night soon after this discouraging hospital visit, Virginia was driving home from a PTA meeting when suddenly, she began to cry. She realized that she was under pressure as head of the Halloween Carnival that year, but it wasn't really the Carnival. She knew that. A deep intuition told her that the tears were for something much deeper.

Tears, more tears, floods of tears, started over again that night and then the next morning. The crying jag lasted for four days and three nights. Virginia was convinced it was the start of a nervous breakdown.

But on the morning of the fourth day, after her husband Ed had left for the bank and the two children for school, all at once she felt power in the air around her. The atmosphere in the quiet living room seemed to hum and crackle as though she were standing in the center of an electric storm.

As she sat in a high-backed chair, through the window she saw a ball of light on the eastern horizon. The light was moving, traveling toward her with incredible speed. It appeared white, yet from it poured all the colors Virginia had ever seen.

Then it was beside her. Although it seemed impossible that anything with such energy could hold still, it took a position at her right shoulder and stayed there. As she stared, she started to smile. She smiled because He was smiling at her. She now saw that it was not light, but a Face.

Even now Virginia finds it hard to put into words a description of that beautiful countenance. His forehead was high. His eyes exceptionally large. But she could never fix the color of His eyes any more than she could have the color of the sea.

More than individual features was the overwhelming impression of life—unhampered life, life so brimming over with power and freedom that all living things she had seen seemed lumps of clay by comparison.

Not for a moment did Virginia hesitate to call this Life at her side Jesus. And two things about Him struck her most. The first was His humor. She was astonished to see Him often break into outright laughter. And the second was His utter lack of condemnation. He knew her down to her very marrow—knew all the stupid, cruel, silly things she had ever done. But she saw that none of these things, or anything she would ever do, could alter the absolute caring, the unconditional love that she saw in those eyes.

It was too immense a fact to grasp. Virginia felt that if she gazed at Him for a thousand years, she could not realize it all.

She did not have a thousand years. She had three months. For as long as that, the face of Jesus stayed before her, never fading, never withdrawing.

For the first two weeks of this great experience, Virginia had given little thought to her father. She felt so joyous and free that there was no way she could have recaptured the previous mood of fretful grief.

Just after lunch one day she was lying on her bed reading the Bible. Growing drowsy, Virginia turned on her side, intending to take a nap. She was looking at a patch of sunlight on the wall thinking of Him, of how wonderful He is. That crackling vitality! When He'd said that He was Life, she smiled to herself, thinking, "Is that ever the understatement of the ages!"

Suddenly her train of thought was interrupted as an X-ray picture of lungs three times larger than life appeared in the middle of the sunlight. Unmistakably, her father's X-ray; she would have recognized it anywhere. There was the unusual figure-eight cavity and the single dollar-sized one at the top of the left lung. There were the same shadows and areas of scar tissue she had seen so often on the hospital X-rays.

Could this be an odd quirk of tree or cloud shadows? Virginia turned to look out the window. No, nothing.

As she turned back to puzzle over the picture on the wall, a white line about three inches wide moved slowly up the wall. As the white line passed the lower lobes of the lungs, it left behind healthy lungs with the scar tissue gone. As it traveled upward over the diseased portion, it left behind healthy tissue—no cavities.

Virginia stared incredulously. What was going on anyway? She hadn't even been thinking about her father, much less praying for him. As if in answer to her perplexity, the entire episode began again. A second time there was the enlarged picture of Roy Wolff's X-ray on the wall, all the familiar and distinctive markings. Once more the same white line appeared at the bottom and traveled slowly up, leaving behind it the shadow print of two perfect lungs.

"Then Dad's well!" Virginia whispered.

In the Face at her side she was suddenly aware of a new dimension of joy. He threw back His head and laughed and the laughter filled the room.

Virginia found herself crying again, only this time it was for gratitude. She wanted to fling herself on her knees to thank Him. For some reason it was the kitchen where she knelt as the torrent of praise poured from her.

She never knew how long she spent there, the linoleum cold against her bare knees, but she does remember that as she got up she looked at the kitchen clock. Twenty minutes after two.

From the wall phone in the kitchen she spoke to her mother. "Mother, this is Virginia. Daddy's well!"

"Yes, honey, his spirit's been wonderful."

"Mother, not like that. Really well. Daddy's healed."

"Yes, dear." Her mother's voice sounded flat and tired. "We mustnt' let ourselves be discouraged."

Virginia stifled her exasperation. "Mother, when are the next X-rays?"

"Next Wednesday."

"Then I'll call you Wednesday evening," she said. "But remember that I told you, Daddy's well." And she hung up.

The minute Virginia heard her mother's voice on Wednesday night, she knew that the truth had begun to surface. "Virginia, the most annoying thing. They got the plates mixed up! Poor Dad's got to go back for more X-rays tomorrow. Why, they sent down pictures of someone who never even had T.B.—"

Virginia almost laughed. "Mother, Dad's O.K. No matter how many X-rays they take, they're not going to find anything wrong."

And of course the next set of X-rays showed no sign of disease either. The sputum tests were negative; the culture test was negative.

By then the doctors were puzzled. Perhaps they had X-rayed from the wrong angle. More chest studies were made, this time from every conceivable angle. No sign of disease in the lungs.

A week or so later Virginia and her sister Doris stood beside a doctor at the sanatorium looking at the latest set of X-rays. "Where are the cavities?" Doris asked in pretended innocence.

A frown creased the doctor's forehead. "Well, I'll tell you— Hmmm . . . Well, there aren't any cavities."

"How do you explain that?"

"I haven't any explanation," the physician admitted. "There are times—. Well, what can I say?"

The sisters left the doctor's office for a long visit with their father, who was still being kept in bed because the hospital couldn't quite credit their own tests. That day the sisters heard the patient's side of the story. . . .

"It happened one day at my nap time—"

Virginia remembered the kitchen clock. "Excuse me, Dad. When do you take your nap?"

"About two—few minutes before, few minutes after—"

Then that was about the same time I was lying in bed, Virginia's thoughts went. *Because twenty minutes later I was in the kitchen—*

"Well," her father continued, "I was just lying here when all at once there was the strangest feeling—like something draining from my body out of my feet. At first it frightened me.

"But there wasn't much time to be scared because the draining sensation was followed by a swoosh of well-being that filled up my whole body. I felt warm and cared-for. Loved—that's it. Loved. Never felt so well in my life. No reason to be here now. I'm going home."

It was soon apparent that Roy Wolff's healing was not just physical. His attitude about Christianity was totally changed. For the rest of his life he was a happy man in love with His Lord. Almost every time the church doors were open, he would be there. He started a Sunday School class to share his growing faith with other men. He was always seeking people out to talk about Jesus. Moreover, many chores he had always disliked—like mowing the lawn or gardening—were now a delight to the new creature Roy was.

The tuberculosis never returned, and Roy lived out his life in thanksgiving to God.

After that Virginia has gone on to a remarkable healing ministry. It is quiet but well-grounded. The healing always includes any sickness of the spirit and the deep mind along with the body. Virginia is given such amazing insights into the depths of human personality that recently professional men—doctors and psychiatrists—have been consulting with her about specific patients.

"And every time," Virginia told me, "I learned the same thing I'd learned with my father—that when healing comes, it's because our eyes have been on Jesus one hundred percent. We can get our attention so firmly fixed on the problem or even on the general topic of healing that we get our eyes off the Healer."

This was where Virginia's story showed me that what I had thought was a contradiction between relinquishment and faith was no contradiction at all. In each of the cases mentioned earlier the sufferer was rushing to Jesus as the Source of help. Each one had faith in *Him*. It was His robe they wanted to touch.

Yet Virginia, like the rest of us, is still groping her way with many questions about healing unresolved. If in our early Christian search we pour forth glib and ready answers, in later years we dare not do so. With the earthly loss of two grandchildren still vivid to me, I know there are no easy, simple answers as to why some are healed in this life and some are not.

But we have learned that God's objective is whole men, wholly dependent on Him. So His Spirit will counteract each time we try to tag, categorize, and pigeonhole Him—for instance, in the direction of rules for healing. Obviously, we are to worship Him rather than a set of spiritual laws.

We resist that because laws are pat and predictable, whereas people are not. Since this is true with human persons, then how much more so with God!

Even as Jesus advised us to begin by taking the lowest seat at banquets, so with healing we are well advised to begin with the lowest place. . . . "Lord, what would You like to tell me about this situation? How do You want me to pray? What do You want me to do?"

188

Relinquishment and such a seeking prayer will always bring His response. Often it is a surprising response that we could not possibly have anticipated.

The twenty-three-year-old daughter of a close friend of mine had been treated for years for attacks which the doctor tentatively diagnosed as myoclonic seizures (often linked to *petit mal*, a form of epilepsy). The girl's mother was told by the Spirit, "Ask the doctor for a blood sugar test." It turned out that extremely low blood sugar (hypoglycemia) had been responsible for the trouble.

In another less serious case, a woman's leg and back pains were submitted to Jesus. "Your white sandals, look at them," she was told. The left sandal had a strap across the instep so tight that it was interfering with circulation. "Throw the sandals away," came the simple, practical order. She obeyed and the pains were gone by the next day.

Does this seem too simple, too obvious even to mention? Not when we understand that our Lord was a carpenter who wore sandals and who knows all about the mundane details of our lives. Often we miss the wisdom He seeks to give us because we are so intent on the high-flown super-spirtuality of our preconceived image of Christ.

Through all of this we need to be careful not to confuse what the old egocentric self wants—to succeed, to get well, to be loved—with that positive, trusting, obedient attitude that wants only God's will for us. . . .

Self will turns the eyes on self and what self strongly wants.
Faith turns the eyes on Christ to ask Him what He wants.

Self will worries about the results.
Faith worries only about obedience, then leaves the result to Jesus.

Until we have heard His directives regarding a given situation, we would do well not to assume healing "on general principles" and run out ahead of the Lord trying to claim healing anyway. If we do, we'll be guilty of the sin of presumption, and not even Jesus—the Son of God—ever dared presume on the Father.[13]

Then how can we tell the difference between presumption and faith? Presumption assumes something to be true in the absence of God's proof to the contrary. Faith hears and receives God's word first-hand via the Spirit speaking to our spirit, and moves forward only on that word.

Jesus meant it when He said, "The Son . . . does only what He sees the Father doing."[14] Notice the word "only" in Jesus' statement. That's altogether different from doing something because God hasn't said not to do it. The latter road is a tangled maze of errors, mapped out by Satan. When we run out ahead of God, an element of daring God and of boldness bordering on impertinence, even unbelief, enters the situation.

But then when we *have* gotten His directives and obeyed them, we no longer have to carry the responsibility for the results. Jesus is the Healer. The results are His.

There will be times when the results are not what we yearn for: not all for whom we pray are restored to health. Honesty and honest sharing is necessary here. The skeptic has a point when he accuses some Christians of sweeping negative experiences under the rug. True, but I have never known a hospital to shut down because it lost some patients. Despite disappointments, the Christian is obligated to pray for the sick because we are bidden to do so[15] and because the crumb of our caring is but a morsel broken from the whole loaf of the Father's infinite and tender love.

With our eyes fixed on Jesus we go forward, knowing that the time will come when the whole person—body and spirit and mind—will be presented unto Him faultless, without spot or blemish.

11.

The King's Treasury

*S*ome years ago a physician's wife took issue with something I had written about daring to trust God for material and physical needs. "That's being selfish," she remonstrated, "and self-centered prayers just aren't answered. I don't think we have any right to pray about anything but *spiritual* things. Besides, the Bible says that God knows what we need before we ask Him, so why should we ask?"

The God I know does not want us to divide life up into compartments—"This part is spiritual, so this is God's province, but that part over there is physical, so I'll have to handle that myself." If we are to believe Jesus, His Father and our Father is the God of all life and His caring and provision include a sheep-herder's lost lamb, a falling sparrow, a sick child, the hunger pangs of a crowd of four thousand, the need for wine at a wedding feast, and the plight of professional fishermen who toiled all night and caught nothing. These vignettes, scattered through the Gospels like little patches of gold dust, say to us, "No creaturely need is outside the scope or range of prayer."

The experience of Edith and Francis Schaeffer beautifully illustrates how material, physical, and spiritual needs are all part of a whole. I first became aware of this couple through reading Francis Schaeffer's *The God Who Is There* in 1971, followed by Edith Schaeffer's *L'Abri*.

In 1945 Dr. Schaeffer, theologian and philosopher, was a pastor in Grove City, Pennsylvania, when he was asked to go to Europe to make a study of the condition of Protestant Christianity. He visited thirteen countries in thirteen weeks, encountering such need as he had never seen and finding this a searing spiritual and emotional experience. Dr. Schaeffer was more deeply stirred by Europe's postwar spiritual devastation than by the shell holes and bombed-out buildings.

Then in August 1953 he became convinced that God was calling him and his family to a higher level of giving, working, and sacrifice; to give up the security of a fixed income for an uncertain, nonstructured work in Europe, possibly with a Swiss base.

After reading Edith Schaeffer's account of all this and pondering it, what interested me was that as the Schaeffers moved on to that higher level of obedience and commitment, God's supply started to work in their lives in a different way—what I choose to call supernaturally. I wondered if I wasn't glimpsing an important principle here.

With a wife and four children to provide for, Dr. Schaeffer knew that this had to be a family decision and a family commitment. As the spiritual head of his home, Francis Schaeffer laid out before his wife Edith and their children all the alternatives. The decision was unanimous—they would say "Yes" to God's call and depend on Him to supply the $1800 the six of them needed for the boat fare to Europe. However, circumstances had created a deadline; if the Schaeffers were to go, they would have to have all of the $1800 in just three weeks, by September 9th when the boat sailed.

Their daughter Priscilla painted a big thermometer on a poster. Within a few days the poster was beginning to show a red line depicting the money received. Opening the mail became the most exciting event of each day. Checks began arriving from the most unexpected sources, most of them for small amounts. The red line on Priscilla's thermometer kept rising. God was giving the Schaeffers a foretaste of what was to become a way of life for this family—trusting the "God who is there" to supply whatever they needed.

Years afterward, Edith Schaeffer would explain this more fully:

> What happens when you pray? God is all-powerful in every realm. . . . One way in which He works is to "move" in the realm of men's minds. . . . God can cause someone to feel a strong "urge" or "conviction" to do something. So when we pray for a certain amount of money, God can cause one person to reach for a checkbook and send that amount, or He can cause a dozen people to send odd fractions of that amount, causing the total to be exact. . . . When that kind of thing happens, you know that you have contacted a *Person* who has replied.[1]

In those days of late August and early September 1953, God the Person replied. During the three weeks, all of the $1800 arrived. It was the opening door to the work that became L'Abri (meaning "the shelter"), a Christian evangelical community in the tiny village of Huémoz high in the Swiss Alps.

In reading *The God Who Is There*[2] I had been intrigued by two strong features of Dr. Schaeffer's approach not usually found in the same person: he is a conservative, committed evangelical who stands upon all the major tenets of the Christian faith, yet his appeal is to the intellect rather than to the emotions.

The notion that we must throw away human reason for leaps of faith in the dark is anathema to Francis Schaeffer. Did not the God who is there create man's intellectual equipment—the ability to think, to reason, to plan, to will? If this seems to be a flouting of the danger of going the Thomas Aquinas route of deifying reason, Dr. Schaeffer's answer is that when Christ redeems us, He redeems the mind along with the rest of us. We have exchanged our fallen intellect for that mind "which was also in Christ Jesus."[3] After that, we are not to belittle or throw away the intellect but keep it subject to Christ who nourishes and upbuilds it, and to His truth revealed in Scripture.

Extremely knowledgeable about the world's major figures who have molded philosophic thought-forms—such as Aquinas,

Calvin, Kant, Rousseau, Hegel, Kierkegaard, Barth, Jaspers, Sartre, Heidegger—Doctor Schaeffer speaks especially to the young, who so often these days are not aware that any intelligent educated person can believe the Bible to be true. Emphasizing "content" (one of his favorite words), he is fond of saying that "honest questions deserve honest answers" rather than the usual dodge, "Don't question, just believe."

I kept hearing that the L'Abri community had become one of the favorite haunts for agnostics, atheists, scientists, and intellectuals, seekers of all nationalities and types—especially the young. But in just fifteen years how had it grown from this one family with no material resources into such a world-renowned community? In the summer of 1972 my husband Len and I decided to find out for ourselves.

That August we flew from New York to Geneva, planning to go on to see the Schaeffers the next day. But even before we got to L'Abri, we had a foolish little experience that pointed up in a ludicrous way a larger truth we would learn later on.

We started out from Geneva for L'Abri in a rented Fiat on a very warm afternoon. All along the road we passed bicyclists and back-packers. I wondered if many of them were also going to L'Abri. If so, how had the Schaeffers handled and supplied so many transients all those years?

With Geneva an hour behind us, Len, quite thirsty, spotted a filling station with a row of refreshment machines and turned confidently into it.

"Swiss francs?" He held out his hand and I dutifully supplied several coins from the envelope marked "Switzerland" out of the packets of foreign change we had purchased before leaving New York.

Len put a coin in the dispenser, then looked puzzled when no drink appeared. He pushed levers, fished around in the coin return, pounded the machine with his fist. Nothing. He shrugged, put in another coin, and tried again. Still nothing. Glowering now at the bright-red machine, he gave up and walked over to seek out the station attendant.

Len said a few words in English, gesturing toward the offending machine. The attendant first shrugged, then scowled and began whipping the air with his hands as words in French poured from him. "*Voilà—mais Monsieur, naturellement cette machine marche—*"

"*Marche?* Not on your life! That machine isn't marching. It's not going anywhere or doing anything. It's broken."

"Brok-en? *Ah, non, Monsieur. L'inspecteur l'a verifié hier. Vous vous êtes trompé.*"

"*Trompé?* That's what I feel like—tromping on it." Then, taking a new grip on his patience, Len said slowly, "Now look, I put in a franc just like it said."

"*Montrez-moi les francs dans votre main—*"

Len held out the Swiss coins. The man took one look. "*Mon dieu!*" He raised his arms heavenwards. "*Monsieur, c'est la France. Vous—êtes—en France.*"

"France!" Len looked incredulous. "I thought this was Switzerland. How can we be in France? We weren't stopped at any border."

The man merely grinned as he turned the palms of his hands outward. "*Oui*, Monsieur, France. *La machine ne prend que de francs français.*"

Len grinned too—weakly—and we drove off, two thoroughly cowed and still thirsty Americans. Sure enough, there on the map I saw that a corridor of France ran forty-five miles along the southern shores of Lake Geneva. French officials simply didn't bother to check passports in and out of this small section of their country.

The absurd experience of the Drink Machine that Wouldn't kept nagging at my mind. Then in simplest terms I saw It: thirsty, we had needed a drink. Not realizing what country we were in, we had sought to buy what was needed in the coin of another realm.

Just so, many of us—even Christians—not realizing that we are living in the kingdom of God on earth, try to buy the fulfillment of our needs with the coin of another realm—earth's coinage, not God's. It doesn't work, any more than the stubborn red drink machine would work.

The Schaeffers seemed to be living in God's kingdom using the coin of that realm. I was eager to see with my own eyes what the coin was and how it worked.

By the time we reached Ollon, now back in Switzerland, the road had begun to climb. Suddenly we were in the tiny remote village of Huémoz. All around us were sparkling sunshine and brilliant flowers cascading from balconies and windows of Alpine chalets. A sharp turn up a steep driveway and we were at Chalet les Mélèzes.

It was a surprise to see that Dr. Schaeffer, born an American, had become so European in appearance, rather like some philosopher-hermit out of the Middle Ages. Not a tall man, his gray hair is casually cut and he wore a trim gray goatee. Kindly intelligent brown eyes dominated his face. He was fond of wearing baggy Swiss tweed knickerbockers, long woolen socks, and brogue-type shoes that should by all rights have been ornamented by a silver buckle.

Edith Schaeffer was a more vivacious, gregarious version of her philosopher-husband. Her mind, her speech, and her body seemed ceaselessly active. As individualistic as her husband, she wore her long dark hair combed straight back, loosely twisted into a chignon. More often than not she was a study in browns— her deep brown eyes set off by one of the brown dresses she is fond of wearing.

Their community consisted of one small church and a series of chalets scattered throughout the village. When Len and I attended the Sunday morning service we saw first-hand what a world crossroads L'Abri really is.

To the pealing of myriad church bells across the valley, we arrived at the church thirty-five minutes early. Even so, we were fortunate to get a seat. The interior was paneled with honey-colored wood; there was a large stone fireplace and a Flentrop organ. Wide windows opened inward to reveal a panoramic view of the Rhône Valley with the peaks of the Dents du Midi in the distance.

When all seats were taken, worshipers sat on the floor before the platform. There were boys and girls in dungarees with knapsacks beside them, together with little girls in fluffy white dresses. A man from India cast off his sandals before he sat on the floor cross-legged alongside a woman garbed in an expensive green pants suit.

With seemingly every inch of the floor covered with bodies, I sat there wondering how the preacher would ever make it to his pulpit. By then the balcony was filled with those who would listen through the open windows. People were even sitting on the platform floor.

Dr. Schaeffer entered and began carefully threading his way between the people, pausing to pat the heads of children, beaming on the hippies and jet-set types, obviously delighted with what he saw. The service was simple, joyful; the message, a penetrating look at Christian commitment.

Our first few hours at L'Abri provided the initial clue as to how God provides material resources for those living in His kingdom on earth: the Schaeffers' part was a total self-giving with every inch of space, every scrap of food, every last franc, every quarter-hour and vestige of strength. Dr. Schaeffer still had no office, nowhere to work privately except the bedroom.[4] It is a rare night one finds no youngsters sleeping on Mrs. Schaeffer's kitchen floor.

That Sunday, as usual, Edith Schaeffer herself cooked a three-course meal for forty-five people. We were seated at tables so crowded that the plates of food had to be passed overhead, then from hand to hand.

During that Sunday meal we heard incredible human-interest stories of how so many different individuals had gotten to L'Abri. This is a working out of the second of the four prayer principles on which L'Abri is grounded: that God will bring the people of His choice to the community. This too depends on prayer alone; L'Abri had never put out any advertising leaflets.

The four principles are:

1. Financial and material needs will be made known to God alone, in prayer, in lieu of sending out any pleas for money.
2. That God will send the people of His choice to L'Abri for work and study.
3. That God will plan the work and unfold His plan day by day. (This is in place of planning for the future in the usual "efficient way," such as committee meetings.)
4. That God will send the staff and workers of His choice for the community rather than L'Abri seeking them through the usual channels of solicitation or pleading.

Here then, was a most important coin of the kingdom—giving God and His ongoing work priority in one's life. Jesus stated it like this, giving us a command followed by a promise:

> Seek ye first the kingdom of God and his righteousness; and all these *things* shall be added unto you.[5]

An example of how magnificently God fulfilled His promise by handling the Schaeffer family's needs is the story of their acquiring the Chalet les Mélèzes. In 1955 they needed $7,366 by May 30th for the final payment on the chalet. Eight days before the deadline they had exactly $4,915.69. Once again Priscilla had made one of her thermometers. The family felt that God had led them to this particular chalet, though speaking humanly (in dollars and cents) purchasing it seemed impossible. Yet each mail brought them unsolicited checks so that the red line on the thermometer kept rising.

There were times when it seemed that the suspense would be more than they could bear. Many a man who has lived by faith has testified that though God moves slowly, He never moves too late. Nevertheless, by breakfast on May 30th, the day the payment was due, the family still lacked over 800 Swiss francs. The last mail was due at eleven o'clock in the morning. Dr. Schaeffer would need to take the two o'clock bus in order to make the required payment. In that last mail there arrived fifteen gifts. When letters were opened, the total filled in the gap on Priscilla's thermometer—exactly $7,366. God had done it again! Jubilantly, the family went to their makeshift living room to pray their thanksgiving.

When Dr. Schaeffer caught the yellow bus for Aigle that afternoon, he was lacking only the notary's fee, and he did not know how much that would be. As he arrived at the Notary's office, he found a special delivery letter awaiting him. Thinking how extraordinary it was for a letter to be sent there, he tore it open to find a letter of encouragement from Mr. X—along with the last check: "Enclosed is something that will give me a small share in the purchase of the house today." That gift was the precise amount of the notary's fee—300 Swiss francs.

In Edith Schaeffer's own words to me, "The miracle was the exactness and the timing and God's arithmetic."

After the family was settled in the Chalet les Mélèzes and had time to appraise what had happened, the totality of it seemed even more remarkable. Over a two-month period, 157 gifts had been sent from all over the world. No giver had any way of knowing how the amount of his gift would fit into the total needed. The smallest gift had been one dollar; the largest, $225, with the exception of a single check for $1,000. Yet the total was so exact and the timing so perfect even though many of the gifts had come from far-flung places. Not only that, but after May 30th the gifts stopped as miraculously as they had started. Not another gift came for the house.

Francis Schaeffer would be the last one to say that he and his family are living by faith in order to prove something to the world about God. The God who is there has no need of vindication by His creatures. Rather, for the Schaeffers it has been a matter of obedience: this is the way God has called them to live.

Why had God chosen to ask this of the Schaeffers—and then proceeded to supply their every need? Here is the heart of their prayer-miracle of supply: they could ask and confidently expect *because they had given everything in advance.* After a few hours at L'Abri, one realizes that Edith and Francis Schaeffer have long since laid everything on the altar, even their privacy.

Why? In Dr. Schaeffer's words, "What we seek supremely here in the L'Abri community is to exhibit in some poor fashion the love of God and the holiness of God simultaneously in the whole spectrum of life."

Even in our short visit Len and I felt God's love as all feel it at L'Abri. We sensed Edith and Francis Schaeffer's deep concern and interest in the young people, especially the hippies and the floaters. They care passionately, totally, with utter self-giving about those who don't know what to believe, who have lost their way in life. That there is truth to be found in the Scripture, that God will see to it that we have that truth—that is the fire in their souls, the light in their eyes, the ring in their voices.

As Len and I were leaving, we witnessed a little scene that remains in my memory as a miniature parable of L'Abri. Walking along with Dr. Schaeffer as he waxed eloquent on some point of homiletics, we were stopped by a little boy outside one of the chalets. He was crying over his tricycle; a wheel had come off. Instantly, the child had Francis Schaeffer's full attention.

First, some comfort tendered by one obviously on the child's wave length. Then a careful examination of the wheel. "Matthew, come here and let's talk about it," Dr. Schaeffer said, drawing the boy into his arms. "Now, I want to show you. I've put the wheel back on, but see this end here?—it's not going to stay on. See, you've lost a part—right here. Understand that?"

The child nodded gravely.

"Now, Matthew, the minute your father comes home this afternoon, you show him what you and I did and ask him please to fix the wheel so it will stay. Will you do that?"

"Oh, *yes!*"

"So, Matthew, ride very carefully now."

Exhibiting the love of God in the whole spectrum of life.

As we take our first timid steps in God's kingdom, we will begin to find the principle of God's supply working for us too.

"But," most of us think, "I'm not as committed as the Schaeffers." True, but we have to begin where we are.

As long as we have a low threshold of expectation limited to our needs and those of our immediate family, we probably won't turn to God for help in this area; our own efforts will handle it. But when we, in obedience to God, decide to be totally His person at His disposal and take on some enormous task He requires of us, then we are going to find ourselves thrown upon His unlimited supply.

Negative situations throw us upon God's supply when we have made a mess of our emotional or financial or material situations. Perhaps we have abused our body or our relationships; perhaps we have family problems, are in debt or some other sorry predicament. In this plight we long to know how God's unlimited supply can start flowing in our direction.

How God supplies is spelled out for us in Scripture. Beyond that, we have the accumulated wisdom of men and women who have tested out those Scriptural principles and promises over the centuries and can provide us with so many illustrations of how faithful God is.

The first step is to get our eyes off our own need, to look instead at God's unlimited supply. One of Christ's fundamental premises was that God the Father controls all of earth's material resources. Simple words, but what a tremendous assertion! Most of us do not really believe this at all. Yet the Bible emphatically declares it:

The earth is the Lord's, and the fullness thereof. . . .[6]

Then we are assured that we are beloved children of this King:

Behold, what manner of love the Father hath bestowed upon us, that we should be called the sons of God. . . .[7]

Since we are His children and all the world's riches belong to the King, it follows that He can and will take care of our physical needs:

But my God shall supply all your needs according to His riches. . . .[8]

So if we really believed that we are children of the King and that we can trust Him to supply all our needs out of His unlimited supply, there would be no reason for a greedy storing up of things. There would be no fear about inflation or money shortages, for fearing would be a sure sign that we did not believe God's ownership of earth's resources. It would be wrong to have a "poverty complex," because to think ourselves paupers is to deny either the King's riches or to impugn our being a child of that King.

To call our Father in heaven a King, in my opinion, is to understate the truth. Consider the prodigality of the Father's world. He did not create a single kind of fern, but some 10,000 kinds; not one type of palm tree, but 1500 different palms. Not one insect, but 625,000 and more that scientists have not yet named. Astronomers now estimate that there are a hundred billion galaxies of stars in the universe, of which earth's Milky Way is but one: There are a million galaxies inside the bowl of the Big Dipper alone.[9] No poverty complex in the Creator of such infinitude!

The magnificence of His handiwork is seen in the tumbling seas, in a sunset slashing the Grand Canyon of the Colorado. Ride to the top of the mountain at St. Moritz, gasp with awe at the snow-covered panorama of rugged peaks spread out at one's feet. Or see the turquoises and blues in the waters around Moorea and Bora-Bora in the South Seas, colors so intense that no painter could capture them on canvas.

How much of this beauty we bring into our homes and our lives is limited only by our appreciation and desire for it and our faith in the King's ability to supply us. Yet always, this must be a personal discovery. The second step in discovering how to become a good receiver of the King's bounty is to invite Jesus into our need. As we see our situation through His eyes we begin to understand how intensely practical God is in dealing with us, His carnate creatures.

Reflecting that practicality, Jesus' directives to us are always specific, never vague and generalized. He would not allow those who came running after Him wailing, "Lord, have mercy," to stop there; He was forever forcing them out of this "General Blessing" area by asking questions like "What do you want Me to do for you?"[10] In other words, "Use your mind, my son. Make up your heart. God is not the Father of sloppy thinking. Nor is He the Lord of generalizing."

At first glance it may seem odd that the more extensive our need, the more important it is to get God's guidance on pinpointing where and how He wants His supply to come to us. It's as if once we find the first right thread to pull, the whole of our tangled problem begins to unravel.

On a certain December day in 1931, an Oregon schoolteacher, Rebecca Euland, found that key thread to pull for her migrant pupil, Billie. It seemed to Miss Euland that the undernourished girl was the victim of more deprivation than any child she had ever known. She thought of that no-breakfast morning when Billie had fainted. Why, the child even lacked shoes. Into the teacher's mind came a picture of the girl's high-laced canvas shoes, 50 cents at the dime store, worn winter and summer. Billie had never slept on a bed, just on a pallet in the family tent beside eight other members of the family. Tangled hair told her that the camper-child was lacking a comb; she also, the teacher suspected, was without a toothbrush.

"What can I do?" the teacher wondered. "With my small salary, how can I make a dent in poverty like that?"

The answer came that same day when Miss Euland noticed Billie squinting over her English book. All at once she was reminded of herself at about the same age. That realization was like a light going on in her mind. Yes, she knew what to do.

That weekend she took Billie to a nice restaurant for lunch, then to an appointment with her own eye doctor. A few days later, Miss Euland pressed into her pupil's hand shiny eyeglasses in a handsome case.

"But I've no money for glasses," Billie protested.

"You don't need to have any," came the reply. "Sit down and I'll tell you a story. . . . When I was your age I needed glasses too. So a kind neighbor took me to lunch, then for an eye examination, just as I took you. She told me that someday I was to pay for them by getting glasses for some other child. So you see, Billie, your glasses were paid for long ago. Some day," she concluded, "you will pay for the glasses of yet another little girl."

The future would underscore what Billie realized even then. . . . Her teacher had given her not only eyeglasses but an even greater gift: her faith that Billie would not always be a subpoverty camper-child, that some day she would be in a position to give to others.

How right Miss Euland was! After some forty different schools near migrant camps, Billie graduated from East Bakersfield (California) High School in 1941, then from Drury College, summa cum laude. Much of the work on her doctorate has been completed. As an author, a lecturer much in demand, an educator, Billie has seen seemingly impossible dreams become reality. The one closest to her heart is the fulfillment of Miss Euland's prophecy, "Some day you will pay for the glasses of yet another little girl."

In 1961 Billie and her husband George Davis were led all the way to Central America to find that particular little girl. Her name was Gloria, a tiny seven-year-old from Costa Rica. The child, born of banana pickers on a plantation near Golfito, weighed only 29 pounds. Her teeth were bloody from malnutrition.

Gloria was legally adopted by the Davises, and it has been Billie Davis' joy to pass on to her not only educational advantages, but also her strong conviction about the power and fulfillment implicit in giving.

Recently, over lunch in our home, I heard Mrs. Davis describe her new adventure as Director of the High School Equivalency Program (HEP) under the United States Department of Labor. In this role, she has become one of the government's Lady Bountifuls to give opportunities for education and job training to many young migrants. Not even Miss Euland could have imagined such glorious fulfillment of giving for her pupil!

Today, looking back to that 1931 turning point Billie Davis realizes that her teacher's faith in one child's future was really part of a larger dimension: faith that the King means for each one of His children to have the fulfillment of becoming a "giving person" with riches of mind and spirit and substance to lavish on others. Once we have that faith, then we are ready to begin using the coin of God's kingdom. He told us what another important coin is: *to receive, one must give, even out of poverty.*

> Give, and it shall be given unto you: good measure, pressed down, and shaken together and running over, shall men give into your bosom. For with the same measure that ye mete withal, it shall be measured to you again.[11]

This is not only a promise, but a fact of the Father's world, part of the rhythm of the universe. In the last century every farmer knew it as he primed the pump by pouring a bucket of water in to start the water flowing. We feel it each time we stand on an ocean beach and feel the tugging rhythm of the tide washing the sand beneath our feet. We experience it when we step out on God's promise and to our astonishment discover that our Father will never allow Himself to be in debt to any child of His.

Here is an exciting principle for all those in life's holes. Of what do we have a shortage? Money? Household possessions? Ideas? Friends? Love? Prayer-power? Creativity? Strength? Health? Whatever it is, when we, under God's direction, give away out of our shortage, like the tide returning we get back abundance—"good measure, pressed down, running over."

There was a time back in 1964 when Ellie Armstrong would have said she had nothing to give—least of all money. With faith and almost no cash she had attempted to buy a $64,000 motel on U.S. Route 6 in the rolling hills of western Pennsylvania.

Ellie knew the truth, that when we set our eyes on Jesus and in obedience attempt a big task for Him, we can trust Him for supply. It was in that framework that she was praying for this motel.

The dream she was given was a motel where Jesus would be the Host. There weary travelers could find a spiritual oasis in their travels. More importantly, people who might not have heard about Him and would not go near a church could meet Him there.

I have visited the Port Allegheny Motel, read the inspirational literature Ellie puts in the rooms, and heard story after story of travelers helped and healed of problems and hang-ups and physical ailments as incredible dividends to their good night's sleep. Each of the fourteen motel units has been dedicated to God for a specific purpose, such as a room for healing, a special room for honeymooners, one for alcoholics, another for the mending of broken relationships, the happiness room. When each traveler checks in, Ellie asks the Host which room He wants them in, then asks Him to be present in that room to meet the guest at his point of need.

But for Eleanor Armstrong, it took many a time of testing, many a crisis situation before her dream about the motel could be fulfilled. She had to learn to live in a state of financial dependence as constant as that of the Schaeffers. When Ellie acquired the motel, one of her prayer-requests had been that she would never fail to meet a mortgage payment on time. One midwinter a $300 mortgage payment was due in a few days and she had only $50 to her name. To make it worse, this was off-season and for five consecutive nights not a single car had stopped at the motel.

Ellie began to pray. At last an inner voice seemed to tell her: "Send the $50 to Dave Wilkerson in New York for his work with young drug addicts." Ellie was as startled as any of us would have been. Surely this was not the time to give away money! But the inner Voice had been very clear. She mailed off the $50 that afternoon to Mr. Wilkerson. That same night nine cars came in, one right after another. As she stood behind the hotel register, she shook her head wonderingly as she remembered Jesus' words, "Give, and it shall be given unto you."

The rest of the week the motel was filled to capacity. The mortgage money was paid on time. Ten years of blessings have followed for the Port Motel as a business venture and as a ministry to wayfarers.

Knowing about this second coin of the kingdom, that to receive we must give, helps us to understand the Scriptural admonition to tithe. Tithing was a practice God asked of the Jewish people back in Old Testament times. It means giving to God through giving to others a minimum of one-tenth of one's gross income or harvest or cattle production or whatever. "Minimum" because even as Christ upholds tithing, He also strengthens it by often asking that we give away more than the base ten percent.

In teaching the practice of tithing to the Jews, God was seeing to it that they would have an unending demonstration of how sound the coin of His kingdom is. To buttress this further He gave them—and us—that magnificent promise:

> Bring ye all the tithes into the storehouse, that there may be meat in mine house, and prove me now herewith, saith the Lord of hosts, if I will not open you the windows of heaven, and pour you out a blessing, that there shall not be room enough to receive it.[12]

Notice God's invitation and challenge to each of us to prove Him, to try out tithing. That when we put Him first, we won't have to worry about our supply.

I remember how pointed a challenge this was to me back in early February 1949. In those early weeks after Peter Marshall's sudden death on January 25th, I was still groping to find what God intended the new basis of my life to be. There was that crucial evening when three men had come out to the manse to discuss business matters with me.

"I've worked it all out," the young insurance salesman said, showing me impressive-looking graphs. "From Dr. Marshall's insurance and the Presbyterian Church's pension fund, you'll have a total of $171 a month for the first eight years, then it will drop."

The men were good friends and were trying to be helpful. Yet all that they said that evening added up to a gloomy prognosis indeed: $171 per month wasn't enough to live on in Washington. I had no specific vocational training and uncertain health. They recommended that I sell our car and the Cape Cod cottage. At the end of the evening the men left troubled because they felt I was not worried enough.

They were right. I had heard their words and seen the neat columns of figures and the graphs. Figures didn't lie. Or did they? Deep, deep inside I felt that these three kind men were reckoning without God.

Looking back, I know it was no spiritual strength or virtue of mine that kept me from accepting gloom and doom and sinking into fear. From a few hours before Peter's homegoing to several weeks afterwards, heaven had opened wide and was carrying me over and above all circumstances. That brief experience showed me what it is like to live in the Kingdom of God on earth: it is glory and joy even in pain, and crystal-clear guidance, and oneness with other people, and a giving and receiving of incredible love.

So my guidance was clear, I was to pick up my pen and edit and write. I was to trust God to provide for me and Peter John so completely that, yes, we would tithe even the inadequate $171 a month.

We obeyed, and God provided all right. I did not sell the car or the Cape Cod cottage. Every need was met on time. There were no debts. For Peter John and me it happened precisely as God has promised, the windows of heaven opened and poured out so many blessings that there was scarcely room to receive them.

There is endless fascination in seeing what has happened to individuals who have picked up God's challenge to tithe. A correspondent-friend Barbara Reynolds, had spent nearly eighteen years in Hiroshima, Japan, as a part of the World Friendship Center ministering to atom bomb survivors and crusading for peace. Meanwhile, Mrs. Reynolds had been offered a scholarship to Pendle Hill, the Quaker study center near Philadelphia. It seemed right to accept. There was only one difficulty: she did not have the money for the trip home. It was at this point, she wrote me, that she read Peter Marshall's sermon "Research Unlimited."[13]

I will never forget the challenge that started me on one of the most exciting adventures of my life: "Suppose, for example that a group of Christians decided to experiment with the Lord's exhortation to tithe for one year. What do you suppose the results would be?"

I had never tithed. Quakers don't even pass the collection plate. . . . Nevertheless, when I finished reading that particular sermon, I felt moved to try.

I began by adding up all the money I had in the world: a few thousand yen in a Hiroshima Bank, a couple of hundred dollars in the United States, and some small change in my purse. I resolved to set aside a tenth in a special purse and the next day, withdrew enough from my bank account to start my Fund for the Lord. I also began to keep a special record of my experiment.

And would you believe it! On January 26th when I began to tithe, I had less than three hundred dollars. When I left Japan two months later (on March 23rd) I was able to turn over, in tithes, more than I had to begin with!

Now a year later, I can report that the experiment which I began without any particular expectations has developed into a way of life which has opened up amazing and un-dreamed-of potential.

I'm sure you know that I am *not* speaking of tithing as a way to get rich quick! No, the amazing effect of my tithing experiment has been twofold (1) It has completely freed me of the panic fear that used to grip me about being penniless. Now I *know* that my needs will always be supplied. And (2) it has helped me to know the joy of being a channel through which blessings can flow to those around me. The Lord's purse is never empty!

When we give God our unlimited "Yes," then we find in our hands yet a third coin of His realm: *each of us has within himself the clue, the secret, and the potential for everything he will ever need.*

The essence of creativity is to seek Him first, making full use of whatever master coin is yours—to give priority to the King-dom of God and His righteousness. Then as we begin living in the Kingdom of God on earth, He will show us how to make the best use of our talents. We begin with a seed idea or a seed talent and create something that other people need or enjoy. That plunges us directly into the stream of the Creator's unending creativity and generosity.

This was the truth God was teaching me. When as a widow I was facing what looked like financial extremity, He told me to begin what I had never done before—editing and writing.

The Schaeffers put God's kingdom first by laying lives, time, energy, privacy on the altar to establish L'Abri Community. For over twenty years God has seen to it that all necessary "things" were added unto them.

Billie Davis found that there is no poverty so grim that the King cannot lift us out of it. He showed her how to use even her poverty as her "seed" asset by writing and speaking of it candidly. That sharing of it, such as a *Saturday Evening Post* article[14] now so famous that it is included in English textbooks, led to myriads of opportunities for yet more giving.

Ellie Armstrong was giving God's kingdom and his righteousness priority when by faith, she undertook the motel on Route 6 to minister to wayfarers. For over ten years God has provided the mortgage payments and running expenses and all other "things."

When Barbara Reynolds decided to obey God by tithing, she was taking a first big step toward putting God's kingdom and His ways first. And she has been blessed accordingly.

So I would have to say to that physician's wife who so strenuously objected to any prayer for personal or material needs and to all those who are afraid to pray about money and those other "petty" things—nowhere in Scripture or Christian experience can I find any justification for the idea that prayer should be limited to spiritual needs. So far as I can understand, Jesus taught us quite the opposite.

It is as if God, knowing full well that while we are in these bodies of flesh and blood, we are going to be physical creatures of this earth and earthy, says to us, "There's only one place and one way you can learn of Me, that's just as you are in your present circumstances. Let's deal with your obvious needs and lacks by looking at your assets—no matter how small. I'll show you step by step how to approach Me, how the coinage of My kingdom is put to circulation, how to hand Me your lack and get back My adequacy. What better demonstration of My reality and My love and caring for you could you have? Come, try it.

"Taste and see that the Lord is good. Prove Me!"

12.

The Dilemma of Our Rebellion

There they were, six little words, staring up at me from the page of the New Testament: "So do not criticize at all. . . . "[1]

But isn't that a little too easy?, my thoughts went. That would knock out all value judgments, all sifting, all screening. "Do not criticize at all. . . . "? *I don't get it.*

What I really meant was "I resist it." I have always prided myself on my critical ability, enjoying the sizing up and analyzing of people and situations. I did it almost in spite of myself, whether I enjoyed it in a particular instance or not. I identified with the eighteen-year-old girl who recently wrote of her parents and homelife:

We could be called opinionated. Certainly we are a hyper-critical family—we don't lavish superlatives on things and places and people. I was raised to look closely, not to accept easily. . . . I couldn't suspend judgment even when I wanted to: it was as if I went through life with X-ray glasses on, seeing through not just the things I wanted to see through but the things I'd just as soon have believed in too. I was old before my time. . . .

The criticism we applied to everything we encountered we applied to ourselves as well. Never "You are bad," but "You could do better." . . .

The critical faculties my parents gave me have made me more demanding than I should be, given me standards that the real, flawed world can't live up to. . . .[2]

But isn't it good to be observing and analytical, to discuss how things can be improved? I can speak from experience here because I might almost have been this girl. My home training was surprisingly like hers, and for much of it I am grateful. But I have lived a number of years on the other side of eighteen. From my vantage point, I can see the underside—or backlash—of such sharpened critical awareness.

In every situation, this girl and I have fallen into the habit of seeing what's wrong with it, not what's right with it. The good qualities, those things well done, are passed over quickly—in time, scarcely noticed—in order to get on with the critique. All encounters in life, every personality, every institution, every relationship, is a mixture of the good and the bad. When we habitually focus on the bad, we are training ourselves in negativism.

We call it by other names. Looking with such analytical eyes must surely be constructive, we tell ourselves, because what we're really asking is, "How can such-and-such be improved?"

But there is a secret cost in such an outlook to one's spiritual and mental health. In my case, I woke up twenty years into adulthood to find myself deeply schooled in serious negativism. That, in turn, can bathe all of life in emotional gloom. When the habit continues into mid-life or later, the dark glasses of critical-ness can lead to long periods of melancholy and even to serious depression.

Exactly this happened to a long-time friend, the author Agnes Sanford. In her case, the depression led to emotional disturbance and thoughts of suicide. In writing of this in her recent autobiography, Mrs. Sanford refers to her escape from this pit of chronic depression as the major healing of her life. But what first caught my attention was her account of how the seeds of the

near-disastrous negativism were planted. The setting was Yang-
cheng in northern China where the young Agnes's parents were
Presbyterian missionaries. On any given Sunday, there would be
worship at the Union Church. . . .

> But on the long homeward drag, my heart would sink, for I
> dreaded the Sunday dinner. . . . The grown people's Sunday
> sport was the tearing apart of the sermon phrase by phrase
> and argument by argument. Dr. Harry Emerson Fosdick
> once preached at our church, and fragments of his sermon
> were scattered over every course. . . .
>   Dr. Fosdick preached on Christian love, but he was not
> *sound* because he did not mention the Blood of the Lamb in
> about every third sentence. This went on and on until
> finally I burst into tears and left the table, to the utter
> consternation of my parents. . . .
>   What was the trouble? I could not tell them. I did not
> know. They were good, they were completely Christ-cen-
> tered . . . but something was *wrong*.[3]

In Agnes Sanford's words, supercriticalness was a "breaking of
the bonds of love." By her teen years, she was beginning to
experience the consequences:

> The deep dissatisfaction with life and with God that had
> begun in me at age eleven was growing. Something was
> lacking, not only in life, but in me. . . . I remembered the
> days when I had come home by the high-road, literally
> dancing, my feet hardly touching the ground for joy. And
> thought, "That was the joy of childhood. Grown people
> never feel like that." Thank God I was wrong!

Yet it was to be many years before Agnes Sanford would be
healed of depression and would finally rediscover joy.

The insistence upon picking apart, upon pronouncing judgment, which Agnes recalls from her childhood, is by no means
unusual in missionaries' and ministers' families. We Protestants
especially belong to a tradition which imposes on every Christian
not only the right but the duty to judge every word spoken from
the pulpit or printed between the covers of a book. Doubtless
this has served as a necessary corrective in the long history of

the Church. But the effect of this constant vigilance upon individuals—and whole denominations—can also be a deficiency of love and a lack of joy.

And it is not only Christians who almost from the cradle are taught to be criticizers. It is not only the spirit of the Renaissance and the Reformation in our religion, but the spirit of eighteenth-century rationalism in our politics which encourages every American to be judge of the men and events around him. Our national heroes, the founders of our country, were precisely those men who refused to accept unquestioningly the world as they found it.

The two hundred years since then have trained us that an uncritical populace is a populace in peril. As in religion, so in the secular world: "eternal vigilance" is the price of what we hold dear. From school days on, each citizen must be responsible, must inform himself, must stay on top of issues.

I wonder if we who form judgments of people and issues over our morning coffee realize how unique in the experience of the world is our concept of good citizenship. In most places on the globe even today people are trained in a kind of docile numb acceptance which is the very opposite of the critical spirit.

During a trip to the Middle East, our party of four took a three-and-a-half-hour drive in Jordan with a guide—clearly an intelligent, well-informed man. In the course of the long trip we asked him a single political question, something about King Hussein and an important meeting to be held that week.

The guide's face went as blank as though a sponge had gone across it. "Oh," he said with finality, "I don't think about those things."

He didn't sound like someone who had been intimidated into silence. His attitude seemed merely to reflect that of the society in which he had grown up. "These are not my affairs."

The opposite, democracy's insistence on each citizen's responsibility to be informed and to judge, is accepted throughout western Europe and North America as a positive thing. Yet judging can also have a negative side. Just as the missionary groups in China (which Agnes Sanford knew so well) regarded themselves as knowledgeable "sermon tasters" and experts in theology, so most of us Americans consider ourselves expert armchair politicians. The result is that any man in public office gets sniped at continually by the public and the press. All of us can be grateful for a free press made operative by reporters like the two *Washington Post* newsmen who, in the face of incredible pressure to "let sleeping dogs lie," brought the Watergate offenses to the attention of the nation.

And yet I recall during the years I lived in Washington, especially during the McCarthy era, more than one man's career was ruined by innuendo, character assassination, and blacklisting. Sometimes the news media seemed to thrive on it—not a needed exposé of wrongdoing, but criticism because criticism is one of our national sports. It can be a dangerous sport.

Critics and protestors insist that dissent is for some good end—"for the exploited"—"for peace"—"for liberalizing university rules." Behind that insistence is the conviction, blown up into a philosophy, that insubordination—mild to violent—is the best technique for reform, a healthy process for necessary change. How often I have felt that way as I have agonized over child labor, the living conditions of migrant workers, our inhuman treatment of the insane, the slum conditions of our inner cities.

Sunday afternoons during college days I used to go with a group who visited in the tenements (since torn down) around the State Capitol building in Atlanta, Georgia. My journal reflects my shock and dismay:

> I had dimly realized that places like that existed, but had never seen any before—squalid, miserable, dirty, ill-ventilated. The broken windowpanes stuffed with paper; the sick child doubled up on the dirty bed; the absurdly young mother wearing red ankle socks of which she was so proud, nursing her baby before us; the drunk woman; the crying children. . . .

If protest rallies and sit-ins at legislators' offices had been the style among college students then, I would have been part of them.

Years afterward our family ran head-on into one of those injustices in our society that scream for reform. In 1956, soon after my mother and father retired to Evergreen Farm in Loudoun County, Virginia, Hank Reid, our black tenant-farmer, was caught in a classic loan-shark trap. The manager of the loan company telephoned saying that they would repossess the Reids' household goods unless their debt was paid up within twenty-four hours.

We managed to postpone the immediate crisis, then dug in to appraise the situation. The original loan, taken out two and a half years before, had not been large; incredibly the loan company claimed Hank now owed twice that much. The apparent interest rate was only 3½ percent, but a clause hidden in fine print enabled the loan company to figure the interest charge each month. That made the real annual percentage rate 36 percent. If Hank defaulted a month's payment, the interest for that month was added to the principal and future interest figured on the total. He could never get out of debt.

What was wrong with our laws, I raged, that exempted dishonest outfits of this type from the Small Loan Act and the strict supervision of bank inspectors? Regularly I drove past a cluster of them with flashing neon signs just across the Key Bridge into Arlington. "Quick cash" . . . "Get your bills paid." The bait dangled hiding the hook.

Hank's plight turned into a family crusade. We made the loan company a proposition: we would pay the total (then take it gradually out of Hank's wages) provided that total was reduced to a fair figure. They refused. We peppered them with letters and phone calls. One morning I was astonished to hear my gentle mother scornfully telling the head of the loan company, "I marvel that you can hold your head in public, preying on the poor and those who don't know better. You're no gentleman, you're a—a—" Here her vocabulary failed. "Horsewhipping would be too good for you."

Finally the man buckled. We paid, demanding a receipt declaring Hank completely free of debt.

And yet there they were, each time I drove into Washington, those neon signs challenging me: what are you doing to root out this evil from your community? One family had slipped through the net so cunningly laid; how many thousands were trapped for the duration of their working lives unless people with typewriters, an education, with acquaintances in the government, mounted some form of protest? How else, my conscience asked me?

"So do not criticize at all." How are we to understand these words? Criticism, protest, even open rebellion, sometimes seem the only ways that essential change can come about. What about the American Revolution—surely there is an example of great good coming out of revolt?

Or . . . is it? I remember my first dispassionate look at this touchstone of the American experience. It came during college days when I earned part of my tuition by doing clerical tasks for Dr. Philip Davidson, head of the History Department, as he prepared his book *Propagandists of the American Revolution.* I remember my surprise at the irrefutable evidence of the extent to which propagandists aided by the Liberty Boys deliberately whipped up the inflamed feelings that led to war with England.

That the American colonies should have received a great deal more understanding and eventual independence is unassailable. The question is, were war, revolution, hatred, and bloodshed the best way to achieve needed goals?

Two hundred years later, may we not still be suffering the results in the American temperament? Perhaps the "good" revolution was not as harmless as we like to think. During the last six years when violent crimes in the United States have increased more than 90 percent, many sociologists and historians have been telling us that the seeds of that violence may well have been planted during the very founding of our country. The National Commission on the Causes and Prevention of Violence asserted:

Our nation was conceived and born in violence—in the violence of the Sons of Liberty and the patriots of the American port cities of the 1760s and 1770s. . . .

These analysts then went on to point out what a large part violence played not only in the launching but in the expansion of the young Republic westward, in our violent and dishonest ways of dealing with the Indians, in the vigilante groups of frontier society. They cite evidence that America's long training in insubordination of the heart is resulting today in a schism-ridden, polarized society with cracks and rifts all through.

Whether analyzing the steps that lead to the breakup of a marriage, or of the high school student who joins a violent revolutionary group, or even what caused the American Revolution—the process goes something like this. . . . Criticalness leads to discontent. Discontent expels appreciation and gratitude. Self-pity moves in and turns the attention inward; surely self deserves something better, we tell ourselves, such as happiness, prosperity, that its ideas and demands be heard and implemented. If what self wants will hurt others—spouse, children, parents, store proprietors, educational institutions, bystanders—well, they asked for it in one way or another. Anyhow, the end justifies the means.

But if rebellion has such built-in dangers, how can necessary change come about?

It is at this point that we can see a clear parting of the ways between the philosophy of dissent and the wisdom of Jesus of Nazareth. How else could we view statement after statement of Christ's? . . .

"Thou shalt not kill."[4]

Then said Jesus unto him, "Put up again thy sword into his place; for all they that take the sword shall perish with the sword."[5]

"Whosoever is angry with his brother . . . shall be in danger of the judgment . . . whosoever shall say, Thou fool, shall be in danger of hell fire."[6]

"Agree with thine adversary quickly, while thou art in the way with him. . . ."[7]

"If ye forgive not men their trespasses, neither will your Father forgive your trespasses."[8]

"Try to show as much compassion as your Father does. Never criticize or condemn—or it will all come back on you."[9]

Yet no one accuses Jesus of a Pollyanna attitude toward the evil and injustice of His time. His fury at the perfidious money changers was a form of violent protest, no question about it.

Studying Jesus' response to evil I began to see three guide lines. First is the question of motivation. We see into the heart of Jesus' motive in one of the most beautiful verses in the New Testament:

Thou [Christ] hast loved righteousness, and hated iniquity; therefore God, even thy God, hath anointed thee with the oil of gladness above thy fellows.[10]

"Loving righteousness," in His case came before "hating iniquity." Does it, I wondered, in our crusades and causes? When we go forth to stamp out sin, disease, poverty, oppression—as He did—do we keep uppermost in our minds the heart-stirring vision of the world as God intended it to be? Or does hatred of the enemy we are opposing gradually fill our horizon?

Then second, He gave us the love test:

"Listen all of you. Love your enemies. Do good to those who hate you. . . ."[11]

Here Christ was making a clear distinction between the iniquity which He hated and the sinner who, even though his own will was responsible for his sin, was nevertheless now the victim of it, bound by it. I saw only too clearly why I could never, relying on my own strength, launch a "just" campaign against the loan-shark industry: my reaction to these businessmen falls so far short of love. Indeed, this command to love our enemies is often not possible for us worldlings; it is a miracle God Himself has to work in the human heart.

Therefore, the third guide line follows inevitably. In the end Jesus chose God's way, not man's, to deal with the iniquity He loathed. Judas Iscariot wanted His Master to use the world's technique by rebelling against Rome. Judas, the classic revolutionary, wanted armed political rebellion against the godless forces of Rome. Jesus deliberately refused, thereby telling us for all time, "No, the end does *not* justify the means." He chose instead God's way of changing men's hearts and minds and lives via the Cross.

Certainly we cannot "love righteousness" and "hate iniquity," then use any of iniquity's techniques. Those who recognize in Jesus of Nazareth the First Rebel, see equally that His weapons were never those of unrighteousness. He will never allow us to do evil with the claim that it's to achieve justice or right.

Part of the problem here may be that we have not understood Jesus' way. When I realized that He was standing against my critical spirit, I felt the need to dig into the Bible to get its teaching as to what's wrong with grumbling and revolt. Right away I found the answer to my questions about that verse which had so startled me, "Do not criticize at all." I saw too why God regards even the lowest rung of protest—complaining and grumbling—not as a petty personality flaw, or even as an offense against another person, but as serious sin against Him directly. The Apostle Paul wrote Stringent words on this.

> And don't murmur against God and his dealings with you, as some of them [the Jewish people] did, for that is why God sent his Angel to destroy them. All these things happened . . . as object lessons to us—to warn us against doing the same things; they were written down so that we could read about them and learn from them. . . . [12]

I found that "all these things" in this passage referred back to the Books of Exodus and Numbers. We read there how God had tapped the reluctant Moses on the shoulder, directing him to lead the Jewish people out of bondage in Egypt to the Promised Land.

As Moses obeyed, remarkable proof of Jehovah's presence and protection was given to the children of Israel time after time: the rolling back of the Red Sea so that they could cross it; a pillar of cloud by day and fire by night to guide them; the provision of food and water in the desert. God made them the solemn pledge that if they would trust Him, He would supply their every need from the smallest to the greatest.

The Israelites had less than two hundred miles between them and their goal. That distance could be covered in weeks. But they did not trust God. From Exodus 14, when they fled slavery in Egypt, to Numbers 14, in the midst of their desert trek, there is the record of a series of "murmurings" against circumstances, against their leaders Moses and Aaron, against the lack of water, the hardships of the journey, the strength of their enemies. They were dissatisfied with the food God provided and longed for the dainty fare of Egypt. Each time the complaints reached the level of mutiny, Moses would intercede with God on behalf of the people. Each time Jehovah would humor His fussing children and stoop to meet their demands. Miracle followed miracle. But rather than being grateful and praising Jehovah for these mighty acts, the people would soon begin complaining again, offering back to God discontented hearts and yet more grievances.

The murmurings reached a climax as recorded in the fourteenth chapter of Numbers. This time the murmurings went too far. The congregation wallowed in self-pity, lamenting and weeping through the night, "Would God that we had died in the land of Egypt!"

By then the Israelites had finally traversed the two hundred miles and were virtually on the doorstep of the Promised Land. In fact, it had already been spied out by a group led by Caleb, who had pronounced it a good land ready to be taken with the Lord's help.

Wearily, Moses once again entreated God with long and eloquent pleading. But this time, though God agreed to pardon, a price had to be paid: a generation had lost the Promised Land by making grumbling and rebellion their way of life. In doing so, they had been steadily acting out a spurning of God and of His promise for them. Therefore they were told, "Tomorrow turn you, and get you into the wilderness by the way of the Red Sea. . . . All . . . from twenty years old and upward, which have murmured against me . . . shall fall in this wilderness."[13]

Thus sadly, on the threshhold of achieving their destination, the Israelites were turned back to wander in the desert for forty years. Their children would enter in the Promised Land—but not those who had started out in such high hopes, those to whom God's glorious promises had first been made.

By this story, my eyes were opened to several truths. From the time the Chosen People first left Egypt, God had been trying to teach them some facts about Himself: first, He was (and is) a personal God. "I will walk in and with and among you, and will be your God, and you shall be My people."[14] Thus as a Father, no detail of His children's lives was beneath His notice—from the dimensions of the wilderness tabernacle or the tassels on the hem of the priests' robes, to the adjudication of the minutest quarrel between neighbors.

It follows that when the Israelites or any of us have really accepted God as our Father in the personal way He means it, then we are going to trust the circumstances He permits us to have. That is why our grumbling about God's provision is at the least attributing more power to circumstances and to evil than to

God. And murmuring and rebellion can lose us our personal Promised Land. Our Promised Land means God's will perfectly done in our life and affairs. It means the supplying of every provision—spiritual and physical—for our every need. We can miss all of it through complaining.

On a larger scale the same principle applies to modern nations just as much as to the Israelites. Greed and lack of gratitude stemming from the grumbling spirit could eventually cost us or any nation the blessings of God.

What the Israelites needed—and what I believe we who build our lives around criticalness need today—is to see that the antidote to negativism is the power of God. It is a transforming power in and over the world He has made. On the reality of that power Scripture never backs down or gives ground. From the time God called Moses to lead His people, through the plagues visited on the Egyptians, through the parting of the Red Sea, through many miracles in the desert, God was saying, "I do have power. I am the God of the supernatural. You are to trust Me for more than you would expect through 'natural' law or 'natural' causation."

Power over what? Precisely those factors about which the Israelites were murmuring—the harsh desert, the difficulties of their trek, physical ailments and illnesses, and the hostility of their enemies. In other words, over the external conditions of life.

Rebellion of a far different sort—against dishonest United States government inspectors—turned into a surprisingly positive experience for two Florida businessmen several years ago. At that time the Meloon family boat business, Correct Craft, Inc., owed $500,000 to 228 creditors and faced financial disaster.[15] The trouble had begun when Walter Meloon and his brother Ralph were awarded a government contract to build 3,000 assault boats.

Shortly afterwards they were called upon by a member of the three-man team who would inspect the boats. "Did you know," the inspector asked Walter, "that you are one of only two companies in the Southeast that does not have someone on their payroll who takes care of their inspectors' expenses?"

Walter shook his head, knowing that the government paid all the inspectors' expenses.

The two brothers talked it over and decided to dismiss the overture as an ill-considered remark rather than as a request. Soon, they learned differently.

Correct Craft, founded in 1925, had always been proud of producing quality boats. But now, as the sleek 18-foot fiberglass boats began coming down the assembly line, great numbers were being rejected by the government inspectors—many for tiny flaws allowable under the contract.

One day the brothers quietly took one of the rejects, cleaned off the inspector's chalk marks and sent it back through the line. It was passed.

It was now clear what they faced. In desperation they went to the inspector's superiors, but to no avail. As the silent war continued, they foresaw financial disaster for Correct Craft and for over a hundred employees and their families.

Temptation whispered to Walter, "Why not pay those men off? It really isn't much compared to what the company stands to lose."

No, it wasn't the money, Ralph knew. Something far deeper. At night he would wrestle with the problem. Trying not to disturb his wife Anne, he would slip out of bed to think and pray.

"Lead me, Lord. Tell me what to do." By the little bedroom lamp, words glowed on the printed page open on the table. "Trust in the Lord with all thine heart; and lean not to thine own understanding. In all thy ways acknowledge Him, and He shall direct thy paths."

To pay off the men would not be trusting the Lord.

Ralph crawled back into bed. "All right, Lord. We'll just try harder to build perfect boats."

Then one gray afternoon came the final blow. A flatcar had just been loaded with forty boats, each stamped "approved" by the inspectors. As Ralph watched the switch engine back up to it, the inspector came out.

"I don't like their looks," he said flatly. "They've got to be unloaded and refinished." Ralph waved the engine away and turned wearily to his car.

The brothers had reached the end of their rope. The contract had already cost them $1,000,000. They had delivered 2200 boats with 600 rejects stacked in their storage yard.

Ralph found himself battling his bitter animosity against the surly inspector. He knew that Christ has told us to forgive our enemies. He tried his best to forgive the man, only to stay awake for hours with his mind seething with fury.

Then one night the Lord spoke. "I love that man too. I died for him as well as for you." The words were like a cooling hand on Ralph's brow. After that, he was able truly to forgive the inspector.

Then what seemed like wild thoughts came to Ralph. . . . *God has allowed the inspectors to reject all those boats. Then God has something that He wants us to learn out of this. We will learn it only when we stop rebelling against all this and begin to look to Him in thanksgiving.*

As the Meloon brothers accepted this concept and acted on it, God answered with an explosion of miracles. First, a loan came unexpectedly from business friends in Norway. The second miracle came from Pakistan. The minister of defense ordered six boats for $139,000. With the first shipment Correct Craft sent along one of their "rejected" assault boats, explaining they had more. Back came an order for 239.

The third miracle came in the form of an idea which God put into Ralph's mind. The brothers were led to set up five factory warehouse distribution centers in different parts of the country. Each would operate as an autonomous company selling Correct Craft boats to dealers in their area. A boating industry innovation, those centers proved successful in tapping new markets. In effect, the five satellite companies acted as flotation barges around a sinking ship, lifting the company to the surface.

God was not only teaching the Meloon brothers how to handle temptation and adversity constructively, He was giving them a basic business lesson: no company can exist on a solid foundation with only one big customer. The government might have stopped buying their boats for a perfectly legitimate reason. . . . Indeed, His ways are wondrous.

Today the business is a healthy and growing Orlando concern. Ralph can say, "As I look back, I praise the Lord for those dark days. They helped us become a much stronger company. More important, our faith has been greatly strengthened to the point where I will confidently walk with Him anywhere."

With an approach like Ralph's and Walter's, we are at the opposite of the critical spirit. Here we have trust and praise as the antithesis of complaint and rebellion.

We have seen this is in so many situations. . . . When Ellie Armstrong faced the crisis of the $300 mortgage payment due with only $50 in the bank and no motel guests for five consecutive nights, she might have felt justified in rebelling against such a predicament. Instead, she acted out her praise of God for His provision by giving away the $50 as He had told her to. That same night the motel filled up, stayed filled, and the payment was made on time.

In my battle of the sleeping pills, when I stopped rebelling and sought God even at the point of sleeplessness, then I was given the praise-filled message of the old hymn:

> Blessed assurance, Jesus is mine! . . .
> This is my story, this is my song,
> Praising my Saviour all the day long.

In retrospect I could see the steps—from rebellion, to acceptance, to praise, to God changing the situation. I began to see more clearly too why God sets Himself so seriously against a disobedient or rebellious or judgmental spirit: this is the precise frame of heart and mind which blocks His loving intervention on our behalf.

The wisdom of Solomon tells us, "Out of it [the heart] are the issues of life."[16] Jesus enlarged on this: the human heart and will are the main problem, He kept explaining. Every true reform in civilization involves a change of heart followed by a change of mind of human beings. So how can we get our hearts set right?

Traditionally men have tried to change the minds of other men in two ways—neither of them Jesus' way. The basest effort is the use of physical force to compel another person or an entire nation to do what the opponent wants. The trouble with this method is that the "victory" usually leaves untouched and unchanged the hearts and minds of the vanquished. No military victory could have been more complete than the Roman legions' over tiny defenseless Palestine in Jesus' day. Yet the Jewish fractiousness and insurgentism were worse than ever.

The second, more civilized technique is to use words and the power of personality to try to change the other person's mind and heart. Governments employ many tools to this end: controlled news media, education biased until it is a mere political tool; every imaginable form of pressure and propaganda, every skill of the advertising profession in what amounts to buying a change of mind.

In our times the art of persuasion has been developed to an all-time high, but there has been a curious result. Though a veritable frenzy of words is being spoken over millions of television sets as well as pouring from the presses, modern men seem less trustful of words than ever. It would also appear that both the spoken and the written word are less effective. "As a poet," W. H. Auden once wrote, "there is only one political duty, and that is to defend one's language from corruption. And that is particularly serious now. It's being so quickly corrupted. When it's corrupted, people lose faith in what they hear, and this leads to violence."

And to obscenity, Auden might have added. As the printed page, along with movie and stage scripts, is increasingly peppered with four-letter words, we can't help wondering: isn't the obscenity really our frustration at the poverty of language that no longer really communicates or works any changes in people's minds and hearts? Perhaps then, the subconscious reaction goes, people can be *shocked* into paying attention—and so the foul words pour out.

There are other signs of the increasing ineffectiveness of persuasion. . . . In the last decade "credibility gap" has become one of our favorite terms.

The lecture method of teaching is increasingly under suspicion.

The great issues before Congress are seldom debated any more on the floor of House or Senate.

Presidential speeches are similar casualties. For a quarter of a century television has provided the unprecedented advantage of intimate chats in every living room. Yet these speeches—almost always written by hired speech writers, tailored to computer-determined political requirements—make us wonder, where have great speeches and speakers gone? What has happened to the passion of a Patrick Henry, the sober sincere honesty of a

George Washington, the homespun grandeur of an Abraham Lincoln, the flaming oratory of a William Jennings Bryan or a William Gladstone, the persuasive logic of a Woodrow Wilson, the person-to-person warmth of a Franklin D. Roosevelt, the rolling thunderous cadences of a Winston Churchill?

It would seem that the harder we have tried our "modern" techniques of persuasion, the more breakdowns in communication we have been experiencing on all fronts—between parents and children, between the races, between government and people, between nations. Our frustration then breeds more rebellion.

Psychologist Paul Tournier in his book *The Whole Person in a Broken World* diagnoses the prevalence of rebellion in our society not as a healthy sign of progress nor a means to needed reforms. Rather, Dr. Tournier sees rebellion as a neurosis of epidemic proportions startlingly comparable to adolescent neurosis.[17]

In normal adolescence, the storms and stresses—the negative self-assertion, the customary disparagement of established mores—are ultimately worked through to integration: adulthood. But in cases where this integration is unduly delayed, psychiatrists call the resulting illness the "neurosis of defiance." "Something like this," Dr. Tournier maintains, "has taken place in the development of human history since the Renaissance. . . ."

He cites the classic signs of neurosis in the individual. First, anxiety. We do not have to look far to see much anxiety today. Restlessness and dissatisfaction with oneself and others are epidemic. In society the flood of criticism may be in part an effort to hide a deep anxiety. Jean-Paul Sartre went so far as to say "Man *is* anxiety."[18]

The second sign of neurosis, individual or societal, is sterility. "Big dreams do not produce the fruit. . . . True values do not play an effective role in the destiny of society. . . ."

The final characteristic of the neurotic is inner conflict—ambivalence; the classic adolescent's awkwardness when everything he tries gets botched, and more often than not he gets the opposite result from the one he sought.

Certainly there are marked signs of ambivalence in our society. We undertake the war in Vietnam to keep peace in Asia and to ensure the good life for the South Vietnamese; we end up with the longest war in American history and the devastation of the Vietnamese homeland.

Protestors of that war march for an end to violence, and clash violently with police.

The present administration sees protestors as traitors to law and order. But the Watergate investigation ends up showing that same administration in flagrant violation of the law.

The government seeks to avoid inflation by controlling the economy; the result is runaway prices and a devalued dollar. . . . The ambivalence and contradictions go on and on.

Since our ways are achieving the opposite of what we intend, perhaps we are ready to ask, what is Jesus' way? The first move, He told His disciples who asked Him the same question, has to be made on behalf of the inner man. You have problems in your lives, problems in society, But you must see that

> ". . . from within, out of men's hearts, come evil thoughts of lust, theft, murder, adultery, wanting what belongs to others, wickedness, deceit, lewdness, envy, slander, pride, and all other folly . . . they are what pollute you and make you unfit for God."[19]

Anger in the heart and the contempt of one human being for another precedes the act of murder. Lust in the heart precedes the act of adultery.[20]

The last thing God wants for us men is conflicts and neuroses that tear us apart. His primary concern is the healthy integration of man's heart and will. This health He measures by whether we are still running from Him in rebellion, or are reunited with Him, having found our way back to our heart's home.

The closer I looked into the dilemma of our rebellion, the more this central truth stood out for me: underlying all cleavage amongst us, behind our broken human relationships, lies a basic break—between God and us. We do not often recognize this, being inclined to blame any dislocation in our lives on other people, or on "circumstances," and to look for the remedy anywhere but in a reconciliation with God.

Since we human beings are rooted in God, rebellion against Him is like revolting against part of ourselves. Of course we are not able to "find ourselves" when we are such divided beings!

That is precisely what our adversary Satan wants for us. He was the original instigator of rebellion. Revolt was Satan's sin too. In the Garden of Eden he succeeded in luring Adam and Eve to join him in rebellion. And ever since Satan has whispered to us that the way to improve our lot is to rebel.

But if this is Satan's way, what is God's way? That was essentially the question the thoughtful scholar Nicodemus came asking Jesus during their quiet midnight talk. The Master's answer was, "Those deep inner changes are never going to come about through men's efforts in trying to change the thinking or patch up the old person. There's only one way, Nicodemus: *'except a man be born again, he cannot see the Kingdom of God.'*"

And when Nicodemus probed and questioned, "How *can* these things be?" Jesus pointed him to a cross. How well He knew that soon He would hang there suspended between earth and heaven. And there, if we will recognize it and allow it to be so, our old selves can die too so that the new person can be born.

Can the way of the Cross do in men's hearts what force and persuasion and all man's artifice fail to do? A few years ago during a trip to Austria I heard a true story which suggests that it can and does. A Lutheran pastor, a former Nazi storm trooper, gave me this account of how he, trained in hatred and destruction, had been changed into a follower of Christ. . . .

In December 1941 the trooper was with the German armies invading Russia. In the Crimea, in heavily wooded terrain, the battle began going against the Germans. As they had to fall back, the German found himself within the Russian lines, separated from his regiment. Alone he made his way through the forest, fearful at every minute of being captured. Suddenly, he saw a thin cloud of smoke coming from the chimney of a hut. Creeping up warily, gun in hand, he knocked on the door. It was answered by a tiny elderly Russian woman.

Shoving past her and searching the hut, he satisfied himself that the woman lived alone. Apparently, her menfolk were off fighting—perhaps had already been killed. To the German's surprise, the woman offered him food and drink. Neither spoke a word of the other's language, but in the end the Russian woman hid the soldier, feeding him and caring for him for three days and nights. The German grew increasingly baffled. Certainly, no worse enemy than he, a Nazi, could have come to the door here in Russia, where Germans murdered more civilians than the total number of Jews killed in all of Europe. The woods swarmed with Russian troops; surely she knew that if she were caught harboring a German she would be shot.

Out of his mounting desire to communicate, he managed through sign language and facial expressions to convey his question, "Why have you risked your life to hide and befriend me?"

The old woman looked at him for a long moment in silence, then turned and pointed to a crucifix on the wall above her bed.

Telling me the incident, the Lutheran pastor added, "After I escaped back to the German lines, try as I would I couldn't forget what had happened. I hadn't known love like that was possible. In the end, I was drawn irresistibly to the One who enabled the little Russian lady to prefer another to herself—even when that other was a cruel and deadly enemy. I wanted to know the power of the Cross in my life too. That's why I'm a Christian today."

The way of the Cross, Jesus' way. The way that puts others ahead of self. What would be the difference in our world today if we began to let the Cross work its change in our hearts?

Ezekiel's prophecy could come true for us individually and collectively as a society,

> A new heart also will I give you, and a new spirit will I put within you: and I will take away the stony heart out of your flesh, and I will give you an heart of flesh.
> And I will put my spirit within you . . . and ye shall be my people, and I will be your God.[21]

Rebellion and mutiny would be seen as a paltry playing at life as we enter into the glorious liberty of the children of God. What that liberty could mean for us was spelled out long ago at the beginning of God's dealings with the Israelites. It is a vision that has haunted us ever since. . . .

The good earth, its seas, lakes, rivers, and streams, the air, the trees, the animals, will no longer be ravaged by man.

Crops would be blessed and be sufficient to end hunger for all mankind. The nation that produces plenty would rush its aid and know-how to those countries with less.

Happiness would reign in homes across the world. Marriage and family life would thrive and be blessed. Once again babies would be wanted and cherished.

In the words of Isaiah, "Violence shall no more be heard in thy land, wasting nor destruction within thy borders."[22] Wars will end.

In real and practical ways, men will recognize that this really is one world. With an effective world organization, destructive and fear-motivated nationalism will disappear. As the nations no longer need to spend most of their substance on armaments, creative research will burgeon. The cure will be discovered for cancer, for rheumatoid arthritis, for multiple sclerosis, arterio-sclerosis, heart disease, emphysema, and the myriad of other diseases that have defeated research and plagued mankind.

In all branches of the arts, the new creativity will bring a renaissance—music, art, writing, the theater, crafts.

Mourning shall be ended as men everywhere begin to understand that because ours is a God of love, submission and obedience to Him is not only our greatest good, but the way "to enjoy Him forever."

13.

Run for the Strong Tower

*R*ecently I opened the newspaper to read headlines on a major article:

VIOLENCE

As Crime Soars, a Puzzled
Nation Asks, "Why, Why?"

The first paragraph read:

It is an age of fear—a stark, pervasive, gnawing, mind-numbing, gut-wrenching fear.[1]

Fear and anger are universally recognized as the two most destructive emotions in man. Yet it seems that year by year fears are growing and striking deeper as we—individually and collectively—are increasingly frustrated in our efforts to deal with our problems. In our newspapers we read almost daily of events like a grocer murdered for $20; rapes and killings of young girls in the Boston area; stabbings and holdups in Washington and in London; a grandmother stomped to death by two youngsters; kidnappings and skyjackings.

Long articles are written suggesting ways the average citizen can protect himself: replace spring-type door locks with deadbolts; put chains and peepholes on doors; have keys made by licensed locksmiths recommended by a city Burglary Squad; install bars or ornamental metal grillwork on windows; buy one of the many burglar alarm systems now on the market; bring into the family unit a trained police dog; keep lights burning in stores, warehouses, and homes throughout the night.

Commonsense precautions are certainly necessary. But there come times when all the safeguards man has devised can't stand between us and the raw evil loose in this world. It is then that we discover a surer protection, the only final protection there is. This was dramatized for me by what happened not long ago to a neighbor in Delray Beach, Florida. . . .[2]

It was a beautiful sunshiny June morning. Gene Klinger started out in her car for Delray Beach to take her final teacher's examination. As she turned from Military Trail down Fourth Street, she noted the time on her watch. It was 8:50. Good! She'd be at school by nine.

Fourth Street near Military Trail is a lonely stretch of road until it runs into the residential area. Just ahead of Gene was a light-colored pickup truck. It slowed down, then pulled over to the side of the road. An arm out the car window signaled to Mrs. Klinger to pull over too. She did so instinctively, wondering if the other driver had noticed a flat coming on in that left rear tire she'd been worried about.

A big burly man wearing a sports shirt open at the neck strode up to her window. "Lady, can you tell me how to get to Dixie Highway?"

Mrs. Klinger was unsuspecting. After all, it was broad daylight. "I'm so sorry. I don't live in Delray. I'm just on my way to school here. Afraid I can't give you directions."

The man was looking at her intently. Suddenly the expression on his face changed. Jerking open the car door, he pressed a hard metal object into Gene's back. When she sat there paralyzed, he shoved her to the other side of the seat and climbed in beside her.

Instinctively, she screamed, then reached over and pressed hard on the horn. But there was not a car or pedestrian around.

He pressed the object harder into her back. "Don't try that again or I'll kill you," the man growled. Fear, panic, terror washed in waves over her.

Gene admits that she has always had many fears. Sensitive, intense, vivacious, she feels deeply. Long ago she determined to face up to her fears and to search for ways to eradicate them. Her search led her to seek God for His help in freeing her from these shackles. She had asked that in certain circumstances He help her do the things she feared or found difficult. This led her to apply for teacher training at the Montessori School.

During an early session there she confided to her instructor that she had not yet learned how to deal with her fears. The instructor gave her a copy of a printed prayer that has been widely circulated. The words soon became part of the fabric of Gene Klinger's life. . . .

The Light of God surrounds me.
The Love of God enfolds me.
The Power of God protects me.
The Presence of God watches over me.
Wherever I am, God is.

Upon arising that June morning, as every morning, she had prayed that prayer of affirmation. Thus at the crisis moment, sitting beside the threatening man in the car, when panic and terror almost overcame her, she discovered in herself this mighty prayer resource. Gene cannot remember the exact words she used, but she knows their essence.

"How can you force yourself on me this way?" she cried. "You are a child of God. God's love is in you. He cares about you. And I am His child too, and completely under His protection. His love and protection surround me. . . . "

As she spoke the words, she felt warmed. "There was a kind of aura around me," she said later. "I could see it, feel it. It was like a soft light."

"Then a strange thing happened," she recalled. "Into my mind there came the clear picture of the face of the janitor at my school, one of the kindest, most gentle men I'd ever known, beloved by everyone. It was as if God was saying, 'You told the man sitting beside you that he is a child of Mine. To help you feel that as well as know it, superimpose the janitor's face and image on this other man.'"

"I followed directions and sure enough, after that, I could actually sense God's love flowing to my abductor."

The result was immediate. The man suddenly appeared confused. Lust seemed to leave him. He removed the metal object from Gene's back. Then she saw that it was a key case.

He started Gene's car and drove on in silence for a while, little trickles of perspiration running down his face as his confusion increased. Then he drew over to the side of the road and stopped. "Get out," he ordered. Quickly Gene opened the door and jumped out. The man turned the car around and drove off, careening down the road.

He was no sooner out of sight than the police car she had so desperately longed for pulled up. "Something the matter, lady?"

She and the officer found her car abandoned on down the road and the pickup truck gone. At the police station she was shown a group of photographs. With a start she recognized one of them as the very man who had halted her. As she opened her mouth to identify him, something on the inside of her would not let her say anything except, "I'm not sure." The man had no police record except a series of traffic violations. "I know it seemed weak, uncooperative with the police," she said later. "I only know something stopped me from identifying him."

Despite the ordeal, Gene Klinger continued on to the school, took her examination, passed it. She was glad to share her experience because she believes it may point to the most important protection for all of us.

"I am the light of the world," Jesus told us. In the past we have usually considered this symbolic, even exaggerated imagery. Now I wonder!

In this era of artificial light and of increasing energy shortage we are very aware of the merit of lighted areas for protection. Banks and business establishments are now commonly lighted throughout the night. A group of women in Indianapolis, crusading for years to make their streets safe again, have discovered that crime goes down as much as 85 percent when street lighting standards go up.

Was Jesus speaking figuratively only when He said:

For everyone that doeth evil hateth the light, neither cometh to the light, lest his deeds should be reproved.[3]

I wonder if Christ means for us to take His "I am the light of the world" more literally than we do. Of course, the statement also points to a theological truth. But He who created the atom and the sun[4] remains the power center, the dynamo of the physical universe. And as Light, He is also Protection—largely unrealized, untapped, unresearched.

An increasing number of people are experiencing Jesus' contemporary Presence in this way. To me it is significant that Gene Klinger felt "a soft light" around her and that her attacker either could not or would not penetrate it.

Let us therefore cast off the works of darkness and let us put on the armour of light.[5]

Could the apostle Paul, so often the target of hostile crowds, have experienced the Light of Christ as actual armor?

In promise after promise, the Bible seeks to teach us that in God and in his resources there is physical protection surer than any weapon or defense known to man. Other descriptions of this protection are given in addition to light, such as this one from the days of walled cities. . . .

The name of the Lord is a strong tower: the righteous runneth into it, and is safe.[6]

Short of magic or hocus-pocus, the question is, how could there be enough power (as the world understands power) in the invoking of a mere name to be a genuine safety factor to anyone?

All through Scripture there is the insistence that a man's name is never just a casual handle for identification purposes. Rather, concentrated in a man's name is the essence and character of the person. Thus when God was allowed to enter a man's life and control it, more often than not the man's name had to be changed because the character-focus of the man was then different. So Abram became Abraham; Jacob became Israel; Simon became Peter; Saul became Paul. Frequently the Bible tells us the meaning of names. Seth, for instance, means "granted"; Noah means "relief"; Isaac denotes "laughter"; Moses means "to draw out (of the water)."

There is great significance in the many names Scripture gives to Jesus Christ, among them:

The Last Adam	Light of the World
Saviour	Bread of Life
The Good Shepherd	Cornerstone
The Door	Counsellor
King of Kings	The Prince of Peace
The Lamb of God	Great High Priest

When we think of Jesus' ringing statement after His resurrection, "All power is given unto me in heaven and in earth . . ."[7] we see why many descriptive words are needed to cover "all power." But all of them are caught up and comprehended in the name of Jesus. Again and again we are assured that the power to save, to redeem, to heal, to guide, to give wisdom, to protect, is wrapped up and focused like a laser beam in this "Name."

And whatever you ask in my name, I will do it, that the Father may be glorified in the Son.[8]

When we pray "in Jesus' Name," we are not simply verbalizing a word or a phrase; rather, our petition is to the complete character of the Lord and all of the power implicit in His Name. The Scripture abounds in "holy mysteries" and the full meaning of praying in the Name of Jesus is one of those mysteries. In heaven, the mystery is understood; on earth, we shall probably never know it fully. Yet as we step out in faith using that Name, we do learn bit by bit. Even some of Christ's first followers, the seventy whom He sent out two-by-two during His earthly ministry, discovered early that His Name had power indeed:

And the seventy returned again with joy, saying, Lord, even the devils are subject unto us through thy name.[9]

Surely here is the real reason that men with evil in their hearts back off so quickly when confronted by this Name: evil has always recognized and reacted against the power of this word, often more incisively than "religious people."

A short time after my friend Gene Klinger's experience, I came upon a similar incident.[10] Roberta Lashley, a young girl of Mount Savage, Maryland, was fortunate enough to have learned about the power of Jesus' Name prior to a desperate crisis-moment. One night she had stayed later than she realized at an interesting church meeting. When the bus let her out on a lonely country road, there was still a twenty-minute walk to the Lashley home.

She thought with distaste of the steep climb to her house on Bald Knob Road. It was not until a car drew up beside her on the dark road that she realized how tired she was. "How about a lift?" a man's voice asked from the car.

In the dim light Roberta assumed that this was a neighbor. She climbed into the car gratefully, then realized she had been mistaken: the driver was a stranger. Even so, in that rural community sharing rides was such an accepted practice that the seventeen-year-old girl felt no alarm. She thanked the driver but noticed that he made no reply.

They drove in silence until Roberta pointed out her house. Still the man said nothing and there was no decrease in speed.

"That's my house," the girl repeated, small prickles of alarm alerting her.

Was it her imagination or were they actually going faster? "There's a lane ahead where we can turn around," she told the driver, trying to keep panic from her voice.

The car was gaining speed, careening up the twisting mountain road. The last house was behind them now.

"Stop the car!" Roberta cried. "Let me out!"

Without slowing, the car swerved up a bumpy side road that led to an abandoned coal mine high on the mountain.

The girl looked wildly at the trees whizzing past them. A person could be killed and hidden forever in one of those deserted shafts. Her hand closed on the door handle.

But as her fingers gripped the handle, suddenly she remembered something she had heard at the church service several weeks before. A missionary to the Philippines had said that Jesus

Christ has dominion over the evil in man, but that we have to call upon that dominion. *We must ask.*

Shutting her eyes, Roberta tried to remember the exact words the missionary had used. Then very slowly and clearly, addressing the evil intent within the man, she said in a firm and clear voice, "I rebuke you in the Name of Jesus Christ."

For the first time the man looked at his passenger. "What do you mean?" he asked. "What's 'rebuke'?"

"I mean," she replied, "that Jesus Christ has absolute authority on this earth and that I am under His protection. He's protecting me this very minute."

They had reached the abandoned mine shaft. The car stopped. Time stopped too as Roberta felt her pulse pounding in her temples. The driver remained motionless, hands still on the wheel.

"I didn't know," he said at last. The force that had gripped him was gone. He started backing up, then turned down the steep mine road to the main highway. The crisis was past; waves of relief washed over Roberta.

"I'm not really so bad," the man went on as he headed the car down the mountain. His voice sounded almost pleading. "I've been to church some. It just never made any sense to me."

The girl beside him was never sure afterwards that all she said to the man in the next five minutes made sense either. But in the time it took to reach her house she poured out her heart-felt conviction of Christ's love for each of us, how much He loved the bewildered man beside her, and of the need for Him in every life.

The car stopped at the Lashley's driveway. With relief Roberta got out, then ran trembling into the house to find her mother waiting up for her.

"God took care of me," was all she could say. "God took care of me," over and over again like a child waking up from a nightmare.

The words Roberta Lashley spoke to her mother stirred a slumbering childhood memory in me. As a little girl, I had suffered what seems now like a long period of fear of the dark. Night after anguished night I would lie rigidly in bed, eyelids screwed shut, afraid to breathe for fear of what lurked in the dark corners.

Looking back I am surprised that I didn't share it with my mother. Pride was fierce in me. And I was much too young to reason out that faith was the opposite of fear. As I tried to handle the fears myself, what helped me most was the chorus of a hymn I had learned in Sunday School:

God will take care of you
Thro' every day, in all the way:
He will take care of you,
God will take care of you.[11]

As I would lie there singing this softly over and over to myself, an ease would flow into me, assurance and confidence that nothing else supplied. For one little girl the childlike words of the hymn became at once both an affirmation of faith and also her response to Him—her prayer.

When I mentioned this childhood experience and the "God Will Take Care of You" hymn in a recent article, to my astonishment letters came flooding in from readers. Most wanted to share a similar experience. My words had apparently evoked half-forgotten scenes and impressions, childhood experiences still charged with so much emotion. Clear impressions rising again to the surface—the panic we felt as children followed by the relief of the particular word of consolation.

Sometimes we like to think of fear as an emotion that belongs to the childhood of the race, or perhaps to the child who still lives in every adult. Yet fear resides in the strongest, the most resourceful of men. They learn to handle fear not by hiding it, but through learning an important fact about evil: it has a cowardly side. I find a striking example of this in the life of David Livingstone, the Scottish missionary-explorer who opened up and mapped so much of Africa.

In 1865 Livingstone was facing one of the gravest perils of his sixteen years in the Dark Continent. He had to pass through the wild country of the local chief Mburuma. The chief was not only hostile himself, but was seeking to rouse the whole countryside against the white man's expedition. Warning after warning had been given to Livingstone by runners going ahead of the expedition. There were reports that warriors were in the jungle creeping toward his camp.

Alone in his tent, Livingstone opened his Bible to the promise on which he had staked his life so often. Then he wrote with such stirring eloquence in his journal:[12]

> January 14, 1856. Evening. Felt much turmoil of spirit in view of having all my plans for the welfare of this great region and teeming population knocked on the head by savages tomorrow. But I read that Jesus came and said, "All Power is given unto Me in Heaven and in Earth. Go ye therefore, and teach all nations . . . and lo, I am with you always, even unto the end of the world.
>
> It's the word of a Gentleman of the most sacred and strictest honour, and there's an end on it! I will not cross furtively by night as intended. . . . Nay, verily. I shall take observations for latitude and longitude tonight, though they may be the last. I feel quite calm now, thank God!

During the hours of darkness nothing happened. The next morning Livingstone, still calm, directed the crossing of the river for his 114 men and their oxen while Mburuma and his tribesmen watched from the jungle's edge.

Deliberately, the missionary reserved for himself the last place in the last canoe. One of the party, fond of Livingstone and fearful of treachery, pleaded with him not to give the chief a chance to shoot him in the back.

"Tell him to observe that I am not afraid," Livingstone replied. Then with dignity he thanked the astonished tribesmen, wished them God's peace and walked very slowly to the canoe, never looking back. No shot was fired, no hand raised against him.

For me the incident has great personal significance. About two years before Peter Marshall's death, one day I noticed a strange inscription carefully written on the flyleaf of his favorite Bible. . . .

> It's the word of a Gentleman of the most sacred and strictest honour, and there's an end on it!
>
> David Livingstone

Then underneath Livingstone's name, Peter had signed his own.

When I asked Peter about the inscription, he told me of the incident in Livingstone's life. It meant much to Peter not only because this giant of the nineteenth century was born in the village of Blantyre not far from Peter's home in Scotland, but also because he too had often staked so much on the trustworthiness of the promises in this Book.

Occasionally God can provide the necessary confident poise to overcome evil with such an overflow of good that it takes on a sort of gay exuberance. That's the way it was for Brother Bryan of Birmingham, Alabama, a man whose memory is almost legend to many Southerners. His real name was James Alexander Bryan, and for more than forty years he was the pastor of the Third Presbyterian Church of Birmingham, located at 22nd Street and Avenue G in a downtown section of the industrial city.

Citizens of all sorts—policemen, firemen, the ill in hospitals, those in jail, the hungry and the poor, the black people, businessmen—had long since stopped caring what denomination the preacher was, what color, what social class, just that he was "Brother Bryan," chaplain to the entire city. Since 1934 there has been at the heart of Five Points in downtown Birmingham with traffic flowing on every side of it, a white marble larger-than-life statue of Brother Bryan. He is kneeling in prayer, wearing a baggy old overcoat with a scarf half sliding off his neck, just as the sculptor Georges Bridges had seen him so often.

For Brother Bryan had a way of praying in most unlikely places at most unlikely times. Many a Birmingham citizen had heard his "Brother, let us pray" and couldn't wait to relate the latest Brother Bryan story. . . .[13]

One Thursday night he had been detained late after a prayer meeting at the church and had to walk home alone. As he was crossing a dark narrow alley between business buildings, a man slipped out, stuck a gun in Brother Bryan's face and ordered, "Hands up." Obediently, his hands went up.

The thief methodically went through the preacher's pockets, extracted all the money he found, and removed his watch. Then he almost dropped the watch when his victim said calmly, "Brother, you and I are going to pray about this right now. . . ." Then the pastor lifted up his face and said, "Lord, here's a man who needs Your help in the worst way. I ask You to show him a better way to live, help him make a new start. Lord, You love this man, make him feel Your love right now."

Slowly the gun was lowered. The thief thrust the money and the watch back into Brother Bryan's hands. "Go on home," he said "The likes of you is not for me."

We might wonder where Brother Bryan's kind of coolheadedness comes from. I know only one possible source—an utter trust in God that turns into a total form of protection.

"Fear not" is one of the most reiterated exhortations in Scripture. The Bible denounces fear over and over and describes this deadly brew as one of humanity's major ills. . . .

For God hath not given us the spirit of fear; but of power, and of love, and of a sound mind.[14]

For ye have not received the spirit of bondage again to fear; but ye have received the Spirit of adoption, whereby we cry, Abba, Father.[15]

It is helpful to understand the basis on which the Bible regards fear as a sin of disbelief in God. Most of us moderns are resistant to the term "sin" since it implies condemnation. Yet Jesus stated categorically that He did not come into the world ever to condemn men and women but to save us.[16] Therefore, if we have God's view of sin, it is "missing the mark," missing out on the good things He wants us to have and experience.

Thus any emotion or attitude that disorients or disintegrates human personality so that we "miss the mark" is certainly therefore a sin—a negative to be gotten rid of. Whether at its simplest level when fear "roots us to the spot" or causes our knees to buckle, or a more sophisticated form of jealousy-fear, or the fear of hardship or disaster in times of economic depression, it destroys coordination, riddles personality, blocks logical thinking, and makes creative solutions to problems impossible.

When we see fear through Jesus' eyes, it is the acting out of our disbelief in the loving Fatherliness of God. By our worrying and fretting, we are really saying, "I don't believe in any God who can help me, and I do not trust Him." Thereby we are sinning against God by impugning His character and calling Him a liar.

At that point there is only one way to get rid of fear; like any sin, we must recognize it, confess it in true repentance, claim God's sure promise of forgiveness, cleansing, and renewal, accept these gifts, rise and get on with life.

As Jesus walked the earth and so frequently felt fear in men around Him, again and again we hear that cry of His, "O men, how little you trust Him!"[17] In the cry there was more than a little rebuke and sorrow along with a sort of marveling astonishment that men could be so blind: "Why are you afraid? How little you trust God!"[18]

Behind Jesus' sharp reaction to our faithless fears lay His consistent viewpoint that this is our Father's world still in His control. Nor did Jesus ever use the word "Father" lightly out of slick sentimentality. He taught that God deals with each of us personally in the way the best of fathers would. Therefore, the kind of love necessary to bring His kingdom on earth is not brotherly love, but fatherly love. When we take Jesus' teachings (for example, the last four Beatitudes) in the light of this fatherly love, what has before seemed hopelessly idealistic becomes practicable and possible.

Our Father never forgets the way we humans really are. He knows well that we, His children, are beset with fears. Therefore, in almost every example of God breaking into life on earth, the opening words are, "Fear not" . . . "Fear not, the Lord will go before thee" . . . "Have no fear, I am with thee" . . . "Fear not, nor be dismayed" . . . and a hundred variations. Our Father knows that, like small children, we need constant reassurance.

Whether small children or grown-up children, we need to develop a sense of dependence on the Fatherliness of God. It may seem to us at first thought that any dependence is the opposite of strength or a mature personality. But when we look closely at Jesus, we see that this is not so. Always the Master gave the impression of a moment-by-moment companionship and dialogue with the Father, yet here was a Man afraid of nothing. Not fearing men's opinions of Him, He spoke the truth bluntly. He was not afraid of unpopularity because He knew that when we are true to our real self, it is impossible to please everyone. He did not cringe when He walked through the mob at Nazareth. Here was a truly dangerous mob-lynching scene. Yet with Jesus' faith in the Father, He strode through the midst of them with such assurance that the crowd simply faded before Him.

When we look at His constant dependence on God alone, we begin to suspect that we may be teaching our sons a false basis for manliness. So long as we are in these bodies, we are going to be subject to the limitations of flesh and we shall always know a degree of loneliness. To ignore these facts of life is not to nurture independent manliness, but to suppress fears and cram them into the unconscious where they do further harm.

The Nazarene asks for strong men—the tensile strength of the inner spirit. He would seem to be telling us that much of our bravado is artificial. He is forever calling us to a simpler, sturdier faith.

Faithlessness makes us suffer multitudinous troubles that we never do, in fact, face. Not many of us are actually going to be called on to face the spears of African tribesmen or look down the barrel of a gun or confront a would-be rapist. But untold thousands suffer diminished lives through the fear of all the things that might happen.

"I . . . have known a great many troubles," the humorist Mark Twain wrote when he was an old man, "but most of them never happened."[19]

Peter Marshall was fond of telling a fairy tale to illustrate how fears have a way of growing smaller and then evaporating when we resolutely face up to what we fear most. It is the story of Miobi, the boy who lived far to the south beyond the Third Cataract, and how he went on his journeys to overcome his fears. . . .[20]

Miobi had come to a village where the people were doing nothing else but moan and wail. The fires were not lit, the goats were not milked, because all of the villagers were expecting to be eaten shortly by the Monster on the Top of the Mountain.

This monster had the head of a crocodile and the body of a hippopotamus and a tail like a very fat snake, and smoke came from his fiery breath.

But Miobi said, "I will go up the mountain and challenge the monster."

There he was, sure enough.

But as the boy climbed and came nearer, the monster looked definitely smaller.

"This is very curious indeed," he said. "The further I run away from the monster, the larger it seems, and the nearer I am to it, the smaller it seems."

When the boy reached the cave, he found no monster— but a quiet little thing as small as a frog, which purred; and he brought it home as a pet.

When the villagers saw him return, they wanted to make a hero of him for killing the monster, but he explained just what had happened and how he had brought the monster home as a pet.

What was its name?

The monster answered, "I have many names. Some call me famine, and some pestilence; but the most pitiable of humans give me their own names."

It yawned and added, "But most people call me What-Might-Happen."

Is Jesus a tower-light of protection against this kind of fear? Yes, because Jesus is Light and that Light can melt and dispel these submerged incapacitating fantasies.

Sometimes it helps to write down one's fears, then hold them up one by one to the light of Christ's clear understanding. Never is Jesus as the Light of the World more clear than in these murky areas of our semiconscious fears, most of them unreal and psychotic. The trouble with the imaginary fears is that they can, if allowed to go on and on unchallenged, really destroy. As we talk over each fear on the list with Christ, He will illuminate for us some steps to expose them for what they really are. . . .

For a woman with husband and children away from home who has always been afraid of spending even one night alone, God may simply tell her to try it for one night and trust Him.

He may provide a man who is terrified of public speaking with an opportunity, directing, "Don't duck it. Step out on faith and make that talk. Trust Me to help you with the flow of ideas and words."

A person who has some physical discomfort and is reluctant to go for a medical examination, fearful of fatal disease, may be told to pick up the phone immediately for an appointment with the doctor. This is the objective attitude, the opposite of that preoccupation with self that is one of the fear-dragon's breeding grounds.

He may simply direct the one who is frightened of flying to make reservations and board a plane.

Not only new confidence but real growth in character follows this facing up to what we fear. Provided we are acting under God's direction.

Scripture tells us that the real enemies we should fear are not what or whom they seem to be. . . .

> For we are not fighting against people made of flesh and blood, but against . . . the evil rulers of the unseen world . . . and against huge numbers of wicked spirits in the spirit world.[21]

The question here is, were Gene Klinger's and Roberta Lashley's real antagonists the men who wanted to harm them? Or were these men merely being used by "the evil rulers of the unseen world"? Were Livingstone's real enemies a group of African tribesmen, or were they spiritual forces using the ignorance of the natives as their tools for evil?

Our spiritual enemies take a variety of forms and use many devices. In our family we experienced a curious example of this in 1968 at Evergreen Farm in Virginia, my mother's and father's home for their retirement years.[22]

During the first years at the farm we had happy times with Bessie and Hank Reid who lived in the tenant house. In the years since they left, the little house on the hill seemed to fall on evil times. It was almost as if the house was drawing people of unhappy, violent temperament to it. . . . There was Mr. K., who turned out to have a vicious temper. It erupted with frightening intensity at anyone not white and Anglo-Saxon.

Then Mr. K. left and Mr. and Mrs. W. came. Soon there was trouble in their marriage. One day Mr. W. came home from his job as manager of a grocery store and found his wife and children gone with their clothes and most of the family furniture. Several months later a man entered the grocery store and shot Mr. W. dead. The police never discovered the murderer or the motive.

Three other couples followed, all of whom had financial and marital troubles. A stretch of ten years of acute unhappiness plagued the Little House.

In the living room at Evergreen the family prayed about it. Part of the prayer took the form of questions. "How can we break the chain of downbeat and tragic events? Is some sort of cleansing needed here?"

We had to wait several months for the answer. Eventually it came in two parts: first, we were sent an unusual couple, the Rodriguezes. They had emigrated from Spain several years before. People with a great spirit, they love family life and love the land. Of course, Isabel and Jacinto knew nothing of the history of the Little House.

Certain that God had sent them to us, we began cleaning the house, repainting and furbishing it for its new tenants. As we scrubbed and painted, our conviction grew that the house had suffered a kind of pollution that oceans of soap and gallons of paint couldn't remove. And we could not bear the thought of the delightful Spanish couple moving in to face any such threats.

"Are we imagining this or being superstitious?" we asked ourselves. How is it that buildings can take on the aura and character of the persons and events that their walls have held? Who can tell! But here is something that most of us have experienced: we step into certain church buildings and we are immediately warmed and blessed; going into others we are chilled and no inspiration flows to us, only sterility.

We walk through the door of some homes even when the occupants are away, and know instantly that love is in this place. On the other hand, I've been in beautiful houses from which I wanted to turn and flee, later to find out that discord, strife, or tragedy of some sort had occurred there.

It must be then that the living patterns of those who dwell in these houses are being affected by those "evil rulers of the unseen world" Scripture warns us about.

We knew well that Jesus' authority is the only one which evil must finally obey. It happened that Edith and Peter John Marshall were at Evergreen at the time, so Peter led our assault on the Little House. Len and I, Peter and Edith, paused for our first prayer at the doorway of the house. There Peter, using the

Apostle John's great words,[23] asked that every sin ever committed within the house to violate the peace and purity and sanctity of a real home, be cleansed "through the blood of Jesus who cleanses us from all sin."

Walking through and around the scrub buckets and paint pails, we went from room to room, in each one pausing for a prayer for cleansing, followed by thanksgiving that all darkness and evil would from henceforward pass over the house. Finally, we asked the Lord to bless the house and its occupants.

All of us felt a strange power in this procedure. We left that day knowing that something important had happened: all would be well. And events since then have borne this out. Light entered that home and abides there still. Jacinto and Isabel and their little daughter Maria Dolores love their home and have known a lot of happiness there. When Mary Elizabeth Marshall, age five, comes to Evergreen, she and Maria spend hours together happily playing "house" there with their tiny china dishes and their dolls.

Faith is the Strong Tower into which we can run for protection today. It isn't a physical place but the Light of a protecting Presence. It makes the unreal fears vanish and gives us literal protection against the real ones.

But something is required of *us*:

Let us therefore cast off the works of darkness and let us put on the armor of light.[24]

In other places in the Bible the pieces of our armor are described. Integrity is our coat of mail, truth is our belt, salvation is our helmet. Our shoes are the stability of the gospel of peace. And above all, faith is our shield.[25] This kind of armor suggests that every hour of every day we are in the thick of battle. Not only must we put on that armor of light, but we must practice walking in it on ordinary days when we think we feel no danger. Gene Klinger was doing exactly that as she daily saturated her mind and heart with the words about the light of God. We are putting on the coat of mail when we resolutely expel dishonesty from our lives. We are sharpening our spiritual sword as we memorize some of the great passages of Scripture and seek out the life-giving promises.

But when evil pursues, challenges, persists—at those crisis-moments we need to seek out His light, and to speak out His Name in ringing tones.

There in the Strong Tower we shall be safe. "It's the word of a Gentleman of the most sacred and strictest honour."

14.

The Helper

That night at the dinner table our son was almost too busy talking to eat. He had flown in from Taylor University that afternoon, having finished his freshman year.

"Pops," Chester's voice was excited, "you wouldn't have believed the scene in the Notre Dame football stadium last weekend."

"Football in June?" his father asked quizzically.

"No—lots of singing and prayer and praising the Lord . . . 25,000 people. It was fantastic!"

"What was the occasion?"

"A big meeting of the Catholic Jesus People. A bunch of us students drove up from Taylor. Six hundred priests came pouring onto the field from where the players enter, singing, carrying banners. The whole place was clapping and singing. I've never seen so many people so excited."

Later that week we read *Time* magazine's coverage of the event. . . . First, men in business suits or sports coats carrying banners aloft: THE SPIRIT OF JESUS AMONG US, emerging from the football team's tunnel onto the Notre Dame field; then the double moving line of priests in white robes and clerical stoles singing, their arms raised heavenward, hands open, palms up. The excitement of the crowd built, erupting into applause. Then as eight Roman Catholic bishops, followed by Leo-Jozey, Cardinal Suenens of Belgium, resplendent in brilliant red chasubles came into view, the clapping exploded into a mighty roar. From 25,000 voices "Alleluia! Alleluia!" rocked the stadium.

Commented *Time*:

> The ceremonies at Notre Dame last week made it clear that the fastest-growing force within the church is that of the Pentecostals—or as many prefer to be called, Charismatics. Originating as an off-campus prayer group at Pittsburgh's Duquesne University in 1967, Catholic Charismatics form the third major group of Pentecostal believers. . . . There are probably more than 200,000 of them in the U.S. today, organized in more than 1,100 prayer groups. The movement has taken root in foreign countries more recently and is growing even faster. . . .
>
> To the crowd of 25,000 in the stadium Cardinal Suenens said, "The Pentecostal renewal is not a movement. It is a current of grace . . . growing fast everywhere in the world. I feel it coming. I see it coming."[1]

One portion of a sentence in that report leapt out at me: "Originating as an off-campus prayer group at Pittsburgh's Duquesne University in 1967 . . . " Yes, I remembered about that. I had heard the story from Kevin Ranaghan, at that time still a Catholic layman.

The seedbed of the Catholic Pentecostal movement was a group of four or five laymen (all members of Duquesne's faculty) who had begun meeting together in the fall of 1966. A book that fell into their hands led them to ask for the gift of the Holy Spirit for themselves: David Wilkerson's *The Cross and the Switchblade*, written by John and Elizabeth Sherrill. The story concerned David Wilkerson and his street ministry to gangs and dope addicts in the New York Bedford-Stuyvesant area.

"By February of 1967," Kevin Ranaghan told me, "the four Catholics from Pittsburgh had received a release of the great gift of the Holy Spirit. They began to witness quietly but joyfully among close friends." Some of these friends were at Notre Dame University. Beginning there with small informal groups on whom the joy of the Holy Spirit has fallen, the movement has gathered momentum like a prairie fire.

The Catholic Holy Spirit movement has the official sanction and approval of the Pope and church fathers. Their attitude is that the baptism of the Holy Spirit is completely scriptural and nothing new; it simply "makes operative" the ancient sacraments of Baptism and Confirmation. This sanction has lent a freedom and an openness to Catholics in the Holy Spirit movement not always enjoyed by their fellow Christians in Protestant churches.

In reporting the June mass meeting *Time* went on:

Catholic Charismatics form the third major group of Pentecostal believers. . . . The "classical" Pentecostal denominations . . . grew up around the turn of the century and are by far the largest group—some 2.4 million in the U.S. alone.

A "Neo-Pentecostal" movement has developed over the past 20 years within mainstream Protestant churches—Episcopal, Presbyterian, Lutheran—and is still spreading.

"Spreading" is right!

It is difficult to estimate how far the Holy Spirit movement has spread. A conservative estimate would be that at least 300,000 members of mainline Protestant churches in the United States have found fresh springs of faith and vitality in the surge of the Spirit. By 1970 so many Presbyterian clergymen were caught up in the movement that the highest governing body of the church, the General Assembly of the United Presbyterian Church, appointed a Special Committee to investigate. The gist of that report, as adopted by the 1970 Assembly was:

(1) We cannot follow the view . . . that the purely supernatural gifts (of the Holy Spirit) ceased with the death of the apostles. . . .

(2) . . . know the misuse of mystical experience is an ever-present possibility, but . . . [see] no reason to preclude its appropriate use. . . .

(3) [believe that when such] experience clearly results in new dimensions of faith, joy, and blessings to others, we must conclude that this is "what the Lord hath done" and offer Him our praise.

The Protestant movement has been quieter than its Catholic counterpart because there has been more resistance—even persecution, with some pastors in various parts of the country asked to leave their churches. One of the earliest (now classic) cases was that of the Episcopal priest Father Dennis Bennett, asked to resign in 1960 from the 2,500 member St. Mark's Church of Van Nuys, California. He went on to a rundown mission church, St. Luke's in Seattle, now large and thriving.

Unprecedented growth has gone on anyway, in spite of such resistance. And perhaps it is time for the whole of this branch of Christendom to ask ourselves if this approach to the topic of the Holy Spirit is healthy and does honor to the Third Person of the Trinity.

Either the coming of the Holy Spirit into individual lives and upon the Church is Jesus' own teaching with His authority behind it, intended to result in sound and fruitful Christians—or else it is heresy that has no place in Christianity at all. I, for one, can see no middle ground.

What then did Jesus Himself tell us about the Holy Spirit?

Back in 1945 a personal health crisis led me to seek an answer to that question. Using a concordance and a notebook, I began methodically looking up all the references I could find on the Third Person of the Trinity. Gradually I worked the findings into a logical outline in the notebook. The part of it directly bearing on the question above could be summarized like this. . . .

During the Last Supper conversation Jesus made it clear that the promises He was making that night were not meant just for the eleven men within the sound of His voice, but for "future believers" as well.[2] And what He promised for the future could scarcely be more exciting:

It was "expedient" that He "go away."[3]

When He went away, He would send the Holy Spirit to be "poured out on all flesh." (In contrast to the Old Testament way of a few chosen people—prophets, priests, kings.)[4]

He Himself would be the Giver (or Baptizer) of the Spirit.[5]

His plan was that this Spirit would dwell (with our permission) in our bodies. This would be God the Father coming closer to man than He had ever been before.[6]

The apostles and all believers who would follow them down through the ages were, from the moment of Jesus' ascension, entering a new era—the era of the Holy Spirit. This would last until His second coming in physical Presence back to planet Earth.[7]

The Spirit would make Jesus' continuing Presence and His teachings real to us. He would always turn the spotlight on Jesus and glorify Him.[8]

The chief hallmark of the Holy Spirit would be *power* for service and ministry to others.[9]

The Spirit would be our Teacher; Guide; Comforter; Counsellor; Prayer-Intercessor; Giver of joy, of freedom, of many spiritual gifts, of eternal life.[10]

The Spirit would not ever be totally operative in an individual alone, but primarily in the fellowship of Christ's Body on earth—the Church.[11]

The apostles and those who would come after must expect a degree of resistance, cleavage, even persecution and expulsion from their synagogues (or churches) because "the world cannot receive Him—the Spirit of truth."[12]

After His resurrection and ascension the apostles were "to go into all the world and preach the Good News to everyone, everywhere. . . . "[13]

They were not, however, to leave Jerusalem or start telling the Good News or attempt any ministry of any kind until *they had received the Holy Spirit.*[14]

Jesus promised that He *would* "manifest Himself to us."[15]
And that He *would* lead us into further truth—all truth.[16]

As I put all of this together back in 1945, it shed new light on the account of what happened next. That story is told in the Book of Acts—really the Acts of the Holy Spirit. The Spirit's first great miracle was to transform the erstwhile timid, cowardly, and contentious disciples into bold men moving with power and authority. Thus the infant Church was born.

Jesus' explicit promises both to manifest Himself to us human beings and to lead us into further truth began to be fulfilled immediately. Old religious mores and set habit patterns had to be broken.

Virgin truth is always unexpected, often shocking. Though Jesus had spoken often of the Holy Spirit to the apostles, I could find no record that He had mentioned details of the Pentecost to come such as the sound of a roaring wind or flames of fire, or the sudden speaking of languages they had never learned. Nor were these disciples prepared for the "further truth" such as that Jewish food taboos were no longer necessary,[17] or that the Gentiles were also beloved by the Father and chosen by Him to receive the Spirit.[18]

In fact, it seemed to me that Jesus' promise of "further truth" gives us clear reason to believe that not all the truth and instruction Christ has to give us is contained in the canon of the Old and New Testaments. How could it be? He who *is* Truth will never find the people of any given century able to receive everything He wants to give. Because the Holy Spirit is a living, always-contemporary Personality, down all the centuries there must be an ever-unfolding manifestation of Jesus, His personality, His ways of dealing with us along with new, fresh disclosures of the mind of the Father. I found this concept endlessly provocative . . . and I still do.

At that point in my study some action on my part was clearly indicated. I had already summarized how we receive the Spirit:

(1) By going directly to Christ for Him.

(2) By asking for the gift of the Spirit.

(3) By receiving the Spirit by faith (the only way to receive any gift from God).

(4) By entering upon the discipline of hourly, daily obedience to Christ and the Spirit.

So very simply, I asked for the gift of the Helper, thanked Him for granting this, and entered upon that fourth step—the daily living out of this new relationship. I experienced no waves of emotion or ecstasy. Even when eighteen years later, I was given the gift of a heavenly language (glossolalia), it was with no particular fanfare; rather as a divine quartermaster might casually hand out a tool for a job, "Here. You'll need this."

When I had asked myself, "Can we expect a manifestation of the Spirit?," I had little idea how to answer. Since the Helper is a Person, I reasoned, then of course He has personality traits, and presumably, these traits will show themselves. How or in what way, I could not guess.

Manifest Himself He did, though not in a way I could have guessed. As I stepped out in faith back in 1945, day by day listening to the inner Voice for instructions, the first discipline He gave me was a leash for my tongue. For others the Spirit may give torrents of ecstatic speech; I needed the discipline of not speaking the careless or negative or discouraging word. For weeks I was put through the sharp training of opening my mouth to speak and hearing from the Teacher "Stop! No, don't say it. Close the mouth."

Many other experiences followed which I have described elsewhere[19] such as the joy of discovering the Helper's concern with guiding us in the details of everyday life; the reality of His guidance; the way He brings us to life at the emotional level. None of this I could have predicted. My experience was rather a solitary one. In 1945 I knew no one who was experimenting along the same line.

I realized that my husband Peter had already been given the Helper along with the unmistakable gift of preaching. Unlike me, he had not been seeking the Spirit per se, rather what God's specific will for his life was. Probably the Helper had come to Peter at the same time he was "tapped on the shoulder by the

Chief," as he liked to put it, and told to emigrate to America to enter the ministry. Having long known the Spirit's presence and help in so many ways, Peter did not feel the need for conscious search that I did.

Later, at the time of my husband's sudden death, I shall be forever grateful that I was able to know the Spirit as Comforter during those days. Without Him, I might have survived, but only as a truncated person and without ever knowing the grace and splendor of the Comforter's presence on this, one of life's starkest frontiers. No only did He comfort me, but in one practical step after another, He showed me how to handle the devastation of widowhood.

By 1950 I was in need of another kind of help. I was under contract to deliver the manuscript of *A Man Called Peter* by May 1st, yet had never had a single course in the craft of writing and almost no practice except scribbling in personal diaries and journals. In that extremity, the Spirit became my Instructor in creative writing. For instance, He took me by the hand and showed me that the opening pages must present Peter Marshall in the framework in which the public knew him—through his Senate chaplaincy. Only then could I flash back (I did not even know the term "flashback") to Peter's early life in Scotland and come forward.

I tried to outline the book and knew that it was not right. When I asked my Teacher the right way of outlining the book, I was told that Peter's biography would have no lasting significance apart from what his life demonstrated about God—His goodness, His revelation of truth, His ways of dealing with men. "Outline the book *that* way," was the instruction. I did, and the material fell into place.

My Teacher showed me how to construct a book, what to include out of the totality of one man's life, what to omit. All the way through He kept insisting on the importance of the light touch and humor as the way to emphasize greatness.

Now I experienced all the emotion I had *not* felt when I'd first asked for His presence—plus much much more. "No creative work," He told me, "has final impact unless it touches the reader at the level of the emotions." As I worked on the manuscript, He poured through me a stream of strong emotion, yet permitted me none of the sentimentality into which I was tempted to slip.

So functional and effectual was the Teacher's guidance that I had fewer editorial suggestions, less outside help with *A Man Called Peter* than with any book since, and I wrote it more swiftly.

Little did I dream that some sixteen years later I would see the rise of a major surge of the Spirit like a groundswell across the world.

It came in 1966-1967 when a rising tide of evil had plunged our world into a mess. The young, already disillusioned with war, were convinced that humanism had failed. High school and college students were more clear-eyed about man's failure than were most liberal theologians. Liberal churches and seminarians who mostly told us what *not* to believe, were still teaching the sad doctrine that any reform—humanitarian, sociological, political, racial, or religious—must be made by human effort alone. To which the younger generation's consistent reply was, "No way! Human effort alone hasn't worked, and never will."

So out of the vacuum of churches "holding the form of religion but denying the power of it"[20] the young groped their way—some of them through the jungle of drugs or the occult or Eastern religions they didn't really understand, to become "Jesus people." They not only carried Bibles, they feverishly read them. They waded into the ocean or into backyard swimming pools to be baptized. All over the world they formed communes or "communities." And throughout the Jesus Revolution ran highly charged emotionalism—hand-clapping, hugging, singing, religious rock music, filled with words like "wow!" and "far-out!"

Of course some of these youthful experimenters were not serious and soon drifted away. Yet many—like Carrie and Jeff Buddington—were permanently healed of long-standing hang-ups and had their lives turned right side up.

Like most adults I've had emotions ranging from delight—to wonder— to perplexity about all this. Yet surely these young people have been saying something important that the rest of us need to hear: we could use more joy and more love in our spiritual lives; perhaps we have become so occupied with worshiping God with our minds that we have forgotten that the rest of our beings, including the physical body, need to worship Him too.

Self-forgetfulness, a sort of joyous holy abandon, is indeed one of the Helper's trademarks. An experience Len had in 1962 is still vividly present with me. . . .

During our Chappaqua, New York years we were part of a group of six or eight couples who met once a week in one another's homes for sharing, Bible study, and prayer. I remember that Len came to a particular meeting that spring discouraged and frustrated. An individual with whom he worked professionally was being difficult. In addition, he and I were having problems with our teenagers.

That evening Len shared some of his problems and asked for prayer. Two members of the group especially seemed led to respond. With obvious concern, they stood by his chair, lightly rested their hands on his shoulders and head, and prayed. The particular request, as I recall, was that the power of the Holy Spirit would free Len of all resentments and antagonism. He told me later that he felt warmth coming from their hands. The prayer ended and he expressed gratitude. The meeting broke up.

Hours later, after we were in bed, Len spoke softly, "Catherine, I hate to wake you up, but I have the strangest feeling."

A little alarmed, I asked, "How do you mean?"

"There's this rushing, headlong joy inside me! It started in the pit of my stomach after I got in bed, then has kept bubbling up right into my head. I've been lying here thinking how silly it is to be so joyous when I should be asleep, but I can't control it. Catherine, I'd like to pray about it."

"Well, fine," I responded sleepily. "Go ahead—pray."

"But it isn't enough just to lie here. I'd like to kneel."

So both of us knelt beside the bed.

Len's prayer began quietly enough. First, he expressed gratitude for the friends who had cared enough to pray for him. Then he thanked God for our life together. After that he expressed love for each member of our family near and far. In between he kept telling the Lord how much he loved him. Heartfelt love rose from the depths of his being for each person who had been a human thorn in Len's side. Afterwards he began God-blessing everyone he could think of, as if this love were so great it had to encompass the whole universe.

Always before Len's prayers had been short, even abrupt. Well thought out, words carefully chosen, but quite unemotional. In contrast, that night words poured from him lavishly, exuberantly repetitious, a geyser of deep emotion, unabashedly expressed. Like a bird uncaged, his emotions were darting, wheeling, soaring, wanting nothing so much as to keep on flying forever.

Minutes passed—half an hour, an hour, as the love and joy kept pouring from Len. Finally, becoming aware of me kneeling there too, Len interrupted himself long enough to say reluctantly, "This isn't fair to you, Catherine. I'd like to go on and on, but you need some sleep."

In the morning he reported, "It was the most cleansing experience I've ever had. I got to thinking it was almost like a car engine being overhauled. It's as though negative emotions—my frustrations and anger—had built up a residue in the body just like carbon deposits foul up spark plugs. That love and joy pouring through me was like fresh warm sudsy water washing away the bitterness. This morning I have—I don't know—a scrubbed feeling."

In the years since, on two other occasions Len has felt the same kind of rushing flowing love. In between time, he has tried seeking it on his own—to no avail. We know now—this kind of love is the Spirit's gracious gift, not something we humans can achieve on our own.

In 1970 I received as a gift a very old (1885) copy of *The Christian's Secret of a Happy Life* by the Quaker Hannah Smith in whom I have been intensely interested for years. As I eagerly turned the yellowed old pages—but what was this? A chapter on the Holy Spirit. I had many editions of *The Christian's Secret* in my library, knew this book practically by heart, and there was no such chapter.

Why the deletion, I wondered?

I couldn't wait to read the chapter. As usual, Hannah Smith first turned to the Bible to summarize what it taught about the Spirit, then took a middle-of-the-road position liberally seasoned with common sense. The gist of her conclusion went something like this. . . .

We make the mistake of looking upon the "baptism of the Spirit" as a single experience rather than a life, as an arbitrary bestowment rather than a necessary vitality.

It is plain from Scripture that we can't possibly enter into a new life in Christ or be a child of God at all without knowing the Spirit.[21] However, there is a big difference between being indwelt by the Spirit and being "filled" with His presence. For years (sometimes a lifetime) a Christian can keep the Spirit at a sub-basement level by the insistence on running one's own life. Then through teaching or need—or both—the person consciously recognizes his divine Guest's presence, opens the hitherto closed doors into certain rooms in his being so that the Spirit can enter there too. Thus the individual now deliberately abandons himself to the Helper's control.

"The result of this when done suddenly," Mrs. Smith explained, "is what many call 'the baptism of the Holy Spirit.'"[22] It can be but isn't always, a very emotional and overwhelming sense of His presence.

"In seeking for the baptism therefore, it is not God's attitude toward us that needs to be changed, but our attitude toward Him. He will not give us anything new; rather we are to receive in a new and far fuller sense that which He has already given at Pentecost. The Holy Spirit is the world's sunlight, its energy and power. Sunlight can be kept out only by erecting barriers against it. All we need do then, is to take down our shutters and barriers and walk out into the sunlight already given."

But then Hannah Smith issues a strong word of warning. "Baptism means," she says, "far more than emotion. It means to be immersed or dipped into the Spirit of God, into His character and nature. The real evidence of one's baptism is neither emotion nor any single gift such as tongues, rather that there *must* be Christ-likeness in life and character: by fruits in the life we shall know whether or not we have the Spirit."

Nor does this mean instantaneous holiness. The disciples had to learn that right after Pentecost, and so do we. Ananias and Sapphira[23] could still lie and cheat, and so can we. In practical fact, our life with the Spirit is a walk, a growth, an unfolding, as we learn to trust Him, and open more and more of our being to His presence and control.

To me this seemed such solid teaching that I wondered all the more why the chapter had been deleted from all more recent editions of the book. Intent upon unraveling the mystery, I sought the story behind this chapter. These are the facts as I dug them out of Hannah Smith's letters and writings and more recent books about the Smith family.[24]

Hannah was born in Philadelphia on February 7, 1832, into a Quaker family who were eminently successful glass manufacturers. Though Hannah grew up a lively girl in a happy home, by age sixteen she was writing of "the aching void in my heart." This was in part adolescent drama, but the spiritual hunger was real enough, so much so that for the rest of her long life she was an eager, open-minded spiritual researcher. Like John Wesley in the century before her, she would listen to anybody with a religious experience to relate; she read constantly, investigated tirelessly.

Such eagerness might have led this Quaker girl straying down dead-ends and into paths of heresy. Fortunately, she possessed qualities to balance her insatiable zeal—a thorough knowledge of Scripture and a high degree of common sense.

Hannah had long since arrived at the conclusion that the only solid ground of our faith is the character of God—who and what He is. The only sure route for us humans to know Him and experience His love and guidance resides "not in the region of the emotions, but in the region of the will—not 'How do I feel?' but always 'What does God say?'" Though initially she had set out on "a feverish search for emotional religion," she soon grew mistrustful of emotionalism in religion.

In 1865 Hannah and her husband, Robert Pearsall Smith, and their children moved to the village of Milltown, New Jersey, where Robert took charge of a branch of the family glass business. There Hannah met a group called "the Holiness Methodists."

Some of the most penetrating and valuable parts of *The Christian's Secret*, a book helpful to generations of Christians, was to come from what Hannah learned from this group. She was able to translate their teaching from its in-language to fresh everyday vernacular. No mean accomplishment!

Eventually Robert Smith was as caught up as his wife in all this. One summer the Smiths went to a ten-day Holiness Camp Meeting at a woodland campsite along the New Jersey coast. The purpose of these meetings, in Hannah's words, was "to open our hearts to the teachings of the Holy Spirit and His coming into seekers' hearts." But it was Robert rather than his wife who received an extraordinary emotional experience. As Hannah later reported it:[25]

> After the meeting my husband had gone alone into a spot in the woods to continue to pray by himself. Suddenly, from head to foot he was shaken with what seemed like a magnetic thrill of heavenly delight, and floods of glory seemed to pour through him, soul and body, with the inward assurance that this was the longed-for Baptism of the Holy Spirit.
>
> The whole world seemed transformed for him, every leaf and blade of grass quivered with exquisite colour. . . . Everybody looked beautiful to him, for he seemed to see the Divine Spirit within each one. . . . This ecstasy lasted for several weeks, and was the beginning of a wonderful career of spiritual power and blessing.

Naturally, this made Hannah renew her efforts to receive similar joy. She described how she "went forward" to the altar night after night in the meetings, then would go with a smaller group to one of the tents, where they would spend hours kneeling in the dark, pleading and wrestling in prayer. For Mrs. Smith all this effort seemed of no avail. Not then or ever did she have an emotional experience of the type that had meant so much to her husband.

At first Hannah was disappointed. Then she realized that what had been given her was a "real revelation of God that made life to me a different thing ever since." She wanted emotions and was given conviction. She "wanted a vision and got a fact."

Later, Mrs. Smith came to feel that the difference between what she and her husband experienced was largely a reflection of the difference in their natures: Robert was emotional, inclined to feel response in physical sensations; Hannah was a more reserved and analytical person.

In 1873 the Smiths emigrated to England to become one of America's most famous expatriate families with their lives intertwined by marriage or friendship with Bertrand Russell, Bernard Shaw, Beatrice and Sidney Webb, Bernard Berenson, the great art critic, and Henry James. For some years the Smiths carried on a remarkable joint lay ministry in England, especially in aristocratic circles. These meetings became known as the Higher Life Movement, and much of their teaching was carried on at house parties in some of England's great country places.

In the spring of 1875 Robert also traveled to Germany, where he held highly successful evangelistic-teaching meetings before large crowds, always in a highly charged emotional atmosphere. "All Europe is at my feet," exulted Robert in a letter to his wife. When engraved pictures of him were offered for sale, eight thousand sold immediately.

Then the blow fell. Gossip began about Robert Pearsall Smith's improper conduct with female admirers. No one then or now knows the exact truth of the matter. The emotionalism so appealing to Smith had apparently gotten out of hand. It seemed that Paul's instruction to "Salute one another with an holy kiss," had here spilled over to the physical.

The rumors got into the press. Meetings scheduled in England were canceled by their sponsors and for a time the Smiths returned to New Jersey. Hannah quietly stood by her husband. She wrote a friend of their "heart-scale" and of the "crushing blow"[26] that had befallen Robert.

And crush him it did. He gave way to discouragement, disillusionment, and to a degree of cynicism. Robert sank into a joyless old age, while Hannah went on from strength to strength, her quiet deep faith carrying her triumphantly over all sorts of trials and difficulties.

With this story as background for the Smiths' experience of the Helper, we begin to see the many forms and results His coming into the life can have. Each opportunity for Christian growth, each step forward, brings new temptations and dangers. In Robert Smith's case, tragedy resulted when he succumbed to the temptation to idolize emotion instead of worshiping Jesus. With Hannah Smith, no ecstasy was apparent but a quieter joy from the fruitage of her convictions about God.

As for the missing chapter, clearly editors had been afraid of the subject. It was fire. Hadn't Robert Smith been burned? Safer to omit it, they must have concluded.

As Len and I pondered Hannah's story, we agreed that the modern surge of the Spirit in America may stand poised at the edge of this same problem—too great a love affair with emotion, too little grounding in Scripture, too wanting in garden-variety discipline, too small an emphasis on purity, strict honesty, morality—Christ's own life living in us.

What is needed, of course, is balance: plenty of solid teaching—but plenty of joy as well. Let's admit that overemotionalism is the last problem most of us face in our mainline denominational churches. We shall achieve a proper balance between the emotions and the mind when we are truly led by the Helper—"always a Gentleman."

It may well be that the missing element in Robert Pearsall Smith's experience was a small corrective fellowship of other Christians like that of the infant Church in Acts 5. What was still missing in the late nineteenth century was a body of wisdom concerning the Holy Spirit movement and the Scriptural teaching of group submission. Recent experience is teaching us that as we go adventuring in the Spirit, we must deliberately make ourselves subject one to the other, be willing to be checked and corrected as well as encouraged and strengthened.

Thinking back to his own bubbling joy that memorable night in Chappaqua, Leonard commented, "It was heady stuff. No wonder people at Pentecost thought the disciples were full of new wine! No wonder Robert Pearsall Smith got himself in trouble! I have no intention of stopping at this point, just with waves of emotion, I mean. The emotion's great, but—well, a quiet day-by-day rooting and grounding in love and obedience is far more important."

The excising of Hannah Smith's chapter on the Holy Spirit points up the real question, why are we afraid of the Helper?

Something that happened to Elizabeth and John Sherrill illustrates just how fearful our society can be. In 1962 the Sherrills published *The Cross and the Switchblade*, the previously mentioned story of David Wilkerson's work with New York drug addicts and warring gangs. For religious circles the book was clearly a departure necessarily depicting foul lives and some raw violence. The question in the Sherrills' minds was, would the public really be interested in reading about drug addiction in the big city? In those years it seemed like a remote sort of subject.

The publisher received a large order from one of the major denominational accounts. However, a condition was attached to the order: two chapters—21 and 22—which described the Baptism in the Holy Spirit, must be deleted "because such material would not be acceptable to our readers." The crime and violence the Sherrills had worried about was apparently perfectly permissible; it was the Spirit who was suspect!

The order was a temptation because the number of books in question was so large and the title was not expected to sell well. However, to Wilkerson and the Sherrills these chapters on the Baptism contained the point of the book, the secret of the amazing success of Wilkerson's work. To hold out a promise of help and then not tell how to obtain it would have been cheating. They declined to make the deletions. As it turned out, *The Cross and the Switchblade*, with the "unacceptable" chapters, became one of the best-selling religious books of the decade—including enormous sales to the denomination in question. To date *The Cross and the Switchblade* has sold a total of eleven million copies, domestic and foreign.

Some of us are afraid. Could we be terrified that if we invite the Holy Spirit into our hearts, we will lose control of our own emotions or the guidance of our individual life? Or are we afraid that the comfortable structures we have known may be altered or even blown to bits? Still others say they want to stay in safe areas that won't offend anybody, thus avoiding controversy and divisiveness.

There are dozens of theological dugouts in which people hide such as, "When I became a Christian I received everything there is to receive." Or "All those experiences in the Book of the Acts were just for the first century. Our time is different. We don't have the same needs today." Or again, one hears over and over, "I want my faith to remain middle-of-the-road *orthodox* Christianity. That's good enough for me."

The odd part of this latter statement is that I can think of nothing more central to Christianity or "orthodox" than the doctrine of the Trinity: God, our Father; Jesus, our Saviour and Friend; the Holy Spirit—Comforter, Counsellor, and Helper, who mediates the Father and our Lord to us. What Jesus Himself taught us must be central to "Christianity." Since He Himself bade us "Be filled with the Spirit" and told us that He personally would be the Baptizer, we can't very well extirpate the Third Person of the Trinity and still be "orthodox."

Part of our fear may also be that instinctively we know that the Spirit means power, and power makes all of us acutely uneasy. We're like people who have always lived with candles and campfires. We've heard rumors of electricity, but because we've never seen electric lights and are not certain we would know how to handle electric power, we'd rather make do with candles all our days.

As for churches, they must choose whether they wish to remain ecclesiastical monuments to Christ as just another historical figure—a great teacher whose brief life was cut short in 29 or 30 A.D. (Those churches would be limited to such things as liturgy, organizations, and a degree of social action.) Or the alternative is the church as the close fellowship of followers of the living Christ, the contemporary Lord, that fellowship made alive and operative by His Spirit, marching to His now-orders.

Until the surge of the Spirit began in the 1960s, far too many churches had chosen to be ecclesiastical monuments. A churchman like Dr. Carl Henry has warned about the danger of making the Holy Spirit "a displaced person": "Whenever the Church makes the Spirit of God a refugee," Dr. Henry wrote, "the Church—not the Spirit—becomes the vagabond."

Once we understand what Jesus told us would happen in the Era of the Spirit, we next ask, are these miracles of grace, restoration, guidance, new teaching, healing, rescuing, and all the rest actually happening today?

The account of what took place in the life of someone like Tay Thomas points up what a resounding "Yes" can be answered to this. Tay is Mrs. Lowell Thomas, Jr.; her husband is the son of the famed radio and television commentator and world traveler. The Thomases live in Alaska, where Lowell is one of Alaska's state senators.

Good Friday, 1964, began as such a happy day for the Thomas family. The snow which had been coming down steadily for two days finally let up. Lowell could fly from Spenard to a meeting in Fairbanks, and get back so that the family could spend Easter together. David Thomas was then six; Anne, eight. The story is best told in Tay's own words:[27]

"The children and I waved goodbye as Lowell drove off to the airport, then shut the door quickly because it was still below freezing outside. About five o'clock, feeling lonesome for him,

Anne, David, and I went upstairs to watch TV. We took off our shoes so we could sit on the bed.

"It was half an hour later that I heard a rumbling sound. Although we frequently hear a similar roaring—the firing of guns at a nearby Army base—I knew instantly that these were no guns.

"I leapt off the bed, yelling 'Earthquake!' Grabbing Anne, I called to David. We had gotten as far as the front hall when the house began to shake. As we ran outside into the snow, David was crying, 'Mommy, I'm in bare feet!'

"We were about ten feet beyond the front door when we were flung violently to the ground, which was jolting back and forth with unbelievable force. The hallway we had just run through split in two. We heard the crashing of glass, the ear-rending sound of splintering wood. In front of us a great tree crashed full length. Our garage collapsed with a sharp report.

"Now the earth began breaking up and buckling all about us. Suddenly between Anne and me a great crack opened in the snow. I stared in disbelief as the trench widened, apparently bottomless, separating me from my child. I seized the hand she stretched out to me in time to pull her across the chasm.

"We were left on a wildly bucking slab. Suddenly it tilted sharply, and we had to hang on to keep from slipping into a yawning crevasse. Now the earth seemed to be rising just ahead of us. I had the weird feeling that we were riding backward on a monstrous Ferris wheel, going down, down toward the water (our house stood on a high bluff overlooking Cook Inlet). The entire face of the bluff had fallen to sea level. A few feet away, at the water's edge, lay the roof of our house.

"All I could think of was that the water would rise as earth tumbled into it and we would be trapped. The cliffs above us were sheer, with great sections of sand and clay still falling.

"The children both were hysterical, crying over and over, 'We'll die! We'll die!' I realized we'd have to find a way up that cliff, but the children were too frightened to walk.

"I looked up at the leaden gray sky, the bleak clouds, and silently cried out, 'Jesus, where are You—I thought You'd be with us at the end.' *Suddenly, I felt a sense of peace so intense that I knew beyond all doubt He was with me—not way up in the air, but right there inside me.* It was a revelation that gave me a tremendous courage.

"We clambered up and down the great slabs of earth and snow, our bare feet aching and raw in the cold. I found a large tree leaning against the cliff and thought for a few moments that we might be able to shinny up it, but we gained only a few feet.

"Suddenly a man appeared above us. 'Help!' we called to him. He shouted down that he would hunt for a rope, then disappeared. As we waited we were aware for the first that we were soaked to the skin, the children shaking and their lips blue.

"At least six or eight men appeared at the top of the cliff. One of them, a stranger to us, started down, finding one less steep spot. The children threw their arms around him as he reached us. He took off his black wool jacket, put it around Anne, then boosted David into his arms and led us all back up along the rope. At the top, when I turned to thank our rescuer, he had gone."

Tay Thomas went on to describe the mounting suspense during the hours when Lowell and his family could not communicate; then the drama of their reunion. For so many hours Lowell had not known whether his family was dead or alive.

The earthquake experience bound families and neighbors together as never before. For Tay it was another in a series of spiritual adventures that have been part of her life's search.

In 1954 she and her husband had flown around the world together in a single-engine Cessna plane named "Charlie." They spent long days with bearded Afghan nomads and Pygmies of the Congo; they sailed in a primitive dhow on the Persian Gulf; they put in an appearance at the birthday ball of the Emperor of Ethiopia.

On the dashboard of the plane Tay had pasted this poem:

> Peace be in thy home
> And in thy heart.
> Or if thou roam
> Earth's highways wide,
> The Lord is at thy side,
> To bless and guide.

In 1958 the Thomases had put three-year-old Anne in "Charlie's" back seat and taken off on three months' work on a television film documentary on Alaska, the new forty-ninth state. It was an area pulsing with vitality, full of the promise of the frontier and of undeveloped resources. Tay's book *Follow the North Star* is a vivid account of traveling in a small plane through wilderness areas with a small child.

Out of this trip had come the Thomases' decision in 1960 to make Alaska their home. Soon Lowell was elected a state senator, Tay to the Anchorage School Board, and to the important Land Use Planning Commission.

Tay's spiritual search had begun two years after the move to Alaska. Her family, the Sam Pryors, had been lifelong Episcopalians in the traditional manner. But intermittent years of roaming the world had deprived Lowell and her of a church home. Suddenly Tay realized that the children were old enough for Sunday School and that the time had come to find a church. Within a few weeks she found Saint Mary's Episcopal Church, a small wooden structure sitting on a hilltop, with windows looking out over Alaska's magnificent mountains. But it wasn't the building that won over the Thomases—it was a warm, loving, informal congregation and pastor. To Tay, Saint Mary's meant the finding of what she calls her "faith ladder."

In 1963 she climbed up the first of two most important rungs. It happened the night she heard the visiting pastor, Dennis Bennett, talk in a crowded school auditorium. Tay's whole life was changed that night. In her own words . . .

While driving home I realized that Christianity wasn't just going to church on Sunday and trying to follow the Ten Commandments—that I actually had to commit my life to Jesus, to give up all of my own personal ambitions and desires and let Him take over, using me in whatever way He saw fit. At first I was frightened, scared to death of letting go the "command" of my own life. But I did, talking to Him while driving, "I am Yours, Lord, do with me what You wish." My fear was suddenly replaced by such a joyful, peaceful feeling that I sang praises all the way home.

Once I had climbed onto that first rung of my faith ladder, life changed in many ways. I was happier, I prayed informally often, all during the day whenever I felt the need for support or guidance, and with missionary zeal I plunged headlong into a massive load of community social work.

I'm so grateful that I had achieved the first rung of the ladder before the trauma of the earthquake. But it was traumatic, and while it taught me that God is a present power, I knew that I needed something more. That was when I embarked on my search for what step would take me up the second rung of my ladder. The second part of the search took almost five years.

One day, after many hours of reading and searching through the Bible, the answer came to me. The original apostles had Jesus as their constant companion and guide, but when He was about to leave them, He promised to send the Comforter, one who would continue to be with them in everything they did—the Holy Spirit. I had always considered the Biblical story of the day of Pentecost as an historical happening, but now, as I read through the letters of Saint Paul, I knew I was wrong—the Holy Spirit had been promised to all people for all time, bringing to all believers the same gifts and fruits of the Spirit as in those earliest Christian days.

I longed to be filled with the Holy Spirit because I could see what His presence was doing for friends and for the many Spirit-filled people I was reading about. But who isn't afraid of the supernatural!

As I prayed more and more about my dilemma, one Sunday our minister announced that there would be a Wednesday evening prayer meeting at the home of a parishioner and his wife who I knew were having real experiences of the Spirit. I had the immediate realization that here was my chance to step up onto that next rung of the faith ladder. I was so excited by Wednesday I was ready for anything—all reticence gone. An uncanny coincidence of timing, perhaps, but I still think that Jesus has His eye on our movements up that ladder.

That night I received the laying on of hands, felt the joyful inpouring of the Holy Spirit. Needless to say, my elation increased until I thought I'd burst with joy, a state of euphoria which lasted for several weeks. Once I had returned to a more normal emotional level, I realized that many startling changes in my life were coming one after another.

I was fascinated to hear from Tay what those changes were. For the first time, she knew Jesus as a close personal Friend, that same closeness which she had experienced briefly during the Earthquake. There was a great strengthening of her private prayer life—she could talk to and praise God in a way and a language she had never known before. Gradually she was learning to listen to that "still small voice." Then there was the new dimension of answered prayer, though not always in the way Tay wanted or expected. She also saw some miraculous healing through prayer and experienced it herself. There was a new relationship to other people, a deeper love and understanding which helped immeasurably in Tay's community work—old habit-patterns of anger, frustration, and irritation were gone, leaving her more energy and enthusiasm.

One of the changes that startled Tay Thomas most had to do with her old reticent Episcopal solemnness toward worship in church. In the beginning she resisted the folk mass, the new liturgy, the general informality of worship. Her inclination had been to go the altar for Communion in reverent silence, to pray quietly by isolating herself in the pew. In her new life she was startled to find herself in the midst of the loudest singing during services, the words of the prayers, old and new, took on a deeper meaning, and she almost danced on her way to the altar. She has laughed and cried during folk masses and at retreats, and along with this great release of emotions, has no hesitation sharing the new growth of her faith with others.

Tay Thomas has been amazed at what has been happening recently in her state. "In just the last five years," she wrote us recently, "the Holy Spirit has roared through Alaska from the Panhandle to the tiny Arctic villages. Many churches are open about the wonderful experiences felt by so many people of all denominations.

"I don't see how this tremendous and exciting Power can be stopped" she told me, "when it is so clearly supported by the Bible and so firmly supported by so many 'conservative' people of traditional background. anyway, as for me I feel strongly that it's time for me to speak up and be counted.

"We're told there was an earthquake on the First Good Friday too. But then dawned the calm and the victory of Resurrection morning. What happened on the first Easter morning made possible all the good that has come out of our Good Friday earthquake, for me perfectly captured in the lines from an old hym:

Speak through the earthquake, wind and fire,
O still, small voice of calm.[28]

There is a sense in which every page of this book is about the Helper. Jesus told us He would send Him to us—and He has. As Comforter and Teacher He was with Edith and Peter John and me in that little Cessna 205, tenderly brooding over Peter Christopher's tiny white casket, saying to us, "I have many things to teach you. Walk softly, with heads up. This too will teach you." . . .

Nancy De Moss's friend Ginny learned what Jesus meant when He promised, "He—the Spirit—will tell you about the future." The Helper knew about that fire. The baby Brandon must be saved. "Go and get Brandon," He directed Ginny.

"It's the risk in *not* obeying the Helper that gives me the shivers now," Nancy De Moss reflects.

That day in the little church, the Spirit came to Pat Baker in His role as Counsellor. He spoke through the young preacher's lips, "He's ready to deal with your problem of nicotine."

How does he know that?

"It started when you were a teen-ager. The problem grew out of the soil of rebellion."

So He does know! Wise Counsellor. . . .

That bitterly cold winter in Oregon it was the Helper who rescued Carrie and Jeff Buddington and their friends by alerting the men up the road in the Christian community, "Go—and saw wood."

"Saw wood, Lord?"

"Yes, saw wood. I was a carpenter, I know all about wood. Remember? But the woodpile will be only the beginning."

Or I think of Gene Klinger and Roberta Lashley who got an intimate look at how swiftly and ingeniously the Helper comes to protect from immediate danger those who ask Him, even as David Livingstone experienced the same protection a century ago in Africa.

And Maude Blanford, so grievously ill of cancer, knows now how surely Jesus fulfills His promises about the Helper. "He, the Spirit of truth, is come, He will guide you into all truth."

"The truth is," the Helper told Maude, "your life is in danger. See, your body-house has no roof. Without Jesus as your covering, you have no protection."

"But how do I get the roof back on my body-house?"

"Here I am—I, the Lord thy God, to loose the bonds, to let the oppressed go free. I will lead you out step by step."

Yes, a healthy Maude Blanford knows that the Spirit is also this, the Great Physician, Lord of the body. . . .

You and I are living in rough times. We must make our way through minefields of evil, booby traps of deception, brush fires of sickness and disease, wastelands of economic disaster, burning deserts of disappointment. "I won't take you out of this world," Jesus told us. "But don't be afraid, because I've overcome that world of dangers. All power is Mine. I promise to be with you always."

"How, Lord? How are you with us?"

"Through the Helper."

It is true. He is here. We who in moments of desperation have asked, "What can I do? What is there left?" have felt His answering presence and experienced His help . . . We know now . . . always He holds out to us the exciting promise of something more.

Notes

Chapter 1   Yes, God Is in Everything

1. Acts 4:20
2. Job 1:21
3. Hannah W. Smith, *The Christian's Secret of a Happy Life* (Westwood, N.J.: Fleming H. Revell Company, 1962), pp. 148, 149
4. I Thessalonians 5:18
5. Hannah W. Smith, *The Christian's Secret of a Happy Life*, pp. 144, 146, 147, 149
6. Romans 8:28
7. Shakespeare, *Hamlet* IV. v. 78
8. This story and other examples of relinquishment are included in Catherine Marshall's *Beyond Our Selves* (New York: McGraw-Hill Book Company, 1961), chapter 6, "The Prayer of Relinquishment".
9. Luke 18:10-14
10. Matthew 10:29-31
11. Matthew 25:37-46

12. Acts 9:4, 5

13. Matthew 18:5

14. Frank C. Laubach, *You Are My Friends* (New York: Harper and Row, 1942), p. 22

15. Mark 1:40. James Moffatt, *The Bible: A New Translation* (New York: Harper & Row, 1935)

16. Matthew 18:12-14

Chapter 2   The Golden Bridge of Praise

1. Merlin R. Carothers, *Prison to Praise* (Plainfield, N.J.: Logos International, 1970)

2. Psalm 22:3

3. I Thessalonians 5:16-18

4. Colossians 4:2

5. See also I Peter 2:9; Philippians 4:4-6; Romans 1:21

6. Hebrews 13:15

7. *The Random House Dictionary of the English Language* (New York: Random House, 1966, 1967)

8. Habakkuk 3:17, 18

9. II Chronicles 20:21, 22

10. The Acts 16:19-40

11. Luke 10:20

12. Isaiah 12:2, 3

13. Philippians 4:11 (*Revised Standard Version*)

14. Philippians 4:4-6

15. II Corinthians 11:23-30

16. Ephesians 5:20

17. This incident has also been told in Corrie ten Boom's *The Hiding Place* (Washington Depot, Conn.: Chosen Books, 1971), pp. 180–181.

18. Though the material here (and at several other places) is set in much the same style as Peter Marshall's sermons, I have borrowed the style but not the material.

19. Both in Greek or Hebrew the most common word for "thank" or "praise" is also often translated "bless": Ps. 63:3, 4; Ps. 69:30; Luke 1:64. Note also the clear thrust of Luke 15:11-32 that man's actions can make God happy.

20. Hebrew for "hand" is *yad*; for "thanks" *yadah. Yadah* is used for

"thanksgiving" 40 times in the Old Testament; for "praise" 53 times; for "confess" 19 times. (King James Version)

21. Scripture's use of the same Hebrew root for "praise" and "confession" makes sense. Confession is the recognition that we have sinned—an offense against God. Thus both praise and confession are an acknowledgment that God is God.

Chapter 3   Forgiveness: The Aughts and the Anys

1. Mark 11:25
2. John 16:8
3. Catherine Marshall, *Beyond Our Selves*, pp. 47–48
4. Matthew 18:18
5. Matthew 22:37, 38 *The Living Bible* (Wheaton, Illinois: Tyndale House Publishers, 1971)
6. Luke 15:25-32
7. Matthew 17:20

Chapter 4   The Law of Generations

1. Deuteronomy 28:41
2. Biblical scholars generally agree that Moses' towering spirit, along with his remembered and recorded words, was the inspiration for Deuteronomy. As usual, there is disagreement about the actual date of the book. Some would place it as late as Josiah's reign, about 638 B.C. Others offer evidence that the book discovered in the Temple and read to the people as told in II Kings 22, 23 was the book of Deuteronomy.
3. Deuteronomy 30:15, 19 *The Amplified Bible* (Grand Rapids: Zondervan Publishing House, 1965)
4. Romans 12:5
5. Exodus 20:5
6. Malachi 4:6
7. Ephesians 6:17, 18
8. Hebrews 4:12
9. Luke 4:18
10. II Corinthians 3:17
11. Romans 8:21
12. Starr Daily, *God's Answer to Juvenile Delinquency* (St. Paul, Minnesota: Macalester Park Publishing Company, 1953), pp. 43–51; 132–142

13. Matthew 18:19
14. Matthew 6:4
15. Starr Daily, *Love Can Open Prison Doors*; (Worster, England: Arthur James, 1943); *Release*; (New York: Harper & Row, 1942); *Faith, Hope, and Love* (St. Paul, Minnesota: Macalester Park)
16. Matthew 6:33
17. Acts 10:28
18. This and the material that follows is taken from Elisabeth D. Dodds' *Marriage to a Difficult Man* (Philadelphia: The Westminster Press, 1971).
19. Exodus 20:6
20. Acts 2:39

Chapter 5 The Joy of Obedience

1. Art De Moss is founder of National Liberty Corporation, a life insurance company.
2. Matthew 7:24,25
3. John 14:21-23
4. Hebrews 5:9
5. John 7:17
6. Matthew 12:50
7. John 14:23
8. John 14:21
9. Acts 5:32
10. James 1:25; I John 3:22
11. John 14:21
12. Titus 3:1; I Peter 2:13-17; Romans 13:1, 2; John 19:11
13. I Peter 5:5
14. Hebrews 13:17; I Peter 5:1-5
15. I Corinthians 11:3
16. Ephesians 5:21-24; I Peter 3:7; I Samuel 3:13
17. Ephesians 5:25-33; I Peter 3:1-7
18. Colossians 3:20
19. C. S. Lewis, *The Screwtape Letters* (New York: The Macmillan Company, 1943), p. 21
20. The existence of both a sleep system and a wakefulness (activating) system in the brain is now generally acknowledged. The sleep-inducing mechanisms have been experimentally demon-

strated in the lower brain stem, the descending limbic hypnogenic circuit, and the neocortex; the reticular arousal system is thought to be in the brain stem. For more on this, see J. Edward Murray, *Sleep, Dreams and Arousal* (New York: Appleton-Century-Crofts, 1965)

21. Such as the sleep experiments of the Sleep Research and Treatment Facility of the Milton S. Hershey Medical Center, Hershey, Pennsylvania

22. Hymn *Blessed Assurance* by Fanny J. Crosby

23. Hannah W. Smith, *The Christian's Secret of a Happy Life*, p. 208

24. Genesis 12:1, 2

Chapter 6 "To Sleep! Perchance to Dream . . ."

1. Numbers 12:6, 8 (*Revised Standard Version*)

2. Matthew 27:19

3. Research typical of sleep laboratories is the research of Dr. Charles Fisher as summarized in "Psychoanalytic Implications of Recent Research on Sleep," *Journal of the American Psychoanalytic Association*, Vol. 13, p. 20 (April 1965)

4. Morton Kelsey, *God, Dreams and Revelation, A Christian Interpretation of Dreams* (Minneapolis: Augsburg Publishing House, 1968, 1974)

5. John A. Sanford, *Dreams: God's Forgotten Language* (Philadelphia: J. B. Lippincott Company, 1968)

6. John 2:25

7. See pages 90–94

8. Glenn Clark, *How to Find Health through Prayer* (New York: Harper and Row, 1940), pp. 105–108

9. Lewis's fiction works (New York: Macmillan) include *Out of the Silent Planet; Perelandra; That Hideous Strength; Till We Have Faces.*

10. See page 87

11. See page 87

12. Joel 2:28; Acts 2:17

Chapter 7 The Fallen Angel

1. C. S. Lewis, *Mere Christianity* (New York: The Macmillan Company, 1943), p. 40

2. Isaiah 14:12-14

3. Revelation 12:4

4. For a summary of current research in an effort to solve the mysteries of memory, learning, and consciousness, see "Exploring the Frontiers of the Mind," *Time* (January 14, 1974).

5. Genesis 3:5

6. Genesis 1:28

7. Hebrews 2:7,8 is quoted from Psalm 8:5, 6

8. Matthew 4:4

9. Edna St. Vincent Millay, *Collected Poems* (New York: Harper and Row, 1934), p. 91

10. C. S. Lewis, *The Screwtape Letters*, pp. 68, 96, 97

11. John 12:19

12. Derek Prince, "Spiritual Conflict" (from the Cassette Teaching Series, Derek Prince Publications, Fort Lauderdale, Florida)

13. John 18:37

14. C. S. Lewis, *Mere Christianity*, pp. 55, 56

15. Ephesians 6:12, 13. (*The Living Bible*)

Chapter 8   The Unholy Spirit

1. Out of this interview also came Catherine Marshall's "An Answer to Drugs," *Guideposts* (May 1970)

2. Lysergic acid diethylamide (LSD)

3. The amphetamine drugs

4. *Life* (July 18, 1969)

5. *Time* (February 11, 1974) and *Newsweek* (February 11, 1974)

6. Zechariah 12-14

7. This and the quotations below from the graduate student and from Professor Eliade are from Andrew M. Greeley, "There's A New-Time Religion on Campus," *The New York Times* (June 1, 1969)

8. I Peter 5:8 (*Revised Standard Version*)

9. John 8:44

10. Luke 13:16; Mark 9:25, 26

11. Job 1:2, 5, 18, 19

12. Job 1:9-11

13. Derek Prince, "Deliverance and Demonology," from the Cassette Teaching Series, Derek Prince Publications, Fort Lauderdale, Florida

14. James 4:7

15. I Corinthians 10:13
16. Matthew 28:18
17. John 8:34
18. John 14:30
19. Romans 13:12
20. Isaiah 9:2
21. Ephesians 5:8
22. Joshua 7:11-13
23. John 3:20, 21
24. Luke 8:28
25. II Peter 2:9 (*The Living Bible*)
26. Luke 10:19
27. Revelation 3:10
28. I John 1:7-9
29. Colossians 2:14, 15 (*The Bible: A New Translation*)
30. Catherine Marshall, *A Man Called Peter* (New York: McGraw-Hill Book Company, 1951) pp. 120, 121

Chapter 9   The Enigma of Healing

1. As this book goes to press Kent Ghost is still an outpatient at NIH in Bethesda, Maryland. The happy ending of the crisis was but one of the many episodes in an eight-year battle with leukemia. The end of the story is not yet. C. M.
2. John 6:38; 14:9
3. Acts 10:38
4. Luke 4:18; Matthew 4:23; Matthew 12:15
5. John 5:1-14
6. Luke 5:12, 13; Mark 9:22-24
7. Matthew 5:3-11
8. III John 2
9. John 14:12. See also Mark 16:15-18; Hebrews 13:8
10. Matthew 8:16-17; Mark 3:7-11; 6:53-56; Luke 6:17-19
11. Mark 3:1-5
12. John 5:1-14
13. Romans 3:23
14. Deuteronomy 9:5
15. Titus 3:5

16. John 5:14 (*The Living Bible*)
17. Ruth Cranston, *The Miracle of Lourdes* (New York: McGraw-Hill Book Company, 1955)
18. One compilation of these case histories: (*The Miracle of Lourdes*)
19. Dr. Carrel's own account of this is: Alexis Carrel, *The Voyage to Lourdes* (New York: Harper and Row, 1950)
20. Catherine Marshall, *A Man Called Peter*, pp. 175-177

Chapter 10   The Roof on the House

1. John 16:13
2. Isaiah 64:6
3. Romans 3:20; Philippians 3:8, 9
4. John 5:19
5. John 8:29; 5:30
6. John 6:38 (*The Bible: A New Translation*)
7. John 4:34
8. For other instances of relinquishment, see Catherine Marshall, *Beyond Our Selves*, chapter 6
9. Fritz Kunkel and Roye E. Dickerson, *How Character Develops* (New York: Charles Scribner's Sons, 1944), pp. 116, 120
10. Luke 8:43-48
11. Mark 2:1-12
12. Luke 18:1-8
13. Matthew 4:4, 6, 7
14. John 5:19 (*The Living Bible*)
15. Luke 10:9

Chapter 11   The King's Treasury

1. Edith Schaeffer, *L'Abri* (Wheaton, Illinois: Tyndale House, 1969), p. 126. Other books by Mrs. Schaeffer describing the L'Abri community are *Hidden Art* and *Everybody Can Know*.
2. Francis Schaeffer, *The God Who Is There* (Downers Grove, Illinois: Inter-Varsity Press, 1968). Dr. Schaeffer is also the author of thirteen other books including *Escape from Reason, Death in the City, True Spirtuality, The Church at the End of the 20th Century, He Is There and He Is Not Silent, Pollution and the Death of Man.*
3. Philippians 2:5

4. In late 1973 after nineteen years of living with almost no privacy in the Chalet les Mélèzes, the Schaeffers now have a private home. Yet typically they wrote me, "At last we have the space to share in a new way with endless teas, meals, conversations, meetings, Bible studies, discussions."
5. Matthew 6:33
6. Psalm 24:1
7. I John 3:1
8. Philippians 4:19
9. *The National Geographic* (May, 1974)
10. Matthew 20:32 (*The Living Bible*)
11. Luke 6:38
12. Malachi 3:10
13. Peter Marshall, *Mr. Jones, Meet the Master* (Westwood: Fleming H. Revell Company, 1949), pp. 63-74
14. Billie Davis first told this incident in "I Was a Hobo Kid," *The Saturday Evening Post* (December 13, 1952)

Chapter 12   The Dilemma of Our Rebellion

1. I Corinthians 4:5 (*The Bible: A New Translation*)
2. Joyce Maynard, "My Parents Are My Friends," *McCall's* (October 1972)
3. This and the quotation that follows are from Agnes Sanford, *Sealed Orders* (Plainfield, New Jersey: Logos International, 1972), pp. 51, 52
4. Matthew 5:21
5. Matthew 26:52
6. Matthew 5:22
7. Matthew 5:25
8. Matthew 6:15
9. Luke 6:36 (*The Living Bible*)
10. Hebrews 1:9
11. Luke 6:27 (*The Living Bible*)
12. I Corinthians 10:10, 11 (*The Living Bible*)
13. Numbers 14:23, 25, 29, 32
14. Leviticus 26:12 (*The Amplified Bible*)
15. *Guideposts* (November 1973)
16. Proverbs 4:23

17. Paul Tournier, *The Whole Person in a Broken World* (New York: Harper and Row, 1947), pp. 2-12

18. Walter Kaufmann, *Existentialism from Dostoevsky to Sartre* (New York: The World Publishing Company, 1956)

19. Mark 7:14-23 (*The Living Bible*)

20. Matthew 5:22

21. Ezekiel 36:26-28

22. Isaiah 60:18

Chapter 13 Run for the Strong Tower

1. David Shaw and Bill Hazlett, *The Miami Herald* (January 7, 1973)

2. *Guideposts* (November, 1966)

3. John 3:20

4. Colossians 1:16; John 1:3

5. Romans 13:12

6. Proverbs 18:10

7. Matthew 28:18

8. John 14:13

9. Luke 10:17

10. *Guideposts* (December, 1965)

11. Hymn *God Will Take Care of You.* Lyric by C. D. Martin

12. Schapera, ed., *Livingstone's African Journal 1853-1856*, 2 vols., (London: Chatto and Windus, 1963), vol. II, p. 374

13. Hunter B. Blakely, *Religion in Shoes* (Richmond, Virginia: John Knox Press, 1953), pp. 89, 90.

14. II Timothy 1:7

15. Romans 8:15

16. John 3:17

17. Matthew 6:30 (*A New Translation of the Bible*)

18. Matthew 8:26 (*A New Translation of the Bible*)

19. Ralph L. Woods, *The Modern Handbook of Humor* (New York: McGraw-Hill, 1967), p. 471

20. (Author unknown) *The Scarlet Fish and Other Stories*

21. Ephesians 6:12 (*The Living Bible*)

22. Catherine Marshall, *To Live Again* (New York: McGraw-Hill Book Company, 1957) pp. 299-325, and *Beyond Our Selves*, pp. 247-256.

23. I John 1:7-9 (*The Living Bible*)
24. Romans 13:12
25. Ephesians 6:16

Chapter 14   The Helper

1. *Time* (June 18, 1973), p. 91.
2. John 17:20 (*The Living Bible*)
3. John 16:7
4. Acts 1:4, 5; 2:17
5. John 1:33b; Mark 1:8; Matthew 3:11
6. John 14:17; Galatians 2:20; I Corinthians 6:19; John 15: 18-26
7. John 7:39; 16:7; Matthew 24:14, 30, 31
8. John 15:26; 16:13, 14
9. Mark 16:15-18, 20 (*The Living Bible*); John 14:12
10. *Teacher*: John 14:26; Luke 12:12; I Cor 2:13
    Guide: Romans 8:14
    Comforter: John 14:16, 26
    Counsellor: Matthew 10:19, 20
    Prayer-Intercessor: Romans 8:26, 27
    Giver of Joy: Romans 14:17; I Thessalonians 1:6
    Giver of Freedom: Romans 8:2
    Giver of Spiritual Gifts: I Corinthians 12:4-11;27, 28; Hebrews 2:4
    Giver of Eternal Life: Galatians 6:8; Ephesians 1:13, 14
11. Ephesians 1:22, 23; Romans 12:4,5
12. John 14:17; 15:20
13. Mark 16:15 (*The Living Bible*)
14. Acts 1:4
15. John 14:21
16. John 16:13
17. Acts 11:1-10
18. Acts 11:11-18
19. Catherine Marshall, *Beyond Our Selves*, chapter 14, "Journey into Joy," pp. 227-246
20. II Timothy 3:5
21. John 3:5, 6; Romans 8:9; Galatians 4:6
22. Hannah W. Smith, *The Christian's Secret of a Happy Life* (Boston: Willard Tract Repository, 1885), p. 249
23. Acts 5:1-11

24. *Philadelphia Quaker, The Letters of Hannah Whitall Smith* (New York: Harcourt, Brace and Company, 1950); Logan Pearsall Smith, *Unforgotten Years* (Boston: Little, Brown and Company, 1939), pp. 29, 30; Ray Strachey, *Group Movements of the Past and Experiments in Guidance* (London: Faber and Faber, Limited, 1928); Robert Allerton Parkes, *The Transatlantic Smiths* (New York: Random House, 1959)

25. This summary of the Smiths' experiences together with the exact quotations is taken from Hannah W. Smith, *My Spiritual Autobiography or How I Discovered the Unselfishness of God* (New York: Fleming H. Revell Company, 1903), pp. 288-296

26. Letter to Mrs. Henry Ford Barclay, June 3, 1876, Hannah W. Smith, *Letters*, pp. 29, 30

27. This portion of Tay Thomas's story was written originally for *Guideposts* (April 1965)

28. *Dear Lord and Father of Mankind.* Lyric by John Greenleaf Whittier

Part II
A CLOSER WALK
A Spiritual
Lifeline to God

I am weak but Thou art strong
Jesus, keep me from all wrong;
I'll be satisfied as long
As I walk, dear Lord, close to Thee.

Just a closer walk with Thee
Grant it, Jesus, if You please;
Daily walking close to Thee
Let it be, dear Lord, let it be.

Acknowledgments

*S*pecial thanks go to Jeanne Sevigny, Catherine's trusted secretary and close friend of fourteen years, who not only did the typing of Catherine's handwritten journal items, but served as advisor on the selection of material used in this book. Also to Regina Trollinger and Yvonne Burgan for their secretarial skills.

A big debt of gratitude to Elizabeth Sherrill, whose book expertise guided Catherine for twenty-two years through the writing of *Beyond Our Selves, Christy, Adventures in Prayer, Something More, Meeting God At Every Turn*, and *Julie,* and who edited the editor of this manuscript with her usual sensitivity and brilliance.

Scripture quotations are from: The Amplified Bible © 1965 by the Zondervan Publishing House and The Lockman Foundation; The King James Version published by the American Bible Society, 1972; The Living Bible © 1971 by Tyndale House Publishers; The Bible, The James Moffatt Translation © 1954 by James A. R. Moffatt; The New English Bible © 1970 by the Delegates of the Oxford University Press and the Syndics of the Cambridge University Press; The Holy Bible, New International Version, © 1978 by the International Bible Society, used by permission of Zondervan Bible Publishers; The New Testament in Modern English, J. B. Phillips, © 1972 by J. B. Phillips; The Holy Bible, Revised Standard Version, © 1946, 1952 by Division of Christian Education of the National Council of the Churches of Christ in the United States of America; Good News Bible, The Bible in Today's English Version, © 1976 by the American Bible Society. We are grateful for use of the lyrics on pages v, 126–27, and 129–30, © Singspiration of the Zondervan Corporation.

Over the years, Catherine Marshall shared many of the insights from her journals with the readers of *Guideposts* magazine. These articles are copyright by Guideposts Associates, Inc. Copyright © 1964, 1965, 1967, 1968, 1969, 1970, 1976, 1977, 1979, 1983 by Guideposts Associates, Inc., Carmel, New York 10512.

Contents

Using This Book . . .
On Your Own Walk

*F*or you—as it has for me—*A Closer Walk* can become not so much a book as a traveling companion, inviting us to share the rough places and the mountain tops with a fellow pilgrim, Catherine Marshall.

In personal journals kept during her most creative years as a writer, wife, and mother, Catherine recorded her encounters with such roadblocks as . . .

> Criticalness
> The Poverty Complex
> Resentment
> The Dry Period
> Chronic Worry
> Illness

Most importantly, she described also the "way through," which she found in the Scriptures.

Throughout her journey, the Bible was the traveler's staff on which Catherine leaned. From every page shines her commitment to daily Bible reading—and her faithfulness in applying what she read to that day's need.

If you're like me, two things will happen as you make this pilgrimage with Catherine. Your own Bible reading will become more focused, more personal, infinitely more exciting. And you will be nudged to start your own "travel diary."

This was exactly the impact on Len LeSourd, after reading the first of these entries. Before he married Catherine, Len recalls today, he had never thought of putting his own spiritual struggles down on paper—certainly not *as* he was living through them.

Shortly after their marriage in 1959, however, a moving van delivered Catherine's possessions to their first home. Len watched in husbandly amusement as Catherine hovered over one particular carton, clearly attaching more value to it than to the clothes, dishes, and pieces of furniture that arrived along with it.

"My journals," Catherine explained.

When Len still looked blank, she drew from the box a dark green volume, four inches by seven, with "Year Book 1934" stamped on the front. Catherine had filled the book with reactions to campus life that sophomore year at Agnes Scott College in Georgia. Three more green journals in the box covered the years through 1937.

There was a five-year diary for 1938–42, recording Catherine's soul-searching as she met and eventually married Peter Marshall. Journals of various shapes and colors detailed her years as Peter's wife: the birth of their son, her own serious illness, the loss of her young husband. As a widow in the 1950s, Catherine entered her spiritual questing in a succession of spiral-bound notebooks.

In growing astonishment, Len helped Catherine store the volumes on a shelf. What discipline and devotion these thousands of pages represented! Where would a person find the time?

Len soon found out. Early in the morning, Catherine would take from a dresser drawer a bright red hardcover *Daily Reminder*. No amount of fatigue from the previous day spent coralling three small stepchildren, no pleas from a sleepy husband, could keep her from this daily appointment-in-writing with God.

When Catherine finally allowed Len to read some current entries, he understood her commitment to the discipline. These were more than simply prayer records, more even than the joyful recording of answers. The act of writing itself was part of Catherine's relationship with God; it helped define her needs, focus her prayers, act out her trust.

Len soon joined her in this early morning time and began keeping a prayer record of his own. His approach was somewhat different from Catherine's. Each individual's format, style, and frequency will of course be unique. But right from the start Len discovered the secret that Catherine had known for years: *putting prayer issues on paper* eliminates the vagueness that so often diffuses personal devotions.

Her lively new family, Len confesses, sometimes made it difficult for Catherine to keep a set time of day for her journal. Before long she was making her entries at any and every moment when the dust settled.

But make them she did. For the next twenty-three years Catherine poured her hopes and dreams, questions asked of God and answers received from Him, into the growing collection of *Daily Reminders*. The current volume accompanied the LeSourds on trips, appeared in the laundry room and at the breakfast table. When Catherine's pen was stilled on March 18, 1983, these journals were her rich legacy to Len, with instructions to disclose the contents with wisdom and discretion.

A Closer Walk is the result.

It will remain only "someone else's story," however, unless you and I come along.

Elizabeth Sherrill

A Woman Called Catherine

The first time I saw Catherine was on December 1, 1955, at a luncheon in the Waldorf Astoria ballroom, where she was to receive the Salvation Army's 1955 Award for her contributions to "the spiritual life of her time." A poll that year had listed her as one of the ten most admired women in America. As the dignitaries, mostly men, filed onto the stage, Catherine, overshadowed by their physical presence, looked small, fragile, a bit overwhelmed.

I stared at her more closely. What was the secret of her sudden propulsion onto the national stage? Writing a best-selling religious book like *A Man Called Peter* couldn't do it alone. Watching her animated gestures as she conversed with master of ceremonies Walter Hoving (president of prestigious Tiffany's), noting her trim figure and stylish grooming, I decided that she was a phenomenon—a devout preacher's wife who had also won the admiration of nonbelievers.

How had she done it?

I listened carefully to Catherine's speech that described the "supernatural intervention of God" at Dunkirk during World War II. *Unlikely subject for a sophisticated New York City gathering*, I thought to myself. But she avoided religious clichés and held her audience. *A high voltage, spiritual woman, but with worldly wisdom*, I concluded.

Some months later Catherine was invited to speak at our Young Adult Group at the Marble Collegiate Church. There, I met her face to face for the first time, bathed for a short moment in her warm smile and controlled intensity. Yet, too, a shyness. In her speech I liked the practical way she applied biblical truths to her personal struggles.

As the editor of *Guideposts*, I wrote and asked her if she would write a piece for our small inspirational magazine, which had just reached a circulation of one hundred thousand. We talked over the phone about it. Her article "How You Can Receive God's Guidance" sparked eager reader response.

In 1957 I was functioning in the role of single parent, trying to rear three small children in Carmel, New York, while commuting over a hundred miles each day to work in New York City. It was a lonely, difficult time for me. One night I poured out my agony to God and laid before Him my need for a wife. Then, remembering Catherine's article on guidance, I took out a yellow pad, prepared to write down the names of any possible mates He might suggest.

Catherine's name popped into my mind.

It seemed almost ludicrous to tie Catherine Marshall to my plea for a partner. "That can't be your idea, Lord," I said, dismissing the thought.

Then I recalled Catherine's book *To Live Again* and the chapter that had entranced me—"They Walk in Wistfulness." In it she had given a poignant answer to a doctor's question about her emotional well-being. I reread the chapter and came to these words:

Do you really want to know what it feels like to be a widow? God made men and women for each other. Any other way of life is wrong; because it is abnormal. The last few months it's been like having a gnawing hunger, a haunting wistfulness at the center of life. I can forget about it for short periods—ignore it sometimes. But it's always there—always—and I'm afraid not even you can prescribe any pills that can cure it.

Elsewhere in that same chapter she wrote:

The need is to love and to be loved—that ultimate of life. Could I, and all those like me who walk the earth in wistfulness, find the way to trust God even for that?

Suddenly I knew that Catherine and I had something in common—loneliness. But so little else, it seemed. The whole idea was ridiculous.

I ticked off the reasons why.

First and foremost, who would want to follow the Peter and Catherine act? Their romance and marriage had entranced and stirred millions of people through her best-selling book; more millions had been captivated by the beautifully-done movie of *A Man Called Peter*.

Why would I want to marry a super-spiritual Christian celebrity? Who was almost five years older than I was?

Even more to the point, why would Catherine, at age forty-four, even supposing she should be attracted to me as an individual, want to marry a man who was rearing three small children?

Looked at logically, the idea of Catherine and me pairing up made little sense from any standpoint.

But . . . a voice deep inside reminded me, God is not bound by logic.

The least I could do was give it one good shot, I decided. If God was in it, I'd soon know. So I called Catherine, said *Guideposts* was looking for another article (true), and asked her if I could come to Washington and take her out for dinner. Requesting a dinner date should signal to her that I had more in mind than just an article.

She parried that proposal with the suggestion we make it lunch.

Strike one.

I took a plane from New York to Washington, rented a car, and drove to her town house just off Wisconsin Avenue. Catherine emerged, wearing a dark blue dress with white collar and cuffs;

silver earrings and a diamond brooch added distinct feminine touches. A lovely woman. Something quickened inside me.

Lunch at a Georgetown restaurant, however, was a letdown. Catherine was friendly and full of ideas for an article. Yet she neatly sidestepped all probing into her personal life. She was the consummate professional.

Strike two.

I drove her back to her town house, prepared to say goodbye and dismiss once and for all any thoughts of a personal relationship. Just before opening the car door, I happened to ask her a question regarding the Holy Spirit. It was as if I had found the combination to a valuable safe. An excited conversation followed that lasted for another half hour. Our two spirits had touched, then been ignited.

I was still at bat.

A week or so later I wrote to Catherine, asking if I could see her on the way back from an upcoming trip to California. With my plans a bit uncertain, I listed two possible dates, told her I would telephone beforehand. There wasn't time before I left for the coast for her to reply.

I did call Catherine from California—several times—but got no answer. The morning I was to fly from Los Angeles to Washington I called again—still nobody there. Then I came to a conclusion.

This is ridiculous. Catherine has no interest in me personally. I'm being silly to pursue this. Besides, she's not even home.

I changed my reservation from Washington to New York, flew home, and decided to forget the inner nudging that I should seek a romance with Catherine.

Strike three?

No, not quite. A foul tip, perhaps, that the catcher dropped. Several days later I received a letter from Catherine. "What happened to you?" she wrote. "You asked me to hold two dates. I did, but you never appeared. Or called. Is anything wrong?"

I was startled. Then stimulated. Catherine was obviously annoyed with me. But that was not all bad. In fact, it was many moons better than indifference.

In a spirit of contrition, I started to call Catherine, then stopped. A new, more direct approach was needed. *Drop your editorial front, Len; don't be defensive. Approach her man to woman.* In this vein, I wrote her a letter.

In *Meeting God At Every Turn* Catherine describes how she reacted to this change of style in me:

There was nothing of the professional editor about the letter I received from Len several days later. "I would like to know you better," he wrote. "How do you react to this idea? We'll choose a day, and then you write on your calendar three letters: F U N. I'll pick you up in the morning in my car and we'll just take off to the beach or the mountains or whatever."

The letter seemed deliberately couched to say, "If you're interested in pursuing this relationship, let's have a go at it. If not, then tell me so right now."

I liked the approach. We set a day in early August. Len telephoned the night before from a Washington motel to say that he would call for me at 10:30 the next morning. He was delighted when I suggested fixing a picnic lunch.

The next morning turned out to be a beautiful summer day, not too hot. When I met Len at my front door, I found myself slipping easily into the adventurous mood he had suggested. He put the picnic basket in the trunk of his car and we climbed into the front seat. "What do you prefer," he asked casually, "ocean or mountains?"

"I would choose the mountains," I replied.

"Which direction?"

I aimed him west toward Skyline Drive. As we drove along, I studied this fortyish editor sitting beside me. He was of medium height; dark hair beginning to gray; lithe, athletic figure. His gray-blue eyes were direct, warm, the lids often crinkling with humor. He was a good conversationalist, probing but relaxed. I relaxed, too. It was going to be a good day.

It was a good day, an amazing day. We talked for almost eleven hours straight. All my resistance to following the Peter Marshall romance, to her "super spirituality" and to our age difference dissolved in my astonishment over Catherine's physical warmth, simplicity, and earthy good humor. I was overwhelmed by the idea that God had perceived all this beforehand and had brought us together. During that one astounding day I fell in love with Catherine and began to think ahead toward marriage.

Catherine was slower in coming to this conclusion. She had to face more obstacles than I did. Mine had been mostly ego problems. Hers were substantive: taking on three small children, turning at a right angle to the life that had seemed to stretch so comfortably and predictably ahead of her—for which her dream house was even then being built. This home in Bethesda, Maryland, was to be ready for occupancy within a few months; Catherine had personally designed it to meet her career-woman needs.

That she was able to overcome these obstacles had to be the Lord's doing. For weeks she prayed, probed the Scriptures. And it was during this time of her intense searching that I began to find answers to the question I asked myself at that Salvation Army luncheon: What was the special charisma in this woman that had captured both believers and nonbelievers?

First, a down-to-earth quality that shunned subterfuge and embraced candor and openness. Ever since the success of *A Man Called Peter*, people had tried to put her on a spiritual pedestal. She resisted, refused to play the role of guru, insisted that she was a struggler for truth like everyone else.

Second, the spirit of adventure. She saw her faith in this light. Jesus was bold, imaginative, unpredictable. God's plan for each life was unique, did not fit any set formula. Both the death of her first husband and the rebirth of love interest in her life were totally unexpected, yet within the illimitable providence of the God she knew.

Third, vulnerability. Catherine was honest about her flaws, admitting her inadequacies in such areas as child rearing and certain social situations. Result: she learned from her mistakes. This quality also made her open to editorial advice in every book she wrote but one, and that one had to be abandoned.

I learned a lot about Catherine during this period, but the deeper secret of her success eluded me. That first date, rambling along the Skyline Drive, was in early August; we were married three months later on November 14, 1959.

Catherine had huge adjustments to make. She sold her Washington dream house to move to Chappaqua, forty miles north of New York City, so that I could continue to commute to my job at *Guideposts* in the city. My children—Linda, ten; Chester, six; Jeffrey, three—had been through a deeply unsettling two years, adjusting to a variety of housekeepers. They had mixed feelings toward moving into a new house, and especially toward "the new Mommie that Daddy's bringing home."

Catherine's son, Peter John, nineteen, was going through a period of rebellion at Yale. It's hard enough for a young person to cope with one celebrity parent, but Peter's father and mother both were "Christian personages." Peter told us one day with a straight face that when he graduated he wanted to be a beach boy at Virginia Beach.

Catherine and I had so many things to pray about that we began to rise an hour early each morning to read the Bible and seek answers together. Her current journal lay open beside us in these pre-dawn prayer times, recording our changing needs, His unchanging faithfulness.

Our togetherness as an author-editor team was tested early in our marriage. Catherine had already been working over a year researching her novel *Christy* and had written some fifty or so pages. One day she handed me her manuscript. Outside of her typist, I would be the first to read it. I started in with much anticipation.

Two hours later I faced a dilemma. The manuscript was wordy, short on action—yes, a bit dull. Conversation between mountain people was almost undecipherable because of Catherine's attempt to spell out the dialect as she had heard it. On the plus side, the characters were truly believable. Should I tell her the whole truth, or just center on the good things I saw in the manuscript?

Drawing a deep breath, I told her the truth as I saw it. She flinched for a moment, then stared at me with a new light in her eyes. "You're right on all counts," she admitted. "I felt it was weak, but hoped somehow I was too close to it to see its strengths." She sighed, "Let's start with the mountain dialect."

Thus did I pass the first crucial test of our professional relationship. If I had been less than honest, she would have eventually gotten the needed critique from Ed Kuhn, her McGraw-Hill editor. But she and I were full collaborators at work, now, as well as in the home.

As the years passed Catherine and I, as a writer-editor team, became more and more productive: between us we were responsible for nearly one hundred *Guideposts* articles and more than thirty published books. There were dozens of appearances as a speaking team; numerous courses conducted together on Christian subjects, highlighting the movement of the Holy Spirit.

I have one major regret about all this. We didn't take enough time to smell the flowers, to learn what it really means to take a vacation. We went from deadline to deadline, from crisis to crisis, dealing with what had to be done, forgetting too often to mark on our calendar those letters F U N. I feel deeply convicted about this, but the truth is that Catherine and I were workaholics.

During our twenty-three years of marriage I did discover the secrets behind her extraordinary gifts of communication. There were two. One came out through the dedication she showed in rearing my three young children—despite lungs that never operated at more than seventy-five percent normal capacity. It emerged as she struggled for the precise descriptive phrase in her writing, as she sought the exactly right color for a living room chair, in her search for tonal perfection in stereo music. She tried to lift the sights of her family and friends by planting dreams in our hearts of achievements that appeared beyond us.

This reach toward excellence was a prt of everything she did.

One example, I'll never forget. Catherine was preparing a dinner party for special friends. The day before, she asked me to drive her to Falls Church just outside of Washington—an hour's trip. "Some errands," she told me.

One errand, as it turned out. At a bakery, which sold a certain kind of macaroons. As we drove about Falls Church looking for this bakery in steamy weather, I fought off a growing irritation.

"Catherine, why are these macaroons so important to you?"

"I have a great recipe for grinding them into a wonderful sauce."

"A sauce! For what?"

"For the fruit compote I'm planning for dessert."

I turned and looked at her in amazement. "We're taking three hours out of a day, in terrible heat, to drive through miserable traffic to buy a bag of macaroons so people can pour a little sauce on their dessert!"

"That's right," she said. "It's the sauce that makes the dessert."

That was Catherine. She gave herself unreservedly to what she was doing, would settle for nothing but one hundred percent, was one-eyed in the scriptural sense whether it was writing, speaking, painting, decorating, preparing meals, building family life.

Her intensity spilled over into everything and I loved to watch it erupt. One night during the late 1960s, she strode into our bedroom where I was reading and began to pace the floor, face furious. "What's happened?" I asked in alarm.

She didn't answer right away, just stared at me with tears in her eyes. "I'm so upset I can hardly speak," she said.

"Over what?"

"Viet Nam? We shouldn't be fighting there. It's wrong . . . wrong . . . wrong. God will punish us for this."

I looked at her in amazement, surprised again at the emotion she poured into her convictions that could focus one moment on a child's poor study habits, the next on a war ten thousand miles away.

But there's another more profound reason for Catherine's extraordinary accomplishments. Her love of Jesus, expressed through a love affair with Scripture.

Bibles were scattered throughout our house . . . all editions, plus reference books and concordances. We often went to bed, turned out the light, and listened to a chapter of Scripture on tape. If she could have found a way to spread Bible passages on a slice of bread, Catherine would have devoured it.

When upset or under spiritual assault or in physical pain, Catherine would go to her office, kneel by her chair, and open her Bible to the fifty-third chapter of Isaiah, or the ninety-first Psalm, or the second chapter of Acts, or the eighth chapter of Romans. She would read, then pray, then read, then pray some more. She liked to pray with the Bible clutched in her hands; it gave her strength. She would rest her case on its promises. Catherine didn't read the Bible for solace or inspiration, but to have an encounter with the Lord. Sometimes she emerged from these sessions contrite, sometimes at peace, sometimes still in turmoil. I think these were the most intense moments of her life.

All of Catherine's Bibles are marked with underlinings; color shadings make certain passages almost leap out at you. Question marks and exclamation points dot page after page. A long comment will be scribbled at the top or bottom or along the side. Sometimes "Yes! Yes! Yes!" indicates Catherine's exuberant confirmation of a teaching.

Some of her happiest moments were when she was preparing a Bible study for one of our classes or for a writing project. She chose our king-size bed for this adventure, propping herself up with pillows, while Bibles, reference books, a thesaurus, a concordance, and yellow pads were spread all about her.

Catherine's passion for the Word permeated her whole life. It undergirded her writing. It formed a base for us as a married team in the making of family decisions. It provided substance to her counseling of people through the mail. I'm convinced it was also the basis for her inner vitality, her charisma, and the mantle of authority she wore with some reluctance.

Her grappling with the Word mostly took place in the early morning hours, as she fed her questions and discoveries into her journals. Material from these writings—her "closer walk" with her Lord—provides the content for this book. They cover our struggles in bringing together two broken homes, learning to relate to children and stepchildren—and later, our relationship to their spouses and our grandchildren.

What shines through Catherine's words is that Christian growth and adventuring never stop. The search for more of the truth is endlessly absorbing: the promises God holds out are worth every moment of struggle, the "walk" never arrives at some static, fixed point, but leads on into ever deeper intimacy with God.

A Closer Walk is the record of Catherine's encounters with the Lord of Scripture along the way, most appearing in print for the first time. The book is divided into six sections that move chronologically from our early life together as a family, through Christian creativity and growth, into spiritual warfare, to the final triumph of her death.

Years before Catherine died, we had talked about the probability that I would outlive her. Since I had worked so closely with her on every writing project, she knew we were in accord on one basic principle—no book of her writings would see print unless it measured up to her standard of excellence. The principal guardians of this standard were to be myself and her long-time friend and editorial advisor, Elizabeth Sherrill, whose talents we both admire so much and who has carefully gone over this manuscript.

May this book bless you who read it, and stimulate you to seek "a close walk" with Jesus.

Leonard E. LeSourd

Section One

The Home As His Classroom

*U*pon returning from our honeymoon in late 1959, Catherine and I confronted all the problems and adjustments involved in bringing together two broken homes. Catherine's greatest self-doubt centered around the responsibility for mothering three young stepchildren. (Her son, Peter John Marshall, was attending college.) Always a perfectionist, she felt she lacked the patient, accepting qualities of an ideal mother.

The early morning time when we sought answers together in the Bible became lifeblood for Catherine. Time and again from Scripture she drew insight and answers. Praying together in advance of the inevitable conflicts and confrontations solidified our marriage. It is hard to stay upset or angry at your mate when you are sitting up in bed side by side, holding hands, reading God's Word.

The setting for the following episodes was an eight-room house in Chappaqua, New York, a suburban community some forty miles north of New York City, where we lived for the first five years of our marriage.

LL

1.

A New Way to See Jesus

As Len and I begin our new life together, I'm enjoying a new way to read the New Testament—undoubtedly a way known to many Christians through the centuries but new to me: during my early morning devotions I'm reading the words as if Jesus were speaking directly to me.

At the time of my discovery, I was going through the Gospels consecutively, desiring above all else to get a vivid portrait of Jesus. And a portrait emerged all right, not so much what He looked like, as the characteristics of His person. I discovered in Him one who is totally alive—physically stalwart, emotionally sensitive. Humor, I definitely found. And grief—not for Himself, but for others' hurts and the tragic havoc that sin brings. And love, an amazing love that pours out of Him with never any effort to hide it or dam it up. Yet it is a love with steel in it.

Over and over I have come upon this steel—a note of stringency in Jesus' conversation and His way of dealing with people that, for the most part, seems alien to the teaching in our churches today. Never have I found a trace of coddling or compromising or self-protectiveness in Him.

For example, there was the Pharisee who asked Jesus to lunch at his house. Jesus accepted. But if there was anything pleasant about the conversation around the table, we were not told so in Luke's account. Indeed, centuries later, the words all but blister the page:

> But woe to you Pharisees! for you tithe mint and rue and every herb, and neglect justice and the love of God . . . you love the best seat in the synagogues and salutations in the market places . . . you are like graves which are not seen, and men walk over them without knowing it.
> Luke 11:42–44 RSV

It is clear that Christ chose to tell this particular man and his guests the simple, straightforward truth rather than keeping quiet or being socially correct. That takes courage of a rare sort, and Jesus must have known full well that it could lead only to a cross.

There is an unexpected dividend from reading the New Testament as if Jesus were speaking to me: when I look away from the problems in my new marriage to turn my full attention to Jesus, He proves Himself alive by concerning Himself with my life, family, and friends and talking to me about these matters morning after morning.

Last week, for example, as I read the twelfth chapter of Luke, it was as though Jesus were saying:

> Beware of pretending before the family to be something you are not, or to have attained spiritual values that you have not attained. This is hypocrisy. And nothing is more futile than trying to keep anything secret. There is nothing covered up among family members that is not going to be uncovered.

Later in the same chapter He seemed to tell me:

> You think that because members of your family believe in Me, all should be peaceful and serene. Not so. My presence

is not going to bring sweet peace and an easy time. On occasions, My thoughts and My way will bring severe discord. Do not be surprised when this happens. Realize that out of temporary disharmony—if it includes honest facing-up—comes growth for each member of the family and a further knitting together in Me.

This new way of letting Jesus speak to me may help me relate to a new neighbor too. She's asked me to assist in a community project in which I do not believe. I was puzzled as to how to handle the situation without hurting her feelings. In the eleventh chapter of Luke I heard:

You think that you do not want to tell your neighbor the truth because you do not want to hurt her. The real reason is that you want to protect yourself from her displeasure, or antagonism. It is wrong to keep quiet because you care more about her friendship (or anyone else's) than you care about her growth in Me. That is just another way of putting yourself first.

What are the results of these meditations? Increased honesty in our family has already led to more openness toward God in the lives of two of our children. I find that I'm less threatened by family arguments. So far I have not found the way or the courage to be honest with my friend. I ducked out of the project through an excuse.

But this I can say—the resurrected Jesus is a continual reality in my life. How can I ever find words to express the joy of His presence?

2.

Stepmothering

*T*his morning I am pondering my bizarre dream of last night to see if the Lord is telling me something through it:

In my dream a small animal emerged from a swelling near my shoulder. Looking more closely, I saw that the animal was wounded. "Those cuts will have to be sewn up," I thought, and then I woke up.

As I listened for God's word about the dream, I recalled how both Len and I have referred to the two small boys as being like bear cubs the way they roll and romp about the family room. Yesterday they broke a vase doing this. I have to admit that sometimes the children "get under my skin." Obviously the Lord is pointing out that changes need to be made in my attitude.

Part of what Len and I have to resolve comes down to the proper order he places on his new wife and his children by a previous marriage. All the stepmother tales in fairy stories and folklore tell us that we are confronting something basic and difficult here.

Len's emotions toward his flesh and blood are *so* stong that perhaps it is against nature for him to try to put his wife first. In his mind, he's done this, but his instinctive emotion is to defend and protect his children. Yet not to put the wife first is to risk disaster in the marriage.

I turned to the nineteenth chapter of Matthew:

For this reason a man shall leave his father and mother and be joined to his wife, and the two shall become one.

Matthew 19:5 RSV

Fortunately, Len and I can pray together and can talk over these problems. I was able to tell him about my dream without fearing he would use it against me. We are learning to admit our weaknesses to each other.

3.

Around the Dinner Table

After much experimentation, Len and I have settled on the evening meal as the ideal time and place for growing as a family. Mornings are too pressured, evenings too filled with school work, meetings, phone calls.

Being at the dinner table each night of the week is a command performance for Len and myself, Linda, Chester, and Jeff. No TV dinners in front of the tube. No dinners for our children at friends' houses except on weekends. A major effort by Len and me to keep our professional activities from interfering with this time.

The meal begins with grace, and the children do most of the praying, learning to overcome shyness until they can talk to God easily. Soon I hope we'll learn to say grace just as naturally when we eat as a family in restaurants.

Len and I try not to dominate the ensuing conversation, but draw out each child. "What did you learn today in school, Chester? . . . Which teacher do you like the most, Linda? . . . Who is your best friend, Jeff?"

Criticism in this setting, we learned, quenches fragile spirits; it's better saved for one-on-one encounters. After dinner there's a reading from Scripture and family prayer around the table. One of our main objectives is to show Jesus as so engaging a Person that we would all enjoy it if He joined us at the table.

"Jesus had a sense of humor," I mentioned once.

This seemed to surprise the children so the next night I came to the table armed with examples from Scripture. About the hypocrisy of the Pharisees He said, "You blind guides, straining out a gnat and swallowing a camel" (Matthew: 23:24 RSV).

This is the humor of exaggeration, I explained, pointing out that Jesus' humor was always for a purpose. Sometimes it was His bridge to an individual He would otherwise have had trouble reaching. Most often it was to illuminate a truth.

There was the occasion when Christ joshed His disciples about spiritual timidity: "Is a lamp brought in to be put under a bushel, or under a bed?" (Mark 4:21 RSV). The point He was making: "I need disciples who don't hide their light."

When the apostles became too impressed with the crowds Jesus was drawing, knowing full well that crowds gather for many reasons, Jesus commented dryly, "Wherever the carcass lies, there will the vultures gather" (Matthew 24:28 MOFFATT).

Once we reread the Gospels, watching for Christ's wit, we find it everywhere. "Can one blind man be guide to another blind man? Surely they will both fall into the ditch" (Luke 6:39 PHILLIPS). Or the comment made about the rich man who valued his possessions too much. "It is easier for a camel to go through the eye of a needle than for a rich man to enter the kingdom of God" (Luke 18:25 NEB).

To awaken people at every level of their being, Jesus used every weapon of language and communication to achieve His goals; most effective were the humorous thrust and banter about those who put on airs and think more highly of themselves than they should. Jesus sees all our incongruities and absurdities, and He laughs along with us.

As the result of these dinner table discussions, we're all finding that our spontaneity and fervor in worshiping Him increase. Our goal with the children: to help them see in Christ an incredible Man with that rare blend found nowhere else—purity, strength, compassion, and sparkling humor.

4.

Loving the Unlovely

As I look out over the bright greenery of our backyard this morning, I realize how hard it is for me to love people, even members of my own family, when I disapprove of their behavior. I know this is wrong, Lord Jesus, because You demonstrated time after time that it is possible, even necessary, to love people without judgment.

There was the woman taken in adultery and about to be stoned when You asked the mob surrounding her, "If any one of you is without sin, let him be the first to throw a stone at her." As You told her to go and sin no more, I could almost hear the caring quality of Your voice. Likewise with the woman You met at the well, the one who had had five husbands. Uncondemning love was in Your manner.

I have no trouble forgiving certain people, but recently I have seen that the forgiveness is not complete in Your eyes until I can love them too.

Ever since we moved here to Chappaqua, Marilyn[1] has been a thorn in my side. She's overbearing, overweight, and always overreacting. Her criticalness rubs me raw. Forgive her, sure. Love her, so hard for me. We can't manufacture love, can we? Until now I haven't even been willing for *You* to love Marilyn *through* me.

Queer about love . . . Is it a quality so of a piece that when we deliberately withhold it from any single human being, we deny love itself and, in the end, are rendered incapable of loving?

So last night, down on my knees in Len's presence, I confessed all this. With Len and You as witnesses, I'm giving You permission to give me the gift of love for Marilyn.

But this morning I'm not willing to stop there; I would like to be able to love people the way You love them. In Your Word this morning I came across some verses that give me a handle on how.

In 2 Peter 1, the apostle rejoices in the "precious and very great promises" by which we may be "partakers of the divine nature." Then he gives us a ladder of seven steps leading to this high goal:

1. To faith, add *virtue*. (v. 5)
2. To virtue, add *knowledge*. (v. 5)
3. To knowledge, add *self-control*. (v. 6)
4. To self-control, add *steadfastness*. (v. 6)
5. To steadfastness, add *godliness*. (v. 6)
6. To godliness, add *brotherly affection*. (v. 7)
7. To brotherly affection will then be added, *love*. (v. 7)

"For if these things are yours and abound," Peter concludes, "they keep you from being ineffective or unfruitful in the knowledge of our Lord Jesus Christ" (v. 8, RSV).

I want to climb that ladder, Lord, to be able to know You and love You more than ever before.

[1]Not her real name.

324

5.

Seeking Excellence

I've been troubled about Linda's schoolwork. Considering her high IQ she's not doing anything like her best. Last night at the dinner table I told her about one of my favorite Bible verses, which appears no less than three times in the Old Testament: He maketh my feet like hinds' feet, and setteth me upon my high places (Psalm 18:32–33, 2 Samuel 22:33–34, and Habakkuk 3:19 KJV).

"What in the world does that mean?" she asked, with a frown on her freckled face.

To answer, I told her about a friend of mine. . . .

When I was six years old, this family friend whom we called "Auntie Chamberlain" purchased the book *Hiawatha* for me. But this was no ordinary copy. It had handcut paper, beautiful illustrations, a pronouncing vocabulary for difficult Indian names, even a section for handicraft projects.

She had searched all over town to find it. And this was so typical of Auntie Chamberlain—a woman who gave herself totally to life. Auntie Chamberlain taught me the importance of doing every task with my whole heart. Soon I discovered that family games—like Parcheesi—were the most fun when played with total enthusiasm and concentration. Piano lessons took on added luster when I not only learned to read a piece of music, but also memorized it. School assignments were more fun when I did more than the minimum required.

I found that something more important than good grades came from this approach: a deep inner satisfaction, a glow, a happiness. And conversely, I discovered that when I undertook any project halfheartedly, the result was usually half successful.

Later on, while living in Washington, I saw to my delight this "Auntie Chamberlain quality" in another individual—Dr. Lida Earhart. She, too, gave all of herself to whatever task she undertook and had been the first woman to attain the rank of full professor at Columbia University. After retiring, she came to Washington to live and regularly attended services at our New York Avenue Presbyterian Church.

One day someone asked Miss Earhart to give a talk on the Book of Job at the monthly meeting of the church women's association. This was probably a tossed-off invitation, with the usual kind of talk expected. But the talk turned out to be far from usual. For two months Miss Earhart had studied the Book of Job. She had researched the archeological features of the time of Job and his contemporaries. She had read biblical scholars' analyses of the book. She had pondered deeply the book's theme: the problem of evil in our world. The result was one of the most memorable presentations I ever have heard.

Even more remarkable, she had done all that work for an ordinary church meeting. Nothing extraordinary had been asked or expected. Yet she knew *the secret of hinds' feet*.

"What is the secret?" Linda asked.

"The rear feet of the female red deer, known also as the *hind*," I said, "step in precisely the same spot where the front feet have just been. Every motion of the hind is followed through with this same single-focused consistency, making it the most sure-footed of all mountain animals."

As the feet of the female deer are to the mountains, I told her, so is the mind of man to the heights of life. "Ask yourself—how many things have I done with single-minded devotion, nothing held back?"

"Not many," she admitted.

"It's not easy in our modern world," I agreed, "to make our lives like hinds' feet. Too much today is done with minimal effort. This attitude can begin with school work done sloppily—but there's no joy in halfhearted efforts."

Linda listened with real interest to this biblical simile. Lord, make it come alive in her life!

6.

The Contagion of Joy

*A*s I absorb the Gospels this September morning, I'm seeing Jesus so clearly as a vital young Man who loved life and was filled with joy.

I'm influenced no doubt by my experience last month [August 1961] at a conference of The Fellowship of Christian Athletes in Estes Park, Colorado, where I spoke to the wives of the coaches and leaders. I never had seen so much muscle and maleness packed into one area. During the entire week there was a virile, vibrant atmosphere. And who was the central figure? Jesus Christ!

Of primary interest to me was the involvement of my son Peter, who had graduated from Yale the previous June. Peter admitted his purpose in coming to the conference was to get close to nationally known athletes. "I'm not interested in hearing any Sunday school stories," He told Len and me. During high school and college to my great dismay he had rejected his Christian heritage.

Instead of Sunday school stories, Peter heard some of the biggest names in sports unashamedly tell how they had found joy in the Christian faith. From the beginning my son was swept along in the excitement of young men singing, shouting, laughing, competing, and praying together. By the fourth day he was literally catapulted into making a personal commitment of his life to Jesus Christ as Savior and Lord.

"It is an awesome thing when you meet Jesus for the first time," he told me later. Gone was his bored, know-it-all attitude, in its place a new aliveness. A decision to enter Princeton Theological Seminary followed a few weeks later.

It makes me eager to take a fresh look at the qualities of the One who has such an attraction for young people—in His time and ours. The Gospel picture of Him is of a joyous man with a buoyant zest for life. The New Testament in one place describes Him as "anointed . . . with the oil of gladness" (Hebrews 1:9 KJV).

As I read through the Gospels, I see that Jesus had quite a bit to say about joy. We are *not* invited to a relationship that will take away our fun but asked to "enter into the joy of [our] Lord" (Matthew 25:21 KJV). The purpose of His coming to earth, Jesus said, was in order that our *joy might be full!* (John 15:11 KJV).

No wonder the young in the full tide of life adored Him and left everything to be with Him! And the young today still respond to the lure of adventure and the giving of their all to a cause. That is why the stringency and the sacrifice called for by movements like the Peace Corps have so much appeal.

I can see that Jesus drew men and women into the Kingdom by promising them two things: first, trouble—hardship, danger; and second, joy. But what curious alchemy is this that He can make even danger and hardship seem joyous? He understands things about human nature that we grasp only dimly; few of us are really challenged by the promise of soft living, by an emphasis on me-first, or by a life of easy compromise.

Christ still asks for one's total surrender and then promises His gift of full, overflowing joy. It was that Spirit of joy that I felt in the young people at Estes Park. It was this Spirit that captured my son and turned his life around.

7.

Quenching a Child's Spirit

*A*fter three years of marriage, Len and I are groping for wisdom in relating to each of our children. Gradually we have become aware that family life is God's classroom for shaping us into the kind of people He wants us to be.

God often speaks to me through dreams. Last night, for example, I dreamed I was talking to Jeff, our irrepressible six-year-old. In my right hand was a bottle of what looked like baby aspirin. Jeff and I were having one of our typical confrontations. In the dream, however, I lost my temper and somehow the bottle hit one of his eyes. He cried and to my alarm I saw on my hand fluid from his eye.

The next scene was of Len carrying Jeff into our bedroom, where I was standing by the window. Sitting on his father's knee, Jeff took his forefinger and ran it around his eye socket. I looked and—to my horror—there was no eye there.

"Let's get him to an eye doctor fast!" I urged.

Len's stance was his usual patient tolerance, though now full of sadness. "It's too late. There's no eye there."

I was overcome with grief—then, to my great relief, I woke up.

This morning when I asked the Lord if He was telling me something through this dream, I was led to one of Jesus' teachings in the Sermon on the Mount.

> The eye is the lamp of the body. So, if your eye is sound, your whole body will be full of light.
>
> Matthew 6:22 RSV

Then came His gentle but firm correction to me. I had been putting out, quenching, some of Jeff's light by the way I had been treating him.

Convicted of my sin, I confessed immediately the specific ways I had been quenching the light in Jeff: (1) Through losing my temper (quite inexcusable); (2) dominating him because I'm bigger; (3) not demonstrating enough love for Jeff.

I asked for and received God's forgiveness for these sins. Then I sought out Jeff, hugged him, and asked his forgiveness.

"That's okay, Mom," he said with a grin. Pause. "Can I have Rodney over for lunch today?"

Several weeks later: I dreamed again last night about Jeff. This time he and Chester were tumbling about on the back porch. Suddenly Jeff lost his balance and fell down the steps, his head striking the pavement below.

The next picture was of Jeff being carried off on a stretcher covered with blankets neatly tucked in, with his head heavily bandaged. And in my dream, suddenly I realized how much *I loved this little guy.*

8.

Malnutrition of the Spirit

The problems that arise in second marriages are more than I could ever have imagined. Being a new mother to three young children is exhausting, leaving little time for creative writing. There are times when life seems to go gray; I have no zest for anything.

When this happened last week I recognized my problem: *malnutriton of the spirit.*

It was Carol, my friend from California, who had made me aware months ago that spiritual undernourishment can be quite as real as physical starvation. When I first met Carol, it was obvious that she had problems, but not the usual ones. She had a happy marriage; no major troubles with her three children; everything fine economically; no health difficulties.

But she felt tired all the time from the daily routine.

"Nothing is much fun anymore," she had said. "I have so little energy that no undertaking seems worth attempting. What's wrong with me?"

An hour and much talk later, I had a sudden inspiration: could it be that Carol's inner spirit was starving to death?

Taking up my Bible, I turned to the Old Testament story of Daniel. I read to her about how Daniel was in exile in the king's palace. "His windows being open in his chamber toward Jerusalem, he kneeled upon his knees three times a day, and prayed, and gave thanks before his God, as he did aforetime" (Daniel 6:10 KJV).

"We have three meals a day." I suggested. "Perhaps we need spiritual food three times a day too."

"But what *is* spiritual food? And how do you take it?" Carol asked.

"Jesus said that His words are spirit and life indeed. He used metaphor upon metaphor to tell us that His Spirit is our life substance. He described himself as 'living water' and 'the bread of life.' Meeting Him in Scripture is like an intravenous feeding from His Spirit to our spirit," I replied.

"So," I challenged Carol, "would you be willing to try spiritual food in the form of life-giving Bible verses three times a day for one month?"

At a Christian bookstore Carol found an "Inspiration Box" of paper capsules, each containing a verse of Scripture. They were to be taken daily as spiritual vitamins. (This word "vitamin" means "life substance.")

Later, with another spiritually undernourished friend, we decided that an additional blessing came when we took the time ourselves to dig through Scripture and put together a homemade card file of spiritual vitamins.

So last week I produced a "Vitamin Box" of dozens of favorite passages for my new family. I used a concordance and looked up words such as *strength, food, bread, water, hunger,* and *thirst.* Other cards were culled from Christ's own words. Now before blessing the food at each meal, we pass the box, and one of the children chooses a card to read aloud. The nourishment is most effective when the life-giving words of Scripture are memorized and so become the permanent possessions of mind and heart.

But they that wait upon the Lord shall renew their strength; they shall mount up with wings as eagles; they shall run, and not be weary; and they shall walk, and not faint.

Isaiah 40:31 KJV

For the Lord disciplines the man he loves. . . . So up with your listless hands! Strengthen your weak knees! And make straight paths for your feet.

Hebrews 12:6, 12–13, MOFFATT

Oh that men would praise the Lord for his goodness, and for his wonderful works to the children of men! For he satisfieth the longing soul, and filleth the hungry soul with goodness.

Psalm 107:8–9 KJV

. . . My grace is sufficient for thee: for my strength is made perfect in weakness.

2 Corinthians 12:9 KJV

By saturating my mind with these and other verses, I find that the grayness lifts, the spirit is infused with spiritual food, and I am ready to meet any difficulty that comes along.

9.

Early Morning Time

Awake my soul, and with the sun
Thy daily stage of duty run;
Shake off dull sloth, and joyful rise
To pay the morning sacrifice!

Shine on me, Lord, new life impart,
Fresh ardors kindle in my heart;
One ray of Thine all-quickening light
Dispels the clouds and dark of night.
Thomas Ken (1637–1711)

As Len and I arise at 6:00 A.M. this morning, I find the above verses help move me from "dull sloth" to "fresh ardors." Then in Psalm 5, I read:

Give ear to my words, O Lord, consider my meditation. Hearken unto the voice of my cry. . . . My voice shalt thou hear in the morning, O Lord; in the morning will I direct my prayer unto thee, and will look up.

Psalm 5:1–3 KJV

God, who created heaven and earth, will hear *my* voice? The King of the universe will consider *my* meditation? Oh, thank You, Lord, for the undreamed-of opportunity of this audience with the King! Anyone who has a favor to ask of an earthly monarch has no chance of having his request granted until he makes his wish known to the king. That *could* be second-hand—generally is, in protocol-bound human societies. What a privilege to have an audience in person! Yet this is the status and the honor You allow each of us, Lord.

Even more privileged is he so in favor with the King that he is allowed as long as he wishes to be with the One he loves, listen to Him, watch Him, bask in His presence. In earthly courts, such a one would be considered favored indeed, and the courts we're invited to enter are of an "infinite majesty." Just to say "Thank You" seems inadequate. This morning I make it a welling, swelling gratitude!

10.

Subject One to Another

T*his* week I've been focusing my thoughts and prayers on the fifth chapter of Ephesians.

Wives be subject—be submissive and adapt yourselves—to your own husbands as [a service] to the Lord. For the husband is head of the wife as Christ is the Head of the church. . . . As the church is subject to Christ, so let wives also be subject in everything to their husbands.

Ephesians 5:22–24 AMPLIFIED

Like many women, I've struggled with conflicting emotions over the current emphasis on "submission." Especially when I hear of a case, as I did last week, of a husband who used this passage in Ephesians to intimidate his wife and force her to accept and condone his own adultery with another woman. An extreme situation, of course, but one of many instances where the basic truth of Scripture is violated or distorted when taken out of context.

For example, the admonition "Wives, submit to your husbands" is coupled in Ephesians with, "Husbands, love your wives, as Christ loved the church and gave Himself up for her" (v. 25). Yet this complementary verse is frequently overlooked.

This week's Bible focus was promoted by a letter:

"I am having a mighty struggle with my role as a Christian wife," the woman wrote. "Something inside of me literally rebels at the words—obey, submit, subject! At times I have considered the apostle Paul to be a male chauvinist. Also, I can't believe that my loving heavenly Father, as I personally know Him, would want me to be as completely and blindly submissive as these Scriptures seem to indicate.

"I realize my resentment and selfishness is sin, yet when I try to submit to my husband, I end up feeling angry and hypocritical. Or like a spiritless dumb animal. How do I understand and accept this teaching?"

To answer this question, I've taken time to review my own relationship as a wife to Len, study the Ephesians chapter, then talk and pray some more with my husband.

When we were first married, Len suggested that I assume spirtual responsibility for our home. This seemed wrong to me. It went against a number of scriptural teachings. Also I doubted that Len's two sons would respond to this; they would perhaps see religion as "a woman's thing." In fact, Chester, the elder son, who is gifted in all sports, sees God the Father primarily through his own athletic father. Once Len and I began to search the Bible together in the early mornings, he saw for himself that he should take spiritual leadership of our home and did so.

But there's more. As we study Ephesians 5, we're beginning to believe that this may be one of the most misinterpreted chapters in the New Testament. Nor do we believe that St. Paul was any kind of male chauvinist.

Much light is shed when we investigate the background against which Paul was teaching. He had come out of Judaism, a patriarchal system where women were considered their husbands' property. Still, Jewish women were better off than most. In the other countries around the Mediterranean basin of Paul's day, wives had no political or social status whatever, were allowed no education, no activity beyond the home. In the Greek world, for instance, groups of single young women were trained to provide the social and sex life of Greek husbands whose wives stayed at home, did the menial tasks, and cared for the children.

In Ephesians, chapters four through six, Paul is speaking out against this immoral system and is trying to teach new Ephesian Christians how they should relate to one another. It is only against this pagan backdrop that we can see how revolutionary Paul's "Husbands, love your wives" was! Not only was Paul not against women, he, like his Master before him, was teaching that women are equally children of the Father and as such are to be respected and beloved. At that time this was a radically new approach to women.

In the end we're discovering that the hub upon which the Ephesian "submission" passages turn is the statement that introduces them: "Be subject to one another out of reverence for Christ" (Ephesians 5:21 AMPLIFIED). This is the irreducible minimum of Paul's instructions to all Christians—male or female.

What is coming out of Len's and my seeking prayers on this subject can be described as a triangle of authority more than a pecking order. God is at the apex of the triangle; the husband and wife are equally positioned at the lower corners. Thus both mates are equal in His sight, equally beloved by Him, equally committed to each other and to Him.

We're finding "Be subject to one another out of reverence for Christ" to be intensely practical. It means a spirit of mutual respect, a willingness to listen. It means giving—and sometimes giving in—on the part of both of us, since sometimes God gives His direction through Len, at other times through me. Most importantly, at the peak of the triangle God Himself has to be acknowledged as the final Authority in the home.

In thinking further about the subject this morning, I realize that I want for our home everything in that Ephesians chapter. I want Len to be its spiritual head. I want him to be a husband whom I can love and trust and submit to in the biblical sense. I want him to love me as Jesus loves the Church, to love me as he would love his own body. I also want to "respect, reverence, honor, love, and esteem him exceedingly."

Section Two

Adventuresome Living

*T*ravel is often called "the door to adventure." Catherine and I had our share of this kind of excitement. During the early years of our marriage we visited Uganda, Kenya, the Holy Land, drove through central Europe, painted with oils on the beaches of Bora Bora and Moorea in the South Pacific, shared stories with missionaries in such remote places as Tonga, Fiji, and Tahiti, ministered to groups in Samoa and Australia.

Yet the real adventure for us was always spiritual: testing scriptural truths, exploring different kinds of prayer, sharing in fellowship groups, teaching together from the Bible. The base for the first five years of our marriage was Chappaqua, New York. When Northern winters caused increasing congestion of Catherine's lungs, we moved to Boynton Beach, Florida, in November 1964.

The first of our children to marry was Peter, who met Edith Wallis at Princeton Theological Seminary. They were married on May 29, 1966, and their daugther, Mary Elizabeth Marshall, was born on March 1, 1969.

During these years life was tumultuous, demanding, often exhausting. With God in charge of our lives, there was the never-ending suspense of wondering what He had in store for us next.

LL

1.

The Prayer of Agreement

I am impressed this morning with the power in a Scripture verse about prayer.

When my son Peter accepted an invitation to give a speech in Kansas City, I had a telephone call from a dentist in that city who was on the sponsoring committee. This man asked me to pray for the meeting and that Peter's message would be God's topic for this particular audience at this particular time.

The dentist and I decided to claim the promise of Jesus in Matthew 18:19–20 RSV:

> "If two of you agree on earth about anything they ask, it will be done for them by my Father in heaven. For where two or three are gathered in my name, there am I in the midst of them."

In heartfelt accord, my caller and I asked God that His word only be spoken at the upcoming gathering.

Peter's talk was in the newly decorated ballroom of the largest hotel in Kansas City, with six hundred people in attendance. The audience were both Christians and non-Christians, a cross section of civic Kansas City.

Len and I learned later that just before Peter was to speak a black man with a powerful voice sang, "There Is a Balm in Gilead." This got to everyone, especially Peter.

On the table beside him were the notes of the prepared speech, which he had in fact planned to use. After hearing the song, he shoved aside his papers, rose, and picked up the theme of the song for his talk. For one hour and fifteen minutes he laid out before that Kansas City audience Jesus Christ as *the* "balm in Gilead."

The room was so quiet (according to the dentist) that not even the usual coughing and respiratory upheavels were in evidence. A doctor friend, not particularly religious, who was there as the guest of the dentist, told him afterwards, "I've never witnessed or heard anything like it. It was so quiet that I was almost afraid to breathe."

I asked the dentist, "But, speaking that long extemporaneously, didn't Peter ramble or repeat himself?"

"Not once," he answered. "However you tie it, Catherine, when anyone can hold six hundred people *that* attentive for an hour and a quarter—that had to be God."

What neither Peter nor the dentist knows is that "There Is a Balm in Gilead" was one of the favorite songs of Peter's father. He had sung it in a quartet during his seminary days. He sometimes sang it as a duet in Westminster Church in Atlanta. When he was pastor of the New York Avenue Church in Washington, it was one of the favorite numbers of Charlie Beaschler's great massed choirs. Now, through the singer in Kansas City, God has used it again to bring His message to a hurting world.

2.

Happiness Is . . .

As I've been pondering the subject of happiness this morning—an elusive and seemingly unattainable state for so many—I am led to these words of Jesus:

If any man would come after me, let him deny himself and take up his cross and follow me. For whoever would save his life will lose it, and whoever loses his life for my sake will find it.

Matthew 16:24–25 RSV

I believe the secret of happiness lies imbedded in those words, painful though they appear to be. How else explain radiant people like the young man who sat in our living room and described how his six-year-old boy had died in his arms from leukemia. Today this man finds fulfillment in giving himself totally to helping college students. Or the woman I visited recently whose husband had turned out to be a homosexual and demanded a divorce. Some years later, this woman also lost her eyesight. Yet she is a cheerful, loving person, fully self-supporting.

You might say that such people almost have a right to be unhappy. That they are not, lies in the way they spend themselves for others.

I have observed that when any of us embarks on the pursuit of happiness for ourselves, it eludes us. Often I've asked myself why. It must be because happiness comes to us only as a dividend. When we become absorbed in something demanding and worthwhile above and beyond ourselves, happiness seems to be there as a by-product of the self-giving.

That should not be a startling truth, yet I'm surprised at how few people understand and accept it. Have we made a god of happiness? Have we been brainwashed by ads assuring us "Happiness is . . ."—usually a big, shiny, new gadget?

Perhaps our national preoccupation with happines dates from these words in the Declaration of Independence:

> . . . All men are . . . endowed by their Creator with certain unalienable rights, [and] among these are life, liberty and *the pursuit of happiness* [italics added].

Now, I have always had immense admiration for Thomas Jefferson, author of these words. And until recently I never questioned them. But (and my apologies to you, Mr. Jefferson) I do question them as I see more and more people interpret "the pursuit of happiness" as a license to grab for power or money or physical pleasure.

The truth, as I see it, is that not one of us has "an unalienable right" to anything, not even to life itself. We did nothing to bring about our birth, and we are dependent for the next breath we draw on the grace of God. How arrogant and ungrateful we must seem to our Creator when we demand our "rights."

I think of Mary and Harold Brinig—a remarkable couple who found the true basis of happiness some years ago. Having moved to Chicago where they had no friends, they became irritable with each other and unhappy. While seeking help from the Bible one day, they were struck by these words of Jesus:

> You did not choose me, but I chose you and appointed you that you should go and-bear fruit and that your fruit should abide . . .
>
> John 15:16 RSV

348

Somehow that passage was like light penetrating their darkness: much of their unhappiness, they realized, was caused by self-centeredness. Could Jesus be choosing them for service? But practically speaking, how could this happen in a big city like Chicago?

The first person they encountered after this revelation was the waitress who served them in a nearby restaurant. She apologized for giving slow service, admitted she was new in the city and miserable. They invited her to visit them in their apartment after work.

"You did not choose me, but I chose you. . . ." A widower in the next apartment was the second person they befriended. Soon a dozen people were meeting together once a week for conversation and prayer.

Out of these meetings grew a project called Adventures in Friendship. Before long, scores of people were involved in seeking the lonely and the shut-ins throughout the whole area. Needless to say, Mary and Harold Brinig had become so absorbed in the needs of others that their own life was enriched beyond anything I can describe. Happiness found them.

This Chicago experience prepared the Brinigs for a thirty-five-year team ministry at the Marble Collegiate Church in New York City that resulted in spiritually rejuvenated lives for thousands of people, including my husband, Len.

3.

The Power of *Let*

While reading a manuscript by Mrs. John Peters (wife of the founder of World Neighbors), I was intrigued by one episode in particular. Losing his footing in the bathroom, her husband struck his head on the ceramic soap dish. One ear was almost severed and he was bleeding profusely when Mrs. Peters heard his cries and came to his aid.

Despite her shock at the sight of so much blood, the Spirit took over and enabled her to speak with authority. She heard herself saying, "Let the bleeding stop immediately. Let there be no infection. Let there be no pain. Let there be no scarring."

Mrs. Peters made no comment on the experience other than to report that, gloriously, the bleeding stopped. There was no infection. Almost no pain. No scars. But something about these "Lets" stuck like glue to my mind.

I realized that it was the same word God had used in creating our world. "*Let* there be light," . . . and so on.

Jesus to His disciples:

Let your light so shine before men, that they may see your good works, and glorify your Father which is in heaven.
                                                    Matthew 5:16 KJV

And if the house is worthy, *let* your peace come upon it; but if it is not worthy, *let* your peace return to you.
                                                    Matthew 10:13 RSV

Paul used it too:

Let this mind be in you, which was also in Christ Jesus.
                                                    Philippians 2:5 KJV

What, I wondered, is the significance of this word for us?

Author Harold Hill gave me the missing insight. "'Let' is a word of tremendous faith with volumes of meaning poured into it," he told me. "It *assumes* the total love and good will of the Father. It *assumes* that heaven is crammed with good gifts that the Father desires to give His children. The 'let' is saying, 'Father, I give to You permission to do so-and-so for us down here on earth. I allow it.'"

It also assumes an almost preposterous humility on God's part—that He should wait for our permission to bestow wonderful gifts on us! How amazing!

Worlds of meaning behind this three-letter world . . . *let*.

4.

The Poverty Complex

I'm going through one of those "money anxiety" periods this morning, Lord, so I know I've taken my eyes off You and placed them squarely on worldly matters.

The sad thing is that I know better. Only the other day I was expressing my incredulity over a famous financier who committed suicide when his wealth diminished from fifty million to ten million. It seemed inconceivable that a man could feel desperate about money when he still possessed ten million dollars. Wealth, clearly, is a matter of attitude.

So once again I go through the process of replacing fear with faith in connection with Your provision.

First, I need to remind myself that You control all of earth's material resources. Most of us do not really believe this. Yet from cover to cover the Bible declares it:

The earth is the Lord's and the fulness thereof. . . .
                                                      Psalm 24:1 KJV

> But my God shall supply all your need according to his riches. . . .
>
> Phillippians 4:19 KJV

If I truly believe that I am a child of a King, then my fear will disappear. Worrying would be the sure sign that I did not believe God's ownership of earth's resources. To think myself a pauper is to deny either the King's riches or my being His beloved child.

Second, I can think about Mary Welch. Born in a log cabin on a run-down farm in west Texas, even after she became a Christian she found it difficult to shed her poverty complex. A turning point for her came when she was in St. Paul, Minnesota, on a speaking trip as the guest of a wealthy woman. As she was preparing to take a bath before dinner, she drew her customary three inches of water in the tub.

Her hostess happened to look into the tub. "You're not intending to take a bath in that tiny amount of water?"

"Why not? That's all I ever use."

"This isn't Texas, Mary," her hostess chided her. "There's no shortage of water here. Minnesota has ten *thousand* lakes."

Mary realized that she had just gotten a sharp insight about herself. She watched the water nearly fill the tub. Then she lathered herself with soap—marveling at all she was wasting. That night before she went to sleep she asked God to register His Perfect Adequacy on her subconscious and clear out all her deep-rooted beliefs in shortages.

Soon after, Mary realized that even her skinny, ninety-pound body looked like a shortage of woman. She took a piece of soft soap and, in a full-length mirror, drew an outline of her ideal measurements. Then she packed most of her size-three dresses to send to an orphanage.

Her mother caught her at the packing and didn't approve at all. "You've never had much. You worked too hard to get those clothes to give them away. Besides, suppose you *don't* gain weight?"

But Mary realized that she could not pray for one thing and make provisions for another. Furthermore, she had discovered what she calls the "law of the Golden Initiative": the secret of receiving is to give—even out of poverty. In fact, the more sunk we are in visions of lack, the greater need we have to start giving.

So the dresses went off to the orphanage. "And within that year," Mary reports, "I measured exactly what I had pictured and prepared for—size nine."

The third thing I'm to do is to remind myself of that moment of decision I faced some weeks after Peter Marshall's death in 1949. The trustees of his church gave me a bleak financial report of how little insurance money there was. They advised me to take a full-time job to support Peter John and myself.

You, Lord, encouraged me to write, with the promise that if I trusted You, all my needs would be met. I took Your challenge and how greatly have You blessed me! Thank you, Lord. Praise You! Forgive me for my lack of faith.

5.

Forward, Like Gideon!

*T*his morning, Len and I dragged ourselves out of bed at 6:00 A.M. for our morning prayer time. After the long drive from Evergreen Farm in Virginia to southern Florida, I'm exhausted. Our suitcases are still packed. But there's a meeting of our church committee on Christian education this afternoon that Len insists we attend.

I'm fighting off resentment as well as fatigue. I want to get back to my writing. Meetings drain me. Bore me. Len wants us to teach a class on the Holy Spirit this winter to a group that is resistant to what is happening across the country today, frightened by the excesses of some of the "Jesus people," by speaking in tongues and so on. Len looks at this class as an adventure. I'm full of doubts as to whether we can handle it.

Is it coincidence that I have been reading the Book of Judges? Today it was the story of Gideon. Such fascinating reading! So jam-packed full of truths and insights!

For instance, Gideon certainly had no idea that he was anyone special in God's sight or in man's. He lived at a low point in

Israel's history when the people had forsaken Jehovah and were worshiping idols.

Yet God sent an angel to Gideon with the message, "The Lord is with you, you mighty man of [fearless] courage" (Judges 6:12 AMPLIFIED).

There's immense humor in this greeting. For the "mighty man of courage" was at that moment hiding out in a winepress for fear of the Midianites.

And his reaction to the angel's appearance was doubt and confusion. "If the Lord is with us, why is all this befallen us?" (v. 13).

The answer was a strange one. The angel did not rebuke Gideon for answering back with unbelief. Instead, he repeated, "Go in this your might, and you shall save Israel from the hand of Midian. Have I not sent you?" (v. 14).

Again Gideon sounds like anything but a hero. He replies, in effect, "Who, me? Save Israel? Surely you must be kidding. My clan is the poorest in Israel and I'm the least in my father's house, the youngest son, the one everyone picks on."

The Lord's answer is, "Surely, I will be with you, and you shall smite the Midianites as one man" (v. 16).

Only after the angel disappears does Gideon seem to realize that he has actually been in the presence of an angel. His reaction to this, characteristically, is downbeat all the way. He might have been thrilled and begun praising God. Instead, he says, "Alas, O Lord God! For now I have seen the Angel of the Lord face to face!" (v. 22).

Never on God's side, however, is there anything but patient understanding of Gideon's doubt and unbelief. "Peace be to you; do not fear, you shall not die" (v. 23).

Then begins a series of clear-cut instructions from the Lord. First, Gideon is to tear down two idols.

The "mighty man of courage" obeys, but does it at night because he's so scared of his own clan, even of his father and brothers.

In fact, his father sticks up for him before the townspeople.

But Gideon is full of doubt still. Only after elaborate further signs and reassurances from Jehovah will he consent to take command of the Israelite forces. And then the point of the story becomes clear: it is God's strength and His alone that delivers us.

For God persuades Gideon to reduce his warriors from 22,000 to 300. And it is this small army that routs the Midianites.

The clear message for today that I receive from this reading is that God is going to show me that I can rely on Him alone—for physical strength as for every other need. So thank You, Lord, for the meeting I will go to this afternoon, hence no nap today. Thank You for the challenge of teaching a class on the Holy Spirit. Full speed ahead, O Gideon!

6.

Small Needs

*A*fter the Bible study I gave last week on praying for all our needs, no matter how small, one woman took sharp issue with me.

"Asking for small things is being selfish," she remonstrated, "and self-centered prayers just aren't answered. I think we should pray only about *spiritual* needs. Besides, the God who runs the universe can't be bothered with individual wishes."

I could only reply that this was not Jesus' viewpoint as presented in the Gospels: both by teaching and by action He impressed upon us that no need is too trivial for His attention.

I've combed Scripture for examples and there are many, such as: The wine needed at a wedding feast (John 2:1–11); a dying sparrow (Matthew 10:29); a lost lamb (Luke 15:3–7).

These vignettes, scattered through the Gospels like little patches of gold dust, say to us, "No creaturely need is outside the scope of prayer."

As if to emphasize the same thought, the apostle Paul adds:

Do not fret or have any anxiety about anything, but in every circumstance and in everything by prayer and petition [definite requests] with thanksgiving continue to make your wants known to God.

Philippians 4:6 AMPLIFIED

Now obviously not all our human wants are genuine needs. Moreover, we are often so selfish and shortsighted that the granting of some wants would not be good for us. But I believe that Scripture invites us to talk over all our concerns and dreams with our Father, then leave the outcome to His wisdom.

Just before Christmas we had a wonderful example of His loving involvement in the everyday-ness of life. My son Peter was laboring to build an elaborate miniature horse stable for his daughter, Mary Elizabeth. Hour after hour, he closeted himself in the basement putting it together. Especially time-consuming was the process of covering the roof with tiny shingles of almost paper-thin plywood. As the laborious work of positioning and gluing proceeded, it became apparent that he was going to run out of shingles.

Peter called all manner of hobby stores in the area. Nobody had any.

He even called the company in Texas that made the shingles. Yes, they could get them to him in time by special plane service for about $100. Too costly.

Finally, Peter found a hobby store up the road that had half of one package. The owner's wife had been using them for some project and had that many left. This was still not enough to complete the roof, but Peter decided to pick up those that were available.

As he drove off I breathed up a quiet little prayer about this. Immediately I had a mental picture—a little drama really—of Peter walking into the hobby store and the owner saying, "I have a surprise for you. I found another package of those shingles."

Peter came back home beaming. What I had "seen" as I prayed was exactly what had happened. He had more than enough to finish the roof.

A very small prayer request for what many would consider a superficial need. Yet this little episode gave all of us a heart-warming glimpse of the Father's careful provision for the small details of our lives—and of the adventure He means each moment in His world to be!

7.

Homemade Bread

I am troubled about a quality of blandness in our nation today, a lack of creativity. It's apparent in our leaders. Most gear their lives to television ratings, are afraid to take stands on issues. Movies and stage plays focus on sex and violence, with little originality. Sex so dominates advertising and the arts that it has become commonplace, almost boring.

Jesus lashed out at the spiritless quality in the people in His time:

> I know thy works, that thou art neither cold nor hot: I would thou wert cold or hot. So, then, because thou art lukewarm, and neither cold nor hot, I will spew thee out of my mouth.
>
> Revelation 3:15–16 KJV

One of our new neighbors is no longer trapped in a bland way of life. Yet for the first twelve years of her marriage, Cynthia felt she was losing her identity in an endless procession of social events and chauffeuring of children.

During one cocktail party, Cynthia decided to limit herself to ginger ale and made some discoveries—not especially pleasant: "I saw our crowd through new eyes," she told me. "No one was really saying anything. Most sentences were never even finished. There was a lot of laughter over—well, nothing at all. All at once I began to ask questions about what we call 'the good life.'

"What was so good about it?

"But," she continued, "what was I to do? If my husband and I ducked those invitations, we'd be thought snobbish and eventually dropped. But if we went, we would have to drink, otherwise how could we stand the emptiness?"

In a search for answers, Cynthia set aside an hour each day for meditation. As she did this over a period of weeks there came to her the realization that she was being met in this quiet hour, at her point of need, by something more than her own thoughts and her own psyche, by Someone who loved her and who insisted that His love must be passed on to her family and her friends.

Cynthia began to bake bread regularly, finding this ancient female ritual deeply satisfying. "You can't imagine how many enemies I slay and repressions I get rid of as I knead that bread," she says.

Instead of letting the children dash away from the dinner table for television, the evening meal has become a time for family sharing. Family Game Night once a week has become a creative substitute for television.

A new strength developed in Cynthia in regard to her children. I have heard her tell her astonished eleven-year-old that he is going to walk to Little League one way each practice day, and calmly state to her nine-year-old daughter that she certainly is not going to buy her any "training" bras.

"I've discovered that real love for our children has to go beyond catering to their every whim—or we turn them into tyrannical little princes and princesses," Cynthia said. "They, too, have to find their own inner resources. And how can they, if I do for them the things that they could do for themselves?"

Recognizing that some of her friends were as bored as she with the typical cocktail party, she began experimenting with some new types of entertaining. One evening after a buffet supper, a hand-picked group listened spellbound to a play on the radio. "The Murder Trial of William Palmer, Surgeon." Cynthia had supplied each guest with a paperback copy of the play to follow as they listened. The evening was a big hit, especially with the men.

"I realized one day that my church had little more meaning for me than did our country club," Cynthia said. "I called our pastor and asked if there was a Bible study."

That's what brought Cynthia and her husband to our house, where eight couples were already meeting twice a month to find ways to relate the Bible to some everyday problems we were all facing. Out of this experience has come a new level of shared concerns for us all and the exciting discovery of answers sought out together.

As I ponder Cynthia's story, I've concluded that we don't have to settle for blandness in life; God, who is the Author of creativity, is ready to make a dull life adventuresome the moment we allow His Holy Spirit to go to work inside us.

Section Three

Christian Growth

T here is a misconception in the minds of many believers that success-ful communicators of the faith speak from some Mt. Olympus of perfection—that it is only because these Christian superstars have overcome their faults and weaknesses that they are able to minister to others in a mighty way.

Not true. Those most used of God often have struggled or are struggling with one or more major weaknesses. It is often just because of a weakness that these people have much to share.

Dr. Norman Vincent Peale frankly admits that only due to his own fears and doubts and tensions was he able to minister so effectively to others with similar problems. A study of Christian leaders down through the ages reveals that most of them battled major weaknesses.

So it was with Catherine. The Lord gave her major gifts in the area of communication that catapulted her into the public eye. But when people tried to place her on a pedestal, she refused, knowing that God alone deserves to be exalted. Instead, she wrote openly about her struggles, her mistakes, her flaws.

In her journals she was ruthless with herself. The following excerpts indicate how hard she struggled to overcome certain weaknesses, how seriously she took the matter of our need to grow spiritually.

A lesson learned was an inadequately thought-through novel she began in 1969 and abandoned two-and-a-half years later. It was titled Gloria. *The loss of time and energy on this manuscript weighed on Catherine for years.*

LL

1.

Dealing with a Major Mistake

*L*ast week I needed to be alone for a few days to think and pray. The mistake I made in deciding to write the novel *Gloria* has shaken my confidence. The shelved manuscript is like a death in the family.

What went wrong?

I needed to find some answers about this—and about other troubling areas in my life. So I made arrangements to spend two days at the Cenacle, a Roman Catholic Retreat House several miles away in Lantana, Florida. Len dropped me off Sunday at 8:00 P.M.

The next morning after breakfast I sat for a while in a lawn chair out under an ancient mango tree. Through the curving trunks of the coconut palms I had a glimpse of the Intracoastal Waterway. The grounds were alive with bird calls.

A sound new to me was the creaking of the tall, tall bamboo that borders part of the property. The bamboo, too, was ancient. The slender branches writhed and creaked as they rubbed against one another in the barely perceptible breeze. The creaking reminded me of the grating of a long-unused hinge, as of a door being opened after many years. The foliage was still delicate and lacy as it was when the bamboo was young.

Leaf patterns were all across the grass. Squirrels raced up and down trees. A cardinal kept whistling. "Cheer! Cheer!"

I had thought that I wanted guidance on certain family matters and whether there was some way to resurrect *Gloria*. But when I talked briefly with Sister Forman at breakfast, her advice was to seek Christ and Him alone and let Him decide what He wanted to talk to me about.

That morning the first thought dropped into my mind was the single word *edification*. "Think on edification," He seemed to be saying, "what builds the members of the family up in love, perfecting them into the body of Christ."

The focus throughout the morning was largely on my home situation. (Perhaps the conclusion to be drawn is that it's essential that I get this right with Christ before I can write *anything* worthwhile.)

Soon I found myself turning to the book of John. As I read, the Holy Spirit showed me that I had fallen hook, line and sinker for one of Satan's oldest and most-used tricks: looking steadily at the difficulty instead of at Jesus. I had listened, really paid attention to Old Scratch's suggestions—every one of them, I fear—as to the size and intractability of my problems. The Comforter told me that all of this had been Satan's technique for discouraging me unduly and that I must *never* fall for this temptation again.

Next I was shown that my husband, my children, and my grandchildren are not mine, but God's. He's not only as concerned as I am for them, but loves them far more than I ever could. Therefore, I was to take my possessive, self-centered hands off—strictly off. So, in an act of relinquishment, I did this.

Then came a beautiful touch. I was reading in the Psalms when suddenly these words leapt from the page:

The Lord will perfect that which concerns me . . . forsake not the works of Your own hands.

Psalm 138:8 AMPLIFED

I could—and did—claim this promise promptly for my family. Years ago the Lord began a work in these lives. It's His business to perfect what He started. He has promised that He will. I've claimed and accepted that promise. It's as good as done. My heart is steadily rejoicing. Weights and weights have been lifted from me.

The focus that afternoon turned from my home situation to my failure with *Gloria.* What do You have to tell me about this, Lord?

I was led to this passage in Numbers:

> . . . the people . . . spoke against God and against Moses, and said, "Why have you brought us up out of Egypt to die in the desert? There is no bread! There is no water! And we detest this miserable food!"
>
> Then the Lord sent venomous snakes among them; they bit the people and many Israelites died. The people came to Moses and said, "We sinned when we spoke against the Lord and against you. Pray that the Lord will take the snakes away from us." So Moses prayed for the people.
>
> The Lord said to Moses, "Make a snake and put it up on a pole; anyone who is bitten can look at it and live." So Moses made a bronze snake and put it up on a pole. Then when anyone was bitten by a snake and looked at the bronze snake, he lived.
>
> Numbers 21:4–9 NIV

It didn't take long for me to get the point: God told Moses that the people were to take that which had hurt them and lift it up to Him. He would then turn even a snake into blessing and victory. Thus the "snake" in our life can be redeemed and turned to power.

In this way does God deal with our mistakes and sins. I had made a mistake in undertaking the novel *Gloria.* I had not heeded the advice of experts like Elizabeth Sherrill and Len; even my mother had expressed strong reservations. But God would find a way to turn a bad experience into good.

Even more to the point: when any one of us has made a wrong (or even doubtful) turning in our lives through arrogance or lack of trust or impatience or fear—or what not—God will show us a way out. Therefore, I am to turn off all negative thoughts about this wrong decision and accept fully my situation as it is now, as God's will for me now. I am to place the present situation in His hands for Him to use fully for my spiritual growth and for the "edification" of all concerned. Further, I am to do this joyfully.

2.

The Servant Role

The message I am getting today from Jesus is the servant role that He wants to play in the lives of every one of us. The following passages reveal to me the extent of His passion to *serve* us because He loves us so much:

. . . the Son of man came not to be waited on but to serve, and to give His life as a ransom for many. . . .
Matthew 20:28 AMPLIFIED

. . . I am in your midst as one who serves.
Luke 22:27 AMPLIFIED

In the early days of my walk with Him, when I was experimenting day by day with hearing the Inner Voice, I had a hard time believing that His guidance was for *my* benefit, never His own. I still can hardly grasp this.

When He wrapped a towel around his waist, poured water into a basin, and began to wash his disciples' feet (see John 13:4-5), Simon Peter objected that this was beneath the dignity of the

Master. *We* the disciples are to be the servants, I want to insist along with Peter. But Jesus answered him, "If I do not wash you, you have no part in me."

This is a stunning and stupendous thought. Unless I can believe in *this much* love for me, unless I can and will accept Him with faith as my servant as well as my God, unless I truly know that it's *my* good He seeks, not His glory (He already has all of that He can use for all eternity), *then I cannot have his companionship.*

What an amazing revelation!

3.

Why Do We Judge Others?

I am determined to dig in on the matter of my critical nature. I do not like it. It's negative; yes, often destructive. Jesus warned us not to be judgmental. So did Paul:

> Then let us no more pass judgment on one another, but rather decide never to put a stumbling block or hindrance in the way.
>
> Romans 14:13 RSV

I have tried to excuse myself by saying that one must evaluate situations and people. It won't wash. It still comes out judging, a haughty superiority, which is the opposite of love.

With Jesus' help I want to go back to my childhood to see if I can find the root cause for this fault of mine:

He is showing me a little girl who was supersensitive in the sense that she would rather die than be laughed at or found unacceptable by her peers, and most of all, by the adults around her. When she didn't make friends as quickly as other children, she tried to persuade herself that she was superior to others her age.

She got by with this superiority syndrome in school because she received top grades, especially in writing and speech courses. She yearned to be like classmates who were outgoing, witty, and popular, but since she had none of these personality traits, she convinced herself that these were lesser qualities while those of the mind and spirit were somehow on a higher plane.

When she left her small hometown for college, nothing changed in her approach to other people. Because she felt inferior socially, she looked with secret disapproval at those who danced, played cards, and went to drinking parties, all denied to her as a preacher's child.

Superiority breeds contempt. And contempt breeds criticalness. And my criticalness cut me off from other people. Even when I said nothing, made no comment at all, people would tell me they could feel my unkind judgment of them. I was miserable about this quality in me, yet trapped by it.

Along with all this, ironically enough, went an acute sensitivity to any criticalness of me. The Holy Spirit pointed out to me how *deeply* the least tiny bit of unacceptance rankles, causing a wound that festers on, year after year. Incidents, so small that a healthy reaction on my part should have been amusement and then prompt dismissal of the incident from mind, are remembered—still with an emotional sting attached—years later.

For instance . . . soon after I was married to Peter Marshall, I remember a woman friend commenting about my hands, "Well, they aren't beautiful, but at least they're capable-looking."

The pronouncement that my hands weren't pretty has stuck; ever since, it made me reluctant to have a manicurist do my nails.

This is, of course, acute oversensitivity, which, in turn, is the sure sign of acute self-centeredness . . . the same hypersensitivity and self-protectiveness that had led me to take refuge in an assumed superiority to others—with the accompanying right to stand in judgment on them.

Being oversensitive, I am quick to pick it up in others and relate to it. Once when a judge at the Junior Miss Pageant in Mobile, Alabama, I found myself intrigued by the contestant with the highest academic average of all fifty girls. When she came to the five judges for her ten-minute interview, I watched her with deep interest.

One question asked her was: "If you could pick out one person in any field of endeavor in our world today whom you admire most, whom would you pick?"

She hesitated a moment and then said loud and clear, "Jesus Christ."

Two of the judges responded almost simultaneously, "Oh, we mean a living person."

The girl felt rebuked. Her eyes filled with tears; she choked up and never could get herself under control during the rest of the interview. I ached for her. I wanted to hug her and tell her I loved her reply, that to me, as to her, Jesus *was* a living person.

Later, though, I wondered if her extreme sensitivity had caused her to put all her efforts into getting top grades—thereby avoiding, as I had, the far riskier confrontation of equal-to-equal.

How do we sensitive, critical people deal with our condition? I had one very direct answer from the Lord recently after I had loosed a blast of angry criticism at one of our national leaders at the luncheon table. God said to me, "Do not criticize at all" (1 Corinthians 4:5 MOFFATT). "You spread negativism around you and pollute your own atmosphere when you do so. Turn your criticism and your indignation to good use by praying for that leader right now."

A good handle for me to grasp!

4.

A Fast on Criticalness

T*he* Lord continues to deal with me about my critical spirit, convicting me that I have been wrong to judge any person or situation:

Do not judge, or you too will be judged. For in the same way you judge others, you will be judged, and with the measure you use, it will be measured to you.

Matthew 7:1–2 NIV

One morning last week He gave me an assignment: *for one day I was to go on a "fast" from criticism. I was not to criticize anybody about anything.*

Into my mind crowded all the usual objections. "But then what happens to value judgments? You Yourself, Lord, spoke of 'righteous judgment.' How could society operate without standards and limits?"

All such resistance was brushed aside. "Just obey Me without questioning: an absolute fast on any critical statements for this day."

As I pondered this assignment I realized there was an even humorous side to this kind of fast. What did the Lord want to show me?

For the first half of the day, I simply felt a void, almost as if I had been wiped out as a person. This was especially true at lunch with my husband, Len, my mother, son Jeff and my secretary, Jeanne Sevigny, present. Several topics came up (school prayer, abortion, the ERA amendment) about which I had definite opinions. I listened to the others and kept silent. Barbed comments on the tip of my tongue about certain world leaders were suppressed. In our talkative family no one seemed to notice.

Bemused, I noticed that comments were not missed. The federal government, the judicial system, and the institutional church could apparently get along fine without my penetrating observations. But still I didn't see what this fast on criticism was accomplishing—until mid-afternoon.

For several years I had been praying for one talented young man whose life had gotten sidetracked. Perhaps my prayers for him had been too negative. That afternoon, a specific, positive vision for this life was dropped into my mind with God's unmistakable hallmark of it—joy.

Ideas began to flow in a way I had not experienced in years. Now it was apparent what the Lord wanted me to see. My critical nature had not corrected a single one of the multitudinous things I found fault with. What it *had* done was to stifle my own creativity—in prayer, in relationships, perhaps even in writing—ideas that He wanted to give me.

Last Sunday night in a Bible study group, I told of my Day's Fast experiment. The response was startling. Many admitted that criticalness was the chief problem in their offices, or in their marriages, or with their teenage children.

My own character flaw here is not going to be corrected overnight. But in thinking this problem through the past few days, I find the most solid scriptural basis possible for dealing with it. (The Greek word translated "judge" in King James, becomes "criticize" in Moffatt.) All through the Sermon on the Mount, Jesus sets Himself squarely against our seeing other people and life situations through this negative lens.

What He is showing me so far can be summed up as follows:

1. A critical spirit focuses us on ourselves and makes us unhappy. We lose perspective and humor.
2. A critical spirit blocks the positive creative thoughts God longs to give us.
3. A critical spirit can prevent good relationships between individuals and often produces retaliatory criticalness.
4. Criticalness blocks the work of the Spirit of God: love, good will, mercy.
5. Whenever we see something genuinely wrong in another person's behavior, rather than criticize him or her directly, or—far worse—gripe about him behind his back, we should ask the Spirit of God to do the correction needed.

Convicted of the true destructiveness of a critical mindset, on my knees I am repeating this prayer: "Lord, I repent of this sin of judgment. I am deeply sorry for having committed so gross an offense against You and against myself so continually. I claim Your promise of forgiveness and seek a new beginning."

5.

Thou Fool

I visited my friend Virginia Lively in Belle Glade, Florida, on Sunday afternoon. Out of several hours of prayer together came—among other things—the conviction that my relationship with and attitude to B—— needs to be corrected by Jesus, especially in the spiritual realm.

This morning, Lord, You brought to my remembrance Your words, "Whosoever shall say to his brother . . . Thou fool, shall be in danger of hell fire" (Matthew 5:22 KJV).

Well, I have certainly been saying that of B——, and thinking it. How clearly I see this now, Lord, as the sin of spiritual and intellectual pride. So I confess this sin of mental and verbal judgment. I ask You to forgive me for my arrogance and to cleanse me. Bring my attitude toward, my every thought of, my every reaction toward, and my every word about or to B—— in line with Your view of her.

Cleanse me of every holier-than-thou stance. Since I am "hidden in Christ," then my opinion of anyone doesn't matter. Only Jesus' opinion matters.

Thank You, Lord, for Your acceptance of this confession. Thank You for Your forgiveness. Thank You for the beginning right now of a new relationship with B——. Thank You for dealing with her in Your all-seeing love. Thank You for lifting the burden of resentment and judging from me. I *do* feel tons lighter already. Thank You!!

6.

Jesus Makes the Decisions

Yesterday I began trying to get back to a real *quiet time* in the early morning. My directive was, "Never mind about reading. Spend the time getting in touch with Jesus directly."

For a couple of days prior to this the Holy Spirit had dropped a curious clause from Scripture into my mind and heart: "And the government shall be upon [Jesus'] shoulder . . ." (Isaiah 9:6 KJV). I had never thought of this in relation to the government of *my* life. Suddenly it spoke volumes to me . . . the responsibility of my life is now His, the burden *He* will carry. He will make the decisions, the right decisions. What a relief: what joy to turn it over to Him.

Yesterday I mostly just asked Him questions, knowing that sooner or later in His time, He will answer them. He well knows my questioning spirit. I don't think He minds that.

Having posed my questions, I left them there, in His hands . . . and felt sweet peace flow into my spirit.

A while ago I was told that I was to refrain from criticism for one month, a fast of the tongue. Now I am directed to extend this curbing of my faultfinding into the thought area.

The Spirit reminded me of Jesus' words, "Sufficient unto the day is the evil thereof." Clearly then, Jesus recognizes the evil all around us in our daily walk. Simply, for the time being, I am not to let my mind dwell there. The Spirit also showed me that the tidiness of my possessions and papers has a direct bearing on my peace on the inside. Rather than let this chore weigh on me as an added pressure, though, I am to let Him direct me *when* to undertake straightening up my things.

7.

The Dry Period

I've been off on a familiar barren road recently and need to get down on paper the steps I took to get back on the main highway. I'm talking about the *dry period*. The state is always much the same for me: shriveled and lonely on the inside. I can't do any writing. I'm unable to accomplish much of anything, just going through the motions of life and barely able to do that. Worst of all—shut off from God.

In her book *Mysticism*, Evelyn Underhill points out that such experiences are a necessary part of the Christian walk.

> For those who have trod the Christian way for some time, a spiritual and psychic fatigue occasionally creeps in and overcomes one. In this state one knows anew the helplessness of us humans. Yet here, for a time, we are in a worse state than at the beginning of our Christian walk. For at that early stage, along with the helplessness, there was the sure and wonderful knowledge of God's adequacy.
>
> Now the skies seem totally deaf; no glorious light breaks through at all. Nothing, inside or outside, seems to work. If

one can ride it through on sheer blind faith, just hanging onto the rock of salvation, *then* it has to pass, and we go on into an advanced state in the spiritual life.

The reason this dry state is necessary, she points out, is that we have to find anew our need, become desperate in a new way, in order to get on with the next stage in our Christian development.

We know that physically and emotionally the developing self advances through a series of growth spurts interspersed with pauses on plateaus. Apparently, the same process holds in the spiritual life.

So the way out of this latest dry period for me began with an admission of my helplessness. And not just a grudging acknowledgment, but a trusting and expectant *acceptance*, relying on Jesus' promise that *His* strength is made perfect in *my* weakness (see 2 Corinthians 12:9).

Next, I was not only to bear this dry and barren stretch of life, but actually to *thank* God for it. My praise to Him lacked enthusiasm at first, but as always the Psalms supplied the words I could not. (Psalms 95, 100, 103 are some of my favorites.) Gradually my cup began to fill and my spirit to loosen.

The last step was to show someone I loved them; in this case it was a visit to a bed-bound neighbor.

Before going back to my writing, I asked the Holy Spirit for specific help in setting up the story sequences in my novel. Soon a wonderful thing began to happen. I could feel my creative nature thrusting down its rootlets in search of the life-giving Water at some deep level in my being. Bit by bit, episode by episode, I watched the lineaments of the story line emerging in my mind. It was as if I could see the bulbs I planted in the ground last fall begin their growth in the cold and the dark. Even the creative process that formed the earth, I reflected, began in *darkness*.

It takes acceptance and praise and outgoing love for me to emerge from a dry period, but, oh, the exhilaration that follows!

8.

To Forgive . . . and Forget

*T*his morning I had to face up to the fact that I still had a bad attitude toward a woman who is constantly attacking me and my writings. On taking it to the Lord, I received two insights:

(1) The reason I am so upset is that *I haven't forgiven her completely.* I've made stabs at this in the past, but as she comes to my mind I have an almost physical sensation, as of iron bars pressing against my chest. The Lord showed me that on the other side of these bars was a woman, a human being, who needed to be freed. So, on my knees before Him, I went through a process of unreservedly forgiving her by an act of my will. I confessed my feelings about her and asked God to make the forgiveness real.

(2) My job was not finished, however, He told me, until *I can forget what she has done.*

"But *how can* I do that, Lord?"

Your will is greater than your memory, Catherine. Rebuke the painful memory and cast it out in the name of Jesus.

I was to "... bring into captivity every thought to the obedience of Christ" (2 Corinthians 10:5 KJV). Then to ask forgiveness for hanging onto these memories (we tend to stab ourselves again and again with old, hurtful episodes), and ask for an alarm system on the door of my mind whenever the memory tries to creep back.

From henceforth I am to look at this woman—*and at anyone else who has ever hurt me*—with eyes of compassion and love, concentrating on the potential they have for good. Only thus will I be able to see them as Jesus does.

"But Lord ... will this approach bring about changes in them?"

That's between them and Me. You will have peace.

9.

The Key to Obedience

*A*m struggling this morning with the seeming contradiction between Jesus' constant stress on *obedience* as crucial to Christian growth, over against the reality of "grace," which is the "unmerited favor of God."

Obedience would seem to be our going up the ladder step by step, not earning our way exactly, while continually dependent on still putting forth our own efforts. Whereas the teaching all through the Bible is that it is God who always takes the initiative with us. All of God's good gifts are given by pure grace; there is no way we can deserve a single one of them.

So—exactly where and how does obedience fit into this?

I'm beginning to see that the missing key here is Love. The chief characteristic of love is wanting to do what pleases the beloved. The analogy Jesus used most often was filial love: He meant His relationship to His Father to be the pattern for *our* relationship to Him (Jesus). Jesus' obedience was not the result of gritted teeth and grim determination, but the natural outworking of love: "I do as the Father has commanded me, so that the world may know (be convinced) that I love the Father . . ." (John 14:31 AMPLIFIED).

When we truly love someone, our focus is on *him* or *her*, not on ourselves. And our constant thought is, "What can I do to give this beloved person joy? To please him? To ease his path? To minister to him?"

It staggers my mind to think that I can in any way minister to Jesus, or gladden His heart. Yet this is the gracious message of the Gospel, which always puts the emphasis on love:

"We love Him, because He first loved us" (1 John 4:19 AMPLIFIED).

God's grace, God's initiative.

". . . If a person [really] loves Me, he will keep My word— obey My teaching" (John 14:23 AMPLIFIED).

Our natural, unforced response.

10.

Worry: Be Gone

*T*his morning I awoke full of worry about the future, with Len having resigned from his job as editor of *Guideposts*. Len and I were in agreement about this step, and he is enthusiastic about going into book publishing with John and Elizabeth Sherrill, but I see so many obstacles ahead, especially when his salary check stops coming.

Then the Lord directed me to the fourth chapter of Phillipians, particularly to verse 8 (AMPLIFIED, italics added):

   . . . whatever is worthy of reverence . . .
     is honorable and seemly . . .
       is just . . .
         is pure . . .
           is lovely and lovable . . .
             is kind and winsome and gracious,
   if there is any
     virtue . . .
       excellence . . .
         anything worthy of praise,

> [we are to] think on
>   and weigh
>   and take account of these things—
> *fix* your minds on them.

Now this might seem to be the worst kind of not facing reality were it not for the fact that earlier in the same chapter Paul has already exhorted us (v. 6) to pray about *everything*, to pour our hearts out to the Heavenly Father with "definite requests."

My problem is that having done this, having laid my concern before the Father, I get the feeling that if I do not frequently return to it in my mind and keep "worrying" it, much as a dog would a bone, then there certainly can be no chance of solving it. It's a feeling that it would actually be irresponsible or frivolous *not* to do this—wrong to think about other things, and go my merry way while a major problem faces us.

I slip into the worry stance in spite of telling myself over and over that God is the problem-solver, that we can confidently leave our situation in His hands. I know what I should do, yet emotionally and practically I do not act out this letting go. This morning God seems to be pointing out chapter four in Philippians as a blueprint for handling crises His way:

1. Regardless of any circumstances, we are to *rejoice in the Lord always.*
2. We are *not* to fret or have anxiety about *anything.*
3. We are to pray about everything, making our needs and wants known unto God.
4. We are to be content with our earthly lot, whatever it is.
5. We are to guard our thoughts, think only upon upbeat, positive things—nothing negative. If we will do the above, then we are promised:
    a. God's peace . . . shall garrison and mount guard over our hearts and minds in Christ Jesus.
    b. Christ will "infuse inner strength into us"—that is, "We will be self-sufficient in Christ's sufficiency.

LL Note: God honored our leap of faith into book publishing. Chosen Books, from its inception, produced books that made a major impact on both the Christian and secular world.

11.

His Peace

This morning the Lord asked me to look up the Scripture verse "the things that belong unto thy peace." With the help of a concordance, I found it in Luke 19:41–42 KJV. The scene is a hill overlooking Jerusalem.

. . . [Jesus] beheld the city, and wept over it, Saying If thou hadst known, even thou, at least in this thy day, the things which belong unto thy peace! but now they are hid from thine eyes.

Lord, what do You want me to understand from this? What are the things that belong to my peace?

Surely, this ties in with the "rest" that was the other message given me this morning.

There remaineth, therefore, a rest to the people of God. For he that is entered into his rest, he also hath ceased from his own works. . . .

Hebrews 4:9–10 KJV

In the midst of disquiet about so many things in our life right now—my trying to make progress on my novel, the Chosen Books situation in general, my declining eyesight due to cataracts, poor sleep, etc., the message Jesus wants me to have today seems to be simply, "Peace! Rest in Me. I am here to give you, Catherine, the precious gift of peace of mind and spirit."

How glorious! He confirms it in Scripture after Scripture (italics added):

May grace (God's favor) and *peace* (which is perfect well-being, all necessary good, all spiritual prosperity and freedom from fears and agitating passions and moral conflicts), be multiplied to you. . . .

2 Peter 1:2 AMPLIFIED

For though the mountains should depart and the hills be shaken or removed, yet My love and kindness shall not depart from you, nor shall My covenant of peace and completeness be removed, says the Lord, Who has compassion on you.

Isaiah 54:10 AMPLIFIED

Praise You, Lord Jesus! Praise You!!

The next day . . .

I discovered yesterday that the beautiful freedom the Lord gave me in His gracious promises of "peace" carried along with it the joy of a moment-by-moment obedience.

That is, during the day I made the discovery that I had departed from the habit of looking directly to Jesus for the answer to small daily decisions; that the only way I will keep a pliable, obedient spirit in the larger decisions, is to look to Him and *to obey* in the smaller ones.

I had slipped badly on that. I'm always getting hung up on the tension, or seeming tension, between freedom in Christ Jesus and obedience.

James, however, makes this connection beautifully:

But the man who looks intently into the perfect law that gives freedom, and continues to do this, not forgetting what he has heard, but doing it—he will be blessed in what he does.

James 1:25 NIV

Or to approach all this another way. I see that Satan has small chance of getting at us—of accusing us and destroying our rest (as he has with me so often over "small" things like sleeping pills, or the lipstick issue I faced years ago on Cape Cod) when we are faithful in present-moment obedience, steadily looking to Jesus, asking, "Shall I do this? Or not?"—and then obeying.

Thus this obedience *results* in liberty—and the two go hand in hand.

12.

Idolatry

A couple of days ago Len and I had a heated discussion about the subject matter for the Tuesday evening Bible class and how we were going to teach it. He did not accept—or even understand—what I was saying, and it annoyed me that I could not get my point across.

That night I had a dream in which I was pursued by photographers. Flattered, I allowed them to take a series of pictures. When they appeared in print, I was horrified. The photos were obnoxious, nasty, almost obscene. To my eyes, the pictures clearly said, "She's a big showoff."

Through the dream I believe God was revealing to me my arrogance and self-righteousness about my *opinions.* I saw that this has always been one of my problems with the children, Linda especially. "Love me, love my opinions!" Ideas are very, very important to me, and I consider *my* ideas uncommonly valuable.

How ironic that the very passage over which Len and I disagreed—the giving of the Law to Moses—included as the first Commandment of all: *Thou shalt have no other gods before me* (Exodus 20:3 KJV).

Before bedtime that night I confessed to God and to Len my idolatry of my own passionately held convictions.

13.

Self-Denial

*L*ast night at bedtime I ate several pieces of candy, which was wrong from every point of view: pure gratification of self's momentary desire.

This morning I could not worship the Lord. Something was coming between us. Then the Spirit spoke gently, *"Deny yourself . . .* pick up your cross daily and follow Me." It was as if He were putting His finger on the words "Deny yourself." I had never noticed them particularly in that passage. I wasn't even certain those two words were there. So I looked up the verse; they were there all right. I also got illumination on the rest of the passage: "For whoever wants to save his [higher, spiritual, eternal] life, will lose [the lower, natural, temporal life which is lived (only) on earth]" (Mark 8:35 AMPLIFIED).

I saw that Jesus is here simply stating a fact of life. If I want to lose weight, I must give up the lower desire for stuffing my mouth in order to attain the higher desire of a fit, healthy body.

If I want to write a book, I must give up the use of my time for other things.

For the first time I glimpse the rationale of certain spiritual exercises, such as fasting.

Lord, teach me!

14.

Self-Denial:
The Teaching Goes On

*A*n insight today on how to make the denial of some small pleasure not only less painful but even an almost joyous event.

Up to this point in my life, whenever I've thought I was hearing the Lord's voice telling me to give up something that I loved, I could—and often would—drag my feet for weeks and months. Often I've had to pray the laggard's prayer, "O Lord, make me willing to be made willing." Almost always I've thought of obedience to the Lord as really quite painful.

But now after so many years of my Christian walk, a change is taking place within me. Jesus is becoming much more real to me as a person. I believe that what has been happening to me recently is the beginning of the direct fulfillment of this passage (italics added):

The person who has My commands and keeps them is the one who [really] loves Me, and whoever [really] loves Me will be loved by My Fther. And I [too] will love him and *will show* (reveal, manifest) *Myself to him—I will let Myself be clearly seen by him and make Myself real to him.*

John 14:21 AMPLIFIED

For quite a stretch I've been getting the message that Jesus was displeased with my 5:00 to 6:00 P.M. "Happy Hour," a time for relaxed reading or listening to music, when I sip a glass of sherry. At first I thought He wanted me to give up the sherry. Lately I've seen that it isn't so much what He wants me to give up, but that He wants me to be active physically during this hour, to walk or work in the garden. I had let myself become too lazy and sedentary, and too rigid about this 5:00 to 6:00 P.M. pattern. *I* like my ruts. *He* wants me active, and above all, flexible.

Then He began teaching me about *how* He goes about changing long-standing habits. It's part of the outworking of the great promise.

This is the covenant which I will make with the house of Israel after those days, says the Lord: I will put my law . . . upon their hearts; and I will be their God, and they shall be my people.

Jeremiah 31:33 RSV

I had never before tied this promise to the problems connected with habit changing. I have no addiction to alcohol or smoking, or sweets, for instance, but I ache for certain persons I know who do. I see now how He helps us with these ingrained patterns when we ask Him for help. What happens is that *our* tastes begin to change. Something that we liked a lot suddenly is not so appealing. When we understand *how* He works and that this *is* the Lord Himself working, then we can stop resisting our own changing tastes, thank Him, and flow with the new direction of the tide.

It's a marvelous plan only He could have thought of, for there is no pain in ceasing to do what we no longer care to do.

15.

The Temptation Of Things

I've been through a small siege of temptation to worldliness that I'm almost embarrassed to write about—and yet feel I should.

From the time I was a small girl I've loved pretty, feminine things, especially jewelry. Nothing very unusual or terribly wrong about that. For most of my life I could not afford jewelry, so it was no issue.

Even when in recent years I could afford some jewelry, the Depression syndrome that permeated my family for many years has kept me frugal. One day a check for several hundred dollars arrived that I hadn't expected. "Now I can get those gold earrings," I said to myself.

So I began making trips to jewelry stores looking for the exactly right earrings. Then an inner restlessness began to ruffle me. So I started to argue with God.

"Lord, are You telling me that earrings are too frivolous?"

Silence.

"It isn't as though I'm buying them from my tithe funds. I mean, the money is extra. I hadn't expected it."

Silence.

"Lord, I've spent much more for a rug or a piece of furniture without this guilt complex. Now, really, isn't this inner disquiet just my Puritan, Depression-born complex?"

Then came the gentle response:

I'm concerned over the inordinate amount of time you've given to this in your thought life.

At once I was led to the apostle John's comment on worldliness and his warning about the "delight of the eyes":

Do not love or cherish the world or the things that are in the world. If any one loves the world, love for the Father is not in him.

For all that is in the world, the lust of the flesh [craving for sensual gratification], and the lust of the eyes [greedy longings of the mind] and the pride of life [assurance in one's own resources or in the stability of earthly things]— these do not come from the Father but from the world [itself].

And the world passes away and disappears . . .

1 John 2:15–17 AMPLIFIED

Here John is taking us into the higher reaches of spirituality. He doesn't use the word "sin"; he doesn't mention Satan. He's concerned with whether we realize the extent of God's love for us—and how much love for God there is in us.

The crux of it: the love exchange between God and me is going to suffer if I focus too much on worldly things.

16.

Fear of Man

*T*he Lord is having me look at something this morning that is very unsettling. It came first through the following verse:

The fear of man bringeth a snare: but whoso putteth his trust in the Lord shall be safe.

Proverbs 29:25 KJV

I don't fear man in a physical way, but do I fear his disapproval of me? In other words, how much do I try to please other people instead of looking to God alone for His approval? Certainly, there is enormous pressure on all of us to be accepted and approved by others. But God wants us to resist this pressure. Consider the tragedy of the religious leaders of Jesus' day:

Among the chief rulers also many believed on him; but because of the Pharisees they did not confess him, lest they should be put out of the synagogue: For they loved the praise of men more than the praise of God.

John 12:42–43 KJV

Even Peter, soon to be leader of the earliest church, denied knowing Jesus at all following His arrest, simply to remain in the good graces of a motley crowd gathered around a bonfire. Peter was no coward. When the soldiers had come to seize Jesus, he had grabbed a sword and cut off the ear of one of them. So it wasn't his life Peter feared for here, but the ridicule and judgment and opinions of others.

We are told that in our daily task—whatever our vocation or profession or daily round—we are to seek to please God more than man:

Servants, obey in all things your masters according to the flesh; not with eyeservice, as menpleasers; but in singleness of heart, fearing God.

Colossians 3:22 KJV

The thought comes that my tendency to be critical of others springs out of the soil of what-people-will-think. What we are, we see in others. I am judgmental, therefore I expect others to be the same.

Jesus was simply stating a law of life when He told us, ". . . judge [and] ye shall be judged: and with what measure ye mete, it shall be measured to you" (Matthew 7:2 KJV). Put this way, judging others constantly cultivates more soil for the thistles of fear-of-man to grow in.

Judgmentalism is an attempt to ward off this fear by standing in a superior place. Self thinks that when it can get there first and judge before others can state their opinions, it can forestall others' criticisms. Of course, self is mistaken, since the very opposite happens—judging draws the judgment of others.

Two passages of Scripture, personalized for this specific fear, are helping me overcome my exaggerated concern for man's approval:

Fear not [the opinions of others]: for I have redeemed thee; I have called thee by thy name; thou art mine.

Isaiah 43:1 KJV

When thou passest through the waters [of ridicule], I will be with thee; and through the rivers [of rejection], they shall not overflow thee: when thou walkest through the fire [of contempt], thou shalt not be burned; neither shall the flame kindle upon thee.

Isaiah 43:2 KJV

17.

Immersed in a Horse Trough

I want to get down in my journal the fascinating experience Len and I had this past weekend. At the urging of our friend Virginia Lively we drove to Clewiston, Florida, about sixty miles from our home here in Boynton Beach. Virginia had gone through what she called a "believer's baptism" in the Episcopal church there. She described it as "a beautiful, cleansing, and healing experience" and urged us to consider doing it.

For months now I have read with fascination about the Jesus people, a California phenomenon. Most seem to be young, former members of the drug culture, who, after a "believer's baptism" in the Pacific Ocean, experience an almost total change of lifestyle.

Virginia's conviction was that every Christian should have the opportunity of undergoing baptism *following* his or her personal decision for Christ. She had been baptized as a very young child in her own Episcopal church and had accepted this sacrament as valid, but she believes that, ideally, we should be "dedicated" to God as babies, then have a "water baptism" later when we are ready to accept Jesus on our own.

I spent a morning digging out Scripture references to baptism, coming on one archetype I'd never noticed:

> For Christ . . . was put to death in the body but made alive by the Spirit, through whom also he went and preached to the spirits in prison who disobeyed long ago when God waited patiently in the days of Noah while the ark was being built. In it only a few people, eight in all, were saved through water, and this water symbolizes baptism that now saves you also—not the removal of dirt from the body but the pledge of a good conscience toward God . . .
>
> 1 Peter 3:18–21 NIV

Since the subject of baptism has always divided Christians, at first Len and I felt a certain wariness about accepting Virginia's invitation. Then John and Elizabeth (Tib) Sherrill (our close friends and associates at *Guideposts* magazine) arrived for a visit and expressed interest. All four of us had been baptized as infants, long before we could remember. We were convinced that the performance of this sacrament on our behalfs had been complete and theologically adequate in every way. We all agreed, however, that we didn't want to miss anything that the Lord might have for us right now. The Sherrills, LeSourds, my friend Freddie Koch, and her daughter Claudia drove from our home in Boynton Beach last Saturday for a spiritual adventure. In Clewiston we located the home of the Episcopal rector. Virginia Lively had arrived there a few minutes earlier.

The first thing that happened was between John Sherrill and me. Our relationship had become strained through some theological differences. While we sat together in the rector's living room, John began speaking about his fear of change. Twice when there had been major upheavals in his life he had developed cancer. He confessed apprehension of a recurrence in the face of upcoming changes in his and Tib's situation.

At Virginia's urging, he recollected his childhood and talked about the little-boy John—skinny, non-athletic, not popular with the "in" crowd—and tears filled my eyes. How I identified with him there. A new love for John filled me and I went over and hugged him. The reconciliation was complete and almost instantaneous.

Next we went to the nearby Episcopal church, a small sanctuary set in a grove of Florida pine trees. In the vestibule of the church had been placed a galvanized iron horse trough, the stickers from the feed store still visible on one end. A hose, connected to a water spigot outside, ran through the open screen door and was filling the trough. This was to be the setting for the baptism.

First, we sat down in the sanctuary and sang some appropriate hymns. The Episcopal priest, in slacks and sports shirt, prayed, then explained the significance of a believer's baptism: that it was not necessary for salvation, but an opportunity for confession, asking and receiving forgiveness, then making a new commitment of our lives to Jesus. This would open us to a fresh infusion of the Holy Spirit with the resulting new love and joy and power that comes when Jesus indwells us.

As we changed into bathing suits, each of us pondered the areas in our lives where confession and foregiveness were needed. This was done quietly with God, with our spouses, or openly with the rector. The Sherrills led the way, first Tib, then John being immersed.

Afterwards John said softly to Tibby, "Now that we have left our old persons at the bottom of the horse trough and are new creatures, don't you think we ought to get married again?"

The two of them, barefoot, water dripping from their hair and bathing suits, stood before the altar, pledging themselves to one another again. Len and I followed . . . into the horse trough and then to the altar for a reaffirmation of our marriage vows, our eyes brimming with tears.

The next morning, after we got home, we found just outside our front door an elaborate "Just Married" sign which Claudia Koch—who had been wide-eyed during the ceremonies—had made and sometime during the night left at our door.

Section Four

His Strength in Our Weakness

*A*t one point during our courtship, Catherine voiced a concern over her health, saying she doubted that she had more than five years to live. I "pooh-poohed" this, pointing to her own mother's robust health at age sixty-seven.

Both of us were wrong. Catherine lived twenty-three years more, but her death at sixty-nine was far short of her mother's life span (Mother Wood is now ninethy-four).

And for all of those twenty-three years Catherine battled a debilitating emphysema that sapped her energy and sometimes left her gasping for breath after even so simple an exertion as climbing a flight of stairs. New York winters brought on severe bronchitis. Our move to Boynton Beach, Florida, doubtless prolonged her life, but it did not solve her health problems. Along the way she won a battle over sleeping pills—until her last years when sleeplessness once more turned her nights into a spiritual battleground.

Prayers for Catherine's healing throughout our marriage lifted her, strengthened her, but never totally healed her. "Why?" she asked over and over. The enigma of why some are healed, some are not, frustrated Catherine all her life.

But she never stopped struggling for answers. And out of the struggle came—not robust health she yearned for, but a daily, growing intimacy with God that became far more precious than any amount of physical stamina. Her constant companion on this closer walk . . . the Bible.

LL

1.

Trusting God

*T*oday this verse in Psalm 37 spoke to me:

> Commit your way to the Lord—roll and repose
> [each care of] your load on Him; trust (lean on,
> rely on and be confident) also in Him, and He will bring it
> to pass.
>
> Psalm 37:5 AMPLIFIED

This is my husband Len's favorite verse of the entire Bible. He has leaned on this passage in recent years while making the switch from editing a magazine to publishing Christian books.

There is much in Scripture stressing our need to have faith in God. The above verse takes us a step further. It not only admonishes us to trust, it promises that when we do, God will act in a supernatural way to answer our need. Dwell on that for a moment. We turst, God acts. A mind-blowing premise.

Yet total, all-out trust on our part is not as easy as it first seems. There are periods when God's face is shrouded, when His dealings with us will *appear* as if He does not care, when He seems not to be acting like a true Father. Can we then hang onto the fact of His love and His faithfulness and that He *is* a prayer-answering God?

Can we get to the point Habakkuk reached: "Though the fig tree does not blossom, and there be no fruit on the vines . . . Yet I will rejoice in the Lord . . . !" (Habakkuk 3:17–18 AMPLIFIED).

Can we, *at the moment* when His face is hidden, exult in the God of our salvation? "The Lord God is my strength, my personal bravery and my invincible army" (v. 19).

Last Saturday morning Len had a chance to demonstrate the principle of trust in a difficult situation. He awoke with a very bad throat condition; could hardly speak. Yet he was supposed to give a talk that morning at a men's prayer breakfast in the local Lutheran church.

Before he left for the church I anointed him with oil, placed my hand on his throat, and asked the Lord to do a healing work in Len for the glory of God.

During the breakfast preceding Len's speech, however, he told me later, his voice got worse and worse until there was little left but a croak. The Lutheran pastor suggested turning the gathering into a discussion group, giving Len the chance to bow out. But no, my husband would at least try.

So Len stood up and uttered a rasping, halting first sentence, literally plunging ahead on faith. Suddenly, he reported afterwards, his voice cleared. From then on, for thirty-odd minutes, the message poured out with no cough, hardly even a clearing of the throat. The Holy Spirit had simply taken over. In the question period afterwards, still no problem with his throat.

But when he returned home, Len's voice was once again a painful whisper.

What fascinated me in this episode is how biblical it is: as the symptoms get worse, the temptation is there to "give up" and not to trust Jesus. We must resist that temptation in the midst of our very real human helplessness, "roll" the entire burden onto His shoulders, as He bade us do, step out and *take the first step* with bare, no-evidence-at-all faith.

And lo, He does take over gloriously, doing what we literally cannot do for ourselves.

2.

Lord, I Resent . . .

*T*hank [God] in everything—no matter what the circumstances may be, be thankful and give thanks; for this is the will of God for you [who are] in Christ Jesus . . .

1 Thessalonians 5:18 AMPLIFIED

Yesterday morning in my prayer time, God showed me that if I wanted more vitality for my work hours, I had to deal with the following resentments that were smoldering inside me.

I resent my lack of social graces in certain situations, which I'm inclined to blame on my childhood years when I too often fled social encounters.

I resent the fact that I'm such a poor sleeper. I can see that resentment produces tension and, of course, accumulated tension through the day is one reason I'm not sleeping better.

Here at Evergreen Farm there are so many stairs to climb, and outside, hills and more hills, which I cannot mount because of my breathlessness. This condition is a constant embarrassment and the central thorn in my flesh. I resent my damaged lungs.

I see this morning that there are deeper resentments still: that of creeping old age, being progressively shut down, as it were, and, of course, out there—death. Have I not always resented the fact of death, even though I have total belief in and expectancy about the life after death?

How can I come to terms with all this?

The answer came in the above verse. I am to praise God for *all* things, regardless of where they seem to originate. Doing this, He points out, is the key to receiving the blessings of God. Praise will wash away my resentments. I've known this, accepted it, even written about praise. But as I began praising Him yesterday, my efforts were wooden.

Then came these thoughts: I was to ignore my feelings and act on the principle. I was to do it despite the lack of joy—simply because God told me to. True praise grows out of the recognition and acknowledgment that in His time God will bring good out of bad. There is the intolerable situation on the one hand and the fulfillment of Romans 8:28 on the other. ("All things work together for good. . . .") By an act of will and through imagination and with faith, I am to turn my back on the bad and face the good, and begin actively to praise God for it as Scripture commands.

Shortly after this insight, my cleaning woman called in to say that she was not coming. Praised God for this, though mechanically.

Following that, joy began spilling over into the tiny everydayness of my life. Walked by a vase of beautiful roses from our garden and buried my nose in the fragrance, saying, "Praise You, Lord, for such beauty!"

Stepped onto our patio for a moment to listen to the birds singing. "Praise You, Lord, for all Your creatures."

Then came the feeling that all these small acts put together—little tricklets of praise—were running together, beginning to form a river of praise.

Continued to praise God for *all* things, good and bad. All setbacks, frustrations, and resentments.

Praise You, Lord, for my awkwardness in certain social situations.

Praise You, Lord, that I have trouble sleeping.

Praise You, Lord, for my weak lungs.

Praise You, Lord, for creeping old age.

Praise You, Lord, for the death that comes to all of us.

This morning I actually woke up with praise swelling in my heart. Only later did I realize I had slept through the entire night! Cannot remember when I last did this! Awakened by the coffee pot going on. Imagine! Praise God indeed!

3.

Do I Really Want to Get Well?

My heart is heavy this morning as I think of Rosalind. She is almost bedridden now with asthma. We went to pray for her healing yesterday, but she was more interested in talking about her ailments than in receiving Christ's love and power. How tragic!

This morning I turned again to the Gospel of John for the story of the man at the Pool of Bethesda who had been ill for thirty-eight years. As I read, I pretended I was there in Jerusalem myself, watching in the shadow of one of those great arched colonnades around the long pool. I could shut my eyes and see the scene as if it were happening today.

The man in this account is a chronic invalid, probably in his fifties or sixties. The stone floor around the large pool is crowded with the pallets of the crippled and the blind. But this man has been there longer than any. He is now the old-timer; his illness has virtually become his career and status symbol.

Now Jesus appears, threading His way through the porticos. He looks into the eyes of the sick man: "Do you want to become well?" (John 5:6 AMPLIFIED).

It seems a ridiculous question on the surface. Wouldn't anyone want to be healed of a physical handicap? But surprisingly, the invalid begins to stammer excuses.

"Sir," he replies to Jesus, "it's just that I haven't anybody to put me into the pool when the angel of healing is present. While I'm trying to get there, somebody else always gets into the water first."

As I read these words I knew that this sick man's problem was Rosalind's problem too. He thought he wanted healing, but even to his own ears his rationalizations must sound hollow. Yet those amazing eyes boring into his hold no contempt. Rather, Jesus issues a loving directive in a voice that rings with authority. "Pick up your bed and walk."

This is the moment of truth. I could picture the emotions moving across the pinched features: surprise, consternation, doubt, awareness, hope, then resolution. The man scrambles to his feet, picks up his bedroll, a well man.

How much this story says to me every time I read it—and can say to anyone who finds his fervent petitions unanswered. The principle here is: True prayer is dominant desire. If the person is divided in his real yearnings, he will experience emptiness and frustration.

I still remember vividly the three years in the 1940s when I myself was bedridden. Little by little I had come to enjoy my quiet life. I thought that I yearned for healing, but in fact I was not ready to shoulder the full responsibilities of vigorous health.

Only when I asked the Lord to mend my inner confusion was I able to go all-out in prayer. The healing of my physical disability followed.

Since that experience, I have been able to perceive this divided self as a major stumbling block to many people. I think of my friend in Washington, Jessie, who had been praying long and hard for her husband to be healed of alcoholism. Jessie was spiritually minded, her husband worldly and cynical. He was contemptuous of his wife's frequent trips to retreats and church meetings.

Several of us met regularly to pray with Jessie that her husband would encounter the living Christ for himself. Thanks to a group of vital Christian men, this came about, gloriously. John became a recovered alcoholic and a changed man.

The surprise was Jessie's reaction. Her criticism of John continued unabated. For the first time we, her friends, suspected the divided will in Jessie. Our suspicions were confirmed one night when one of the women suggested that Jessie thank God for so great an answer to our prayers for John.

Jessie could not do it. The words would not come. Then we understood. For years Jessie's prayers for John had gone unanswered because she had enjoyed standing above John on her pedestal marked "spiritual." Admired by friends for her suffering and patience with an alcoholic husband, she came to enjoy her martyr role. Therefore, the unsuspected desire of her deepest being had canceled out the prayer of her lips for John's conversion. Only when she was able to see this divided self and surrender it to God was she able to work out a better relationship with her husband.

It is so clear to me this morning. The divided self can defeat us in every area. Like finding the right job. When we hear the job-seeker insist on a string of specific conditions regarding salary, hours, pension, geographic location—we will often find a cleavage in his aspirations.

Fortunately, there is something we can do about the contradictions inside us.

First, we can present our long-standing, unanswered prayers to God for analysis. If there is any division of will deep inside, He will put His finger on it. This will hurt. We will be shocked—even as the man at the pool was, even as Jessie was.

Second, we can acknowledge this inner inconsistency and present it, without cringing or making excuses, to God for healing, asking Him to bring our conscious and subconscious minds into harmony. At this point He will almost always issue us a directive as Jesus did the man at the poolside. He asks that we prove our wholeheartedness by obedience. The moment that we rise to obey Him, we discover a great fact: that the word of God and the work of God are one. His words *are* life—with power to restore the atrophied will, to quicken pallid desire, to resurrect us from the graveclothes of a half-dead existence.

4.

To Live in the Present Moment

Iwant to record this morning that I did something yesterday, November 5, 1978, I do too seldom. For a period of time I lived fully in the present moment. What a healing this was for my spirit.

It happened in church. Six members of our family were sitting in the same pew.

Beside me was my tall son Peter, then his beautiful wife, Edith, and their two children, Mary Elizabeth and Peter Jonathan; on my other side, Len—so faithful, so solid. And we were all healthy and together and of one mind in the Lord. Great surges of gratitude washed over me and I was happier than I have been in a long time.

The Spirit seemed to say, "Bask in the moment. No matter that the future may hold problems. This is yours."

I did bask. It was golden.

My thankfulness flowed beyond the church walls. I thanked Him for my mother—now eighty-seven—who is still with us with her serene, cheerful disposition. How blessed I am, Lord, to have had You choose such a woman to bear me! I thank You for her lifelong gentleness . . . her womanliness, her unwavering faithfulness, her vision that always could lift our dreams on wings and send them flying beyond drudgery or mundane circumstances.

And for Len's three children, grown now, all Christians, each on the right path to his or her own fulfillment. How grateful I am for what they have taught me.

At that beautiful moment God seemed to be shining a light on each member of my family, saying, "See what I have wrought. Enjoy them, be thankful for them, for everything I make is good."

And my response this morning is to thank Him and praise Him in these words I find in His book:

Give thanks to the Lord, for he is good; his love endures forever.

Psalm 107:1 NIV

O Lord my God, you are very great; you are clothed with splendor and majesty.

Psalm 104:1 NIV

Shout for joy to the Lord, all the earth. Worship the Lord with gladness; come before him with joyful songs. . . . Enter his gates with thanksgiving and his courts with praise; give thanks to him and praise his name.

Psalm 100:1–2, 4 NIV

Thanks be to God! He gives us the victory through our Lord Jesus Christ.

1 Corinthians 15:57 NIV

5.

Helplessness

When I was still not asleep last night about 1:00 A.M., I swallowed one mild sleeping pill. No sleep! At five minutes to three, feeling empty, I got up, went to the kitchen, ate two Ritz crackers with peanut butter, drank a paper cup full of milk, and went back to bed.

Still no sleep! About 4:00 A.M., I took a second sleeping pill. It had no effect at all. I saw dawn break and finally got up.

I got down on my knees and prayed something like, "Lord, You have promised to talk to Your friends. Would you tell me what this is all about?"

I drank a cup of coffee in bed, had my quiet time—Bible reading, etc. No answer from Him. Dead silence.

Got down on my knees again and prayed. No response.

Or . . . was I simply not listening to the message He was speaking? As I was dressing, light began to dawn: He wants to demonstrate to me that I really am helpless without Him, that I really am dependent on Him *even for the sleeping pills to work.* Jesus put it this way:

Apart from Me—cut off from vital union with Me—you can do nothing.

John 15:5 AMPLIFIED

Since I am stubborn, He has been forced to bring this oh, so-very-basic truth home to me the hard way.

It was on the subject of sleep—the subject *I* wanted to know about—that He was silent. He did not promise me a thing, not that I would sleep beautifully without the sleeping pills, nor that I would sleep *with* them, this afternoon or tonight; nothing. Apparently, He wants me to place this whole area trustingly into His hands, believing that He loves me and wants me to be full of the vitality that comes from adequate sleep. Total dependence, that's the all-important lesson He wants me to learn. For regardless of what I do or do not do, whether I'm in a period of trusting Him or of pulling away, *He* never forgets that I belong to Him, that my life has been paid for with a price. *He* never lets me go!

This is such a *tremendous* base fact to know and to build on and to lean on.

Praise God for this tough experience!

6.

Spiritual Preparation for Surgery

*T*his morning I can look back over the past weeks and see clearly how God works in adversity. It began over a month ago with the doctor's words. "You're going to need surgery. . . ."

The procedure was "routine," he assured me, the problem most likely "minor," but no casual approach could soften the impact of the next sentence: "Of course, we never know what we'll find." Statistics on cancer then followed. "With this type of ovarian cyst, the percentage of malignancy is . . ."

Thus began a month's battle with fear. As I drove home from the doctor's office that beautiful September afternoon, the brilliant color of the autumn leaves seemed tarnished. How is it, I marveled, that bad news has a way of invading human life so suddenly? Trouble rings no warning bells. Adversity and sorrow stalk into life on rubber soles.

"Fear is lack of faith," I told myself. "It dishonors God." But then I discovered that I could not handle fear any more than I could mastermind any other strong emotion.

As Len and I talked over my situation, our first reaction was the very human one: "Is this operation really necessary?" However "routine" such surgery might be for the doctor, my inadequate lungs make any use of anesthesia a questionable risk. On the medical level, a second opinion seemed the wise course. We pursued this; the second examination confirmed the first.

Next came our conviction that we needed to pose the same question in prayer: "Lord, what is Your will? Do You want to handle my case through prayer alone?"

After all, Scripture provides clear directives and means of grace, which we ignore to our own detriment. From James 5:13–15: prayer with a group of fellow Christians, followed by the laying on of hands and/or anointing with oil by church elders or spiritual leaders. From 1 Corinthians 11:23–30: prayer at the altar rail of a church by a priest or pastor, with the laying on of hands and/or Communion.

How wonderful it is when God wants to move in this direct manner, and the way is clear for Him to do so! This is what happened to John Sherrill back in 1960 when a suspicious lump was discovered in John's neck and an operation scheduled to remove it. Since a melanoma cancer had been surgically removed from his ear two years before, John asked his rector for the ancient laying-on-of-hands ministry of the Episcopal Church.

Twenty-four hours later, when the famous cancer specialist at New York's Memorial Hospital operated, all he could find was a tiny, dried-up nodule. No lump, no malignancy. I know of other instances equally dramatic, where God has chosen to heal without medical intervention.

In my case, a group of fellow Christians began to meet with Len and me for prayer at 7:30 each morning. My crisis was their crisis. After two weeks in which we sought God's healing, I went for still one more examination. The doctor found no change. More intensive prayer followed; with it came the assurance that I was to go ahead with the operation, that my lungs would withstand the strain, and that there would be no cancer.

Apparently this was one of those times when God wishes us to make use of the skilled hands of surgeons. (God may have other purposes too, of course, such as some personal contact in the hospital He wishes us to make for Him.)

The next step in preparation came over the long-distance telephone from a Christian physician in North Carolina. "Over several years," he told me, "I have seen an incredible difference in the patient's post-operative condition between those who saturate surgery with prayer and those who don't. Most anyone facing surgery has fears. We can't just will them away. But God can handle our fears.

"Another thing," he went on. "Those undergirded with prayer often escape sticky little complications and just sail through the recovery. They even heal faster."

What helped me most of all during those long hours the night before the operation were two Scripture verses. The first promise spoke to fear:

> Fear not, [there is nothing to fear]. . . . For I, the Lord your God, hold your right hand; I, Who say to you, Fear not, I will help you!
>
> Isaiah 41:10, 13 AMPLIFIED

The second Scripture was a promise from the Psalms:

> Though I walk in the midst of trouble, thou wilt revive me . . . thy right hand shall save me.
>
> Psalm 138:7 KJV

As I read these reassuring words, a clear picture was dropped into my mind, childlike in its simplicity: the Lord would be standing on the right side of the operating table, facing me, looking into my eyes.

Of course. He would have to be in that position since the Isaiah promise was that He would hold my right hand, and the promise from the Psalms was that by *His* right hand, He would save me. *How beautiful!* I thought.

At ten minutes to eight the next morning, Len and our daughter, Linda, who had flown down from Washington, arrived at my hospital room just as an orderly appeared to roll me to the operating room.

"A quick prayer," Len said. He had no sooner said, "Amen" than the telephone rang. It was our dear friend, the Reverend Joe Bishop. "I can't believe this split-second timing," I told him. "The orderly is here to take me to surgery."

"Then time for one more prayer," Joe said. His loving benediction was all around us as we left the room.

All through the corridors Len and Linda walked beside the stretcher, right up to the anteroom.

As I was wheeled into the operating room I was given a beautiful three-part promise, one from each Person of the Trinity:

God the Father would hold me in His everlasting arms.
Jesus would take my right hand in His.
From the moment I lost consciousness, the Holy Spirit would be my Breath of life.

After that, suddenly I found that fear was nowhere around.

LL Note: The cyst was benign. Catherine had a recovery as swift and uneventful as the North Carolina doctor predicted.

7.

My Yoke Is Easy

For many years I have pondered the following words of Jesus, wanting to bear them out in my life, repeatedly falling short:

Come to Me, all you who labor and are heavy-laden and over burdened, and I will cause you to rest—I will ease and relieve and refresh your souls.

Take My yoke upon you, and learn of Me; for I am gentle (meek) and humble (lowly) in heart, and you will find rest—relief, ease and refreshment and recreation and blessed quiet—for your souls.

For My yoke is wholesome (useful, good)—not harsh, hard, sharp or pressing, but comfortable, gracious and pleasant; and My burden is light and easy to be borne.

Matthew 11:28–30 AMPLIFIED

Then at age sixty-five I was given a whole new perception of these verses through my friend, Roberta Dorr, author of the novel *Bathsheba*. During a visit at our home, she told me of the miracle-healing of her doctor-husband from supposedly incurable Hodgkins disease.

The diagnosis was made while her husband, David, was still in surgical residency. Having a laid-back temperament, David accepted the verdict of a very limited life span and went about his work.

But Roberta has a different nature—always seeking to understand, always questioning, always a fighter. She resisted the idea of losing her beloved husband and seeing their three small children grow up without a father. She and her husband had just filled out the final papers and were ready for an appointment to a hospital in Africa when the diagnosis was made final. Why, she asked over and over, had this happened?

No answer came. Until at last, with total relinquishment she asked God the right question, "How do You want me to pray about my husband?"

One morning shortly afterward, this thought was planted in her mind: "Pray that your husband will be able to *use* for the good of others the medical training he has been given."

As soon as Roberta prayed *this* prayer, the tremendous burden lifted from her heart. She had discovered that the yoke Jesus offered really did bring peace; by praying *His* prayer, sharing with Him His concern for all of suffering humanity, she was able to repose her load on His great strength. One year later the doctors at Johns Hopkins were astonished during a periodic test to discover no trace of disease in David. They were frank to say that they did not understand what had happened. Three years later, they dismissed him entirely, still unable to explain it. The disease never reappeared, but during the four years of "waiting," David completed a surgical residency that was to change his life. Instead of going to Africa, he went to the Gaza Strip where he was desperately needed as a surgeon.

It was while the Dorrs were on a medical mission to the Middle East that Roberta had further illumination about what it means to be yoked together with Jesus. (The Dorrs spent a total of seventeen years in Yemen and Gaza.) Perhaps seeing double-yoked oxen working the fields helped bring the truth home to her.

Roberta had always thought of these verses in Matthew as a metaphor of Jesus helping her with *her* projects, *her* life—plowing *her* field, so to speak.

Then one day the Lord said to her something like this: "No, you have it all wrong—backwards. Drop your plans. At the beginning of each day simply ask to be yoked with Me for *My* work, to plow *My* field. Then you will find that the yoke fits perfectly and that the burden truly is light."

I've thought a lot about Roberta's experience. First, David's healing. Did it happen in part because David was so involved in ministering to other people that he didn't have time to dwell on his own illness? Did he not only find refreshment in serving his Lord, but healing as well?

Not the whole answer, of course, but a clue toward that great mystery of how and why miraculous healings take place.

Second, there's much for me to ponder about the injunction Roberta received to "drop her plans" and listen for God's plan for her.

Again I'm back to relinquishment. Time after time I've laid my concerns, questions, doubts, plans, on God's altar. The problem for me is leaving them there.

At age sixty-five I still have that determination to take charge of my life, to prove that I can still do everything I did when I was twenty. I still want God to applaud my good works. It's so ridiculous! No wonder I have trouble sleeping and breathing.

Meanwhile, God waits patiently for me to come to Him, forgetting my agenda, so that I can hear what He has in mind for me.

Is it possible for an opinionated woman in her autumn years to become like a child and sit at the feet of Jesus with one idea—to hear what He will say?

8.

The Joy of the Lord
Shall Be Your Strength

For weeks now I have been so discouraged about the quality of my writing that I wonder if I am capable of doing another novel. Is *Christy* to be the only one?

The new novel I've been working on is set in western Pennsylvania during the 1930s. So far it seems lifeless. The characters aren't real to me yet.

Yesterday was the low point as I struggled to get words on paper. I had a mental picture of myself as a lost, crying sheep at the bottom of a very deep pit. Then with startling clarity these words of Jesus flooded my thinking:

> I tell you the truth, I am the gate for the sheep . . . whoever enters through me will be saved. He will come in and go out, and find pasture.
>
> John 10:7–9 NIV

How like Jesus to rescue people like me, not because we have done, or are currently doing, one solitary thing to deserve it. I sought Him and last night He reached down and, with His shepherd's crook, physically and spiritually lifted me out of the pit. Today He is comforting me even as He puts renewed strength into me.

It happened through a dream, fragments of which remained in my mind upon awakening.

In the dream I had a basket in my hands decorated around the rim and sides with flowers and leaves. I was having to "redo" the decorations. As I took off the old ones I was surprised to find how easy they were to remove. But there was an even greater surprise: I *expected* the flowers to be artificial ones, but found them not only real flowers, but surprisingly fresh.

When I awoke there was a joy and a release springing from deep in my spirit and my heart was full of praise.

The message of the dream appeared to be not only my own readiness to begin work on the novel again, but even divine approval of the timing. And the ease with which the bunches of flowers were removed from the basket and the fact that they were *fresh*, seemed to say, "The task of revision will not be as difficult as you have thought, and you will find the material fresh."

I have long known that my writing is never truly on target unless I feel at some point, while in the process of getting words on paper, that certain hallmark of joy within. The scene I am attempting to write may be quite a serious one, but the touchstone of joy must be there—or else I'm working in my own strength, not His.

It will take a little while to turn around a habit of negative thinking about this book—but Jesus is beginning to do that for me this morning. In fact, He who *always* gives to us "more abundantly than we could ask or think" has given me a glimpse of *His* vision for this novel.

I had been realizing the last few days, as I have been doing a quick rereading of the words already written, that I am at the same point in this book I was with *A Man Called Peter* when I received the devastating critique: "You haven't yet gotten *inside* the man Peter."

It was after I fell into a pit of discouragement over that remark that God told me, "No man's life has ultimate significance apart from what that man's life shows about God." So I re-outlined Peter's story *that* way.

Now God is telling me to think of the novel like this: We are living in a time when evil and trouble seem rampant. Every person I know has *trouble* of some kind.

So I am to separate the strands of the different kinds of trouble in the novel, and see what God's solution is to each one. For instance, we have

Economic trouble—I am writing of the Depression times, the 30s.

Emotional depression—Ken, the father, with his conviction that he is a failure.

Ecological trouble—powerful financial interests ignore environmental danger signs.

Natural disaster—the final flood. What is God saying here? To us today?

I'm going to have to listen to the Inner Voice *very* carefully to "get" all this, but praise God, oh, how I praise Him for this revelation! For He is saying, "Yes, yes, of *course* I want you to write this book. Yes, yes, it has an important message for our time."

Oh, thank You, Lord. Thank You for the return of joy to my life!

9.

The Intercessors

Yesterday this Scriptural passage seemed to leap out at me:

And he [the Lord] saw that there was no man, and wondered that there was no intercessor. . . .
Isaiah 59:16 KJV

Then came a rather startling bit of guidance from the Lord (I want to check this out with others). He seemed to be asking me to set up an intercession ministry that would consist chiefly of people with the desire and the faith to pray for others, and the time to devote to it—like many of the elderly, or handicapped, or those who earnestly want to be used by God but can't figure out *how* to be useful within the limitations of family demands, geographical location, etc.

To these intercessors would be forwarded the letters and requests we receive from those who need prayer—with names removed, of course—to whom it could mean everything to know that other people are lifting them up. My conscience hurts me when people write for prayer and I can give so little time to each one, for there are so many.

It would mean an incredible job of collation and feedback, a lot of postage, probably a newsletter with real input on the subject of intercessory prayer. Since this is a phase of prayer about which I know least, I'm surprised the Lord would lay this upon me.

LL Note: This was Catherine's first journal notation (June 1, 1980) about intercessory prayer; her guidance grew stronger with the passing weeks. From this single verse in Isaiah has grown the Intercessors prayer movement, launched in the fall of 1980 as part of the nonprofit organization Breakthrough, Inc. (Lincoln, Virginia 22078). As of April 1, 1986, there were 1500 intercessors enrolled to handle the thousands of prayer requests received each year. The newsletter (put out eight times a year) was being mailed to 12,000 people involved in intercession.

Section Five

Spiritual Warfare

*E*arly *in our marriage Catherine and I went through periods when we seemed to be up against a kind of unexplained opposition: there would be a series of breakdowns in our household equipment; times when all the children misbehaved for no apparent reason; work would be constantly interrupted; and we would feel a heaviness in our spirits. At first we tried to examine these happenings logically; then as we learned more about the dark powers and principalities at work in the world we realized that on occasion we were under a form of satanic attack.*

When Catherine was writing Beyond Our Selves, *she reported the spirit of opposition in her office as being almost palpable. No wonder, since this book more than any other of hers helped people move from unbelief or an uncertain faith into making a commitment to Jesus Christ as Lord.*

As we learned more about "the enemy" and his cohorts, we were able to pray against those dark spirits, reducing their effectiveness. But we were never free from them. In fact as the years went by, we accepted the fact that for all of us engaged in Christian service, there is never-ending spiritual warfare.

In the final years of her life, as her body weakened from a series of ailments, Catherine had a daily battle with the dark forces. Rebuking the enemy in the name of Jesus was the best weapon for reclaiming the creative atmosphere to do our work, to minister to others, to protect our home environment.

But we could never relax our vigilance.

LL

1.

Fear

*L*ast night I had a vivid dream. . . . While driving a car, I became terrified of what was ahead. With no clear idea of what the problem was, I could not seem to keep from doing the very worst thing possible—*closing my eyes as I drove.*

Then I was driving over a concrete road with about three inches of very clear water on it. There was still overwhelming fear in me. I awoke in panic.

As I pondered it this morning, the message of this dream would appear to be that my actual danger is very small—shallow water. Thus my real problem is fear itself. Fear of many things, including God Himself.

He scolded me for this—gently—this morning, reminding me that fear is one of Satan's tools. The *fear of God*—the wrong kind, that is, fearfulness rather than awe—is something I have struggled with for so many, many years. And I sense that many believing people are like me, unable to love and praise their Heavenly Father fully because of fear—often a fear of punishment.

Then I remembered something that Jesus did. Knowing that all people struggle with fear, He often prefaced what He was about to say to His fellow humans with the words, "Fear not."

Therefore my prayer is, "Lord, I hand my fears over to You, fears of all kinds. Fear of You is actually a kind of blasphemy against Your character. I'm sorry. Forgive me."

In answer to my prayer, a line from an old hymn, "Take it to the Lord in prayer," began running through my mind. The Spirit said very clearly, "Why do you think I am reminding you of these words? *Pay attention to every line of these verses.* Learn to bring everything directly to Me instead of allowing so many worrying wonderings."

> *What a Friend we have in Jesus*
> *All our sins and griefs to bear!*
> *What a privilege to carry*
> *Everything to God in prayer.*
> *O what peace we often forfeit,*
> *O what needless pain we bear,*
> *All because we do not carry*
> *Everything to God in prayer.*
>
> *Have we trials and temptations?*
> *Is there trouble anywhere?*
> *We should never be discouraged—*
> *Take it to the Lord in prayer.*
> *Can we find a friend so faithful*
> *Who will all our sorrows share?*
> *Jesus knows our every weakness—*
> *Take it to the Lord in prayer.*
>
> *Are we weak and heavy-laden*
> *Cumbered with a load of care?*
> *Precious Saviour, still our refuge—*
> *Take it to the Lord in prayer.*
> *Do thy friends despise, forsake thee?*
> *Take it to the Lord in prayer;*
> *In His arms He'll take and shield thee—*
> *Thou wilt find a solace there.*
> *Joseph Scriven (1819–1886)*

2.

Fear of Death

Avisit from Betty Malz this week has forced me to do something I keep putting off—examining my attitude about death.

After returning to life from twenty-eight minutes of being dead (*My Glimpse of Eternity*), Betty is so full of *details* of what life will be in eternity, as well as bubbling over with stories of remarkable answers to prayer, that being with her is like a feast.

Yet our conversation several nights ago highlighted my own wrong emotional orientation to death. Though I know intellectually that Jesus *did* conquer death, though I believe with my mind in immortality, my emotions deny this. Somewhere back in my childhood certain experiences planted firmly the conviction that death is our enemy, to be hated and fought every step of the way. By the time I was in my teens, I was writing poetry full of emotional rebellion about the brevity of our lives here and how pathetically unfair that is.

I slept almost none at all night before last, finding in myself a deep unrest about all this.

Yesterday morning as I prayed about it, I remembered a New Testament verse about those "who for fear of death are in bondage all their lives." This seemed such an exact description of me that I thought, *I'd like to take a look at that verse.* Whereupon the Helper clearly said (in my thoughts), *Look in Hebrews.*

So I turned to that book, not having the least idea *where* in Hebrews. I found the verse in the second chapter, fifteenth verse.

Verse fourteen talks about what Jesus did for us on the Cross:

. . . that by [going through] death He might bring to nought and make of no effect him who had the power of death, that is, the devil.

Verse fifteen:

And also that He might deliver and completely set free all those who through the (haunting) fear of death were held in bondage throughout the whole course of their lives.

AMPLIFIED

How to the point! I decided that I had been in emotional bondage to the fear of death long enough, that Satan had used this as a way of stirring up doubt and confusion in me. All of which interfered with my having full fellowship with the Father.

So I made a date with Betty Malz and Len for 4:30 yesterday afternoon and in prayer together we claimed my freedom, asking that Jesus fulfill His promise "to deliver and completely set free."

Last night at the church meeting where Betty spoke, one of the hymns we sang was "Be Still, My Soul." The words were like a Night Letter straight from the heart of God in answer to my claiming prayer in the afternoon (italics added).

Be still, my soul—the Lord is on thy side!
Bear patiently the cross of grief or pain;
Leave to thy God to order and provide—
In every change He faithful will remain.

Be still, my soul—thy best, thy Heavenly Friend
Through thorny ways leads to a joyful end.

Be still, my soul—thy God doth undertake
To guide the future as He has the past,
Thy hope, thy confidence let nothing shake—
All now mysterious shall be bright at last . . .

3.

Self-dissatisfaction

*L*ast night I dreamed I was making a telephone call from a department store pay phone. There was immense trouble, though, about finding the number. I could not locate the yellow pages of the directory. Then I thought that I might have the number written in one of two notebooks in my handbag. But the two notebooks kept getting mixed up, and as I would find the page, someone else would push into the phone booth ahead of me, and my finger would slip out of place in the little notebook. Once I located the number, only to find it so blurry that I could not read it.

The message my unconscious seems to be playing back to me—confusion. Not enough order in my life, or even in my pocketbook.

This morning as I sought answers in prayer to a number of problems, the same spirit of confusion seemed to settle upon me. Quickly I asked for His help. After a few moments I was led to Psalm 78. These verses hit me:

He divided the sea and led them through. . . . He guided them with the cloud by day and with light from the fire all night. He split the rocks in the desert and gave them water as abundant as the seas. . . . But they continued to sin against him rebelling in the desert against the Most High. They willfully put God to the test by demanding the food they craved.

vv. 13–18 NIV

. . . and his wrath rose against Israel, for they did not believe in God or trust in his deliverance.

vv. 21–22 NIV

Was I full of doubts and questions and criticism like the Israelites? Yes, I had to admit I was. How can I be free of this, Lord?

These words of reassurance came:

"Thou art my beloved child, Catherine. Rest in that love. . . . Simply rest in it. Bathe in it. Stop asking so many questions. Stop all this probing, taking your spiritual temperature. Does the Lord want me to do this? Or that? Is this right? Is that right? This is the source of the confusion you are feeling.

"You *are* My child, My disciple. I accepted you long ago—*as you are*—as you are growing.

"You are *still* accepted. Nothing is between us from My side, only yours! Grasp that by faith and all else will follow.

"The nervous probing is Satan's doing, to unsettle you, to confuse you, to knock you off the base of your belief.

"Let My joy flow through you unimpeded, even though you do not feel it at first. *Let it flow. Be not afraid.* That joy will sweep away your fear and uncertainties.

"Stop accusing yourself, Catherine. Turn any such thoughts over to Me instantly. They come from Satan, not from Me.

"Place yourself in My hands as though you were an infant. Let *Me* handle your questions, the tattered remnants of your unbelief, your growth in My *grace*—not My stringency.

"Grace . . . grace . . . grace. Love . . . love . . . love. I came *not* to judge or to condemn. *All* accusation comes from the enemy.

"Open the floodgates that My love can bathe you and that the living water may flow through you to others."

4.

Free from Bondage

*S*arah, a woman in our Tuesday night group at church, told us the following experience.

For years she had been struggling to quit smoking. She would get down to two packs a week, then back up to three, endlessly defeated. Her conscience hurt her about the grip that cigarettes had on her.

Sarah sat on the front row the night Len did a Bible study on how the Holy Spirit can free us from any habit that binds us and keeps us from a close relationship to Jesus. The Scripture he focused on:

> For if you live according to the sinful nature, you will die; but if by the Spirit you put to death the misdeeds of the body, you will live, because those who are led by the Spirit of God are sons of God.
>
> Romans 8:13–14 NIV

In his talk, Len included alcohol, drugs, cigarettes, food, and sex as pitfalls for the compulsive personality. Sarah told us later that she began to associate Len with her cigarette struggle.

One night Sarah had a short, vivid dream in which Len was present. Then she saw a hand with a lighted cigarette between the fingers. The fingers began vigorously and repeatedly tamping out the cigarette. With that the dream ended.

When Sarah awoke the next morning she pondered whether the meaning of the dream could be as obvious as it seemed. Scarcely thinking, she reached for her package of cigarettes. There was a single cigarette left. She lighted it, but it tasted different, not at all good. She tamped it out and has had no desire to smoke since. Her tastes, her desire-world itself, had been transformed by the Spirit.

Later Len and I shared with the group the following steps we use in praying for someone in the grip of addiction:

1. In the name of Jesus move against the powers of darkness that have attached themselves to R——'s mind and will.
2. With Christ's authority, drive these forces back a day at a time. Persist. No matter how long it takes; refuse to be discouraged.
3. Once you have captured any piece of ground in R——'s mind from the enemy, occupy it with a declaration of faith, telling Satan he cannot return.
4. When R—— has been released from an addiction, pray for his salvation and his infilling by the Holy Spirit.

We also suggested that anyone who, like Sarah, has been released from addiction, hold onto the following verse:

Stand fast therefore in the liberty wherewith Christ hath made us free, and be not entangled again with the yoke of bondage.

Galatians 5:1 KJV

5.

Satan's Best Weapon

*T*here is an oft-repeated story about the time Satan gathered his co-workers together for a strategy session. The purpose: find more effective ways to tempt Christians into sin.

One evil spirit said, "Let's set before them the delights of sin."

Satan shook his head. "That works up to a point, but not with the strong believers."

Another incubus suggested, "We can show them that virtue is costly."

Satan again shook his head. "They know that the rewards are worth it."

The third little demon had a knowing look in his eye. "Let's bring discouragement to their souls."

"Now you have it!" cried Satan. "Discouragement is the weapon!"

How true it is! Right now I am worn down by lack of sleep. I thought I had won a victory over sleeplessness and dependence on sleeping pills six years ago. But lately I've been in the pit of despair. Nor has going back to a mild sleeping pill helped.

This morning I want to put on paper what it is like to try and sleep. I go to bed fatigued, yet am not able to let go. The sleep mechanism of the frontal lobe of my brain is apparently all askew. It's as if the stay-alert function is working overtime— night and day. Even at moments when, out of total weariness, I am about to drop off, the brain sends the message, "Wake up!" and I jerk to.

There is a constant tiredness behind my eyes, lids are heavy as if pressing the eyes back into the head.

I cannot find any comfortable position in bed. Make elaborate arrangements with pillows and sheet, but no sooner settled than I am moving again. What to do with the arms to keep them from aching? How to place my neck?

My face itches and I must scratch. There's a cramp in one leg and I flex and unflex my toes. The sheet is scratching my chin. Right arm is hot. Finally, I tumble to the fact that there can be no sleep until I lie perfectly still for a while. Yet it's agony to force myself to do so.

The nights seem endless. How can they be so long?

When I do—toward dawn—drop off, the "sleep start" wakens me abruptly. A muscle in a leg gives a sudden jerk.

I have come to hate the bed, yet am drawn to it, always hopeful. Isn't it man's *natural* state to sleep? Lord, I'm exhausted and discouraged.

So many times discouragement has been the doorway through which the powers of evil have flooded into my situation. For discouragement says, "My problem is bigger than God, who is not adequate to handle my particular need. So herewith I take my eyes off God, bow down before my problem, and give myself to it."

In digging through Scripture on this subject, I have discovered that no matter how difficult the situation, Jesus' attitude was always a calm, "Courage, My son, My daughter. Have no fear. There is nothing here that My Father cannot handle."

It was not that Jesus minimized the problem, but rather that His faith was a magnet for God's power. He knew that *no* problem was any match for the Lord God Almighty.

I confess now that I am discouraged because I have been relying on myself rather than on You, Lord; I have expected something from myself and am deeply disappointed not to find it there. I want to think that I can handle things myself . . . succeed better . . . do more than others.

In *The Practice of the Presence of God*, Brother Lawrence writes that he was never upset when he had failed in some duty. He simply confessed his fault, saying to God, "I shall never do otherwise, if You leave me to myself; it is You who must hinder my failing and mend what is amiss." After this admission, he gave himself no further uneasiness about it.

What the devil wants us to do, of course, is to focus on our failure rather than on Jesus. For when we keep our eyes on Him, we find that no problem—of the 1st century or the 20th—has ever defeated Him.

Jesus never encountered a human situation that discouraged Him. Sickness and disease? Jesus healed a man blind from birth . . . a woman who'd had an issue of blood for twelve years . . . another bent double with arthritis for eighteen years. At not one of these cases did Jesus look with despairing heart.

Did sin get Him down? Never, no matter how heinous. Jesus insisted that He had come into the world not to condemn us, but to save us (John 8:15; 12:47). His attitude was that any time spent in condemnation, in wallowing in old sins and regrets, in recriminations, in kicking ourselves around, is wasted time.

The woman taken in adultery, He forgave and restored—immediately.

Zaccheus had spent a lifetime in greed and grasping. Yet Jesus told him, "*This* day has salvation come to thy house."

Jesus' word in any situation was one of encouragement.

To the paralytic borne by four: "Courage, My son!"

To the ruler of the synagogue whose daughter was dying: "Have no fear, only believe, and she shall get well."

To Martha, grieving over her dead brother: "Said I not unto thee, that if thou wouldst believe, thou shouldst see the glory of God?"

Hear that, Satan? In the name of Jesus, I kick you and discouragement out of my life.

6.

The Other Side of the Mountain

Yesterday David Hill from Dallas telephoned and was on for forty-five minutes. David has had an escape from some sort of cult. He is unmarried, thirty-two or thirty-three, and has been a Christian for eight years. *What* a mature Christian he is for an eight-year-old!

He has had quite a bit of experience with spiritual warfare, and one of the helpful facts he gave me is that when we're engaged in these battles energy is sapped from us and we are *very* prone to depression. *Exactly* my state for the last two months!

He also painted a very vivid picture of Genesis 22. As Abraham and Isaac were toiling up Mount Moriah, Satan must have been tempting Abraham every few minutes. "Surely you did not hear God correctly! Sacrifice your son and heir? Why should you do such an evil thing? Why, Isaac was God's special gift to you in your wife's old age. You're probably just getting senile, etc., etc."

But at *that very moment* that Abraham was struggling with his thoughts, the ram was traveling up the *other* side of the Mount, and God was preparing the way of escape.

David's message was, God always is working on the "ram part"—the escape, God's own way out.

7.

Knowing the Enemy

*H*ow much better we will withstand Satan's assaults when we're wise to his tactics! Thus, these past few days I've been searching the Bible for insights as to the forces—within and without—arrayed against us.

The Serpent's Strategy:

First of all the serpent's objective was to call God a liar, to contradict His Word, to tell Eve—and us—"His Word is not so." It was because Eve believed the serpent as over against God that the Fall came (Genesis 3:2–4).

The serpent's second strategy was to tell Eve, in effect, "God is out to take away or withhold something good from you."

The third trick was to tempt the woman into letting the forbidden fruit play upon her senses. She put herself in the way of the temptation, walked around it, looked at it, toyed with it (Genesis 3:6).

Three curve balls—and Eve struck out.

The Immediate Results of her sin:

1. Eve wanted fellowship in her disobedience. She felt at once the sense of isolation that sin brings. Inevitably when we do wrong we want to drag other people down with us. So Eve gave the fruit to Adam to eat (v. 6).
2. Innocence was gone. Both the man and the woman knew they were naked.
3. They had no desire for fellowship with God; ran from Him; in fact, hid themselves from Him (Genesis 3:8).
4. They knew fear (v. 10).
5. They knew shame (vv. 7–10).
6. Each blamed his sin on someone else:
   Adam—on Eve (v. 12).
   Eve—on the serpent (v. 13).

The Far-reaching Results:

1. Woman is reduced to a subordinate position to man.
2. In sorrow and pain and difficulty will the reproduction process take place. Moreover, woman will be something of a slave to her sexual desire for her husband (v. 16).
3. Man shall till the ground, which will be stubborn in producing for him. He will get food by the sweat of his brow (vv. 17–19).
4. Death enters life—"To dust thou shalt return" (v. 19).
5. Adam and Eve begin to wear clothing, symbol of perpetual loss of innocence (v. 21).
6. They are driven from the Garden and the Tree of Life (vv. 23–24).

How seriously did Jesus take demons?
Apparently very seriously indeed. When He sent the first group of disciples on the first mission, His charge to them was:
First: Preaching
Second: Casting out demons (Mark 3:14–15).
The demons always seemed to have recognized:

1. *Who Jesus was* (Mark 1:24, 34; 3:11; 5:7).
2. *That Jesus was against them all the way.*
3. *That they had to obey Him* (Mark 1:25–28, 5:12–13).

Jesus' dealing with demons:

1. He rebuked them (Mark 1:25).
2. He then gave them a direct order (Mark 1:25, 5:8).
3. He charged them not to reveal who He was (Mark 3:12).

The result for the possessed individual:

1. He is often buffeted and thrown about (Mark 1:26).
2. But the demon obeys Jesus and departs (Mark 1:26).

These further insights have come as I pondered Satan's inroads into my own heart and will:

1. When we rejoice over, or look for, or repeat with relish negative news, then we have placed ourselves on the side of evil.
2. It is possible to take this negative stance so often with regard to situations and persons that this becomes a way of life. Negative thinking is really a weapon of Satan. *We* call it "realism"; Christ calls it "not believing the truth."
3. We do not realize how definitely our mind-set—that is, what the mind picks out from all the news to highlight—reveals *whose* side we're really on.
4. Even after we have accepted Jesus and asked Him to come and live within us, Satan will keep trying to persuade us that the flesh is dominant and must be obeyed. Satan will also feed us the lie that "that's human nature" and there's nothing we can do about it.
5. The response to Satan's attacks has to be *faith*. When I became Jesus' woman, a series of marvelous things happened—whether the effects are visible yet, or not. Among them, as I accepted the atoning work of Jesus for me, I was unshackled on the inside from my bondage to the flesh, freed from the ascendance of flesh over spirit (Romans 8:2). Paul says that when we accept this wonderful liberation by faith, and begin to live it out, we find that the flesh now *has* to obey the spirit, that Satan has been subdued, overcome, deprived of his power (Romans 8:3). Realizing this, we need only allow the Holy Spirit to lead the way, step by step, obedient act by obedient act, like a conquering General victoriously marching ahead (Romans 8:9–16).

8.

Offensive Warfare

Yesterday, I read a pamphlet by Ralph Mahoney, editor of *World Map Digest*, who makes the following powerful points about spiritual warfare:

1. "On this rock I will build my church, and the gates of hell will not overcome it" (Matthew 16:18 NIV).

Now, gates are stationary. *They* are fixed in place, stay put. Therefore, the "gates of hell" cannot move against us. So Jesus has to mean that His church is to take the offensive against the citadel of Satan.

The picture (according to Mahoney) is of a victorious Church laying siege to hell and breaking down the gates to release its prisoners.

2. "That enemy of yours, the devil, roams around like a lion roaring [in fierce hunger], seeking someone to seize upon and devour" (1 Peter 5:8 AMPLIFIED). Peter did not write those words to scare us to death, says Mahoney.

For the key word is *like* the lion. Satan is always an imitator, a fake, a bluff, a counterfeit. He *isn't* a lion. His claws were drawn out at Calvary.

3. The real Lion is Jesus, "the Lion of the tribe of Judah" (Revelation 5:5 AMPLIFIED). We Christians have no strength or ability in ourselves for fighting Satan, or for pulling down gates, or anything else.

But as we allow the Lion of Judah to live in us, we take on the nature of Him who is the real Lion. Our weapons—fickle and weak of themselves—pass through God and become mighty enough to make hell itself tremble with fear.

9.

Conversations with God

LL Note: *As she learned more and more about confronting Satan with his lies and deceit, rebuking him daily, and seeking to hear the voice of the Lord, the answers from Him became clearer and clearer. Here are excerpts from Catherine's 1981 journal:*

"Lord, I need Your help in so many areas. How can I better hear Your voice?"

You need to begin listening in the absolute quiet as you did during that summer long ago on Cape Cod. Remember how you lay on the daybed in the living room, pen and notebook in hand, in absolute stillness? I spoke to you then—and will again.

A morning Quiet Time should be that—not simply reading in this book or that. What I, your Lord, have to say to you is more important than the best wisdom of any author.

"Lord, my novel goes so slowly. The words I put on paper seem so wooden. I need Your Help."

I am glad you have asked Me to be your editor. Turn to Me each time you begin writing for specific directions. If you want real creativity, follow My inner directives.

Now, start reading 2 Corinthians and I'll have more to say to you.

"Lord, I wince at 2 Corinthians 2:9: obedience in all things. How do I achieve that? I feel like such a failure in that area."

Child—you always take life too seriously—with too heavy a spirit, too anxious a mien. A true child of Mine has no need to worry so. You act as if you think you have to do everything yourself, as if I, your Burden Bearer, am not with you at all. Do you really think that honors Me?

Do you not see the egotism in all this? Satan has gotten a toehold in this attitude-area in you, and you have failed to recognize it so that you can deal with it. He is the one who wants you burdened down, fatigued, feeling overwhelmed with work.

"Lord, what a gorgeous revelation! Thank You, thank You. . . . But how do I kick the old boy out and let You turn these wrong attitudes around?"

By recognizing Satan's lies. For example, he wants you to think that your everyday life is monotonous and dull. The very opposite is true. Satan's aim is always to turn your eyes to the world. That's not for you. Even during that brief period in Washington when you thought you were making a little progress into Washington social life, it wasn't for you and would have garnered you husks had you achieved it. Forget it! Permanently! Your life is fascinating, with pleasant surprises every day. Praise Me for the richness of the life I have given you.

Each time you feel a negative attitude building up inside yourself, refuse to accept it. Recognize the satanic source of it, reject it, and turn to Me.

"Lord, there are doubts in me this morning. I admit it. Doubts that what I am writing down here is really You speaking and not just my wishful thinking or what I think You would say. How can I be sure?"

Proof in the world of the spirit never comes in the same way as in the material world. Don't try to transfer the techniques of what you call "evidence" from the one realm to the other.

Trust the Holy Spirit to be the link between us, to speak My words, transfer them to you—and He will. Was there not a sureness and a joy and a knowledge of My benediction on you yesterday that you have not known in a long time?

"Yes, there was, Lord. But there are so many things I want and need to talk over with You that it's going to take all eternity to do it."

Your endless curiosity, which at its best is real seeking, is from Me. Don't fight it. Those who seek Me, do find. Remember? "The poor in spirit". . . . Always I am ready to receive any questing. I bless you and love you beyond comprehension.

"Lord, I know that discouragement is from Satan, that I have no business being discouraged under any circumstances. But I am troubled about my novel. I don't feel I can finish it. How do I keep from giving into those down feelings?"

Patience, Catherine, patience. Don't be dismayed. What's happening to you is only a ripple, a little wave on a big sea. This too will pass. The hostages do come home. The prodigal does return. Joy cometh in the morning.

Take a deep breath, look to Me, and be glad. Smile again. The sky has not fallen in.

In other words, keep at it.

"Thank You, Lord. And thank You that the Spirit gave me this verse from Psalm 31 yesterday: 'My times are in your hand' (v. 15 AMPLIFIED)."

* * *

"Lord, what I read in Tournier's *The Healing of Persons* is exciting to me because I have long sought the answer to the problem of 'scruples,' of why I am the sort of person who is always finding some one little thing wrong in my life that I am convinced stands between me and You. I feel very guilty about having to go back to sleeping pills, even though they are the mildest available. So, Lord, the question I ask today: Am I exaggerating a minor problem, my scruple of the moment—sleeping pills—in order not to have to face up to something much more important that You really want me to look at?"

Do you not see that your love of sleep and your desire to escape into sleep is, in large part—and always has been—because you are reluctant to give more of yourself in love for others?

"What a revelation, Lord! But how do I go about letting You change something as ingrained in me as this? It would be asking You to change a lifelong habit pattern. Also, I'd be afraid that going the people route really would knock out my writing."

I told you that My yoke is easy and My burden is light, didn't I? My burden was and is and always has been love of people, love of you, Catherine. You've never believed Me that this burden is light. You'll find that this is so only as you allow Me to take you by the hand and lead you out. Are you willing?

"Yes, Lord."

"Lord, are there other sins You want me to look at, which I have perhaps avoided facing up to, by the smoke screen of small 'scruples'? What I long for is that love of You, and the realization of Your love for me, become the motivating factor in my obedience."

Ah, if only you knew how much I love you! If only you knew what love surrounds you from the "cloud of witnesses" here with me—your father, your brother, and Peter. If only you knew how many prayers are constantly flowing for you. How grateful you should be for the waves of good will flowing to you constantly from those who read your books.

Relax into My love. Allow Me to love you. There are times when a mother wants to hold her child. No words need pass between them, just the feel of love. This morning let Me love you like that. Let all spiritual strain and tension go. Relax in Me.

"How beautiful, Lord. I do!"

"Lord, is there any particular word You want to speak to me this morning?"

Your life has become unbalanced, Catherine, hence your boredom. You need to cook, to garden, to shop, to exercise more, to be with people more. The more you retreat into the idea-world away from people, the more unreal your Christianity and your relationship with Me will become—even though in such retreat you might think that you were being more spiritual.

"I had almost no sleep last night, Lord. This morning I am full of fears again."

Read the 91st Psalm, Catherine, and absorb it into your bone and marrow and bloodstream and mind and heart and spirit.

I will deliver Catherine. . . .

I will set her on high because she knows and understands My name, has a personal knowledge of My mercy, My love, My kindness. You, Catherine, are to trust and rely on Me, knowing that I will never forsake you.

You, Catherine, will call upon Me, and I will answer you; I will be with you in trouble, I will deliver you and honor you.

One fearful of the water can never get over the fear by standing on the bank shivering, consumed by the fear. . . .

I will not force one to do anything. . . .

Take the first step toward Me. Trust My love for you. Trust . . . trust!

SECTION SIX

The Final Victory

Early in 1982 Catherine realized her time on earth was limited. The emphysema in her lungs had been slowly reducing her vitality. Walking up a flight of stairs was a major undertaking. Talking to people, meetings, shopping drained her.

Saddest of all to see was how her growing breathlessness affected her mornings, the cream time for manuscript work she looked forward to so much. I would watch her go resolutely into her office at 9:00 A.M. Forty minutes later I would hear her return to our bedroom. Once I confronted her there as she lay listlessly on the bed.

Tears welled up in her eyes. "I try to concentrate," she said. "The inner drive is gone. I don't have it anymore."

Then she would rail at herself for being a quitter, get up, and try again. My dilemma was: Should I prod her into doing what was painful and hard, or let her drift into invalidism?

The answer soon became clear. Catherine's basic competitiveness, her battling nature, her spirit of adventure, and her curiosity about life could not, should not, be allowed to die. Catherine would never have forgiven me if I had encouraged her to let go of all this.

So we waged spiritual war against the forces of darkness and the enemy's subtle enticements to give in to weakness. The coffee-pot alarm continued to be set for 6:30 A.M. The day began with an hour of Scripture reading, prayer, and journal entries. During the morning, work continued on the novel Julie. Commitments to our prayer and fellowship groups were kept. We ended the day in prayer, when I anointed Catherine with oil, taking a stand against ill health, asking for sharpness of thinking and a healing of body and spirit.

LL

1.

His Unfinished Work in Me

reamed last night about death. I don't relish putting this one on paper, but since it *has* to be worked through with the Lord, I suppose I must.

I was in a country where certain citizens were being exterminated by order of the state. One got one's notice and came to a special "office" in which were three booths, side by side. In one of these you were given a shot, like a dog being "put to sleep." Afterwards you were carted off to a back room where the bodies were stacked.

Apparently my number had come up. When I got to the office, I noticed that there were stacks and stacks of dirty dishes in the three booths. I sought to stall my death by offering eagerly to wash all the dishes. The attendant said, "Sure, go ahead. I don't blame you. Just don't tell any of the others that I agreed."

I started to wash a stack of plates, saying to myself, "There's always the chance of something happening to intervene, a national emergency or something." Then I woke up.

So now that I have put this dream on paper, Lord, what does it mean—and what do I do about it?

As I waited for some response, a name came to mind— *John Wesley.* Tuttle's book on Wesley was in the stack of unread books on my night table. I picked it up and soon discovered that Wesley and I shared a dread of death as the Great Enemy. Wesley's fear surfaced dramatically in 1735 during a crossing of the Atlantic to Georgia. There were heavy storms at sea and the small wooden ship at times seemed doomed. Most on board, including the crew, were terror-struck. The only ones who remained calm were a group of German Moravian Christians.

Seeing the strength of these Christians as they faced death, Wesley knew he must work through his problem. In reviewing his walk of faith, he realized he had espoused a life of *asceticism*, which took four forms:

1. Self-denial. (He lived frugally in order to give money to the poor.)
2. Solitude.
3. Works of charity. (Including visits to the terrible prisons of the time where he prayed with condemned men.)
4. Interior life as exemplified by the great mystics.

Now Wesley had to admit that while each of these disciplines had a place in Christian life, not one of them dealt with his fear of death. Finally he began to see that this fear was not from God, as the mystics maintained, but from Satan.

Soon after these discoveries John Wesley had his personal experience of the Holy Spirit at Aldersgate. He was back against the basic New Testament proposition: There is no road to God except via faith in the finished work of Jesus Christ on the Cross. Joy flooded in and gradually his fear of death dropped away as the totality of these triumphant words of Jesus sank into his being:

In My Father's house there are many dwellng places (homes). If it were not so, I would have told you, for I am going away to prepare a place for you.

476

And when (if) I go and make ready a place for you, I will come back again and will take you to Myself, that where I am you may be also.

John 14:2-3 AMPLIFIED

I know that the Holy Sprit has much unfinished work to do inside me about my attitude toward death. I need this, and I will myself to desire it.

2.

Our Servant Role

I was the recipient of a beautiful and touching act last night that reverberates through my prayer time this morning. Myra Gertz, a friend and member of our church fellowship group, asked if she could drop in for a short visit.

As we talked I could see that she had something on her mind and was struggling how to say it. Finally she did.

"Catherine, I feel a bit foolish, but the Lord told me to come over and wash your feet. I don't know what this is all about and I've never done this before, but the Voice was very emphatic."

I was startled. My inner reaction was, *Oh, no! Surely, this is not necessary.* But our group had been learning to respect these nudges from the Spirit. "We certainly want to obey the Lord, Myra," I agreed.

Soon she was on the floor in front of me with towels and a basin of water. She removed my stockings and shoes and gently began washing my feet.

Tears filled my eyes as I felt the presence of the Lord through Myra. He had instigated this, just as He had done with His disciples two thousand years ago.

I was the needy one all right. My fatigue level had never been lower.

"Catherine, the Lord wants you to know He loves you deeply," Myra said as she finished drying my feet. "May I pray for you now?"

"Of course."

She did, asking for a healing in every part of me—mind, spirit, emotions, and body. A deep feeling of peace spread over me. "Thank you for being faithful, Myra," I said as she left.

This morning I read through the Scripture account of this act by Jesus in the New Testament book of John:

> When he had finished washing their feet, (Jesus) put on his clothes and returned to his place. "Do you understand what I have done for you?" he asked them.
>
> "You call me 'Teacher' and 'Lord,' and rightly so, for that is what I am. Now that I, your Lord and Teacher, have washed your feet, you also should wash one another's feet. I have set you an example that you should do as I have done for you. I tell you the truth, no servant is greater than his master, nor is a messenger greater than the one who sent him. Now that you know these things, you will be blessed if you do them."
>
> John 13:12–17 NIV

I have set you an example that you should do as I have done for you. . . . Myra had been obedient to this instruction of Jesus, although I can imagine what she went through, wondering if it would seem overemotional to me.

And it did, at first. But how I needed it. I was hurting. Jesus knew this, wanted to demonstrate His love for me and chose Myra as His vessel. If she had not been faithful, a beautiful inner healing experience would not have happened.

3.

Body Language

*I*beseech you therefore, brethren . . . that ye present your bodies a living sacrifice, holy, acceptable unto God, which is your reasonable service.

Romans 12:1 KJV

Reading the Bible yesterday afternoon, I felt an inner nudge to stop and reread this verse. I was conscious that I resisted this idea of offering my body as a sacrifice. Why? Because I suspected it could mean more speaking and traveling, more stress and pressure, with consequent loss of sleep at night, and no chance to recoup with daytime naps.

What is so bad about this is that I'm not really trusting the Lord with my physical body—and that's an awful confession. God expects his followers to be willing to be expendable; I've been circling around this point of total trust in a kind of spiritual holding pattern, unwilling to lay down my body as "a living sacrifice." I'm constantly protecting myself, succumbing too quickly to the temptation to stop my work and lie down for a while.

The conviction then came that I must be willing—and tell God so—to have the self with which I was born, the particular bundle of talents, predispositions, preferences, tastes—all that constitutes me—nailed to the Cross with Jesus, actually die and be buried with Him.

But, a voice inside me argued, *didn't I do just this when I became a Christian?* Jesus assured me, however, that this was a new step of dying to the self that so loves body comforts and beautiful things, that longs to escape the demands and entanglements of other people.

Much of that self *I dislike* (Romans 7:15–25). But a lot of what constitutes "me" I like very much. I've been "me," and lived with "me," and put up with "me" a long time. To lay this self on the altar would indeed be a death.

I remembered Jesus' words about "counting the cost" (Luke 14:28). Was I really willing to take myself to the Cross, die and be buried—not having any idea what sort of person would rise with Jesus on the third day?

I went through agony thinking about this, with a lot of tears.

Scripture says that Jesus resolutely and willingly turned His face to the Cross for "the joy that was set before Him" (Hebrews 12:2).

I finally told Jesus that I was going forward with this because I knew He *was* going to have His way with me, now or in the next life.

I got down on my knees in my office by the daybed at 4:40 P.M. and offered up my body to Him as a living sacrifice.

As a result, I must now be obedient hour by hour, day by day, and *not* hold back. This means seeing the indwelling Spirit so residing in my mortal flesh that I am willing to spend myself totally for others, as He did. It means letting *all* self go—everything in my desire world—whenever it cuts across His higher priorities.

No wonder we can do no mighty works until the surrender is this complete. Until Jesus has been allowed to come and make His home in me like *that*, I will be praying for others, doing His work, in *my* name and in *my* nature rather than in His.

The apostle John puts it this way:

He laid down His [own] life for us; and we ought to lay [our] lives down for [those who are our] brothers in [Him].
1 John 3:16 AMPLIFIED

LL Note: Six months of creativity followed during which Catherine made an important breakthrough with her novel Julie, ministered to several in our prayer group, made several speeches. The two of us drove together from Florida to our farm in Virginia for a month, then flew back to Florida to continue work on her novel.

4.

Self-pity

*T*his morning I took to the Lord a matter that has troubled me for the past two years or so. Sudden tears. I've never been a person who cries often. I generally keep my emotions in check, perhaps more than I should. Recently though, bouts of unpredictable weeping.

The Lord has graciously shown me this morning the why of tears being just under the surface of these past weeks—*self-pity*. In reality, I am weeping for myself.

I weep because of what is happening to me physically. First, my energy level has again dropped to such a degree that it is literally a chore to put one foot before the other. Added to that, worse breathlessness than I've ever known. Sometimes even sitting or lying in bed, I wonder if I'm going to be able to take the next breath. This makes the stairs and hills at Evergreen Farm an agony.

Most puzzling, after years of battling sleeplessness, suddenly I can hardly stay awake. I must check out with the doctor whether this is an overreaction to the new arthritis drug they are giving me.

Or is it possible that, through lack of oxygen to the brain, I am coming into early senility? Hideous thought! For the first time since early girlhood I have no desire to read at night. During church yesterday, I could scarcely keep my eyes open.

Lord, help!

I am led to this verse:

> . . . I know . . . Whom I have believed . . . and I am [positively] persuaded that He is able to guard and keep that which has been entrusted to me and which I have committed [to Him] until that day.
>
> 2 Timothy 1:12 AMPLIFIED

Since self-pity is a sin, then clearly it has to be dealt with as a sin. A sin because since I belong to Jesus, it is He who has control over my life. Thus he overrules everything that He "allows" to happen to me—overrules it for *good*.

My part is to trust Him as a loving Heavenly Father in each of these adverse circumstances. I am to watch expectantly for the "good" . . . the new adventure He has for me . . . the open door I am to go through toward the better way to which He is leading me.

So, given all that, what is there to have self-pity about?

I see that there is a self-discipline to practice during the days ahead: Each time I am tempted toward despairing self-pity, I am to rebuke it, reject it, and turn immediately to praise.

5.

Crisis Time

On July 9, 1982, Catherine was so weak that we had her taken by ambulance to Bethesda Memorial Hospital in Boynton Beach, Florida. Tests showed an alarming carbon dioxide content in her body because of shallow breathing, and she was placed in the Intensive Care Unit. Respirator tubes led through her mouth to her lungs; she was fed through an IV tube in her nose. Machines handled all her body functions. Family members could visit her for no more than fifteen-minute periods three times a day.

Because the tubes in her mouth and nose made it hard to wear glasses, she found it difficult to read the small print of her Bible. A gray 10 by 7-inch notebook that she had filled over the years with Bible promises (see p. 515) in large handwriting became her spiritual lifeline.

The prognosis for her recovery was not good. Doctors could offer no hope that her breathing capacity would improve enough for her to be taken off the respirator. It appeared that Catherine's last days would be spent in the Intensive Care Unit, unable to speak, communicating only through a note pad. Here is a sample of her scribbled comments as the painful weeks passed:

I never knew how frustrating it can be not to be able to speak a word.

I can only move my head about six inches because of that tube in my nose. Lying all night in that one position is torture.

Each little thing is so difficult. It's tough to be getting weaker and weaker and thinner and thinner.

The progress from day to day depends on the blood gases test they take . . . they're running out of places on my arms to draw blood, I bruise so easily.

Remember those old-fashioned cardboard fans people used in church? See if you can find one at home. It gets so hot here at night.

This has been a lonely day. Shifting personnel each with little knowledge of my situation. Sense some are hostile toward Christians. Wish I was a better witness to them for Jesus.

I'm taking twice as many breaths per minute as I should. How do I retrain my body?

I feel that something has to give today. I'm so miserable that I don't see how I can take much more.

It seemed that the Lord was promising me last night that Romans 8:28 would be fulfilled and that I was to begin praising Him. "I believe. Help my unbelief."

Had a crisis with the IV. They spent two hours trying to get it to work. When I began praying they found the answer.

Prayed about my dread of nights. Discovered why I can't really relax. I'm a chronic thinker and a "what-if-er." Prayed to change.

Imagine, four weeks without a shampoo! I dare not look in the mirror. Will be horrified.

Last night the simple thought, "Be still and know that I am God," pulled me through.

On July 24 at 7:30 A.M., my telephone rang: a male nurse reported that Catherine wanted to see me right away. "Don't be alarmed," he said. "It's not a medical emergency. Your wife has something to tell you that she feels is important."

I awoke Peter and Jeff (the family members then on hand) and we drove immediately to the hospital. Catherine greeted us with great excitement in her eyes and reported through written notes that during the night she had felt the Lord's presence there in her Intensive Care cubicle! With His presence came the assurance that she was being healed.

Confirmation came in the next blood tests, which showed a definite decrease in the carbon dioxide content in her body. Day by day the improvement continued. Just as doctors had been unable to explain Catherine's sudden loss of breathing capacity, so too were they baffled when it returned. One doctor said it had to be the power of prayer.

One by one the tubes came out. The ventilator was wheeled away. On August 11, Catherine was moved out of the Intensive Care Unit; she had been there thirty-two days. Nine days later, on August 20th, a rejoicing husband brought her home.

Catherine had been through a dehumanizing process in Intensive Care and had lost twenty-five pounds. The recuperation was agonizingly slow as members of the family took turns coming to Florida to help her recover. Meanwhile, Catherine resumed her journal entries.

LL

6.

Crucified with Jesus

*I*n many ways my thirty-two-day stint in the Intensive Care Unit of Bethesda Hospital was a crucifixion experience. Soon after I arrived there, the Lord reminded me of the act I had performed (through Romans 12:1) of offering forever my defective body, along with all my faculties, as a living sacrifice on His Cross.

While lying on my back, hour after hour, unable to read or talk, I had plenty of time to reflect on the study I did awhile ago on the "Humanity of Jesus." Through it I saw that His humanness for thirty-three years on earth was *real*; that He was as helpless, as "out of control" of circumstances, as we are. All this was in order for Him to be the Wayshower, the true and very practical Captain of our salvation.

I also perceived that during this earthly walk, *the* guiding principle of Jesus' life was "what pleases My Father in heaven, never what *I* want to do."

In the intervening months since I made this study, several things have been happening: (1) the Holy Spirit has been doing a steady softening and melting process within me. This has meant that the plights of other persons presented to me, mostly through correspondence, have been laid on my heart with a new urgency; (2) During this same period my own circumstances have not only been taken out of my control, but also have gone in directions contrary to anything I would wish.

At what point in the Christian walk are we *actually* "crucified with Him"? At what point is the moral self dead on His cross and buried with Him?

In my case, I concluded, dying to self has been going on for some time. For me it has been a slow, torturous, lingering death indeed—no doubt because I have been resisting all the way. I'm reasonably sure that it need not be this drawn out and this painful, if the believer really understands what is going on and why, and assents to it in his will. Yet I do think it's something we have to walk through all the way and *feel*. Death on a Cross hurts.

Early the morning of July 24 (fifteen days after entering the hospital) the climax came for me. I was in a semiconscious, dreaming state when I felt myself literally hanging on the Cross with Jesus. There was no pain from the nails in my hands or feet; only a suffocating, crushing weight on my chest as my entire body dragged downwards. I knew I was close to death, but strangely there was absolutely no fear.

As the weight on the rib cage grew unendurable, however, I was aware of a dark presence, as well as that of Jesus. A fierce struggle with some evil force ensued. Again and again I rebuked the dark power and ordered him to be gone. He didn't leave easily, but leave he did at last.

Then—so gently—Jesus picked me up and removed me from the Cross. As He did so, three words came to me: "The Great Exchange." Later I realized this is what theologians call "the substitutionary atonement," meaning that every sinful thing in our lives was dealt with in Christ's finished work on His Cross. At the moment I knew only that the crushing weight had lifted from my ribs.

I awoke the next morning very excited, feeling that a miracle had taken place in my body. This is the note saved by Len I wrote to the nurse: Please grant me this one request! I want to see my family, now! My husband first. Please call him. 732-6352.

My husband, my son Peter, my son Jeffrey. I want all of them. I want no medication before they get here. I'll "calm down" to suit you.

When Len, Peter, and Jeffrey arrived, through notes I told them about my death, that at one point in my struggle with that dark force, it seemed my body parts were burnt up and lying in pieces around the room. The turning point came when way down deep I cried, "Jesus! Lord. My Lord." And He came and was with me. And He healed me.

My family was very responsive, but I think they wondered if it was a hallucination brought on by low oxygen levels in the brain. The key would be the next blood gases test.

When the doctor arrived at my bedside the next day, he was all smiles. "The carbon dioxide is way down!" he reported. And then we all celebrated!

What transpired on the Cross two thousand years ago has taken on sparkling new meaning for me. We are accustomed to thinking that Jesus carried only our sins on the Cross, but Scripture makes it equally clear that He bore all our sicknesses and diseases there too. . . .

When evening came, they brought to Him (Jesus) many who were under the power of demons, and He drove out the spirits with a word, and restored to health all who were sick; And thus He fulfilled what was spoken by the prophet Isaiah, He Himself took our weaknesses and infirmities and bore away our diseases.

Matthew 8:16–17 (Isaiah 53:4) AMPLIFIED

Len asked me the other night what I considered the chief significance of my crucifixion experience.

"I'm not sure yet," I replied. "I was close to death and the Lord returned me to life. He must have had a reason."

"Do you know what that might be?"

"There are a number of things I'm supposed to do. Finish my novel was one. Even more important: work on some bruised relationships." Then it struck me. "I've had a crucifixion, but not a resurrection."

Len wouldn't accept this. "You emerged from a dark valley into the light. Wasn't that a resurrection?"

"Not entirely. My breathing was restored to what it was last spring, but that's far from normal. My lungs have still not been completely healed."

"Consider this, Catherine," Len replied. "You've operated with little more than half your normal lung power for almost forty years. But look at all you've accomplished. Maybe, like Paul, God's given you a thorn in the flesh for a reason."

Lord, how much more I have to learn!

7.

Doing Grief Work

*H*ow grateful I am for Robert Bonham's[1] visits during my recuperation! What a sensitive counselor and friend! His gifts of wisdom and discernment are balm to my spirit.

After I told him how discouraged I am over the slowness of my recovery and the suspicion that my voice may be permanently damaged, it came out last week that Bob feels I am doing *grief* work.

The minute he spoke the word "grief," it rang a bell within me. He said that whenever we encounter a major shift or change in life, of necessity it involves separation from things well-known and comfortable (whether completely desirable or not), and this entails loss.

When I asked him to spell this out as he saw it in my situation, he ticked off the following:

[1]At the time the Reverend Robert Bonham was Director of the Christian Institute of Healing at New Covenant Church, Pompano Beach, Florida.

Loss of identity in the Intensive Care Unit (ICU). Rings, bracelets, etc., removed and placed in hospital safe. Only individuation is a plastic identification bracelet on patient's left wrist.

Loss of dignity. Emergency conditions in ICU rule out privacy. Tendency on part of nurses is to deal with bodies, not persons.

Loss of speech for so long. Respirator tubes in mouth mean communication is curtailed.

The possibility of loss of life. Death is common and frequent in ICU. Dependency on machines underscores the fragility of life.

Loss of mental ability and memory. Reduced oxygen in brain brings on confusion.

As he talked a flood of emotion ran through me. I saw the physical stripping of possessions that takes place in any hospital as more devastating than I had acknowledged. It says, in part, that any so-called success one has had is now of no consequence. That comes off too. Raiment is a hospital gown—the same garment for everyone. One is just a *body* headed for life or death.

I know now what my husband Peter meant when he was asked what he had learned from his first heart attack. His reply, "I have learned that the kingdom of God can go on without Peter Marshall."

In the same way I learned in the hospital that everyone can get along quite well without my opinions or "insights" or teaching. Even my wedding ring, symbol of marriage to Len, the closest earthly relationship, was taken away. The experience left me feeling not only helpless but worthless—a digit. The danger here, of course, is that this sense of nonentity can lead one into the pit of despair. It can render one unable not only to accept God's unqualified love, but also the love of other people.

Bob's complete assurance that "this too will pass" was very heartening. He had no answer, though, to my question as to what I can do to make the grief work shorter. Simply that I am to trust God and listen.

This morning I had this word from the Spirit. He tells me to praise and rejoice. He brings to mind the Scripture song we've sung so often at church:

Rejoice in the Lord always; again I will say Rejoice.
                                        Philippians 4:4 RSV

Rejoice!
That I can enjoy music again through my stereo record-player.
I actually got up and played the piano a bit—"Breathe on me,
breath of God. . . ."
Rejoice!
Telephoned T. and confessed my lack of love and understand-
ing about several matters. A time of renewed fellowship and
reconciliation.
Rejoice!
For patient Len and faithful family . . . for the Intercessors . . .
for all who prayed . . . for my doctors and the hospital personnel.
Rejoice!
Linda and I are so close now. She drove down to be with me
for a week, bringing a gift of four mats and four napkins for the
dining-room table. "Use them," she urged. The point is that Len
and the doctor have insisted on my getting out of bed and eating
at the table.
Rejoice!
Mary Moncur discovered a tree with mangos out of season.
Also fresh grapefruit. And our lime tree is so full that Mary will
spend all morning squeezing and freezing them.
Praise You, Lord, for Bob Bonham giving up half of every
Saturday to be with me.
Praise You, Lord, for bringing out all the fears that are cling-
ing around the fear of death—so that I can deal with them.
Praise You, Lord, for allowing me to have those experiences in
Intensive Care, and for pulling me back from death.

8.

Receiving Love

*G*od continues to heal me. This morning He gave me a walloping message about the fact that I have not always been able to receive other people's love and so cannot receive Jesus' love. This revelation was sparked by a hassle with Len last night in our bedroom when I was complaining about members of the household who are shielding me about family situations, finances, and decisions that involve my manuscripts and affairs.

Len became quite agitated; finally with tears in his eyes he said, "Catherine, the doctors have told us that you need time to recover from being at death's door. What we're doing is for your protection, out of our love for you. Don't you realize that we almost lost you?" With that, his voice broke with a show of emotion such as I have rarely seen in our marriage.

This morning I awoke with the full impact of Len's deep feeling sweeping over me. How often, I wondered, do men in our society shortchange themselves and their families by letting a "macho" front cover up a sensitive nature underneath? The conviction came too, though, that I have not been open enough to love. I've often had trouble accepting the feelings Len did express. The affection and gratitude of friends and readers, too.

"Read 1 Corinthians 13," the Spirit nudged.

Those verses lay it out for me even more stringently than Len did last night:

> Love is patient, love is kind. It does not envy, it does not boast, it is not proud. It is not rude, it is not self-seeking, it is not easily angered, it keeps no record of wrongs. Love does not delight in evil but rejoices with the truth. It always protects, always trusts, always hopes, always perseveres.
>
> 1 Corinthians 13:4–7 NIV

I see further that, while my act of laying my body on the altar as "a loving sacrifice" was a good first step, it was not enough for: "Though I give my body to be burned and have not love, it profiteth me nothing" (v. 3).

Now comes further revelation, even as I write. Following the 1944 experience of Jesus' healing Presence in my room after I was bedridden for almost three years, I nevertheless lacked something. I've always supposed it was sufficient faith to make the healing complete.

But suppose it was *love* that was missing, not faith. Oh, obedience was not altogether there either, but obedience would have followed love.

"Lord, I rejoice. Lord, I capitulate. Lord, let Your love—and Len's and the love of those around me, each member of my family, and all the love of far-flung friends through my books— *take over.*"

9.

Grief Work Continued— The Healing of Memories

*T*oday I shared with Bob Bonham what I have only flicked at with Len: that is the strange negativism I'm feeling about myself. Lately I keep seeing the underside of things, tend to concentrate on the downbeat.

I'm aware too of a loosening of the hold that *things* have on me. I could care less about fixing up Evergreen Farm or the Florida house—redecorating, repairing, restoring—whereas I used to be very much on top of all of this.

Bob interpreted these observations positively by telling me that this is a normal part of recuperation, that the "grief work" needs to go on. He sees too that God is showing me how to *die to self*. The indifference to *things* is simply one manifestation of this. As the culmination of this process, Bob sees that self will eventually be given back to me in a new way.

Even as I write this, the Spirit gives me a further insight—I am to take the lassitude, the wanting to lie down and take oxygen, the lack of motivation and will power to get on with diaphragm exercises, as part and yet another proof of this "death." The crucifixion experience at the hospital was real.

The above, positively seen, is that Catherine is dead and my dependence upon *Jesus'* motivation and *His* strength is more real than ever.

After reassuring me that my negativism is a part of the recovery process, Bob Bonham then sought to lead me through the healing of some memories that lie at the root of my fear of physical death.

Bob asked me to begin this session by seeking "contact" with Jesus. For example, I might ask to feel the touch of His hand on mine. Then I was to let Jesus lead me back to the memory He wanted to heal.

The first one, curiously, was the time I was walking in the woods as a young girl and stepped on something in the leaves. To my horror I saw that it was a dead bird. The dread of that experience has obviously clung to me ever since.

The second was the time our family went to a relative's funeral in Johnson City, Tennessee. The body of Uncle John Herndon was in a coffin open for viewing. This was my first look at a dead person. The stark coldness of my uncle's face numbed me.

The third was a real surprise—the "living death" of my grandmother Sarah Wood for whom I was named. Grandmother, for the last part of her life, stayed in her bedroom, where she would allow no window opened. To me she appeared sealed in a tomb.

Bob had me continue to seek contact with Jesus who repeatedly reassured me that death was a doorway experience, that the body was shed as an old, worn-out garment while the inner person, the essential being, went joyously through the door into eternal life.

The whole process took over an hour.

After Bob Bonham left I remembered that Agnes Sanford in her book *The Healing Gifts of the Spirit* had a chapter entitled "The Healing of the Memories." I found the book in my library, turned to that chapter and was stopped by this sentence:

"The truth is that any wound to the soul so deep that it is not healed by our own self-searching and prayers is inevitably connected with a subconscious awareness of sin."

We find the same connection in the Bible! Jesus died for our *sins*. Yet in Isaiah 53:4 we are told, "Surely he hath borne our griefs."

So there is a sense in which sin equals, or is tantamount to, grief.

Which is why the healing of memories is bound up with the forgiveness of sins.

While pondering all this, I recalled my mother's statement to me several years ago, how it distressed her, after Peter's death, the way I would spend hours talking over lofty "spiritual matters" with our housekeeper while my nine-year-old son, Peter John, playing alone in his bedroom, desperately needed my attention, time, and love.

A picture came to mind. It is an actual photo. Peter John is half-squatting on the floor of his bedroom, his toys around him, his big eyes solemn, bewildered, seeking.

With sudden tears I confessed my "heavenly-mindedness" as a sin and asked Jesus' forgiveness.

Next I asked Jesus to go back in time and take that little boy with the hurt, bewildered eyes in His arms. Then to sit there on the bedroom floor beside him, playing with him, ministering the healing needed to Peter John's lonely heart.

"Thank You, Lord, that all time—past, present, and future—is 'right now' with You. Therefore, that little boy is available to Your healing presence, even as the little girl Catherine is. I claim especially Your power to 'cleanse me from all unrighteousness.' Thank You for Your great promise 'to restore . . . the years that the locust has eaten' (Joel 2:25 AMPLIFIED), both for Peter and for me."

After this prayer I felt the love of Jesus washing over my body like a benediction.

What the Spirit has been doing for me through Bob Bonham is remarkable. Each time I believe I have plumbed the depths of peace and joy in the Christian life, there is more . . . more . . . more! My spirit bounds and leaps and overflows with thanksgiving so that I struggle for any way at all to express it! The fact that Jesus would love each individual *that much*—me—regardless of worth, regardless of performance turned in, regardless of anything, is *so* amazing. No wonder He was raised to the right hand of the Father and crowned with glory and honor!!

10.

Keeping My Eyes Upon Jesus

*F*ell on my face yesterday. Breathing was laborious. Did very little walking. Could not do the exercises. Was discouraged and disheartened and bored.

I knew the cause of all this. A letter came from my doctor, putting names and tags to my "chronic" illness for use in Medicare forms. It sounded so final that I began looking at *this*, accepting it, settling down to it.

I also opened the door to fear. Not so much fear of death because I've actually, finally worked through that. This time it was a fear that I would let down the readers of my books who expect me to be an example of victorious faith.

In my session with Bob Bonham we traced the roots of this fear of letting people down, back to my childhood. What came out was that my father's praising me so highly when I played the piano for his prayer meetings, or made top grades in school, eventually created in me the feeling that I *had* to achieve in order to have his love.

As the years passed this feeling was extended to other members of my family, to friends, even to God. Added to this was the belief that because I have been so public in my life as a Christian, if I did not measure up to what Jesus expected of me, I would not only let Him down, but that people "out there" would think less of *Him*; that Jesus' reputation would actually suffer.

Put in so many words, this is obviously ridiculous! But that's what came out. So yesterday was a total setback for me.

This morning I sought the Lord's forgiveness and was told something like this, most emphatically:

"Catherine, take your eyes off yourself, off your symptoms, off your fears and center your attention on Me. Look at *Me*. Keep looking at Me.

"Allow Me to be your Doctor. This is My will. I *do* know how to give you health. I made you. I know how to mend you.

"Why do you think I healed everyone who came to Me in the days of My flesh? Out of overflowing mercy. I had only to see any human being blind or crippled or sick or in pain to want to set the wrong situation right as quickly as possible.

"I have told you in My Word (Hebrews) that as man's High Priest I am able—and want—to '*run*' to the assistance of those who cry to Me."

In my answering prayer, I said, "Lord, I do cry to You. I give You permission to change me on the inside, to strengthen my flabby spiritual muscles, to reverse the direction of my gaze, to make me eager to look at You only.

"I know You want a resurrection thrust inside me and an end to my doubts and negative thinking. In the wake of this will come new life and health. If not on this earth, then I will go into the next life with the differentness that You want for me."

Then Jesus led me to the sixteenth chapter of John where I was stopped by this magnificent verse:

... it is profitable—good, expedient, advantageous—for you that I go away. Because if I do not go away, the Comforter (Counselor, Helper, Advocate, Intercessor, Strengthener, Standby) will not come to you—into close fellowship with you ...

John 16:7 AMPLIFIED

These are the blessed functions of the Holy Spirit promised by Jesus:

Counselor (He gives wisdom to the simple.)
Helper (He lifts us over every obstacle.)
Advocate (He is our personal lawyer to "take us on" and plead our case.)
Intercessor (He stands before the throne of grace.)
Strengthener (He gives us vitality and courage.)
Standby (He is always at our side.)

How can a one of us get along without any of those things! Then glorious verse 33 (italic added):

I have told you these things so that *in Me* you may have perfect peace and confidence. In the world you have tribulation and trials and distress and frustration; but be of good cheer—take courage, be confident, certain, undaunted—for I have overcome the world. —I have deprived it of power to harm, have conquered it [for you].

11.

Resurrection

*T*hanks to Pastor Robert Bonham and the ministry of other loving friends and family, Catherine made good progress during September, October, and November 1982. To my amazement she decided we should accept the invitation to fly to Cape Cod to spend Thanksgiving with her son, Peter, his wife, Edith, and their three children, Mary Elizabeth, thirteen, Peter Jonathan, nine, and David Christopher, two. Mother Wood, ninety-one, insisted she would go too.

There were moments of hilarity en route. Since Catherine and her mother both needed wheelchairs to traverse airport terminals, I took over when porters were not available, jockeying both wheelchairs through gates and up and down ramps.

It was Catherine's first visit to the Marshalls' new home, a joyous family time with four generations interacting, sometimes peacefully, sometimes through tensions that bubbled with creativity.

At Christmastime, our own home was the scene of another family reunion. Chet and his wife, Susan, arrived with our new grandson, Jacob LeSourd, joined by Linda and Phil Lader and our younger son, Jeff. Christmas had been a time when the perfectionist in Catherine ran her ragged with holiday *preparations. Now for the first time in twenty-three years, Catherine let others run the show and simply enjoyed herself. Gift-giving and elaborate meals had been reduced, allowing more time for games and family talk.*

At the beginning of 1983 Catherine set several goals for herself. An 800-page draft of the novel had been completed, but needed months of work to sharpen characterization.

She wanted to resume writing for each issue of The Intercessors *newsletter.*

And do an article about her mother for a Guideposts *series on aging.*

At the end of January, however, she underwent a cataract operation. From her journal:

February 9th . . . I am staggering under what the eye surgeon said to me yesterday during a routine checkup following the cataract surgery: "You are sick from head to toe." I did not have to accept this verdict, but I did. Now I really have to ditch it—with the Spirit's help and by God's grace. This verse has truly helped me:

And if the Spirit of Him Who raised up Jesus from the dead dwells in you, [then] He Who raised up Christ Jesus from the dead will also restore to life your mortal (short-lived, perishable) bodies through His Spirit Who dwells in you.

Romans 8:11 AMPLIFIED

February 24th . . . Have hit a new low. I am quite out of breath—indeed, gasping for air—just in walking from room to room. My doctor could find no obvious cause for the trouble yesterday. Today it hit me . . . Once again the doctors neither know what is wrong, nor how to help me. So . . . I am backed up against Jesus' help.

March 9th . . . In my Quiet Time, this thought: my hospital experience of the crucifixion was centered on the matter of breathing. This morning the Holy Spirit reminded me once again: "Jesus took your breathing problem into His own body on the Cross so that from henceforth *He* is your life-breath."

With great heaviness of spirit I drove Catherine to Bethesda Memorial Hospital on March 11th, where she was admitted for more tests. We made light of it. "Just a few days," I assured her.

Silently, however, I was recalling another hospital episode almost twelve years before. A daughter, Amy Catherine, had been born to Peter and Edith Marshall and been given her grandmother's name. The baby, however, was genetically damaged in lungs, kidneys, and brain. Doctors at Children's Hospital in Boston offered no hope.

Friends from around the country gathered to pray for little Amy's healing. God answered the prayers, but not the way we expected. Healings occurred . . . in the people who came to pray. Amy Catherine died.

Catherine was desolate for months. "What went wrong?" she wept.

Eventually, she saw it—nothing went wrong! God is a sovereign God. We can plead with Him, bargain with Him, rail at Him, and claim anything and everything in His name. In return God overwhelms us with His blessings, but retains the decisions about "times and seasons" in His hands.

Here is Catherine's last journal entry made in the hospital:

March 12th . . . The blood test yesterday showed carbon dioxide level in my blood too high, but not dangerous; not enough oxygen in the blood, however. Another problem seems to be anemia.

This morning Jesus told me once again: "Keep your eyes off yourself and look steadily at Me. I love you. I know how to mend you."

That very day Catherine was taken to the same Intensive Care Unit where she had spent so many weeks last summer, and put on a respirator. Shortly after midnight on March 18, Catherine's heart stopped beating. The Lord had come to take her with Him to experience the joyous resurrection she missed last summer.

In the hours and days that followed, the Lord seemed to place all of us in the family under His special love and protection; plus a necessary degree of numbness. The calls, letters, cards, flowers, and food that flowed in warmed and nourished us.

Two triumphant occasions followed: the burial service in National Presbyterian Church, Washington, D.C., conducted by its pastor and Catherine's close friend, Dr. Louis Evans, Jr., with her son, Peter John Marshall.

And the memorial service at the New Covenant Presbyterian Church, Pompano Beach, Florida. Pastor George Callahan along with Dr. William Earnhart (church elder and Catherine's personal physician) shared their memories of a great lady.

Robert Bonham, the man who for so many hours ministered healing to Catherine as pastor and friend, spoke these words at this same service:

"During Catherine's funeral in the National Presbyterian Church, my eyes went to some beautiful stained glass windows through which the sun was shining. I thought of Jesus telling His disciples, 'You are the light of the world.' Catherine as a 20th century follower put her light on a lamp stand so that all might see.

"I looked at the glass in those windows and thought about all the pieces therein. There were dark pieces and light pieces, all kinds of colors blended together. I thought about the suffering experiences that Catherine had early in her life and recently in the hospital. These were deep, deep colors. Her body never was able to keep up with her mind and her spirit. It always hauled her back.

"There were, of course, the brighter colors, the rose tints of love and warmth—the giving of her heart to those in her family and to everyone she touched. Those colors went out across the United States and throughout the world. I remember years back when I was at the University of Illinois, one of the professors there had a hydrocephalic child. He told me that he had called Catherine up long distance and had asked her to pray for his child. She did and the child was healed. All the way to Illinois, and other places far and near, went those pieces of radiating light— warm, bright, healing colors falling on the lives of people.

"There were so many pieces in her life—the books that she and the Lord wrote—the articles for *Guideposts* and other magazines. She wrote nothing that did not have all of her heart and mind in it as well as the heart and mind of Christ. Starting *The Intercessors* not long ago, she and Leonard mobilized prayer warriors across the nation to bring help to many people. Her family represents warm, glowing pieces of glass in the mosaic of her life. Likewise her many friends who kept calling when she died and could not believe that this had happened.

"A surprising thing about a stained glass window is that when the light is not shining through, it comes across as dull. Have you ever looked at a stained glass window when there is no light behind it? You cannot see what is in it. Catherine always had

Christ's light shining through her life. As the light of Jesus radiated through the stained glass mosaic of her life, all of us who were within sight of it got blessed.

"When the sun goes down, the horizon stays bright for a long time. There is going to be a long afterglow to Catherine Marshall LeSourd's life. The books that were written will go on to become classics in Christian literature. The articles will go on helping people. There are things she has written that will yet find their way into print to bless us. Her touches on our lives will live on, ministering to my children, and my children's children.

"In the last page of her book *To Live Again*, Catherine wrote these words as she faced life without her husband, Peter: 'At moments when the future is completely obscured, can any one of us afford to go to meet our tomorrows with dragging feet? God had been in the past, then He would be in the future, too. Always He had brought adventure, high hopes, unexpected friends, new ventures that broke old patterns. Then in my future must lie more goodness, more mercy, more adventures, more friends. Across the hills, light was breaking through the storm clouds. Suddenly, just ahead of the car an incandescent, iridescent rainbow appeared, hung there shimmering. I hadn't seen a rainbow for a long time.' And then Catherine's last sentence, 'I drove steadily into the light.'

"Catherine is doing that right now—moving steadily into the Light."

Catherine's Scriptural Lifeline

*E*arly in her marriage to Len, Catherine formed the habit of copying into a gray 10 by 7 inch notebook the Bible verses that helped most in health or household crises. Over the years the pages filled to become a kind of scriptural lifeline. In the summer of 1982, when she was in the Intensive Care Unit, too ill to read the handwritten entries herself, a member of her family or close friend would read them to her. Here are 41 verses[1] to which she clung with ever-growing assurance:

Behold, I am the Lord, the God of all flesh; is there anything too hard for Me?

Jeremiah 32:27

The grass withers, the flower fades, but the word of our God will stand for ever.

Isaiah 40:8

[1]All passages from the Amplified Bible unless otherwise noted.

He has bestowed on us His precious and exceedingly great promises, so that through them you may escape (by flight) from the moral decay (rottenness and corruption) that is in the world because of covetousness (lust and greed), and become sharers (partakers) of the divine nature.

2 Peter 1:4

God is faithful—reliable, trustworthy and [therefore] ever true to His promise, and He can be depended on; by Him you were called into companionship and participation with His Son, Jesus Christ our Lord.

1 Corinthians 1:9

So shall my word be that goeth forth out of my mouth: it shall not return unto me void, but it shall accomplish that which I please, and it shall prosper in the thing whereto I sent it.

Isaiah 55:11 KJV

And if the Spirit of Him Who raised up Jesus from the dead dwells in you, [then] He Who raised up Christ Jesus from the dead will also restore to life your mortal (short-lived, perishable) bodies through His Spirit Who dwells in you.

Romans 8:11

So too the (Holy) Spirit comes to our aid and bears us up in our weakness: for we do not know what prayer to offer nor how to offer it worthily as we ought, but the Spirit Himself goes to meet our supplication and pleads in our behalf with unspeakable yearnings and groanings too deep for utterance.

Romans 8:26

And we know that all things work together for good to them that love God, to them who are the called according to his purpose.

Romans 8:28 KJV

I know that whatsoever God doeth, it shall be for ever: nothing can be put to it, nor anything taken from it: and God doeth it, that men should fear before him.

Ecclesiastes 3:14 KJV

For the Lord is our judge, the Lord is our law-giver, the Lord is our king: He will save us.

Isaiah 33:22

For I, the Lord your God, hold your right hand; I, Who say to you, Fear not, I will help you!

Isaiah 41:13

For God's gifts and His call are irrevocable—He never withdraws them when once they are given, and He does not change His mind about those to whom He gives His grace or to whom He sends His call.

Romans 11:29

When the enemy shall come in like a flood, the Spirit of the Lord will lift up a standard against him and put him to flight—for He will come like a rushing stream which the breath of the Lord drives.

Isaiah 59:19

But God is faithful [to His Word and to His compassionate nature], and He [can be trusted] not to let you be tempted ... beyond your ability and strength of resistance and power to endure, but with the temptation He will [always] also provide the way out—the means of escape to a landing place—that you may be capable and strong and powerful patiently to bear up under it.

I Corinthians 10:13

The Lord redeems the life of His servants, and none of those who take refuge and trust in Him shall be condemned or held guilty.

Psalm 34:22

Though I walk in the midst of trouble, You will revive me; You will stretch forth Your hand against the wrath of my enemies, and Your right hand will save me.

Psalm 138:7

The Lord also will be a refuge and a high tower for the oppressed, a refuge and a stronghold in times of trouble [high cost, destitution and desperation].

Psalm 9:9

And He will establish you to the end—keep you steadfast, give you strength, and guarantee your vindication, that is, be your warrant against all accusation or indictment—[so that you will be] guiltless and irreproachable in the day of our Lord Jesus Christ, the Messiah.

1 Corinthians 1:8

He will swallow up death in victory—He will abolish death forever; and the Lord God will wipe away tears from off all faces; and the reproach of His people He will take away from off all the earth; for the Lord has spoken it.

Isaiah 25:8

Fear not; for I am with you; do not . . . be dismayed, for I am your God. I will strengthen and harden you [to difficulties]; yes, I will help you; yes, I will hold you up and retain you with My victorious right hand of rightness and justice.

Isaiah 41:10

I have called you by your name, you are Mine. When you pass through the waters I will be with you, and through the rivers they shall not overwhelm you; when you walk through the fire you shall not be burned . . . nor shall the flame kindle upon you. For I am the Lord your God, the Holy One of Israel, your Savior . . .

Isaiah 43:1–3

For though the mountains should depart and the hills be shaken or removed, yet My love and kindness shall not depart from you, nor shall My covenant of peace and completeness be removed, says the Lord, Who has compassion on you.

Isaiah 54:10

For thus saith the Lord God, the Holy One of Israel; In returning and rest shall ye be saved; in quietness and in confidence shall be your strength.

Isaiah 30:15 KJV

In the world you have tribulation and trials and distress and frustration; but be of good cheer—take courage, be confident, certain, undaunted—for I have overcome the world. —I have deprived it of power to harm, have conquered it [for you].

John 16:33

I assure you, most solemnly I tell you, the person whose ears are open to My words—who listens to My message—and believes and trusts in and clings to and relies on Him Who sent Me has (possesses now) eternal life. And he does not come into judgment—does not incur sentence of judgment, will not come under condemnation—but he has already passed over out of death into life.

John 5:24

Do not fret or have any anxiety about anything, but in every circumstance and in everything by prayer and petition [definite requests] with thanksgiving continue to make your wants known to God. And God's peace . . . which transcends all understanding, shall garrison and mount guard over your hearts and minds in Christ Jesus.

Philippians 4:6–7

But they that wait upon the Lord shall renew their strength; they shall mount up with wings as eagles; they shall run, and not be weary; and they shall walk, and not faint.

Isaiah 40:31 KJV

Whoever takes a drink of the water that I will give him shall never, no never, be thirsty any more. But the water that I will give him shall become a spring of water welling up (flowing, bubbling) continually within him unto eternal life.

John 4:14

My sheep hear my voice, and I know them, and they follow me: And I give unto them eternal life; and they shall never perish, neither shall any man pluck them out of my hand. My Father, which gave them me, is greater than all; and no man is able to pluck them out of my Father's hand. I and My Father are one.

John 10:27–30 KJV

Keep and protect me, O God, for in You I have found refuge, and in You do I put my trust and hide myself. . . . my body too shall rest and confidently dwell in safety.

Psalm 16:1,9

In the day when I called, You answered me, and strengthened me with strength (might and inflexibility) [to temptation] in my inner self.

Psalm 138:3

Now the Lord is the Spirit, and where the Spirit of the Lord is, there is liberty—emancipation from bondage, freedom.

2 Corinthians 3:17

(For the weapons of our warfare are not carnal, but mighty through God to the pulling down of strongholds;) Casting down imaginations, and every high thing that exalteth itself against the knowledge of God, and bringing into captivity every thought to the obedience of Christ.

2 Corinthians 10:4–5 KJV

Behold God, my salvation! I will trust and not be afraid, for the Lord God is my strength and song; yes, He has become my salvation. Therefore with joy will you draw water from the wells of salvation.

Isaiah 12:2–3

Rejoice in the Lord always—delight, gladden yourselves in Him; again I say, Rejoice!

Philippians 4:4

Although the fig tree shall not blossom, neither shall fruit be in the vines; the labour of the olive shall fail, and the fields shall yield no meat; the flock shall be cut off from the fold, and there shall be no herd in the stalls: Yet I will rejoice in the Lord, I will joy in the God of my salvation. The Lord God is my strength, and he will make my feet like hinds' feet, and he will make me to walk upon mine high places.

Habakkuk 3:17–19 KJV

Heal me, O Lord, and I shall be healed; save me, and I shall be saved; for You are my praise.

Jeremiah 17:14

Thou wilt keep him in perfect peace, whose mind is stayed on thee: because he trusteth in thee.

Isaiah 26:3 KJV

Our inner selves wait [earnestly] for the Lord; He is our help and our shield. For in Him does our heart rejoice, because we have trusted (relied on and been confident) in His holy name.

Psalm 33:20–21

. . . for He (God) Himself has said, I will not in any way fail you nor give you up nor leave you without support. [I will] not . . . in any degree leave you helpless, nor forsake nor let [you] down [relax My hold on you]. —Assuredly not!

Hebrews 13:5

For I am persuaded beyond doubt—am sure—that neither death, nor life, nor angels, nor principalities, nor things impending and threatening, nor things to come, nor powers, Nor height, nor depth, nor anything else in all creation will be able to separate us from the love of God which is in Christ Jesus our Lord.

Romans 8:38–39

About the Author

Catherine Marshall is the author of four great best-sellers, *A Man Called Peter*, *To Live Again*, *Beyond Our Selves*, and *Christy*. Her books have sold two and one-half million copies in hard-cover editions alone; they include several collections of sermons and prayers by her late husband, Peter Marshall. She is now married to Leonard LeSourd, for twenty-eight years the Editor of *Guideposts* magazine. Her son, Peter John Marshall, is a minister, serving a church in New England. Catherine's life is centered on writing and family activities. (The LeSourds have three children: Linda, Chester, and Jeffrey.) She also finds time to serve as a roving editor for *Guideposts*, to handle a voluminous correspondence, to paint tropical scenes, and to make a few speaking appearances. She is widely known over the country as an attractive, provocative, and inspiring personality.